UNIVERSITY OF CAMBRIDGE
DEPARTMENT OF APPLIED ECONOMICS

MONOGRAPH 21

BRITISH MONETARY POLICY, 1924–1931
THE NORMAN CONQUEST OF $4.86

UNIVERSITY OF CAMBRIDGE
DEPARTMENT OF APPLIED ECONOMICS

Monographs

This series consists of investigations conducted by members of the Department's staff and others working in direct collaboration with the Department.

The Department of Applied Economics assumes no responsibility for the views expressed in the Monographs published under its auspices.

The following Monographs are still in print.

1. The Measurement of Production Movements
by C. F. CARTER, W. B. REDDAWAY *and* RICHARD STONE
4. The Analysis of Family Budgets
by S. J. PRAIS *and* H. S. HOUTHAKKER (*Reissue*)
5. The Lognormal Distribution
by J. AITCHISON *and* J. A. C. BROWN
6. Productivity and Technical Change   *by* W. E. G. SALTER
Second edition, with Addendum by W. B. REDDAWAY
7. The Ownership of Major Consumer Durables   *by* J. S. CRAMER
8. British Economic Growth, 1688–1959
by PHYLLIS DEANE *and* W. A. COLE (*Second edition*)
10. The Economics of Capital Utilisation   *by* R. MARRIS
11. Priority Patters and the Demand for Household
Durable Goods   *by* F. G. PYATT
12. The Growth of Television Ownership in the
United Kingdom   *by* A. D. BAIN
13. The British Patent System   1. Administration   *by* KLAUS BOEHM
14. The Wealth of the Nation   *by* JACK REVELL
15. Planning, Programming and Input-Output Models
Selected Papers on Indian Planning   *by* A. GHOSH
16. Biproportional Matrices and Input-Output Change
by MICHAEL BACHARACH
17. Abstract of British Historical Statistics
by B. R. MITCHELL *in collaboration with* PHYLLIS DEANE
18. Second Abstract of British Historical Statistics
by B. R. MITCHELL *and* H. G. JONES
19. Takeovers: their relevance to the stock market and the
theory of the firm   *by* AJIT SINGH
20. New Commodities and Consumer Behaviour
by D. S. IRONMONGER

BRITISH
MONETARY POLICY
1924-1931

THE NORMAN CONQUEST
OF $4.86

D. E. MOGGRIDGE

Assistant Lecturer in Economics
in the University of Cambridge
and Fellow of Clare College

CAMBRIDGE
AT THE UNIVERSITY PRESS
1972

Published by the Syndics of the Cambridge University Press
Bentley House, 200 Euston Road, London NW1 2DB
American Branch: 32 East 57th Street, New York, N.Y. 10022

© Cambridge University Press 1972

Library of Congress Catalogue Card Number: 76–169576

ISBN: 0 521 08225 0

Printed in Great Britain
Willmer Brothers Limited
Birkenhead, England

CONTENTS

FIGURES

TABLES

NOTE

The contemporary origin of the sub-title is noted on page 228.

In the case of Public Record Office Documents used in this study, only their call numbers appear in the footnotes. However, a complete list of call numbers and full titles appears at the beginning of the bibliography.

Ellipses in the text of quoted matter are the author's, except where otherwise indicated.

PREFACE

This study represents the conclusion of the larger programme of research into Britain's inter-war gold standard experience to which I referred in the acknowledgements for *The Return to Gold 1925: The Formulation of Economic Policy and its Critics*. As such, it is a sequel to that short preliminary study.

However, the past two years have given me time for further reflections and discussions on the subject matter in *The Return to Gold*, and, as a result of these, a revised version of the major part of that study appears in Chapters 2–4. The revisions that have occurred, often as a result of the work of many helpful reviewers, represent, in the main, slight changes in emphasis and interpretation. Therefore, those interested in that particular decision alone will still find most of what they need in the earlier study.

The period of research which lies behind this study has found support, both moral and financial, from many sources, in particular the Provost and Fellows of King's College, Cambridge, the Master and Fellows of Clare College, Cambridge, the Houblon–Norman Fund, the Canada Council, and the Department of Applied Economics, Cambridge. The search for documents and statistics found active support from the late Mr Randolph Churchill, the Bank of England, the Federal Reserve Bank of New York, H.M. Treasury, Mr P. Sraffa, and the staffs of the Marshall Library of Economics, Cambridge, and the Public Record Office. Dr John Atkin allowed me to examine the worksheets from his study of inter-war British overseas investment in connection with Chapter 9. Mrs Silk and her typists in the Department of Applied Economics, Mrs Susan Macdonald and Mrs Margaret Butler, successfully worked various drafts into their already heavy schedules. John Eatwell helped with proofs.

The intellectual debts accumulated during the period of research and surrounding this study are vast. Professor Lord Kahn, who supervised an earlier version as a Ph.D. dissertation, and Professor Joan Robinson have encouraged me from the start and have always been sources of valuable comments and stimulation. Professor W. B. Reddaway has repeatedly made himself available as an informal sounding board for ideas and approaches and has inevitably left traces of his common sense on the subjects discussed. Mr S. V. O. Clarke of the Federal Reserve Bank of New

York, Mr J. A. C. Osborne and Professors R. S. Sayers, N. Kaldor, I. M. Drummond, C. P. Kindleberger, H. G. Johnson and Sir Ralph Hawtrey have all read parts of various drafts and have provided useful comments and encouragement. Any failures to follow so much advice and, of course, any remaining errors are my own.

For permission to cite documents, I would like to thank the following : Lord Kahn (Keynes Papers), the Federal Reserve Bank of New York, the Bank of England, the Bank of France, the Deutsche Bundesbank, and the Reserve Bank of Australia (Federal Reserve Bank of New York Archives, Strong Papers and Harrison Collection), the Controller of Her Majesty's Stationery Office (Public Record Office and Crown Copyright materials), the Chartwell Trust (Chartwell Papers) and Mr P. Sraffa (Pigou Papers in the Marshall Library of Economics, Cambridge).

Earlier drafts of part of Chapters 8 and 9 appeared in the *International Review of the History of Banking*, No 5 and *Essays on a Mature Economy*, the proceedings of the Mathematical Social Science Board's Harvard Conference on the 'new economic history' in Britain published by Methuen in 1971. I would like to thank the editors of both of these publications for permission to use parts of these drafts.

Finally, I should like to thank my wife Janet, who in the course of the last five years has seen me through the research, travel, writing and revision stages of each part of this study with unfailing support and good humour. If this book is at all intelligible to non-economists (or even to economists) it is a reflection of her persistent questioning, criticism, comments and common sense. To her this book is dedicated.

D.E.M.

April 1971

1. INTRODUCTION

'But before I come to the prospects of 1925 I have an important announcement to make to the Committee. It is something in the nature of a digression and yet it is an essential part of our financial policy.'[1] Thus on 28 April 1925, just before 4 p.m., Winston Churchill, the Chancellor of the Exchequer, began to tell the House of Commons of the decision, effective immediately, to return to the gold standard at the pre-war parity of $4.86.[2] That decision marked a watershed in Britain's inter-war economic history. From 28 April, for as long as the Authorities were willing and/or able to defend the new exchange rate, the return to gold closed certain policy options both for the Authorities and, in many respects, for their critics. Thus, for example, Keynes, who had opposed the return to gold at $4.86 in 1925, shifted his ground after the decision and criticised subsequent official policy in the light of a given exchange rate.[3] Until early August 1931, he did not suggest that the 1925 decision be reversed or that the exchange rate be altered.[4] This general acceptance of the exchange rate, coupled with existing levels of unemployment and almost continuous exchange pressure, most certainly led to the examination of second-best solutions, or expedients other than devaluation, which would neutralise some or all of the effects of the 1925 decision, which, as we shall see, substantially over-

---

[1] 183 H. C. Deb. 5 s. column 52. The whole gold standard statement is in columns 52-8.

[2] The actual par was $4.86656 or 4.86\frac{21}{32}$, but throughout the text $4.86 finds use as a reasonable approximation.

[3] See for example J. M. Keynes, *The Economic Consequences of Mr. Churchill* (London, 1925), 27-31.

[4] Committee in Finance and Industry (Macmillan Committee), *Report*, Cmd. 3897, (London, 1931) para. 255-7, Addendum I, para. 323; Cab. 58/2, Economic Advisory Council, 13th Meeting, 16 April 1931, 4; Keynes Papers, Letter to J. R. MacDonald, 5 August 1931. The most persistent critic of the 1925 policy who appears to have suggested devaluation was Ernest Bevin. See, for example, Cab. 58/2, Economic Advisory Council, 13th Meeting, 16 April 1931, 4; Macmillan Committee, *Report*, Cmd. 3897, Reservation to Addendum I, Reservation by Sir T. Allen and Mr Bevin.

valued sterling.[1] This examination had substantial repercussions after September 1931, when, although sterling's fall from gold made their adoption unnecessary, several expedients, such as tariffs and controls on capital movements, found adoption and further disrupted the international economy.

The return to gold and the financial policies subsequently adopted are also important as episodes in British monetary history whose interpretation, despite several recent biographies,[2] autobiographies,[3] and special studies[4] is still 'largely composed of the old skins thrown off by the snake of controversy'.[5] The most effective phrases thrown off by the controversialists of the period still dominate our understanding of 1925 and the years thereafter.[6] They do so largely because until very recently the history of the period could be written only from secondary sources which included and commented upon the controversialists' interpretation of events. True, past studies have narrowed the gap between controversy and fact, but their documentation has been incomplete, if only because the Treasury papers for the period have been unavailable. This study, although limited by the unavailability of the Bank of England's records for the period, attempts to rectify some of these omissions, particularly with respect to the return to gold in 1925 and subsequent monetary policy, and to reduce the dominance of snakeskins in this area of monetary history. It also attempts to chronicle a period of unintended, and largely unnoticed, innovation by the Bank of England and the Treasury which laid the groundwork for the peacetime use of instruments of financial policy that proved important in the 1930s and that still find common use today.

However, before beginning this history of certain aspects of Britain's

---

[1]The classic expedient here is, of course, protection. For a full programme see Keynes' presentation to the Macmillan Committee in its discussions of 20, 21, 28 February, 6 and 7 March 1930 (Keynes Papers).

[2]L. V. Chandler, *Benjamin Strong, Central Banker* (Washington, 1958); Sir Henry Clay, *Lord Norman* (London, 1957); A. Boyle, *Montagu Norman* (London, 1967).

[3]Sir F. W. Leith-Ross, *Money Talks: Fifty Years of International Finance* (London, 1968); Sir P. J. Grigg, *Prejudice and Judgement* (London, 1948); E. Moreau, *Souvenirs d'un Gouverneur la Banque de France* (Paris, 1954); H. Schacht, *My First Seventy-Six Years* (London, 1958).

[4]S. V. O. Clarke, *Central Bank Cooperation 1924-31* (New York, 1967).

[5]R. S. Sayers, 'The Return to Gold 1925', L. S. Pressnell (ed.), *Studies in the Industrial Revolution* (London, 1960), 313.

[6]Thus it is rather amazing that, 44 years after the event, Keynes' *Economic Consequences of Mr Churchill* (London, 1925), which is essentially a political pamphlet, should completely dominate discussions of the events of 1925. See for example Clay, *Lord Norman*, 156ff.; R. Skidelsky, *Politicians and the Slump* (London, 1967), 4; S. Pollard, *The Development of the British Economy 1914-1950* (London, 1962), 219-20; P. Mathias, *The First Industrial Nation: An Economic History of Britain, 1700-1914* (London, 1969), 441-2.

inter-war financial experience, let us first look backwards in time to the pre-war adjustment mechanism used by Britain.

The Pre-war Gold Standard

The power to become habituated to his surroundings is a marked characteristic of mankind. Very few of us realise with conviction the intensely unusual, unstable, complicated, unreliable, temporary nature of the economic organisation by which Western Europe has lived for the last half century. We assume some of the most peculiar and temporary of our late advantages as natural, permanent, and to be depended on, and we lay our plans accordingly.[1]

In no aspect of Britain's economic life in 1914, or in 1919 for that matter, was Keynes' statement more apt than with respect to international currency arrangements. At the time of the outbreak of war in 1914, Britain had been on the gold standard, *de facto* or *de jure*, with the Mint price for gold at 77s. $10\frac{1}{2}$d. per standard ounce, since Newton had set the price in 1717, with the exception of an interval during and after the Napoleonic Wars. When the post-Napoleonic Wars decision to return to gold occurred with the Acts of 1819 and 1821, there had been relatively little debate as to the exchange standard or the ultimate exchange rate, only one as to timing.[2] By the 1830s, the gold standard had become an unquestioned article of faith to most economists and bankers, and so it remained, with occasional rumblings to the contrary, until 1914. Thus it had been a normal and unquestioned part of the economic environment throughout the working lives of those influential in Britain's economic affairs in the years after 1914 and of their predecessors.[3] Moreover, during this period, the standard had appeared to operate successfully for Britain and for the international economy.

The reasons behind the pre-war gold standard's successful operation are particularly relevant, for one of the significant underlying factors in the decision to return to gold at $4.86 in 1925 was Britain's pre-war experience on that standard and a belief that the adjustment mechanism under gold standard conditions worked swiftly and easily – so easily in fact that sterling had remained effectively fixed since 1821 and all other major international currencies had remained effectively fixed for

---

[1] J. M. Keynes, *The Economic Consequences of the Peace* (London, 1919), 1.

[2] F. W. Fetter, *Development of British Monetary Orthodoxy 1797–1875* (Cambridge, 1965), Ch. II–IV.

[3] To take but one example, Montagu Norman's paternal grandfather became a director of the Bank of England in 1821, the year of the first return to gold, and his maternal grandfather became a director in 1866. Thus the family's experience on both sides stretched back through three generations of gold-standard-dominated City life (information from Clay, *Lord Norman*, 3–10).

the 30–40 years before 1914, despite the vast changes which had occurred in international economic relationships during the period.

That the pre-war system of adjustment was effective and appeared to
work well to most influential observers of the pre-war world is beyond
doubt. That there were not widespread public discussions in Britain as
to alternative exchange rates or exchange systems is, to a considerable
extent, an indication of the system's successful operation.[1] Another
indication lies in the range through which the variables of financial
policy moved. In the 463 months between January 1876 and July 1914,
Bank Rate moved within a relatively narrow range, with all measures
of central tendency lying between 3 and 3.36 per cent.[2] In only 43
months, or 9.3 per cent of the time, did it stand at or above 5 per cent
and never for longer than 26 weeks.[3] Open market rates for fine bills
were similarly low.[4] Long-term interest rates were also remarkably stable,
that on Consols moving only twice in the 50 years before 1914 by $\frac{1}{4}$
per cent or more within a single year. This made Consols an extremely
liquid investment and even a medium for banks' secondary liquidity
reserves.[5] This overall stability and relatively low level of interest rates
suggests that monetary policy was rarely severely troubled by balance-
of-payments problems, an impression heightened by the relative lowness
of London rates as compared to those in other centres.[6] Moreover,
these low rates of interest were accompanied by relatively high levels
of employment. In the 33 years after 1880 trade union unemployment averaged 4.7 per cent and in 21 years stood below that level.[7]

[1] The bimetallist debates of the 1870s and 1880s are the exception. See Sir A. Feaver-
year, *The Pound Sterling: A History of English Money*, rev. ed. (Oxford, 1963), 309–11.
This is not to deny that considerable controversy often existed as to possible
directions of improvement within the existing system. See for example L. S. Pressnell, 'Gold Reserves, Banking Reserves, and the Baring Crisis of 1890', C. R.
Whittlesey and J. S. G. Wilson (eds.), *Essays in Money and Banking in Honour of
R. S. Sayers* (Oxford, 1968).

[2] O. Morgenstern, *International Financial Transactions and Business Cycles* (Princeton
1959), Table 83.

[3] Ibid.; R. G. Hawtrey, *A Century of Bank Rate* (London, 1938), Appendix I. The
comparable figures for the period March 1925–September 1931: average Bank
Rate 4.46 per cent; percentage of months at or above 5 per cent, 38.4; longest
period at or above 5 per cent, 16 months.

[4] 1876–1914 average 2.68 per cent; 1925–31 average 4.00 per cent. The difference
between the pre-war and interwar differential between Bank Rate and the three
months bill rate (0.68 per cent and 0.46 per cent) is also an index of changed
circumstances and greater pressures. Below, Ch. 9.

[5] E. V. Morgan and W. A. Thomas, *The Stock Exchange: Its History and Functions*
(London, 1962), 190.

[6] O. Morgenstern, *International Financial Transactions*, Tables 9, 83, 115.

[7] B. R. Mitchell and P. Deane, *Abstract of British Historical Statistics* (Cambridge, 1962),
Labour Force 3. 1925–31 average, calculated on a different base, 13.1 per cent.

Throughout the pre-war period, there is no evidence of demand deficiency of the inter-war Keynesian type operating for extended periods.[1] True, on other grounds, modern statistical research has found areas where pre-war performance compared unfavourably with that between the wars,[2] but it is understandable that the exchange system of the pre-war period appeared to work well to contemporary British observers and did not appear actively destabilising.

To find the reasons for this state of affairs, one must first turn to the international environment in which the pre-war gold standard system operated. The major trading nations were growing at reasonably respectable rates and international trade grew more quickly than output.[3] Moreover, the growth of the international economy was much more stable than in the inter-war period, an important factor in the British experience for British trade has never expanded in the face of declining world trade.[4] To this relative stability was added a strong parallelism in movements of economic indicators.[5] This extended from financial variables to exports, imports and trade balances.[6] These circumstances provided a much more favourable background against which the adjustment mechanism could operate than in the inter-war gold standard period.

Moreover, the pre-war international environment provided strong links between the constituent parts of the system which reduced the probabilities of the emergence of sustained disequilibria between advanced industrial countries. Trade was relatively free and the econo-

---

[1]R. C. O. Matthews, 'Why has Britain had Full Employment since the War?', *Economic Journal*, LXXVII (311), September 1968, 556, 564–6.

[2]R. C. O. Matthews, 'Some Aspects of Post-War Growth in the British Economy in Relation to Historical Experience', *Department of Applied Economics Reprint No. 240*; D. H. Aldcroft, 'Economic Progress in Britain in the 1920s', *Scottish Journal of Political Economy*, XIII (3), November 1966; 'Economic Growth in Britain in the Inter-war Years: A Reassessment', *Economic History Review*, 2nd Ser., XX (2), August 1967.

[3]A. Maddison, 'Growth and Fluctuations in the World Economy 1870–1960', *Banca Nazionale del Lavoro Quarterly Review*, June 1962, 140–4.

[4]I. Mintz, *Trade Balances during Business Cycles: U.S. and Britain since 1880* (New York, 1959), 51, 54, Chart 9. The value of world trade fell in seven years between 1880 and 1914 (three years between 1924 and 1931), while the volume of world trade fell in two (two years also between 1924 and 1931). Maddison, 'Growth and Fluctuations', Tables 20, 24, 25.

[5]O. Morgenstern, *International Financial Transactions*, 40–53.

[6]This parallelism in trade components occurred in both volume and value terms. Thus, for example, between 1890 and 1913 the value of exports and imports in Belgium, France, Germany, Britain and the U.S. moved in the same direction in 72.9 and 73.9 per cent respectively of the years observed. The trade balances of these countries moved in the same direction 68.7 per cent of the time. (Raw data from Maddison, 'Growth and Fluctuations', Tables 19, 20, 22, 23).

mies of the advanced industrial countries were closely interconnected by trade flows.[1] There interconnections, plus competition in third markets reduced the possibilities for the emergence of large international disparities in prices and costs.[2] In addition, the currency arrangements of the advanced countries, which normally combined the internal circulation of gold coin with note circulations also linked to gold, provided a stabilising influence.[3] These arrangements meant that relatively excessive (from an international point of view) internal expansions tended to have effects similar to balance-of-payments pressures, as far as the managing Authorities were concerned, and to result in situations where rates of domestic expansion were moderated in the short run. The obverse was true in periods of recession. These links, plus official concentration on reserve ratios tended to remove conflicts between domestic and external stability.[4] At the same time, however, internal banking developments and the growth of financial facilities generally prevented the link between gold and domestic activity from hampering long-term growth.[5]

However, these favourable conditions existed primarily among the advanced countries rather than throughout the international economy. The peripheral countries in the system, heavily dependent on earnings from exports of primary products and on new foreign investment for balance-of-payments stability, gained somewhat less stability from the pre-war arrangements. Export receipts, in the short run, were heavily dependent on levels of activity and demand in the industrialised centre, particularly as demand and short-run supply were price inelastic. Foreign borrowing was dependent on lending and financial conditions in the advanced countries and was unstable both in aggregate and by destination.[6] In these circumstances, particularly given the parallelism in trends in the advanced centre, peripheral areas were much more likely to have to either face large domestic adjustments or alter exchange rates as a

[1]A. Maizels, *Industrial Growth and World Trade* (Cambridge, 1963), Table 4.4.

[2]M. Friedman and A. J. Schwartz, *A Monetary History of the United States 1867–1960* (Princeton, 1963), Chart 63; E. H. Phelps Brown and M. H. Browne, *A Century of Pay* (London, 1968). 126ff, Fig. 18.

[3]R. Triffin, 'The Evolution of the International Monetary System: Historical Reappraisal and Future Perspectives', *Princeton Studies in International Finance No. 12*, 10–11.

[4]A. I. Bloomfield, *Monetary Policy under the International Gold Standard 1880–1914* (New York, 1959), 37–9.

[5]Triffin, 'Evolution', 16–20; P. Barrett-Whale, 'A Retrospective View of the Bank Charter Act of 1844', *Economica*, N. S., xi (44), August 1944.

[6]M. Simon, 'The Pattern of New British Portfolio Investment 1865–1914', J. H. Adler (ed.), *Capital Movements and Economic Development* (London, 1967); A. I. Bloomfield 'Patterns of Fluctuation in International Investment before 1914', *Princeton Studies in International Finance No. 21*, Charts 1 and 2.

result of external developments than the industrialised countries.[1]

To understand the role of London in this system, one must first grasp the immensely strong underlying position of Britain in the international economy. In the century before 1913, in every year but two, Britain had been in surplus on current account.[2] This implies that the natural tendency of sterling was to exert a strongly favourable pull over the foreign exchanges which was offset by new overseas lending both at long and short term. Consequently any balance-of-payments adjustment problem in the short run (i.e. before income effects had time to work their way through the system) largely consisted of tailoring the capital account to the current account rather than vice versa.[3] Moreover, the changes involved were invariably small[4] so that the adjustment required was never that great, although it was of some import in comparison with the Bank of England's gold reserve.

The tailoring process that characterised the British pattern of adjustment was made easier by the fact that London was the world's premier money, capital and commodity market. At any point in time foreigners had large balances in London to meet commitments on bills outstanding, on interest and dividends for foreign borrowing, etc. Moreover, the rise of colonial and overseas banks in London meant that many foreign banks' liquid reserves were held in London.[5] Similarly, the rise in official overseas foreign exchange holdings also increased the volume of funds in London.[6] At the same time, London's short-term overseas lending provided an additional means of adjustment, particularly as it totalled approximately £350 million in 1913.[7] The exact balance between London's short-term assets and liabilities is somewhat uncertain,[8]

---

[1]Moreover, in periods of international financial stress, the patterns of dominance tended to pull short-term funds in a series of waves away from peripheral centres towards London. See P. H. Lindert, 'Key Currencies and Gold, 1900–1913', *Princeton Studies in International Finance No. 24*, 46–57.

[2]Mitchell and Deane, *Abstract*, Overseas Trade 16.

[3]J. Robinson, 'Monetary Policy Again: Comments', *Bulletin of the Oxford University Institute of Statistics*, XIV (8), August 1952, 283–4.

[4]Mintz (*Trade Balances*, 39) notes that the U.K.'s trade balance changed, on average, by £2.9 million per quarter between business cycle turning points. The current account declines experienced by the U.K. on occasion between 1880 and 1913 averaged £11.4 million per annum (Mitchell and Deane, *Abstract*, Overseas Trade 16).

[5]D. Williams, 'The Evolution of the Sterling System', Whittlesey and Wilson, *Essays in Money and Banking in Honour of R. S. Sayers*, 270–2.

[6]A. I. Bloomfield, 'Short-term Capital Movements under the Pre-1914 Gold Standard', *Princeton Studies in International Finance No. 11*, 13–14; Lindert, 'Key Currencies', Ch. 2.

[7]Committee on Finance and Industry (Macmillan Committee), *Minutes of Evidence* (London, 1931), Q. 1273.

[8]Bloomfield, 'Short-term Capital Movements', 71ff.; Lindert, 'Key Currencies', 56–7.

and detailed (or indeed any) statistics on London's short-term capital position over time are unavailable. Thus we must of necessity guess the exact means of operation of the adjustment mechanism. However, given the volume of funds with which we are concerned, there can be no doubt that the Bank Rate mechanism had ample avenues of operation at the short end.

Given a deterioration in Britain's balance of payments in the short term, we must now speculate as to the operation of the adjustment mechanism. In all probability, the deteriorating position would be masked for a short time as foreign banks, colonial banks and official bodies increased their sterling balances.[1] This reshuffling of deposits, however, would have its limits in the short-run without changes in the inducements to hold funds in London in that wealth holders were probably risk averters.[2] Thus, eventually, the exchanges would probably begin to fall towards the gold export point. The Bank, because of an inability to make a higher Bank Rate effective or because of an unwillingness to raise borrowing rates to domestic industry,[3] might first attempt to protect the reserve by using the gold devices.[4] If these failed to alleviate the pressure by inducing a speculative inflow of funds as the exchange fell below the market's current gold export point,[5] then the Bank would

[1] This would be most particularly the case if the proximate cause of the imbalance was over-lending in the short period, where the funds called would normally be held in London by their new foreign owners until actually disbursed.

[2] The build-up of foreign balances through deposit reshuffling would be constrained as well by actual declines in short-term rates as these funds sought appropriate credit instruments. This would be the case particularly if foreign asset holders had markedly different asset preferences from domestic holders and were inclined to hold their funds in, say, the discount market rather than in bank deposits or idle hoards.

[3] E. V. Morgan, *The Theory and Practice of Central Banking 1797–1913* (Cambridge, 1943), 216; R. S. Sayers, *Bank of England Operations 1890–1914* (London, 1936), 125–7.

[4] These 'devices' involved the alteration of the gold points, and hence the possible range of exchange rate movements, through changes in the costs of private arbitrage. The 'devices' included paying out light, but legal, coin, raising the selling for foreign gold coins, refusing to sell bar gold or raising its price to exporters, and exercising moral suasion against resident brokers and arbitragists so as to raise the commissions normally payable for gold arbitrage. On the other occasions, the Bank might use such tactics as interest-free loans to importers or increases in its open market gold price to increase the volume of gold reaching its vaults through a reduction in the gold import point. The skilful use of such 'gold devices' could alter the gold points by over a cent (i.e. 0.2 per cent). P. Einzig, *International Gold Movements*, 2nd ed. (London 1931), 89; Sayers, *Bank of England Operations*, Ch. IV; Sir John Clapham, *The Bank of England: A History* (New York, 1945), II, 348, 379; Morgan, *Theory and Practice*, 199, 216–7.

[5] The gold points are functions of interest rates, commissions, freight rates, shipping speeds, etc. At any time, they may differ for various individuals engaged in gold arbitrage. Einzig, *International Gold*, Appendix I; Morgenstern, *International Financial Transactions*, 169ff.

be inclined ultimately to raise Bank Rate and make it effective in the market.[1]

A rise in Bank Rate, with the exchanges at or below the gold export point, would create pressures which would affect the assets and liabilities sides of the short-term capital account. Risk-averting investors, faced with the prospect of almost certain exchange gains plus higher interest earnings, would tend to accumulate additional funds in London and to delay the repatriation or transfer to third centres of existing balances. Higher interest rates, through their short-run congestion effects on the Stock Exchange, would tend to discourage long-term foreign borrowing in London, a move which would have a tendency to reduce short-term liabilities.[2] British balances abroad would tend to be repatriated to earn both higher interest and a capital gain on subsequent exchange movements. Short-term borrowing on commercial bills would be unlikely to be greatly affected as there were few alternative sources of finance available and as foreign commercial borrowers would be reluctant to alter long-standing lines of credit or banking connections, although higher interest rates plus almost certain exchange profits would mean that a larger proportion of such bills would probably be held in London with foreign funds.[3] However, drawings of finance bills were quite sensitive to changes in interest rates, and as these represented over one half of the total outstanding in 1913, small changes in interest rates could be extremely effective.[4]

Given these changes in behaviour, and given that at any time London would have an overhang of trade and finance bills outstanding that would be repaid in up to three months, the effects of a rise in Bank Rate on short-term financial flows could be quite powerful, and to some extent self-reinforcing. As these alterations in financial flows affected the exchanges, newly mined gold would be retained in London and in some circumstances gold would be attracted from foreign centres, often for defensive reasons.[5] Thus the Authorities would be able to halt

[1]Making Bank Rate effective in the market would be a difficult task for the Bank on particular occasions and this was an area of innovation during the last years of the pre-war gold standard. Sayers, *Bank of England Operations*. Ch. II; Morgan, *Theory and Practice*, 217–18.

[2]Hawtrey, *A Century of Bank Rate*, 176–7; J. M. Keynes, *A Treatise on Money* (London, 1930), I, 204, II, 376–9; W. A. Brown, Jr, *The International Gold Standard Reinterpreted, 1914–1934* (New York, 1940), I, 663; Lindert, 'Key Currencies', 46–7.

[3]Bloomfield. 'Short-term Capital Movements', 75; Macmillan Committee, *Evidence*, Q.1273.

[4]Ibid.

[5]A. G. Ford, *The Gold Standard 1880–1914: Britain and Argentina*, (Oxford, 1962), 34–40; National Monetary Commission, *Interviews on the Banking and Currency Systems of England, Scotland, France, Germany, Switzerland and Italy* (Washington, 1910), 26–7; Clapham, *The Bank of England*, II, 388; Morgenstern, *International Financial Transactions*, 572.

the drain and possibly even rebuild their exchange reserves to some extent. However, any exact statistical balancing of the part played by the international assets or liabilities sides of the short-term national balance sheet in this process is almost impossible.[1]

Domestically, changes in monetary policy and interest rates seem to have had very slight direct effects on domestic activity.[2] Evidence to support this view, to a considerable extent, comes from a survey conducted by *The Economist* in November 1907 when Bank Rate stood at 7 per cent, its highest level since June 1873.[3] At the time of the survey, Bank Rate had stood at 5 per cent or above for 27 of the previous 56 weeks and had just risen from $4\frac{1}{2}$ per cent in the 8 days after 30 October.[4] Thus both the height and the recent range of movement of Bank Rate were abnormal by pre-war standards. In this particular instance, it is interesting to note the variety of replies or reactions revealed by the survey. The reactions of the 47 firms or individuals surveyed are summarised in Table 1. The total number of replies (69) exceeded the number of returns owing to multiple responses. The emphasis on inventories was almost completely confined to markets in raw materials (jute, grain, sugar, metal, cotton, etc.) where higher carrying costs, plus an expectation of lower prices, had resulted in reductions in stocks and a fall in prices. The emphasis on expectations was also significant and stronger. What is most interesting in this respect was how changes in Bank Rate were expected to affect one's customers but not oneself, i.e. Bank Rate may have been effective in this instance simply because people believed it to be effective. The references to future investment demand expectations centred on particularly long-lived capital goods where external finance was important (railway electrification, tram extensions, housebuilding and shipbuilding). Cost of funds and availability effects appear to have affected very few of those concerned in the inquiry directly. Throughout the survey, the general impression created was that American conditions, plus a belief that Bank Rate changes affected one's customers or one's suppliers, were the most powerful agents of change in the situation.[5] To these expecta-

---

[1]See the excellent discussion by Bloomfield, 'Short-term Capital Movements', 71–7.

[2]R. S. Sayers, 'Bank Rate in Twentieth Century', *Central Banking after Bagehot* (Oxford, 1957), 63–5; A. G. Ford, 'British Economic Fluctuations, 1870–1914', *The Manchester School*, XXXVII (2), June 1969, 110–14.

[3]23 and 30 November 1907.

[4]The 1907 average Bank Rate, 4.93 per cent, represented the highest annual average Bank Rate of any year between 1867 and 1913. The 1906 average rate was 4.27 per cent, the fifth highest annual average during the same period.

[5]The emphasis on expectations is understandable, for expectational effects might be very powerful, particularly when the defense of the exchange rate is the major goal of financial policy, in that businessmen may assume that any rise in rates is the first step in a process that will continue until the necessary results occur.

TABLE I.   *Analysis of replies: 'Effects of Dear Money on Home Trade'*

Effects noted	Number of times noted
Adverse expectations resulting from American crisis	9
Adverse expectations as to future consumption demand	1 1
Adverse expectations as to future investment demand	5
Generalised uncertainty	1
Significantly higher working capital costs	7
Significantly higher fixed capital costs	2
Availability of credit reduced	3
Reductions in raw material prices as stocks realised owing to higher working capital costs	1 5
Buyers expectations of lower prices reducing raw material demand and prices	3
No significant effects	4
Not applicable	9

tional effects, the references to inventory effects on traders in raw materials, working either at home or abroad, appear to have been the other major influence operative in the situation.

As the 1907 situation was exceptional in that it represents one of the most extreme movements in Bank Rate during the pre-war period, it provides perhaps an upper bound for the possible impact of financial policy. As a result the implications of this one survey in one year for our analysis are relatively clear. The direct internal effects of changes in Bank Rate along traditional cost and availability of credit lines seem to have been relatively slight, except perhaps with respect to inventories and raw material prices, although in this latter case expectations often appear to have played a larger role than costs. In many respects, this is understandable, if only because few changes in Bank Rate ever lasted, or were expected to last, long enough to have any great effect on long-term interest rates. As Hawtrey notes for the period 1900–10, the relationship between Bank Rate and yields on Consols 'seems to have been very slight and capricious', although there was some rise in yields under the influence of generally higher Bank Rates than during the

During the interwar period, the emphasis on expectations formed an important part of the Bank of England's view of the operation of the adjustment mechanism, A. T. K. Grant, *A Study of the Capital Market in Britain from 1919–1936*, 2nd ed. (London, 1967), 10–11; Committee on the Working of the Monetary System (Radcliffe Committee), *Principal Memoranda of Evidence* (London, 1960), III, 181, para. 11; J. R. Hicks, 'Monetary Policy: A Symposium', *Bulletin of the Oxford University Institute of Statistics*, XIV (4–5), April/May 1952, 158; Macmillan Committee, *Evidence* Q. 3328–30; Keynes Papers, Macmillan Committee, Notes of Discussions, 5 December 1930, 20; Macmillan Committee, *Report*, para. 218.

previous decade.[1] The expectational effects would depend upon the circumstances prevailing at the time of the change in monetary policy, 1907 in this respect being rather unusual. However, they were probably the primary source of changes in economic activity resulting from marked changes in the direction of monetary policy.

Let us now turn to the inventory effects mentioned in the survey. These related particularly to imported raw materials. On several occasions,[2] Professor Triffin has suggested that increases in Bank Rate affected primary product prices as the increased costs of financing international trade in commodities led to forced sales by traders. As the demand for primary products was price inelastic, these sales led to considerable pressure on primary product prices which in turn provided relief to the British balance of payments through an improvement in the terms of trade.[3] As the discussion of *The Economist*'s survey above indicates, this may have been the case in 1907. However, there is considerable evidence against the normal operation of this mechanism. First, City experts of the period normally asserted that the volume of commercial bills drawn was insensitive to changes in interest rates, given the existence of long-standing lines of credit and banking connections and the small bill business of other centres.[4] Thus for the effect to be operative, changes in propensities to hold stocks would have to push stocks into the hands of those who financed their activities primarily through commercial bills rather than bank overdrafts and thus leave them holding a larger volume of raw materials at reduced prices. This seems unlikely. Second, attempts to plot annual series for the U.K. terms of trade against average levels or ranges of fluctuations in Bank Rate are inconclusive,[5] particularly given the strong parallelism between movements in economic activity and in discount rates both within and among advanced countries which suggests that cyclical factors may have been as powerful an influence.[6] Finally, an attempt to compare

[1]Hawtrey, *A Century of Bank Rate*, Ch. 5, 162. The stability of yields on Consols within given years, as noted above (p. 4), would also point to the same conclusion. This coincides with Tinbergen's overall conclusion 'that the influence of interest rates on investment activity... is only moderate. A rise in interest rates depresses business activity, but only to a modest extent'. J. Tinbergen, *Business Cycles in the United Kingdom 1870–1914* (Amsterdam, 1951), 133.

[2]R. Triffin, 'National Central Banking and the International Economy', *Review of Economic Studies*, XIV, 62–3; 'Evolution', 6.

[3]I. Mintz (*Trade Balances*, 4) suggests that the terms of trade hypothesis implies an absolute improvement in the British balance of trade during slumps, but there is no need to go that far for the effect to be important.

[4]Macmillan Committee, *Evidence*, Q 1167, 1273, 1792; Brown, *International Gold Standard*, I, 652–3. 665–6.

[5]See for example the chart in P. B. Kenen, *British Monetary Policy and the Balance of Payments 1951–57* (Cambridge, 1960), 60. See also Lindert, 'Key Currencies', 44–6.

[6]Morgenstern, *International Financial Transactions*, Chart I, Table 94.

monthly series for the terms of trade with sharp changes in Bank Rate reveals that the process described was not a normal part of the adjustment mechanism, although it was operative in 1907.[1] The short-run adjustment mechanism seems to have hinged almost entirely on capital movements rather than real factors.

Thus throughout the period before 1914, the effectiveness of the Bank of England's management of the gold standard system, from the U.K.'s point of view, depended heavily on certain elements of the prewar British situation in a favourable underlying trend in the international context. It was these elements – Britain's basically favourable balance on current account, the premier financial position of London in relation to other centres, the common money market instruments of the time, particularly finance bills, and the willingness of other centres to let gold go in the short run,[2] secure in the knowledge that it would return once the crisis was over – which made the Bank Rate mechanism seem so effective to contemporary observers[3] and to the Cunliffe Committee after the war.[4] At the same time, with adequate supplies of international liquidity – the determining factor, in many cases, of central banks' willingness to lose reserves – the mechanism could operate effectively without interest rates remaining at high levels for long periods as a result of competitive bidding for reserves – bidding which would have resulted in deflationary pressures on domestic activity in the countries concerned.[5] The effectiveness of the monetary mechanism meant that changes in Bank Rate and financial policy rarely, by themselves, had significantly large effects on domestic activity. Nor were they required to do so to be effective from the Bank's point of view. The trade or credit cycle phenomena of the pre-war period, insofar as they existed, had their roots much more in the operation of underlying trends or swings in the international economy than in the Bank Rate mechanism, which did little more than tailor a strong underlying balance of payments to those swings, perhaps damping them slightly in the process.[6]

[1] Lindert, 'Key Currencies', 44–5.

[2] In particular, one should note the willingness of the Bank of France to take active measures to ease London's position in periods of severe stress. Clapham, *The Bank of England*, II, 329, 388, 392; Sayers, *Bank of England Operations*, Ch. v; National Monetary Commission, *Interviews*, 214ff.

[3] National Monetary Commission, *Interviews*, 26.

[4] Committee on Currency and Foreign Exchanges after the War (Cunliffe Committee), *First Interim Report*, Cd. 9182 (London, 1918), paras. 4–7. The years of Lord Cunliffe's active involvement in the affairs of the Bank before 1914 were those during which the Bank Rate mechanism was used most confidently and appeared most automatic. Sayers, *Bank of England Operations*, 137–8.

[5] Triffin, 'Evolution', 17; Bloomfield, 'Short-term Capital Movements', Chart I; Lindert, 'Key Currencies', Fig. 1.

[6] A. G. Ford, *The Gold Standard*, Ch. IV; A. J. Brown, 'Britain in the World Economy 1870–1914', *Yorkshire Bulletin of Economic and Social Research*, XVII (1), May 1965,

Pre-war experience did not reveal whether the mechanism or the system of adjustment in which it operated would prove effective in a different environment, with different tasks.

An Outline of the Chapters to Follow

As it is from an idealised view of the pre-war gold standard system's operation that official thinking took its lead and much of contemporary discussion made its departure, Chapter 2 concerns itself extensively with the effects of the war on Britain's international economic position and the environment in which any post-war system of adjustment would have to operate, paying particular attention to the year 1924 when conditions were beginning to take on an aspect of normalcy. This chapter also pays some attention to official post-war thinking on the stabilisation problem, beginning with the Cunliffe Committee, and early efforts at financial reconstruction, thus setting the stage for the final discussions surrounding the decision to return to gold at pre-war par – to 'look the dollar in the face'.

The next chapter, 'The Decision to Return', examines the deliberations and the movements in opinion of the last year before the return to gold on 28 April 1925 as they occurred in the Treasury, in the Bank of England and in the Committee set up by the Treasury which publicly reported on the advisability of a return to gold on the day Britain returned. In this chapter, the emphasis is on the quality of the advice the Chancellor received – on the expectations of those involved, on the nature of the evidence and on the models of adjustment to the new parity used. From this discussion, it should be possible to decide whether one particular historical snakeskin should be cast aside – Keynes' charge that Churchill, lacking an instinctive judgement to prevent him from making mistakes, was 'gravely misled by his experts'.[1] It will also help us to evaluate Governor Norman's view of the events of 1925 and thereafter, best expressed in two statements to foreigners, Per Jacobsson of the Bank for International Settlements and Adolph Miller of the Federal Reserve Board:[2]

Yes I have made mistakes also. I am now accused for having gone back to the gold standard. It was probably a mistake. And still in those circum-

56ff. The effects of changes in Bank Rate, 'an important "Index" of economic prospects', (R. S. Sayers, 'Bank Rate in the Twentieth Century', 65) on expectations might be important in this respect, particularly as high Bank Rates (on average) and peaks in economic activity tended to coincide.

[1]Keynes *The Economic Consequences of Mr Churchill*, 10.

[2]E. E. Jucker-Fleetwood, 'Montagu Norman in the Per Jacobsson Diaries', *National Westminster Bank Quarterly Review*, November 1968, 68; letter to the author from J. A. C. Osborne, former Secretary of the Bank. In his letter, Mr Osborne added after the quote to Adolph Miller, 'But of course the Deity may not be an Economist.'

stances I should do the same thing again. It is easy to see it afterwards. But a great deal of what has happened in the meantime was not necessary but depended on policy. It might have been different.

Only God could tell whether it [$4.86] was or was not the correct figure.

From these matters of decision-making, the discussion naturally turns to the implications of the decision from the point of view of 1925 and Britain's international economic position. The examination of these implications and of possible paths of adjustment occupies Chapter 4 and Appendix 1.

Given the implications for Britain of the decision to return to gold at $4.86, attention then turns to an examination of how the Authorities made a go of 'looking the dollar in the face' whilst 'standing on tip-toe'.[1] To set the stage, Chapter 5 examines developments during the years 1925–31 from three perspectives – that of the Bank of England, that of the balance of payments and Britain's international economic position, and that of the domestic economy. Chapter 6 examines the role played in the period after 1925 by the traditional instruments of central bank policy – interest rates and aggregate credit control measures buttressed by official debt management operations. As the use of these instruments appears to have been limited relative to the tasks which the Authorities set themselves by deciding on gold at $4.86 in 1925 and to the pressures revealed in the previous chapter, there ensues an attempt to examine why the Bank, and to a lesser extent the Treasury, did not proceed further along conventional lines and how the stage was set for operations in directions unanticipated in 1925. This examination, along with a preliminary glance at possible avenues for the development of alternative policy instruments, occupies Chapter 7.

The actual development of the resulting instruments – some involving the use of moral suasion, some extending pre-war practice and some involving new departures in the Bank's or the Treasury's operations in peacetime – occupies Chapters 8 and 9. In these chapters, the processes through which these instruments came into use and the various situations in which they came to find employment are the main subject for discussion. In addition, in these chapters, the effectiveness of these new devices, most of which were essentially palliatives which helped to reduce the need for domestic deflation or to widen the Bank's range of manoeuvre in given situations, comes into consideration. With the examination of these instruments the study comes to a close and a final chapter attempts to outline some of the general conclusions arising from all the aspects of the interwar gold standard episode in Britain considered in the previous discussion.

[1] G. Crowther, *An Outline of Money*, 2nd ed. (London, 1948), 310.

2. THE WAR OF 1914 AND ITS CONSEQUENCES

Although few contemporaries realised it at the time, the First World War effectively shattered the bases of the old gold standard order, even though its external forms remained intact in the laws of the belligerents.[1] Initially, a complete breakdown of international financial markets and settlements carried sterling well above $5.00 on the foreign exchanges, as London ceased to undertake new foreign business and unwound old, and as increased risks for shipping and thus higher insurance rates, later coupled with a refusal of the Authorities to include gold under the war risks insurance scheme, made the gold points irrelevant as far as shipping gold was concerned. However, as the Authorities agreed to pay sterling for gold deposited with the Canadian Minister of Finance in Ottawa, the sterling exchange soon returned to more normal levels. But this calling of funds was a once-for-all operation and sterling soon fell below the pre-war gold export point on the dollar exchange as resources were increasingly devoted to the war effort, as British prices rose and as British and Allied demands for American goods rose while exports declined. At the same time, the major Allied currencies depreciated against sterling.[2] In the course of 1915, the exchanges were pegged by official borrowing and intervention with the proceeds, the British Government's pegging of the dollar exchange beginning in August 1915 after the failure of an earlier effort by a committee of London bankers. Ultimately, the intervention peg came to be 4.76\frac{7}{16}$ and, with an official Defence of the Realm Act, prohibition of the melting of gold coin in December 1916[3] and a widening net of controls

[1] Brown, *International Gold Standard*, I, Ch. 2.

[2] These relationships between sterling, the dollar and Continental currencies arose from the fact that most transactions between the Continent and the United States were settled through London.

[3] This would do more to prevent domestic hoarding than exports. A reduction in hoarding would leave more gold in circulation which the Authorities could tap to increase their own reserves. Thus the legal existence of the gold standard during the War depended, *ceteris paribus*, on the unavailability of insurance coverage which protected the reserves by preventing private arbitrage at the pegged rate.

on all types of foreign transactions, the Authorities settled down for the duration with the gold standard legally intact. This pegging of the exchange involved the use of substantial resources, official support totalling $2,021 million between the financial year 1915–16 and the financial year 1918–19 and private support remaining substantial.[1] At roughly the same time, the Allies also pegged their exchanges near their pre-war gold standard pars and it was behind this facade of normalcy on the exchanges that international cost and price levels diverged substantially under the impact of war.[2] At the end of hostilities, however, the question of Britain's future exchange policy required a solution.

As a part of its planning for post-war reconstruction, the Government, towards the end of the war, appointed a number of committees to examine the problems of the transition from war to peace and to suggest appropriate policies for both the transition period and the post-war world. As a part of this process, the Treasury and the Ministry of Reconstruction, in January 1918, appointed a Committee on Currency and Foreign Exchanges after the War, under the chairmanship of Lord Cunliffe, the retiring Governor of the Bank of England, 'to consider the various problems which will arise in connection with the currency and the foreign exchanges during the period of reconstruction and report upon the steps required to bring about the restoration of normal conditions in due course'.[3]

Initially, the official conception of the Committee was that its members would have, for the most part, the necessary information so that it would not need to call witnesses.[4] Eventually, however, the Com-

[1] E. V. Morgan, *Studies in British Financial Policy 1914–1925* (London, 1952), 356.

[2] Some indication of the divergence in price levels that had occurred during the war comes from an examination of wholesale prices in March 1919, the last month during which the Authorities pegged the sterling–dollar exchange. Converting the indices to a common gold basis and taking 1913 or 1914 = 100, the indices appeared as follows: Sweden 354, United States 196, United Kingdom 217, France 336, Italy 325, Germany 274. Other indices of the divergences can be obtained from an examination of exchange movements after the cessation of pegging. Brown, *International Gold Standard*, i, 206, Table 15.

[3] Cunliffe Committee, *Final Report*, Cmd. 464 (London, 1919), 2. The terms of reference were later extended to include the words 'and to consider the working of the Bank Act, 1844, and the constitution and functions of the Bank of England with a view to recommending any alterations which may appear to them to be necessary or desirable'. For a study of other efforts to prepare for peace see P. B. Johnson, *Land Fit for Heroes: The Planning of British Reconstruction 1916–1919* (Chicago, 1968).

[4] Most of the proceedings of the Committee are available in three bound volumes at the Public Record Office as T185/1–3. Volumes i and ii (T185/1–2) represent the main discussions and evidence taken by the Committee on currency and foreign exchange questions plus certain memoranda. The third volume (T185/3) contains the hearings and report of a sub-committee on subsidiary silver coinage. References to the proceedings will be by volume and page: thus T185/1, 83 refers to page 83 of

mittee in the course of its extensive private discussions decided to call a series of witnesses.[1] In the end, the Committee heard 18 witnesses and received several additional memoranda, the most interesting for economists being those of Professors J. S. Nicholson and H. S. Foxwell.[2] As with later Committees, much of the discussion ranged over such matters as the Bank Act of 1844, the relations between the Bank of England and the clearing banks and the Bank of England itself.[3] Thus only bits of the evidence and private discussions concerned themselves with the problem which is of interest to us – the post-war international currency policy of the U.K.

Throughout its discussions, the Committee *assumed* that Britain would return to the gold standard at the pre-war par, and members of the Committee and witnesses did not question this assumption by either considering alternative gold standard rates or alternative currency policies.[4] Thus interest centred on the transition to gold from conditions in which the exchange was supported by foreign borrowing and by formal and informal restrictions on gold movements and most international transactions while British prices were above foreign prices by unspecified amounts.[5] The Committee in its discussions expected that the transition to normal in all respects would take approximately ten years.[6] To successfully conclude that ten-year period with the exchange at pre-war par and with the operation of the Bank Act of 1844 restored in its essentials – the Treasury currency note issue amalgamated with the Bank of England note issue and a central gold reserve of £150 million[7] – the Committee and its witnesses accepted the need for some measure of post-war deflation.[8] They accepted that the process of deflation would be difficult, especially right at the end of the war with its reconversion demands, pressures for changes in social policy and the like,[9] although

the first volume, the point at which Sir John Bradbury stated that the Treasury did not expect that the Committee would need to call witnesses.

[1]T185/1, 146.

[2]The Nicholson memoranda appear in T185/1, 206–12 and T185/2, 496–503. The Foxwell memorandum appears in T185/2, 474–6.

[3]For a discussion of the background to these banking questions see Pressnell, 'Gold Reserves, Banking Reserves, and the Baring Crisis of 1890', 219-28; L. J. Hume, 'The Gold Standard and Deflation: Issues and Attitudes in the Nineteen-Twenties', *Economica*, N.S. xxx (119), August 1963, 229–32.

[4]Cunliffe Committee, *First Interim Report*, para. 15; Clay, *Lord Norman*, 112.

[5]T185/1, 96, 207–8; Cunliffe Committee, *First Interim Report*, para. 18.

[6]Ibid., para 1; T185/1, 178; T185/2, 506.

[7]The sum of £150 million was first mentioned in passing by Cunliffe (T185/1, 106). It was then the subject of memoranda by Pigou and Bradbury (T185/1, 100–2, 116–21) before it was agreed by the Committee (T185/1, 122, *First Interim Report*, para 41).

[8]T185/1, 94, 95, 96, 106–7, 141–2, 208; T185/2, 497–8, 577.

[9]T185/1, 98, 120, 208; T185/2, 497.

Professor Pigou saw that the task of currency restoration might be eased by American inflation.[1]

However, the Committee was very uncertain as to how the transition from a wartime regime of an exchange rate pegged by foreign borrowing and restrictions to one of gold and no restrictions was to be handled. To some extent, this resulted from uncertainty as to the degree to which sterling, to use a later phrase, would be overvalued at the pre-war parity. It also reflected uncertainty as to exactly how long the basic transition period – i.e. that period until sterling returned to pre-war par on the exchanges – would last and as to how the period of transition immediately after the war would be handled. Pigou's analysis of the situation for the Committee ran as follows:[2]

[I]t is obvious that *ultimately* unless we are prepared to lose all our gold and go upon a pure paper currency, discount rates here will have to be raised sufficiently to stop the tendency of gold to be drained abroad. The raising of the discount rates required for this purpose will involve a contraction of credits, a fall of prices and an inflow of notes from the circulation into the reserves: and equilibrium will be established with a discount rate and a level of prices more or less equivalent to the world gold level. The notes brought into the reserve must not, if equilibrium is to be maintained, be used as an excuse for lowering the discount rate: for, if they are so used, credits will be expanded again, the equilibrium destroyed and gold again set going abroad. They can be, and should be, cancelled by being exchanged against Government securities and no new ones being issued except in exchange for gold or old notes. This policy *must* come about ultimately and any attempt to defeat it would involve subsidence to a pure paper currency. But it is a policy which can be *postponed* by a continuation of loans [from] abroad and the restriction of gold export. This is in effect what is being done at the present time: and it is arguable that the present policy of postponing the return to equilibrium should be continued for some little time after the war ends; i.e., that the first few months of the reconstruction period should be treated as a continuation of the war period. If it is decided to do this, it will be necessary, when the natural restriction of gold export due to submarines has disappeared, to create an artificial restriction. If this is not done, the policy, even though adopted only for a short time, would threaten the disappearance of all our gold. Furthermore so long as we are paying for imports by credits specially enacted by the Government, there is obviously a strong case for continuing rigid control of capital investments abroad and restriction of unessential imports.

Assuming the policy of low discounts and a restriction of gold exports

[1] T185/1, 96; Cunliffe Committee, *First Interim Report*, para 18.
[2] T185/1, 98–9. After the word 'desirable' in the last paragraph, Pigou added the following footnote: 'It is possible that in the reconstruction period the relation between credits and circulation may for various reasons be rather different than it has been during the war, but this does not affect the main argument'.

to be adopted for a short period, it is open to the Banks during that period to make the discount rate such as to involve either (1) increased credits and the need of more notes in circulation or (2) the same volume of credits as at the end of the war and the need of the same volume of notes in circulation or (3) a diminished volume of credits and a diminished need for notes in circulation. It is plain that the more discounts are lowered and credits and note circulation expanded during this short period of restriction of gold export, the greater the wrench will have to be in raising discounts and contracting credit when the temporary expedients proper to the period are brought to an end. It will, therefore, be desirable, if possible, not to add to 'inflation' but rather to begin the process of deflation, bringing up the discount rate and bringing down credits and circulation towards the level they will have to assume when gold exports are released and equilibrium restored. It may well happen that this policy will prove less difficult than is often supposed. When the war ends, Government payments on contracts will continue and it may be that Treasury bills will so fall off that they do not nearly absorb the balances created in favour of Government contractors. These contractors may use their balances to buy War Loan held by the Banks, and in this way may reduce their balances considerably. There should, therefore, be a very large margin available for reconstruction loans, before total credits are raised above their war level.   (Italics in the original).

Professor Nicholson, albeit somewhat ambiguously,[1] also accepted the need for restrictions on gold exports and a gradual transition[2] as did the Federation of British Industries[3] and Walter Leaf.[4] However, the Chairman opposed such restriction 'if we could help it'[5] as did Cockayne, the Governor of the Bank.[6] Instead, they both favoured borrowing abroad and/or gold exports. Sir Felix Schuster, on the other hand, simply favoured gold losses by themselves.[7] However, most of the members of the Committee saw with Pigou the need for import restrictions and restrictions on the export of capital to keep the exchange rate up over the transition.[8]

There was, as a result, some disagreement as to the pace at which deflation should occur. Professor Nicholson stood at one extreme, along with most of the Committee, taking the view that 'the process of deflation ought to begin as soon as peace is restored'.[9] Lord Cunliffe tended towards the same point of view,[10] while Bradbury[11] and Pigou[12] saw that there might be reasons for avoiding deflationary measures of

---

[1]T185/1, 212.   [2]T185/2, 500.
[3]Ibid., 571.   [4]T185/1, 287–9, 293.
[5]Ibid., 166, 122, 317.   [6]T185/2, 516, 517–18.
[7]T185/1, 174–6, 177, 190.
[8]Ibid., 83, 110, 197, 198, 288; T185/2, 577; Clay, *Lord Norman*, 112.
[9]T185/1, 208.   [10]Ibid., 95.
[11]Ibid., 120–1; T185/2, 531.   [12]T185/1, 98–9.

any serious sort immediately after the war. The F.B.I., on the other hand, represented the opposite pole with its suggestion that deflation should not occur until most of the debt incurred at inflated wartime prices had been repaid.[1]

Thus the Committee might be said to be somewhat divided and uncertain as to the best short-term policy but united on long-term goals. This division and uncertainty, plus an understandable lack of sureness as to the state of the world immediately after the end of hostilities,[2] probably go far towards explaining the structure and tone of the *First Interim Report*, which centred upon 'broad principles upon which the currency should be regulated'[3] and left matters of timing and procedure undeveloped except as regards the currency note issue.[4] Thus the Committee satisfied itself with recommending in summary:[5]

In our opinion it is imperative that after the war the conditions necessary to the maintenance of an effective gold standard should be restored without delay. Unless the machinery which long experience has shown to be the only effective remedy for an adverse balance of trade and an undue growth of credit is once more brought into play, there will be a grave danger of a progressive credit expansion which will result in a foreign drain of gold menacing the convertibility of our note issue and so jeopardising the international trade position of the country.

The pre-requisites for the restoration of an effective gold standard are:

(a) The cessation of Government borrowing as soon as possible after the war...

(b) The recognised machinery, namely, the raising and making effective of the Bank of England discount rate, which before the war operated to check a foreign drain of gold and the speculative expansion of credit in this country, must be kept in working order. This necessity cannot and should not be evaded...

(c) The issue of fiduciary notes should, as soon as practicable, once more be limited by law, and the present arrangements under which deposits at the Bank of England may be exchanged for legal tender currency without affecting the reserve of the Banking Department should be terminated at the earliest possible moment.

When the *First Interim Report* was made public just before the end of the war, these recommendations were met with general acceptance. *The Economist* welcomed them in a leading article entitled 'Back to Sanity' which referred to the *First Interim Report* as 'an eminently sound document'.[6] This opinion was, with few reservations, echoed in many other quarters.[7] The Committee's views, moreover, were repeated

[1] T185/2, 577.
[2] Cunliffe Committee, *First Interim Report*, para. 1.
[3] Ibid., para. 1.   [4] Ibid., para. 33.
[5] Ibid., para. 47.   [6] 2 November 1918, 618–19.
[7] Hume, 'The Gold Standard and Deflation', 228–9.

by the *Report* of the Committee on Financial Facilities, which unlike the Cunliffe Committee had contained a majority of industrial and commercial representatives.[1]

However, despite the welcome given to the Cunliffe *Report,* when the Armistice came on 11 November 1918, the Authorities lacked a short-term currency policy integrated with the achievement of long-term goals. The Bank of England, following the thrust of its evidence to the Cunliffe Committee, proposed that the Authorities make an attempt to bring sterling to pre-war par in the brief period between the end of the war and the signing of a peace treaty, and it pressed the Government repeatedly to allow interest rates to rise and to fund short-term debts.[2] However, the Government hesitated to follow this advice, if only because it feared the effects of a deliberately engineered trade depression at the start of the peace being added to the dislocations arising from reconversion.[3] Moreover, the Government had not as yet settled its priorities for the period of reconstruction.[4] Keynes, who was still attached to the Treasury at the time, suggested a programme[5] to his superiors which would have possibly settled the dispute between the Bank and the Government by allowing free export of gold immediately with such exports subject to a duty of 10–15 per cent, the amount by which Keynes believed sterling to be depreciated from its pre-war parity. The scheme would have restored a free gold market, by allowing importers negotiable duty rebate certificates for a similar amount of gold exports. The duty itself could not be increased except by Act of Parliament; whereas, it could be reduced by Order-in-Council. Gold would be freely obtainable at the Bank for export 'without questions asked and with no more direct or indirect hindrance than existed before the War'.[6] Such a programme would have restored 'the *natural* forces which regulated the flow of gold before the War' (italics in the original) and 'would allow a large part of the mechanism of freedom to come into play without any violent transition from the existing regime'.[7] Keynes' plan would have moved in the direction of the Cunliffe Committee's recommendations in an ingenious manner, but it fell by the wayside in the ensuing discussions. In the interim, the pegging of the exchange at 4.76\frac{7}{16}$ continued.

Eventually, as the cost of pegging the exchange was very high, the

---

[1]Cd. 9227, (London, 1918).
[2]Clay, *Lord Norman*, 113–16; Boyle, *Montagu Norman*, 125–6.
[3]A. C. Pigou, *Aspects of British Economic History 1918–1925* (London, 1947), 146; Johnson, *Land Fit for Heroes*, Ch. 11, 13–15 (esp. 389–90).
[4]Ibid., 364–8 provides a good example of one effort to settle post-war priorities.
[5]T170/129, Keynes to Bradbury, 4 January 1919. This document is dated January 1918 in the files, but internal evidence, particularly its use of exchange quotations for 30 December 1918, suggests a January 1919 date.
[6]Ibid., 3.   [7]Ibid., 2 and 5.

Authorities decided to solve the transitional problem in another manner. On 20 March 1919, official exchange support ceased and on 1 April official regulations under the Defence of the Realm Act prohibited the export of gold without official permission. This latter step occurred despite the protest of Cockayne, who would have welcomed gold losses and the resulting deflationary pressure on financial policy, but other bankers gave it unanimous support.[1] Norman, at that time the Deputy Governor of the Bank, appears to have supported the Governor.[2] In the course of the rest of the year, restrictions on various current and capital transactions were relaxed, Treasury borrowing on Treasury bills in New York was halted and, through a licensing system, a semblance of the free London market in gold was restored in September 1919. The surrounding administrative regulations were ultimately consolidated in the Gold and Silver (Export Control) Act 1920, which (as is normal in such cases) was due to expire after five years, on 31 December 1925. Finally, in the course of 1919 most of the economy was removed from wartime controls. Thus by late 1919, the Authorities could gain an accurate picture of the depreciation of sterling which had occurred in the course of the wartime inflation and gauge the task ahead.[3] About the same time, amidst the post-war restocking boom, the Bank obtained Treasury agreement to a 6 per cent Bank Rate and a limitation on the currency note issue along Cunliffe Committee lines. By April 1920, Norman, now Governor of the Bank, had persuaded the Treasury to agree 'reluctantly' to a 7 per cent rate.[4] At about the same time, the post-war boom began to break in both Britain and America.

Having formally left the gold standard, the Authorities had as their primary aim a return to gold. As Sir Otto Niemeyer put it, the policy implications were as follows:[5]

If we are to get back to an effective gold standard with a free market for gold, which was the policy of the Cunliffe Committee and of the Committee consisting mainly of representatives of Commerce and Industry on Financial Facilities after the War which reported soon after the date of the first report of the Cunliffe Committee, and which has been and still is the policy of His Majesty's Government, it is certain that there must be some deflation, some fall in the proportion borne between spending power on the one hand measured in terms of pounds sterling, the best indices of which are the figures of legal tender circulation and bank deposits, and on the other hand the output of goods and services...

If we recognise this, and remember that though the war has made us

---

[1]Clay, *Lord Norman*, 116–17.   [2]Boyle, *Montagu Norman*, 126.
[3]For a good discussion of these see Brown, *International Gold Standard*, I, 177–90.
[4]Clay, *Lord Norman*, 138.
[5]T175/6, Niemeyer, 'Memorandum on Deflation', undated but position in file suggests the summer of 1921.

poorer, it has also won for us our freedom to go forward on our traditional lines of development to new successes, we need not feel unduly depressed.

However, the amount of deflation necessary for a return to the pre-war parity depended on developments abroad, particularly in the United States, the only country to return to gold quickly after the war. Thus the American exchange, not domestic conditions, became the official index of the Cunliffe policy's success. Any restrictive American policy actions had to be matched in London for the exchange to remain where it was and when no American restrictive action took place, British policy still had to be restrictive to work the exchange back to par.

At the same time, the Bank of England had to regain control of its own markets to make its policy effective. At the end of the war, Government expenditure was running far ahead of revenue, the 1918–19 deficit totalling 65.5 per cent of total expenditure; the banking system and the public were highly liquid and heavy creditors of the Government; the initiative for interest rate changes lay largely with the Government whose rate for tap Treasury bills served as the corner-stone of the system of market rates; and with almost one-third of the national debt at maturity under five years (almost one-fifth under three months) the problems of refinancing and debt management loomed large. In this situation, the Authorities had to run very hard to remain in the same place: every loss of control, unless parallel to one in America, made the task of returning to gold more difficult.[1]

The struggle for control lasted from the end of the war until 1922. During that period, the Government's financial policies were sharply reversed, despite the depression that occurred from mid-1920 onwards.[2] Central government expenditures fell by almost 60 per cent while revenues rose by 27 per cent. A deficit of £1,690 million in financial 1918–19 was transformed into surpluses of £237.9 million in 1920–1, £45.7 million in 1921–2 and £101.5 million in 1922–3.[3] By March 1922, debt under five years had fallen from almost a third to just over a fifth of the national debt.[4] The clearing banks' cash reserves were

[1] For a full discussion of the 1918–19 position see Morgan, *Studies*, 114–15, 138–56, 202–7; Clay, *Lord Norman*, 109–34.
[2] The post-war boom of 1919–20 must primarily be regarded as a restocking or a conversion boom. However, its extent was to a considerable extent determined by the availability of funds (bank advances rose by over £350 million between January 1919 and April 1920, or by 81.1 per cent, while new issues also surged ahead [Pigou, *Aspects of British Economic History*, Appendix, Section IV, Table II, 173–4] although a rise in velocity also occurred). On the whole episode see pp. 169–97 of Pigou's book.
[3] Mitchell and Deane, *Abstract*, Public Finance 3 and 4. Morgan (*Studies*, 104) suggests that these figures represent a lower bound to the size of the surpluses.
[4] Pember and Boyle, *British Government Securities in the Twentieth Century*, 2nd ed.

reduced from 14.3 per cent of deposit liabilities in 1919 to 11.7 per cent in 1922, their secondary reserves falling from 27.3 per cent to 25.3 per cent of deposits during the same period.[1] The money supply remained above its 1919 average level, but by December 1922 currency in the hands of the public had fallen by 14 per cent from the level of April 1920, while bank deposits had fallen by 2 per cent. Non-financial clearings during the same period fell by almost 40 per cent.[2] All of these indices, plus the existence of a 7 per cent Bank Rate for over a year (6 per cent or above for eighteen consecutive months), provide clues as to the deflationary pressures emanating from the public sector that characterised the period. Their results appear, along with those emanating from the concurrent international slump, in the price and unemployment statistics: by December 1922 the Board of Trade wholesale price index and the Ministry of Labour cost of living index stood at 64.5 and 79.1 per cent respectively of their November 1918 levels and 48.0 and 64.4 per cent respectively of their 1920 peak levels, unemployment among trade union members, which averaged 2.4 per cent in 1919 and 1920, averaged 15.2 per cent in 1922.[3]

By 1922, the Bank of England had also regained control of financial markets. The December 1919 Treasury Minute limiting the fiduciary issue of currency notes and the Treasury's policy of adding Bank of England notes to the currency note reserve both served to transfer internal expansionary pressures to the Bank's reserve and hence give it motives for action. The reinstitution of the tender system for Treasury bills in April 1922 was even more significant. Prior to 30 April 1922, Treasury bills had only been available at fixed rates controlled by the Treasury. This fixed tap rate had inhibited independent movements in Bank Rate, for an increase in Bank Rate by itself merely produced a refusal by the market to take up Treasury bills at the old tap rate, a shift to commercial bills and a rise in official borrowing on Ways and Means Advances from the Bank, which was expansionary as it increased the reserves of the banking system. The resumption of tender sales in April, plus the virtual ending of tap sales in July 1922, meant that market rates were once more determined by the total supply of bills in the market as compared to the total supply of funds. As the Bank had the advantages of a new instrument of market control, open market operations in Treasury bills, and new contacts with market institutions formed by wartime operations,[4] the 1922 decisions, along with the

(London, 1950), 395, 401. Excluding external debt the figures are 39 per cent and 25 per cent respectively.
[1]Macmillan Committee *Report*, Appendix I.
[2]Pigou, *Aspects of British Economic History*, 158–9.
[3]Mitchell and Deane, *Abstract*, Labour Force 3.
[4]Clapham, *Bank of England*, II, 421–2.

totality of other events which had occurred since 1920, meant that the Bank's operational position was potentially much stronger than pre-war. In the summer of 1922 the Bank began to use this new power by embarking on active open market operations to control the assets of the market, at first in a slightly expansionary direction.

Thus at the end of 1922, with the economy in the doldrums,[1] the exchange at $4.63½ – a far cry from the low of $3.40 in February 1920 – the Authorities were in a position to begin serious consideration of the tactics for a return to par. The cost of the period since the end of the boom in 1920 had been high as the index for non-financial clearings, a reasonable guide to the level of activity, noted above indicates to some extent. Real Gross Domestic Product had fallen by 6 per cent between 1920 and 1922,[2] unemployment stood at 12.6 per cent, money wages had fallen heavily – by almost 40 per cent or an average of 28s. 6d. per week for those affected – although real wages had risen slightly, and 102 million man-days had been lost in industrial disputes.[3] In 1922 consumers' expenditure, in real terms, stood below the level of 1910 and G.D.P. at factor cost in real terms stood at its second lowest in this century, the lowest being 1921.[4] It was from this level that the final struggle for par ensued. The Bank and the Treasury still regarded the Cunliffe Report as their 'marching orders'.[5]

For over a year, from mid-1922 onwards, domestic considerations took priority over exchange considerations. The series of Bank Rate reductions to 3 per cent 'owing to domestic reasons'[6] and the mid-1922 series of open market operations which saw the Bank's holdings of Government securities rise steadily and the market's indebtedness to the Bank fall somewhat are all indications of this orientation. By July, Bank Rate was 1 per cent below the Federal Reserve Bank of New York's discount rate, and even then it was ineffective as market rates fell as low as 1¾ per cent early in July. In August, the market rate was pushed up to 2½ per cent through open market sales, and it remained in this area for several months before falling away in the second quarter of 1923. A deteriorating exchange position, resulting from rising British prices and the final phases of the German inflation (which saw funds leaving Europe for America over the sterling exchange) brought a rise in Bank Rate to 4 per cent in July 1923, but the new rate was generally ineffective with market rates rising only slightly and remaining

[1] The phrase is Pigou's (*Aspects of British Economic History*, 7).
[2] London and Cambridge Economic Service (L.C.E.S.), *The British Economy, Key Statistics 1900–1966* (London, n.d.), Table B.
[3] G. Routh, *Occupation and Pay in Great Britain 1906–60* (Cambridge, 1965), 114–15.
[4] L.C.E.S., *Key Statistics*, Table B.
[5] J. M. Keynes, *A Tract on Monetary Reform* (London, 1923), 195.
[6] Clay, *Lord Norman*, 140.

close to 3 per cent. The rise occurred despite Treasury opposition.[1] There was some slight pressure in clearing bank reserve ratios, largely through secondary assets, but this was not severe. The situation remained roughly unchanged in spite of the effects on the exchanges of the inflation scare caused by the speech of a Conservative Junior Minister and of the elections which brought the first Labour Government to power.[2] At the end of January 1924 sterling stood at $4.27½ and the gap between U.S. and U.K. retail prices had widened slightly.

During the period from mid-1922 onwards, although the Cunliffe Committee's goals remained paramount, the Authorities were largely waiting upon events. The Bank was awaiting a settlement of war debts and reparations, uncertainties over which bedevilled the exchanges during the period and affected sterling.[3] British war debts to the United States were settled in February 1923, while other debts, reparations and Central European instability were continual objects of official efforts during this period, but with few results, except in Austria, before the end of 1923.[4] Moreover, both the Bank and the Treasury were expecting the influx of gold in to the United States which had occurred after 1920 to lead to inflation there which would obviate the need for further British deflation to restore sterling to par.[5] In the course of 1923 there was considerable discussion of a proposal to accelerate this process by shipping a large amount of gold to America, the sum suggested being £100 million, thus effectively altering the composition of the U.K.'s exchange reserves and incidentally ensuring funds for war debt repayments.[6] The proposal which Niemeyer admitted would 'cause a flutter in the dovecots both here and in America'[7] and which R. G. Hawtrey believed would be 'a very effective substitute for those "great gold discoveries" '[8] was discussed at various intervals and in various forms

[1]Ibid., 145–6; T176/13, Niemeyer to Norman, 23 June 1923.

[2]It is of interest to note that the Junior Minister's speech, the exchange effects of which were to prove so important during the 1924–5 discussions, had limited effect on forward rates (or speculative confidence in sterling), which prevented spot sterling from falling as heavily as it might have otherwise. See R. Z. Aliber, 'Speculation in the Foreign Exchanges: The European Experience, 1919–1926', *Yale Economic Essays*, II (1), Spring 1962, 194.

[3]F.R.B.N.Y., Norman to Strong, 21 March 1923; Clay, *Lord Norman*, 141.

[4]Ibid., 173–210.

[5]Ibid., 143. Between 1920 and 1924 the U.S. gold stock rose from $2.6 billion to $4.2 billion. Federal Reserve Board, *Banking and Monetary Statistics* (Washington, 1943), Table 156.

[6]Clay, *Lord Norman* 146–8; T176/5, Niemeyer to Chancellor, undated but internal evidence indicates 1923; T176/13, Niemeyer to Norman, 23 June 1923; T176/5, R. G. Hawtrey, Memoranda of 31 October and 17 November 1923; Niemeyer to Norman, 20 November 1923; Norman to Niemeyer, 21 November 1923.

[7]T176/5, Niemeyer to Chancellor, undated.

[8]T176/5, Hawtrey, Memorandum of 31 October 1923.

before November 1923 when Norman finally rejected it as impractical and unlikely to be successful.[1] Just before this, the Committee of Treasury decided that the policy of waiting should continue and that 'any attempt to reconsider the Report of the Cunliffe Committee, at any rate until after a complete settlement of Reparations and inter-allied debts, should be resisted.'[2] Thus at the beginning of 1924, the Authorities were still determined to wait.

Britain and the International Economy in 1924

By 1924, the United Kingdom was well on the way to recovery from the slump of 1920–2. Manufacturing production which had reached 93.6 lin 1920, surpassed that level in 1924 when it reached 100 (1913 = 90.8).[3] It is true that some industries (chemicals, textiles, shipbuilding, drink and tobacco, miscellaneous metal goods) were producing below their 1920 output levels, but generally industries were well above it. All industries, other than coalmining which reflected the drop in coal exports after the Ruhr settlement of almost 18 million tons (or double the year over year fall in output), were producing more than in 1923. With the rise in manufacturing output, employment rose. The number of man-years in civil work was 240,000 above the 1923 level, of which 130,000 were in manufacturing (the rises since 1921 were 830,000 and 560,000 respectively).[4] Unemployment, although considerably above the 2.1 per cent average of 1913 for trade union members, stood far below the strike-affected June 1921 peak of 20.6 per cent, reaching a low of 7.0 per cent in May.[5] On the basis of the Unemployment Insurance returns, the coverage of which was wider, unemployment had fallen from its May 1921 peak of 2,549,395 or 23.0 per cent of those insured to 1,044,540 or 9.2 per cent in May 1924.[6] Among males, the 1924 levels represented the lowest figures for the decade after December 1920. This unemployment was unevenly distributed among trades. Taking the figures for June 1924, when the overall average was 9.3 per cent,[7] one finds above average percentages in the metal industries, including their suppliers and users other than electrical manufacturing, non-electrical engineering, shipbuilding, textiles, public works contracting,

[1]T176/5, Norman to Niemeyer, 21 November 1923.
[2]Clay, *Lord Norman*, 148.
[3]K. S. Lomax, 'Production and Productivity Movements in the United Kingdom since 1900', *Journal of the Roual Statistical Society*, Series A, cxxii (2), 1959, 192–3.
[4]L.C.E.S., Key Statistics, Table E.
[5]Pigou, *Aspects of British Economic History*, Statistical Appendix, Section I, Table VI.
[6]Ibid., Statistical Appendix, Section I, Table IX.
[7]Ministry of Labour, *Eighteenth Abstract of Labour Statistics of the United Kingdom*, Cmd. 2740 (London, 1926), 70–3.

and transport, especially shipping and docking. Given that public works contracting and docking were notorious for the high levels of unemployment associated with their casual systems of labour hiring, it is significant to note that the high unemployment industries tended to concentrate in the export sector. The lowest unemployment industries, on the other hand, tended towards the domestic market. This distribution of trades also accords roughly with the indications provided by the statistics of industrial production, and existed despite a tendency for the number of workers in the depressed trades to decline. It also coincided with the distribution of wage rates, which tended to remain higher in sheltered trades and had moved against the unsheltered trades since 1920.[1]

This tendency towards divergent patterns of behaviour in the sheltered and unsheltered industries becomes clearer if we compare the 1924 components of G.D.P. with those of 1913, dealing in real terms throughout. Taking 1913 as 100, real G.D.P. in 1924 stood at 91.7, consumers' expenditure at 99.5, public consumption at 114.5 and gross fixed capital formation at 132.5. Real exports of goods and services, however, stood at 72.0 while imports had reached 100.3.[2] If we compare the behaviour of British exports and imports of goods only with that of world and European exports, the relatively poor British export performance and the high level of imports is more apparent. Again taking 1913 = 100, British exports and imports of goods stood at 80.1 and 111.2 respectively, while the volume of world exports had recovered to 107.4 and European exports to 82.2 (both of the latter series including the U.K. figures).[3] Thus even in a period when most of Europe was recovering from the ravages of wartime damage and post-war disorganisation, British exports had done relatively badly.

The problems of British foreign trade in 1924 were highly concentrated in her traditional industries: iron and steel, textiles, coal, shipbuilding and machine tools, although much less so in the last. Steel exports (including under this head iron and semi-manufactures) in 1924 had reached only 77.5 per cent of their 1913 level; whereas imports had risen to 104.7 per cent of that base.[4] Similarly, exports of cotton piece goods, which suffered heavily from Indian and Japanese competition in Far Eastern markets, in 1924 stood at only 64.8 per cent of their 1913 level.[5] Coal exports had also fallen off as a result of the slow growth of international trade, increased efficiency in fuel utilisation, the growing use of oil-fired ships and competition from other sources of

[1]Routh, *Occupation and Pay*, 109–15; Pigou, *Aspects of British Economic History*, 48–52, 206–7.
[2]L.C.E.S., *Key Statistics*, Table E.
[3]Maddison, 'Growth and Fluctuations', Tables 25 and 27.
[4]Mitchell and Deane, *Abstract*, Iron and Steel 9 and 10.
[5]Ibid., Textiles 4.

energy, and even the disruption of Ruhr production in 1923 and 1924, which gave a boost to exports, only pushed them to 80 per cent of their 1913 level.[1] Shipbuilding, which felt the effects of world over-capacity after the war, of international trade below its 1913 level and of increased Scandinavian competition, found its 1924 output for U.K. citizens or companies at only 80.3 per cent and its exports even lower at 35.2 per cent of their 1913 levels.[2] As this particular group of exports accounted for almost 40 per cent of the value of 1913 exports, its difficulties had a significant impact on the U.K.'s overall post-war export performance.

TABLE 2.   *The current account of the balance of payments of the United Kingdom, 1907, 1911, 1913, and 1924.*

Item	1907	1911	1913	1924
Trade deficit	−128	−123	−134	−337
Invisible income:				
Net shipping income	+ 85	+ 90	+ 94	+140
Net investment income	+160	+187	+210	+220
Net short interest and commissions	+ 25	+ 25	+ 25	+ 60
Net other invisibles	+ 10	+ 10	+ 10	+ 15
Excess of Government overseas				
expenditure	n.a.	n.a.	n.a.	− 25
Balance on invisibles	+280	+312	+339	+410
Balance on current account	+152	+189	+205	+ 73

n.a. = not available and assumed 0.
Source: *Board of Trade Journal.*

This rather disappointing export performance, combined with strong import demand had, along with other influences, an important effect on the balance of payments. The change in Britain's overall international position is best seen in Table 2. In these years as in every year since 1822 the visible trade balance was in deficit and the income from invisibles was necessary to cover this deficit and allow for short-term lending and long-term foreign investment. Given the pre-war position, any factors tending to increase the deficit on the balance of trade or to decrease the surplus on invisible would, given the desire and the organisation of the London market to lend abroad, tend to weaken London's international position.

The war transformed London's capital position. Between 1914 and

[1] Ibid., Coal 5.
[2] Ibid., Transport 2; Board of Trade, *Statistical Abstract for the United Kingdom 1913–33*, Cmd. 4801 (London, 1935), Table 227.

1919 the cumulative total of transactions on capital account appears roughly as follows:[1]

U.K. Government loans	−£1,825 million
Private loans	−£260 million
U.K. Government borrowing	+£1,340 million
Sales of foreign securities by U.K. Government[2]	+£270 million
Private sales of securities repayments, and net contraction of London's short-term position	+£530 million
Net change (or sales of assets)	+£55 million

The deterioration implied by these transactions is greater than meets the eye, for, as O. T. Falk observed,[3] the Government loan position made the United Kingdom a 'debtor to strong countries and a creditor of the weak', as the borrowing and security sales were largely American while the lending was largely to France, Russia and Italy and subject to varying degrees of default.[4] The net effect of these transactions on the current position in any post-war year would be roughly as follows:

(1) The sale of approximately £500 million of privately held securities − £270 million in privately held securities were vested by the Authorities and sold by the American Dollar Securities Committee and private sales were probably of the same order of magnitude[5] − assuming these yielded 5 per cent on average, would have reduced Britain's income from overseas investment by £25 million.[6]

(2) The decline in London's short-term position as either a net or gross creditor[7] from 1913 by approximately £250–£300 million,[8] assuming short-term interest rates of between 2 and 5 per cent, would have reduced invisible earnings by, say, £5–£15 million. The change in the net short-term balance sheet position and in certain credit instruments in addition affected the effectiveness of certain instruments of monetary policy, as we shall see below, and made the conduct of policy more difficult.[9]

(3) Government borrowing abroad, combined with the default of governments to which the United Kingdom was a creditor and the slow-

[1]Morgan, *Studies*, 342–3.

[2]These securities were either requisitioned or purchased by the British Government from private holders. They were predominantly denominated in dollars.

[3]O. T. Falk, 'Currency and Gold: Now and After the War', *Economic Journal*, XXVII (109), March 1918, 49.

[4]The Russian war loans defaulted totalled £423 million. *The Economist*, 'Reparations and War Debts Supplement', 23 January 1932.

[5]Morgan, *Studies*, 330–1.

[6]If anything, this estimate may be a bit low. Royal Institute of International Affairs (R.I.I.A.), *The Problem of International Investment* (London, 1935), 160.

[7]For some discussion of London's pre-war position see: Morgan, *Studies*, 332, 343; Bloomfield, 'Short-term Capital Movements'. 66, 76; Lindert, 'Key Currencies', 56–7; P.M. Oppenheimer, 'Monetary Movements and the International Position of Sterling', *Scottish Journal of Political Economy*, XIII (1), February 1966, 92–5.

[8]Morgan, *Studies*, 342–3.   [9]Below, pp. 34–6.

ness of other debtors to fund their war debt payments, meant that British Government payments abroad rose faster than income. The 1924 deficit of £25 million on Government account, as compared to a probable position of rough balance in 1913, partially reflected this fact.

The war also meant large merchant shipping losses for the U.K., and in 1924 the tonnage of British registered shipping was almost 700,000 below that of 1914. This too would imply a decline in invisible earnings if utilisation rates remained unchanged.[1]

Given these basically unfavourable influences that operated on the pre-war balance-of-payments position, even without any other unfavourable events, substantial changes would have been necessary in other items to restore the pre-war position. If any price increases took place, these changes would have had to be more substantial, for with equal changes in export and import prices from their pre-war levels the deterioration in the balance of trade in money terms, assuming no volume changes, would have been substantial owing to the pre-war deficit position.[2] Inflation would also imply some deterioration in the real value of the U.K.'s income from overseas investments as these were predominantly in fixed interest form.[3] Inflation would not affect the income on other invisible items as much, for shipping freights would, to some extent, move with the general price level and short interest and commissions income would reflect price changes in that, with rates unchanged,[4] the same percentage of larger sums borrowed or insured as a result of inflation would increase earnings. Thus, even with no changes from pre-war volumes of exports and imports, wartime inflation and changes in the long and short-term capital positions resulting from the war would have implied a deterioration in Britain's international position from that of 1913 or any other typical pre-war year.

The balance-of-payments estimates for 1924 presented in Table 2 above, reflect all of these influences, plus the deterioration in Britain's trading position. The rise in prices since 1913 reflected itself in the net shipping income item where the increase of £46 million is almost an exact reflection of the increase in tramp freight rates from 68 in 1913 to 121 in 1924 (1869 = 100)[5] and the decrease in British tonnage. The same influence, plus new overseas issues of £440.3 million between

[1]Mitchell and Deane, *Abstract*, Transport 1.

[2]Although there would be no change in 'real' terms, the change in money terms would be significant given the limited elements in the invisibles account that were inflation-proof.

[3]B. Thomas, 'The Historical Record of International Capital Movements', Adler (ed.), *Capital Movements and Economic Development*, 15.

[4]T. Balogh, *Studies in Financial Organisation* (Cambridge, 1947), 244–5, indicates that rates for acceptances actually fell.

[5]Mitchell and Deane, *Abstract*, Transport 4.

1920 and 1923, the wartime sales noted above and Russian revolution and other losses of over £150 million,[1] made itself felt in the net investment income which stood £10 million above the 1913 level. The estimate for short interest and commissions reflects inflationary developments, wartime losses, and the twin influences of changing financial instruments and falling commission rates on some parts of London's business. However, the most important change, in many respects, appears at the top of the series, for the increase in the merchandise deficit swamped improvements in the invisibles position in money terms. In real terms the deterioration in both the trade and invisible accounts is striking. The value of the surplus on invisibles in terms of 1913 import prices was £250 million, or £89 million below that of 1913; while the trade deficit at 1913 import and export prices was over £160 million above that of 1913. The deterioration of the U.K. position implicit in these volume changes had been reduced by an improvement in the terms of trade by 25 per cent.[2] It was in this light that the 1924 balance-of-payments position should have disturbed contemporary observers.

Between 1913 and 1924 the balances in particular markets had also changed in a fashion which made the multilateral settlement of the overall British position more difficult. Before the war, Britain had depended on heavy current account surpluses in her transactions with India, the rest of Asia, Australasia and Africa to cover deficits in Europe and America.[3] Between 1913 and 1924 the trade position between Britain and various groupings of her trading partners changed as outlined in Table 3. During this period, the British position deteriorated substantially with respect to North and North-East Europe, the United States, British North America and Latin America. The only major improvement occurred in Central and South-East Europe where British exports and re-exports to Germany grew although her imports were halved, thus changing the position from one of a deficit of £19.9

[1] R.I.I.A., *Problem of International Investment*, 131. The annual rate of new lending during 1920–3 was well below the pre-1913 level in both real and money terms.

[2] L.C.E.S., *Key Statistics*, Table K. If one probes beneath the change in the trade deficit that occurred between 1913 and 1924, in the full knowledge that such partial equilibrium exercises do not tell us anything about causation, one finds the following:

Year	Actual trade deficit at current prices	Hypothetical change in trade deficit due to changes in:		
		Volume	Prices	Terms of trade
1913	134			
1924	337	−166	−173	+131

For a discussion of the problems and methods involved in such calculations see below, p. 122, and C. P. Kindleberger, *The Terms of Trade: A European Case Study* (New York, 1956), 276–84.

[3] S. B. Saul, *Studies in British Overseas Trade 1870–1914* (Liverpool, 1960), Ch. III.

million in 1913 to a surplus of £35.4 million in 1924. This situation could hardly be stable, as the recovery of German industry and the need of Germany to export or to reduce her imports in order to transfer reparations or debt service would tend to reduce the British bilateral surplus and result in a reversion towards the 1913 position. Within Asia, the Indian surplus had declined from £23.3 to £12.8 million and only increased surpluses with other Asian areas prevented this greatly affecting the aggregate. However, the key area of deterioration was

TABLE 3.   *Bilateral trade balances, 1913 and 1924 (£ million)*

Area	1913 Balance	1924 Balance	Change
N. and N.E. Europe	−35.8	−65.1	−29.3
W. Europe	−16.9	−29.0	−12.1
Central and S.E. Europe	−21.2	+22.1	+43.3
S. Europe and N. Africa	+ 6.1	+ 0.6	− 5.5
Turkey and Middle East	− 8.5	−22.0	−13.5
Rest of Africa	+19.8	+ 7.8	−12.0
Asia	+35.7	+31.5	− 4.2
U.S.A.	−82.2	−162.6	−80.4
British N. America	− 3.2	−35.2	−32.0
West Indies	+ 0.2	−12.4	−12.6
Central and S. America	−17.2	−61.2	−44.0
Australasia	− 8.7	−18.7	−10.0

Source: B. R. Mitchell and P. Deane, *Abstract of British Historical Statistics* (Cambridge, 1962). Overseas Trade 12. (These figures are for imports, exports and re-exports of goods.)

what might be called the dollar area, the Americas, where the trade deficit rose by £156.4 million. When to this deterioration is added the decline in dollar incomes on invisible account through the sale of dollar securities during the war, war debts and the shifting of many financial services from London to New York, a potential source of post 1924 strain in the system of multilateral payments becomes immediately apparent. The British pattern of multilateral international settlements and the British balance of payments were more involved in the American economy and its successful management than previously, given Britain's need to finance her larger bilateral deficit by earning sufficient surpluses in third countries.

To these overall changes in the balance of payments and the pattern of settlements, one must finally add changes in the effectiveness of monetary policy between 1913 and 1924–5, for such changes significantly affected Britain's international position. The first major changes involved an alteration in the nature of the short-term securities in the London market. Before the war the sterling bill was supreme as a source of international trade finance. On the other hand, the Treasury bill represented the 'small change' of the London market, the total out-standing in 1913 being no more than 1 per cent of the value of commercial bills outstanding.[1] After the war, changes in methods and sources of trade finance meant that the value of commercial bills rarely rose far above the pre-war level of £500 million, despite the rise in prices;[2] whereas the value of Treasury bills outside the Government Departments and the Bank of England stood between £425 and £575 million.[3] Within the class of commercial bills the type of bill predominating changed, for, whereas 60 per cent of the pre-war prime acceptance outstanding were finance bills, after the war the Bank of England discouraged finance bills which became rarer as the Bank was less prepared to discount them and as the growth of forward markets in London and the widespread use of telegraphic transfers made them less necessary.

These changes in the bill market had important effects on monetary policy. First, the factors determining the volume of bills changed. Before 1914 the volume of bills depended largely on the level of business activity and the level of prices; whereas, after the war the volume of bills became heavily dependent on the budgetary position and the debt management policy of the Authorities. Second, the deposit-compelling nature of the volume of bills on London changed. Commercial bills normally carried with them sterling deposits as acceptors had to carry working balances with their London acceptance houses and as the latter had to be in funds to meet acceptances before their due date.[4] The relative decline of the commercial bill meant that the volume of funds automatically in London was reduced. The Treasury bill, by itself, did not compel foreign deposits to come to London. Third, the change in the volume of finance bills affected the effectiveness of Bank Rate and high interest rates. The volume of commercial acceptances in London was relatively inelastic to interest rate changes; whereas finance bills were very sensitive to such changes.[5] Before 1914, a rise in Bank Rate would induce a reduction in the number of finance bills drawn on London and this, plus the maturing of existing finance bills, gave considerable relief from exchange pressures. After 1918, with the decline of the finance bill, this type of relief from exchange pressure no longer existed and the Bank Rate mechanism depended much more on the attraction of funds from abroad. Thus to achieve a given exchange improvement after the war, the Bank had to pursue a more active policy than previously, for it had to attract much larger deposits rather

[1]Balogh, *Studies*, 174.   [2]Ibid., 165–8.
[3]T175/46, Treasury Bill Figures, undated.
[4]Macmillan Committee, *Evidence*, Q. 1147, 1159; Balogh, *Studies* 233–4.
[5]Brown, *International Gold Standard*, 1, 652–3, 666; Macmillan Committee, *Evidence*, Q.1273.

than rely on a combination of a fall in the volume of finance bills plus an increase in deposits. True, the Bank's position was somewhat stronger in that the Treasury bill gave it an ideal instrument for open market operations and the connections developed with market institutions during the war increased the areas of consultation and the degree of confidence. However, the larger post-war floating debt and the continual need for official refinancing somewhat reduced the short-term freedom of the Bank to pursue its policy goals, and one must place this loss against the gaining of a new policy instrument by the Bank for use in the changed market conditions of the 1920s.

The second major change in the background factors affecting the conduct of monetary policy lay in the rise of New York as an important international financial centre. This change from a relatively centralised to a more decentralised financial system increased the need for foreign balances and foreign exchange transactions for any given volume of business activity. It also complicated London's international position as the sterling–dollar exchange remained the main channel for remittances between New York and areas outside the Western Hemisphere. This meant that changes in the attractiveness of New York as a deposit centre for secondary money markets or changes in New York's volume of lending affected the sterling exchanges independently of the position of the British pattern of settlements and balance of payments at the time. Such exchange changes, under gold standard conditions, would have effects on gold flows which could be troubling to the Authorities, for they could necessitate changes in credit policy unrelated in the balance-of-payments position. Finally, the existence of a second major money market, where interest rates were much less tied to international than to domestic conditions and where official policies were often likely to be domestically rather than internationally orientated, when combined with the reduction in London's deposit-compelling ability meant that the exchanges were open to potentially greater strains than they had been before 1914. Whether these additional complications would matter to London's policy makers depended largely on the underlying strength of London's position. If it was strong, although the additional strains would make life more complex they would not force frequent conflicts in the policy goals; if it was weak, these new strains might prove extremely troublesome.

These changes in the international position of Britain and the associated developments in the domestic economy formed the backdrop against which the 1924–5 discussions concerning the return to gold took place. Most of them had some relevance to the policies actually followed and the exchange rate actually chosen. As to their impact on the participants in 1924–5, an examination of contemporary thought and opinion best tells the story.

3. THE DECISION TO RETURN

The final series of discussions that led to the decision to return to the pre-war parity in 1925 began just over a year before Churchill took that decision. On 19 March 1924, Governor Norman drew the attention of his Committee of Treasury (or the executive committee of his directors) to answers to House of Commons' Questions in which the Chancellor, Philip Snowden, stated that the Government was still guided by the Cunliffe Committee's conclusions as to the desirability of a return to gold at the pre-war parity and that the Government saw advantages in the amalgamation of the Treasury controlled currency note issue with that of the Bank of England. The Committee was then invited to express opinions concerning the advisability of appointing an expert committee to consider the amalgamation of the note issues.[1] The Committee of Treasury must have approved of the idea, for on 16 April Norman wrote to Sir Otto Niemeyer of the Treasury suggesting that the Treasury appoint such a committee.[2] This committee would almost inevitably bring up the question of the return to gold, for the Cunliffe Committee, which would almost certainly be its point of departure, had recommended that amalgamation await at least a year's experience on the gold standard with a minimum gold reserve of £150 million.[3] Norman went on to suggest the possible membership of such a committee – an ex-Chancellor of the Exchequer as Chairman, Niemeyer, Sir John Bradbury, Sir Basil Blackett, 'an Economist (e.g. Professor Pigou)' and a banker.[4] This matter was discussed with the Chancellor and decided early in May,[5] and invitations went out to the membership which was

---

[1]Clay, *Lord Norman*, 149.
[2]T160/197/F7528, Norman to Niemeyer, 16 April 1924.
[3]*First Interim Report*, para. 41, 47.
[4]T160/197/F7528, Norman to Niemeyer, 16 April 1924.
[5]T160/197/F7528, Niemeyer to Fisher and Chancellor, 5 May 1924. This note is dated 5/4/24, but as it appears in a file opened 16/4/24 and as it attached Norman's letter of that date, it seems likely that the date should be 5/5/24. T160/197/F7528, Niemeyer to Chancellor, 19 May 1924.

as follows: Sir Austen Chamberlain (Chairman),[1] Sir John Bradbury, Sir Otto Niemeyer, Professor Pigou and Gaspard Farrer. All the members, except Chamberlain and Niemeyer, had been members of the Cunliffe Committee.

The Deliberations of the Chamberlain–Bradbury Committee, June–October 1924

The Committee met for the first time on 27 June, and before Governor Norman, the Committee's first witness, appeared it discussed its terms of reference: 'to consider whether the time has now come to amalgamate the Treasury Note Issue with the Bank of England Note Issue, and, if so, on what terms and conditions the amalgamation should be carried out'.[2] The Chairman opened this discussion by drawing the logical conclusion implicit in the terms of reference. He[3]

pointed out that the question before the Committee was inseparable from the much larger question of the restoration of a free gold market, which has become very prominent since the publication of the Dawes Report and in view of recent discussion. The Chancellor of the Exchequer would probably desire the Committee to consider this wider question, and to hear evidence from the representatives of all classes affected, for instance the views of industrial as well as of financial experts should be invited.

If anything, this drawing of a conclusion implicit in the Committee's terms of reference should have been expected. However, the Committee, when inviting witnesses to appear before it, did nothing to make this implication as clear to potential witnesses as it had to itself through a list of questions – the practice of the Cunliffe Committee – or otherwise. Instead, witnesses were given only the terms of reference of the Committee and a copy of the Cunliffe Committee's *First Interim Report*.[4] This meant that the evidence that the Committee received primarily concerned currency note arrangements and that witnesses were generally unprepared[5] for questions on the large issue of the return to gold. Thus the summaries of the evidence concerning the return to gold are of necessity an amalgam of answers made on the spot rather

---

[1] Chamberlain became Secretary of State for Foreign Affairs in the Baldwin Government of November 1924 and Bradbury replaced him as Chairman; hence the Committee is often known as the Chamberlain–Bradbury Committee.

[2] Treasury Minute, 10 June 1924.

[3] Pigou Papers, Committee on the Currency and Bank of England Note Issues, Minutes of First Meeting.

[4] Keynes Papers, N. E. Young to Keynes, 4 July 1924.

[5] Only the F.B.I. provided the Committee with a written memorandum before the appearance of its representatives. All other witnesses relied on oral statements which generally ignored the larger question of a return to gold.

than positions prepared in advance. This, moreover, partially explains Keynes' and Professor Cannan's surprise at the form of the Committee's *Report*[1] despite their experience of having given evidence. However, if they had perceptively read the transcripts of evidence which they, in the course of things, had to correct, they could have gathered more of the Committee's intentions and through such things as supplementary memoranda made their views coherently known.[2]

Governor Norman appeared before the Committee as its first witness. Prior to his appearance he had discussed his evidence with his Committee of Treasury and, as Sir Henry Clay records it,[3] he had suggested the immediate amalgamation of the note issues, the deferment of any attempt to settle for the time being the amount of the fiduciary issue and the ending of the prohibition of gold exports with the expiry of the enabling legislation at the end of 1925. However, before the Chamberlain–Bradbury Committee, he was to take a slightly different tack on the all-important gold standard question.

He began his evidence by noting that if he had been asked to give evidence three months previously he would have concerned himself solely with the issue of amalgamation, for at that time currency expansion and a lack of domestic monetary control resulting from rising American prices affecting British prices through rising raw material costs were his main concerns. However, these questions had since become 'entirely subsidiary' and the gold standard question had become a 'practical one'.[4] The reasons behind this change in attitude were, according to the Governor, as follows: (1) 'the continued depreciation of the exchange'; (2) 'the shrinking from sterling of which I have experience from many parts of the world'; (3) 'the lack of confidence which we ourselves have and have engendered in others in the future of sterling'; (4) the recent reductions in Federal Reserve discount rates; (5) the restoration and return of other areas to gold or near gold.[5] He noted that although his colleagues were in agreement with him on these factors and on the ultimate goal of a return to gold at the pre-war par, they were 'not all precisely agreed as to the machinery of doing certain of these things'.[6]

Governor Norman then set out his proposals for the restoration of the gold standard.[7]

[1] J. M. Keynes, 'Notes and Memoranda. The Committee on the Currency', *Economic Journal*, xxxv (138), June 1925, 299; E. Cannan, 'Review of T. E. Gregory, *The Return to Gold*', *Economic Journal*, xxxv (140), December 1925, 615.
[2] See for example Keynes' behaviour noted below (p. 42, n.1.). The proceedings of the Committee suggest that Keynes was unique in his provision of any supplementary material for the Committee or its members.
[3] Clay, *Lord Norman*, 149.
[4] Pigou Papers, op. cit., Evidence of M.C. Norman, 1–2.
[5] Ibid., 2–3.   [6] Ibid., 7.   [7] Ibid., 6–7.

D

I think the first thing to do is that you should decide a date on which the export [of gold] should be permitted and I think the next thing to do is to announce it as a fixed and immutable date beyond all possibility of change and to leave me to work towards it . . . I believe it would appear much more reasonable to the public at large and to the community to fix so long a period as three years, and I believe the result would be no less quickly reached than if you fixed a short period. But I think it is extremely valuable camouflage and appears far more reasonable than to fix a short date. Therefore I do not mind a long date, in fact, I favour it.

He admitted that it would be possible to reach par before the expiry of the prohibition legislation, but he did not think that an average exchange rise of 1 per cent per month after the Committee reported, assuming here a report in the autumn of 1924, was 'a reasonable proposition to put before the man in the street'.[1] He expected that the mere announcement of a definite policy would cause a rise in the exchange because it would show confidence in the exchange,[2] and he thought that the exchange would probably go to par quickly enough to give the Bank some experience at $4.86 before freeing exports of gold, although he was unsure whether the exchange would stay permanently at par and anticipated that the Bank would 'be very apt to back and fill'.[3] He admitted that the transition would not be easy and that this was one reason for his desire for a period longer than eighteen months.[4] Although the Governor did not think that the return would have 'quasi catastrophic'[5] effects on industry, he thought it would 'lead to higher rates here undoubtedly, and to contradiction here undoubtedly'[6] and he expected 'a long period of dear money'.[7] The exact effects of a return would depend on American money rates, on European developments, especially in Germany, and on the reduction in British foreign lending that would be part of the process.[8] The Governor did not look to salvation through a rise in American prices, for, as he put it, 'the Federal Reserve people have complete control of their prices'.[9] Thus there was an element of sacrifice in a return to gold which Norman believed the businessman must make for stability, 'for the good of his business and for his future success'.[10] The exact amount of this sacrifice was uncertain, as it depended on developments elsewhere. Norman could not be specific in his estimates of the necessary price adjustments for a successful restoration, for he did not know what the balance between psychology and price adjustment was in the existing exchange value of sterling and he was unsure of purchasing power parity calcu-

[1]Ibid., 10.   [2]Ibid., 9.
[3]Ibid., 10.   [4]Ibid., 14.
[5]Ibid., 16.   [6]Ibid., 11.
[7]Ibid., 19.   [8]Ibid., 11–12.
[9]Ibid., 17.   [10]Ibid., 13.

lations and whether he 'would really believe such calculations if they were made'.[1] Throughout his evidence, the emphasis was on the need for a target date for the return to gold, for a decision and for the freedom to take the measures necessary to make the announced decision a reality. Time was of the essence only for the decision and a public statement of official intentions.

Norman's evidence was followed on 27 June by that of another Bank of England Director, Sir Charles Addis, a member of the Cunliffe Committee and 'the Bank Director on whose advice Norman relied and whom he used most in his discussions on international cooperation with other centres'.[2] Addis was less prepared to wait for the return to gold. He argued that the Government should announce that the legislation restricting gold exports would not be renewed after 31 December 1925, and that the Bank then take the steps necessary to make such an announcement a success, using the Government statement as 'the reason, and if necessary the excuse', for those steps.[3] He believed that any period longer than the eighteen months to December 1925, such as that proposed by the Governor, would not be credible and as such would be dangerous.[4] Eighteen months would also be sufficient, in his opinion, to allow some adjustment in contracts and to take some of the sting out of the price falls implicit in the return to parity.[5] The amount of deflation necessary for a successful return to parity was uncertain, for he expected some rise in American prices to reduce the existing gap of 10 per cent between the American and British price levels.[6] He was not averse to falling prices as such, so long as changes were not sudden, and he pointed to the experience of 'the latter part of the last century' when 'the trade of this country was never more prosperous, nor were the working people ever better off . . .'.[7] Addis saw 'further social disturbances, further strikes and discontent' as more likely to accompany the rising prices that a failure to follow his policy of returning to gold would entail than to accompany a return to gold and a fall in prices.[8] He admitted that an increase in Bank Rate and credit contraction would be necessary to make the statement of policy credible and to increase confidence in its successful outcome, but, as he put it :[9]

admitting a sacrifice even though we may differ as to the amount, even if it should be the full amount, I think it would not be too high a price to pay for the substantial benefit of the trade of this country and its working

[1]Ibid., 19.
[2]Clay, *Lord Norman*, 138. See also Governor Strong's comment (below, p. 51).
[3]Pigou Papers, op. cit., Evidence of Sir Charles Addis, 58–9.
[4]Ibid., 60.　　　　　　　　　　[5]Ibid., 45.
[6]Ibid., 44–5, 57–8.　　　　　　[7]Ibid., 45.
[8]Ibid., 45–6.　　　　　　　　　[9]Ibid., 45–6.

classes, and also, although I put it last, for the recovery by the City of London of its former position as the world's financial centre.

Thus Addis' evidence differed little from Norman's on the issue of return to gold, except in matters of timing and of the necessary degree of adjustment. Even in matters of timing the difference was very slight, as Norman expected sterling to be at par long before the transition period was over, thus effectively telescoping the necessary adjustments into a comparable period. The difference, in many ways, was merely a matter of public relations.

The evidence presented by the other witnesses who appeared before the Committee in the course of its meetings in the summer of 1924 can be treated in a much more summary manner. The remaining witnesses divided themselves into three groups: (1) those who were more or less opposed to a return to gold at any time; (2) those who were in favour of a return to gold as soon as possible, and (3) those who favoured an ultimate return to gold at the old parity, but had doubts as to the wisdom of such a policy in the existing circumstances. To the evidence of each of these groups I now turn.

Keynes and McKenna were the only witnesses who appeared before the Committee who could be classed as opposing the return to gold, but there were complexities[1] in the policy implications of their evidence. Keynes argued that the embargo on gold exports should remain in perpetuity and that both imports and exports of gold should be subject to licences which might be generally available for long periods.[2] Within this context he argued that the goal of monetary policy should be price stability, a policy goal which he noted many people who did not agree with him on longer term objectives supported for the transitional period 'until there has been some final decision as to what our ultimate currency policy is going to be'.[3] He argued that a return to parity at the present time would require 'a drastic credit restriction', that it would raise the prices asked for British exports in terms of foreign currencies so 'that in a great many cases ... our export trade would be absolutely cut from under our feet for the time being', and that it would lower import prices so that 'we should also tend to buy more, and the extent to

---

[1]Keynes reinforced the thrust of his evidence to the Committee by forwarding to the chairman an advance copy of his article 'The Policy of the Bank of England' (*The Nation and Athenaeum*, 19 July 1924). This article echoed the tone of his evidence, as it is outlined below. McKenna agreed with this article and said that it followed his evidence to the Committee. Keynes Papers, Chamberlain to Keynes, 18 July 1924; McKenna to Keynes, 19 July 1924. In many ways it is unfortunate that the Committee did not question Keynes closely on his position, for even through his oral evidence and his articles he did have some effect on the Committee's Report intended for the Labour Government (below, p. 47).
[2]Pigou Papers, op. cit., Evidence of J. M. Keynes, 15.
[3]Ibid., 4.

which we should do that would depend on the confidence in this policy being permanently successful'.[1] He admitted that the fall in import prices would limit the rise in export prices in foreign currency in industries that used large amounts of raw materials, but this relief would be limited and would not obviate the need for a fall in costs, largely wages, of about 12 per cent.[2]

In the longer term, however, Keynes foresaw problems of an entirely different character. He argued that the pursuance of a policy of price stability would 'almost certainly lead to a restoration of the parity of the sovereign, because I find it very hard to believe that American prices will not rise in time, unless, they do improbable things'.[3] In fact, Keynes suggested that American inflation would, if sterling was convertible at the old parity, result in Britain being swamped with gold imports, and that this, plus economy in the use of gold, would lead to inflation.[4] As he desired price stability and wanted to prevent this inflation and as he was worried by American financial instability and the power of New York over the international economy, Keynes was opposed to a return to the gold standard.[5] However, if the authorities desired to return to gold, he suggested that they retain the embargo until it was made useless by other policies, particularly American inflation, and that they retain the power to close the Mint or lower the price of gold to prevent inflationary pressures from abroad pushing British prices up.[6] However, throughout his evidence, it was clear that from his point of view this was a second best policy.

Reginald McKenna's evidence to the Committee was also somewhat complex (as well as ambiguous) in its policy implications. He admitted that his basic goal was stability in the prices of goods and services.[7] He would guide monetary policy solely with regard to the price level and pay no attention to the exchanges.[8] McKenna believed that such a policy would not affect the business of London as a financial centre, as it could look after itself on the basis of its own attractions of size, price and quality of service.[9] However, once he had said this McKenna more or less concluded his evidence against the gold standard as a long-term goal of policy, for generally he could see few objections to returning to gold at the old parity, if sterling returned to par as the result of external events. He saw three advantages in the gold standard: 'the average man's confidence in a currency when it is convertible into

---

[1]Ibid., 14.   [2]Ibid., 14.   [3]Ibid., 16.
[4]Ibid., 16, 23.
[5]Ibid., 18–19; see also Keynes, *Tract on Monetary Reform*, 174–6.
[6]Pigou Papers, op. cit., Evidence of J. M. Keynes, 16–17. In other words, Keynes believed that it was probable that the exchange rate compatible with price stability might actually be above $4.86.
[7]Pigou Papers, op. cit., Evidence of R. McKenna, 1, 21.
[8]Ibid., 24.   [9]Ibid., 26.

something which he can see or handle', the Imperial interests involved in having most gold production in Empire countries, and the prospect of a repetition of the gently rising prices of 1901–4 which would result if gold found use as a basis for credit and which would be good for trade.[1] He had no fears of a shortage of gold 'because the output today is very great and on any increase in the value of gold the output would be extended'.[2] The only objections McKenna could find against the gold standard in theory were the costs of supporting the price of a commodity whose output was greater than demand and the unsettled position of war debts. As he put it in conclusion, 'On the whole, therefore, if you could get a conference and if you could get the cost of purchasing gold distributed over the whole world, I should be in favour of reverting to the gold standard.'[3]

However, McKenna was unwilling to force the adjustment in prices necessary to revert to the gold standard through domestic policy. As he put it:[4]

You can only get back to a gold standard by a rise in prices in the United States relative to our price level. There is no other means of getting back. The notion that you can force down prices here until you get to the level of the United States if they remain constant is a dream . . . The attempt to force prices down when you have a million unemployed is unthinkable . . . You cannot get on the gold standard by any action of the Chancellor of the Exchequer . . . He could cause infinite trouble, infinite unemployment, immense losses and ruin, but he could not balance his Budget while he was doing it, and he would have to begin again to borrow.

As he expected American prices to rise, owing to the Federal Reserve's shortage of suitable earning assets to offset the gold inflow, he argued that the Authorities should merely keep British prices stable in the interim.[5] As the Americans had an interest in the United Kingdom's return to gold, he argued that there might be a possibility of obtaining an agreement with the United States on war debts as a condition for returning.[6] What he did not advocate was a deflation in the United Kingdom to achieve parity. Thus McKenna concluded his evidence on the gold standard. As to longer-term policy it was rather ambiguous, for, although he accepted the Keynesian position, he could see little wrong with the gold standard as a system, largely because he expected the general international environment in which it would work to be somewhat inflationary. This same expectation had coloured much of Keynes' evidence to the Committee, and as we shall see it had its effects on the results of the summer's deliberations.

Those who favoured a return to gold in the very near future, Walter

---

[1]Ibid., 11–12.   [2]Ibid., 21.
[3]Ibid., 12–13.   [4]Ibid., 14–15, 17.
[5]Ibid., 15–16.   [6]Ibid., 22–3.

Leaf of the Westminster Bank, Sir George Paish and Professor Edwin Cannan, did so for somewhat differing reasons. Some accepted the logical case for a managed currency along Keynesian lines, but thought it impracticable. As Professor Cannan put it: 'I quite agree that managed currency is superior if you get the proper people to manage it under all sorts of circumstances, but I don't think it is practicable for this country at present'.[1] However, among the three there was some disagreement as to the timing of a return in the near future and as to the need and degree of adjustment required. Sir George Paish argued that the embargo should be removed at once.[2] He believed that the exchange would go to par and thought a rise in Bank Rate might be unnecessary to keep it there, although it might be used as insurance. He argued that the balance on current account was favourable and that the need for the embargo no longer existed.[3] In fact, Paish suspected that the embargo was inhibiting the accumulation of gold reserves in the United Kingdom, that its removal would lead to an influx of gold, and that restoration would also lead to an increase in foreign balances.[4] Foreign lending, he thought, provided no problems, even in the short run, for, as he put it, 'We do send the credit in goods and not in gold'.[5] Professor Cannan, although he agreed with Paish on timing, thinking 'that if these things are to be done at all they should be done quickly and get it over', thought that there would be some adjustment strains.[6] He admitted that higher rates for money would be necessary and that there would be unemployment, but as he noted of the former, 'That is a thing we have very often had to put up with in the past, and it has not done any great harm.'[7] The important thing is to make the change quickly and suddenly, for that way he argued you would get over the unemployment 'quickly', although he expected that wage reductions would be more difficult to achieve now that unemployment insurance made the unemployed 'more comfortable nowadays than they used to be' and took pressure off trade unions to accept reductions.[8] Walter Leaf was a more transitional figure, more the McKenna of this group than anything else. He assumed that sterling was undervalued at the time and argued for a bold policy, a return to gold 'at the earliest possible moment'.[9] He would pay some regard to the condition of trade in that he 'would not put up the Bank Rate to about 10 per cent in order to do it', but he would increase Bank Rate immediately to aid the transition by attracting foreign balances to London on an interest and exchange profit basis and by

[1]Pigou Papers, op. cit., Evidence of Professor E. Cannan, 5–6. See also evidence of Sir George Paish, 24.
[2]Ibid., 10.   [3]Ibid., 10.
[4]Ibid., 14, 34.   [5]Ibid., 19.
[6]Pigou Papers, op. cit., Evidence of Professor E. Cannan, 4, 7.
[7]Ibid., 5.   [8]Ibid., 5.
[9]Pigou Papers, op. cit., Evidence of W. Leaf, 4, 7.

reducing the volume of foreign lending.[1] He admitted that such a change would not be popular in the City, but he argued that it would not cause a 'calamitous fall' in prices, that many trades would be relieved if prices fell and that a higher exchange would bring lower import costs which would benefit trade.[2] Leaf reported his discussions with the Governor to the Committee, stressing most particularly that Norman believed that a return to gold could be effected with a 5 per cent Bank Rate through a gradual rise in the exchange over a period of several months, and Leaf thought it could be achieved before the expiry of the embargo with Bank Rate at that level.[3] In that generally vague state he left matters, refusing to be any more specific as to timing and procedures. However, he deserves inclusion in this group of witnesses because he favoured a return in the fairly near future, within slightly over a year, and because he was not particularly worried about the effects of a return to gold or policies associated with it on industry.

The remaining witnesses before the Committee, Sir Felix Schuster, Sir W. H. N. Goschen, The Federation of British Industries, Messrs Goodenough and Currie and Sir Robert Horne, all favoured a return to gold at some time 'in the interests both of the financial position of this country and also for its advantages and benefits to the industry and business of this country',[4] but they believed that 'a British initiative in restoring the gold standard at an early date . . . would be premature and inadvisable'.[5] They all accepted that there was a considerable adjustment in prices and costs necessary before the gold standard could be successfully restored and that a return would require very dear money.[6] The necessary adjustments would dislocate trade and increase unemployment, and, as the F.B.I. put it, administer 'a severe check' to exports.[7] Sir Robert Horne went so far as to suggest that the announcement of the Government's intention to return to gold would cause a recession through its effects on expectations.[8] Both Horne and the F.B.I., who were the most pessimistic of this group of witnesses, argued that the necessary wage adjustments a deflationary resumption would require 'would . . . seriously increase the difficulty of maintaining industrial peace'[9] and would result in 'turmoil, unrest and strikes'.[10]

[1]Ibid., 3, 4, 18–19.   [2]Ibid., 3, 6.   [3]Ibid., 3.
[4]Pigou Papers, op. cit., Evidence of Sir R. Horne, 1; Evidence of Mr Currie, 8–9; Evidence of Sir F. Schuster, 32; F.B.I. Statement, 1; Evidence of Messrs Chisholm and Glenday, 1.
[5]Pigou Papers, op. cit., F.B.I. Statement, 4.
[6]Pigou Papers, op. cit., Evidence of Mr Currie, 5; Evidence of Mr Goodenough, 4, 20; Evidence of Sir R. Horne, 4; F.B.I. Statement, 2.
[7]Ibid., 3.
[8]Pigou Papers, op. cit., Evidence of Sir R. Horne, 6.
[9]Pigou Papers, op. cit., F.B.I. Statement, 3.
[10]Pigou Papers, op. cit., Evidence of Sir R. Horne, 5.

Witnesses in this group were also uncertain as to whether any deadline for returning to gold that would be credible could be met, and they were also uncertain about future political and economic conditions which would influence the success of any policy determined at the present time.[1] Some of the bankers were not averse to a gradual fall in prices,[2] but as there was a general expectation that American prices would rise they were loath to begin deflation at present. Thus the witnesses as a group were, for somewhat differing reasons, in favour of a 'wait and see' policy for the present with general price stability as the short-term goal. However, if this policy did not produce results, or if, as the F.B.I. put it, 'considerations of high finance might make it so important that we should have to take the risk',[3] the witnesses were prepared to reconsider their views.[4]

This emphasis on waiting, with its normal expectation of rising American prices, that was characteristic of the majority of witnesses appearing before the Committee seems to have had its effect on its members. Thus, on 24 July when the Committee had heard all its witnesses except the F.B.I. and Sir Robert Horne, who if anything were more alarmed about the difficulties and costs of deflation than any witnesses other than Keynes and McKenna, Bradbury wrote to Farrer:[5]

I am so far impressed by the views of McKenna and Keynes as to think that it may be wise not to pursue a policy of restoring the dollar exchange to parity at the cost of depressing home prices. The odds are that within the comparatively near future America will allow gold to depreciate to the value of sterling—particularly if she realises that it is the only way by which parity will be restored.

My present feeling is rather in favour of pursuing a credit policy which will aim at keeping the exchanges in the neighbourhood of 4.40 while American prices are steady or falling, and working it back to par when prices rise.

I doubt the wisdom – at any rate unless and until we are nearer a general economic settlement than seems likely on present indications – of a cut and dried policy at the moment.

These are not, however, 'settled conclusions', and I am quite willing to modify them after discussion.

This letter, with its emphasis on exchange stability and semi-price stability in the short run, seems to have summed up the general feelings of the Committee when it came to the first major discussion of its

[1]Pigou Papers, op. cit., Evidence of Mr Currie, 4; Evidence of Sir W. N. Goschen, 6; Evidence of Sir F. Schuster, 13; Evidence of Mr Goodenough, 4.
[2]Pigou Papers, op. cit., Evidence of Sir F. Schuster, 28–9; Evidence of Mr Goodenough, 22.
[3]Pigou Papers, op. cit., Evidence of Messrs Chisholm and Glenday, 11.
[4]Pigou Papers, op. cit., Evidence of Sir R. Horne, 17.
[5]T160/197/F7528/01/1, Bradbury to Farrer, 24 July 1924.

report early in September, a reworking by Professor Pigou of an early draft by the Secretary.[1]

The Pigou draft accepted that 'as a practical present day policy for this country there is, in our opinion, no alternative comparable with return to the former gold parity of the sovereign'.[2] It then moved on to a discussion of whether this restoration was 'a matter of immediate urgency'[3] and concluded that, although a continuation of the Gold and Silver (Export Control) Act 1920 might affect the prestige of sterling, although there was a risk that sterling might be isolated by the development of a European bloc of countries after the adoption of the Dawes report and the adoption of a gold exchange standard by Germany and although the Dominions might take action to restore the pre-war gold parity individually, there was 'no immediate and pressing urgency' for a British decision to return to gold at pre-war par, even though a return as such was a highly desirable goal of policy.[4] The draft report then went on to consider the three possible means by which the pre-war parity of sterling could be restored: (1) price stability in the United Kingdom while American prices rose, (2) deflation in the United Kingdom sufficient to reduce prices sufficiently to raise the exchange to par, or (3) an immediate removal of the embargo on gold exports which would result in a loss of gold and necessitate the adoption of course (2).[5] The second and third courses of action were separated because the bodies taking the necessary decisions were different in the first instance. The draft admitted that the latter two possibilities would involve a discouragement to industry and a threat to British employment which would be 'undesirable to set in motion if there is a reasonable hope that, within a short time, America will permit of our goal being attained by the first of the three routes . . . a route which does not involve any enforced recession of sterling prices'.[6] As an increase in American prices was likely, the goal of the Bank of England should be price stability for the time being, particularly as the contingencies that might make stronger action necessary to preserve the exchange value of sterling, a rise in sterling prices beyond the Bank's control or a fall in American prices due to a change in Federal Reserve policy, were remote.[7] Therefore, the draft concluded, 'for another year, the Government should wait upon events. If at the end of 1925 the dollar has not approximated to parity, deliberate Government action to secure that result may become necessary'.[8]

[1]T160/197/F7528/01/1, Young to Chamberlain, 23 August 1924; T160/197/F7528/01/2, Committee on the Currency and Bank of England Note Issues, Second Draft of Report.   [2]Ibid., para. 5.
[3]Ibid., para. 6.   [4]Ibid., para. 7-10.
[5]Ibid., para. 11.   [6]Ibid., para. 12.
[7]Ibid., para. 13-14.   [8]Ibid., para 14.

The other members of the Committee, although generally speaking with Pigou, found him a bit too hesitant in the longer term. Bradbury, as usual, seems the best at expressing the feelings of the majority:[1]

The general impression ... which ... [Pigou's draft] leaves in my mind is that it is rather flabby. 'For the moment we propose to wait and see which way the cat jumps. If she jumps one way, and we can avoid jumping after her – and whether we can or not remains to be seen – everything will probably be all right. If it isn't, we shall be prepared to be a good deal braver than we are at the moment.'

I think that we ought to make it perfectly clear that we regard a return to a free gold market at the pre-war parity without long delay as of vital importance, but that as it involves either a fall in sterling prices or a rise in gold prices, and as there are indications that a rise in gold prices may be imminent, we think it better to wait for a short time and see whether gold adjusts itself to sterling before taking the steps necessary to adjust sterling to gold, but that we do not propose to wait indefinitely, and if our expectations in regard to American prices are not realised in the near future, we shall be forced to adopt the other alternative.

I would at the same time lay rather more stress than is laid in the draft report as it stands on the importance during this interim period of holding fast to the improvement of sterling which has already been effected, and in particular the necessity of extreme caution in regard to new foreign investments ... I believe there is a real risk that the success of the policy we recommend may be jeopardized by excessive foreign lending ...

Farrer and Chamberlain also wanted to take a somewhat stronger line than the draft,[2] and even Pigou was not averse to stronger measures, for as he wrote the Secretary to the Committee in the covering letter to his draft:[3]

On the main issue, which is one of practical politics rather than economics, whether the Government should take the plunge now or denounce no renewal of the embargo, I am only *just* on balance in favour of a 'wait and see' policy. It would be very inappropriate for me as an academic person to *press* for heroism; but if the rest of the Committee had been in favour of it, I doubt if I should have opposed.   (italics in the original).

Thus a marginally more emphatic draft resulted, 'B. in P.' as Chamberlain called it,[4] and this draft was sent to the Governor and discussed with him early in October.[5] In it the Committee accepted that sterling could be forced to par immediately and that it was strong enough in

[1]T160/197/F7528/01/2, Bradbury to Young, 11 September 1924.
[2]T160/197/F7528/01/1, Farrer to Young, 24 August 1924. T160/197/F7528/01/2, Chamberlain to Young, 11 and 13 September 1924.
[3]T160/197/F7528/01/2, quoted in Young to Bradbury, 12 September 1924.
[4]T160/197/F7528/01/2, Chamberlain to Young, 13 September 1924.
[5]Ibid.; T160/197/F7528/01/2, Young to Norman, 18 September 1924.

an underlying sense to allow a successful return to gold.[1] However, given the necessity of adjusting sterling prices to gold prices by closing a gap of 10–12 per cent and given the domestic 'inconveniences' of deflation, the Committee suggested that the Government wait for up to twelve months for a rise in American prices to reduce the gap while maintaining the current value of sterling and restraining excessive foreign lending either selectively or generally.[2] The draft concluded by recommending that the whole situation be reconsidered in the light of the progress made 'not later than the early autumn of 1925'.[3]

But for the fall of the Labour Government in October 1924, this draft would probably have marked the end of the work of the Committee. Although the resulting report would have been somewhat averse to forcing an immediate return to gold, there was no doubt as to the Committee's ultimate goals and its preparedness to place the achievement of these goals above some level of 'inconveniences' to the domestic economy. However, in the early autumn of 1924, with sterling below $4.50, the members of the Committee were still sufficiently uncertain as to the timing of the resumption of gold payments – and were prepared to wait upon events for an unspecified period.

If the Government had not fallen and if it had accepted the Committee's Report, expectations of an early return to gold would have been dashed and the speculative rise in the exchange which followed the election of a Conservative Government and the issue of the Dawes Loan would have been avoided. In these circumstances, in the autumn of 1925, when the time came for a reconsideration of the Report and the issue of a return to gold, sterling *might* not have risen much above $4.50 and the Authorities would have again faced the decision as to whether to force sterling to par in the ensuing few months before the expiry of the 1920 Act – something they were not prepared to do over a longer period a year earlier – or whether to extend the 1920 Act. If domestic conditions were prosperous, the Authorities might have been loath to create 'inconveniences' deliberately, particularly as any deflation would have been politically unpopular and the connection posited between the gold standard and prosperity by many observers would have looked rather tenuous, and they might have consented to an extension of the embargo. If, on the other hand, domestic conditions were less prosperous than in 1924 as a result of the revival of German competition in export markets, particularly coal, the Authorities, who in the past had displayed a certain tenderness towards domestic conditions, might have been even more loath to force a return to $4.86. Once

---

[1] T160/197/F7528/01/2, Committee on Currency and Bank of England Note Issues, Third Draft Report, 14 September 1924. para, 8–9.
[2] Ibid., para. 11, 15, 18, 20–30.
[3] Ibid., para. 37.

through the 'deadline' of 31 December 1925, conditions might have been completely different, as France and Belgium might have moved farther towards stabilising their internal situations and as Germany's undervaluation and competitive threat would have become even more apparent. In these different conditions, a return to gold at $4.86, involving as it did an appreciation of sterling, might not have been attempted – unless, of course, the Authorities were so completely committed to a return to gold at $4.86 that domestic repercussions of that policy would be ignored, something that the evidence of 1922–4, the Cunliffe Committee's ten year 'reconstruction' proviso, and the Chamberlain–Bradbury Committee's hedging on the issue of forcing a return do not suggest.

Central Bank Attitudes, April–October 1924

Now that we have followed the development of opinion within the Chamberlain–Bradbury Committee, which included the Chancellor's most influential advisers on monetary policy other than the Governor of the Bank – Bradbury and Niemeyer – among its membership, we must turn to the development of central bank opinion on the return to gold. In this area, we are fortunate in having the correspondence of Governor Strong of the Federal Reserve Bank of New York, one of Norman's closest international colleagues as well as a friend. Governor Strong had spent part of the spring of 1924 in London with Norman, and their letters thereafter provide some clues as to internal developments and opinions.

While abroad, Strong wrote a series of letters to Pierre Jay, Chairman of the Federal Reserve Bank of New York, which indicate the development of his ideas. Those of 11 and 23–8 April are of greatest interest:[1]

Very confidentially, I have a strong conviction, after an all afternoon discussion with Norman, Revelstoke and Addis (the real ones here) that if the Dawes Report is accepted, we can find a way to deal with the London – New York exchange that will finally do the job. But it is all in future and depends upon that big 'if'.

Now ... you may gather that I am always considering our old bugbear, 'gold' and the gold standard, — and how these new developments fit in our picture. This can only be written out in the crudest sketch. It is too complicated for pencil and paper.

First, of course, all depends on the fate of the Dawes' plan. If it is successfully launched I would look for two years or so during which Germany would balance her budget and stabilize her currency, – it is not

[1] F.R.B.N.Y., Strong to Jay, 11 and 23–8 April 1924.

impossible that she might take a little of our gold. That would leave the pound and the franc afloat. The British would view (and do) the former with consternation. The French will be more *complaisant*. So what is the problem as to dollars and pounds? It seems to me to have become simplified in so far as the urgency will grow in London to get back to Orthodox ways as soon as possible; and that feeling has gained a new impulse because of the Dawes' plan.

Without elaboration, our interest lies in the earliest possible return to the gold standard, by all nations, especially Great Britain, so that we may escape these arbitrary controls on which we now rely. England's interest is to return to gold payment, for the ultimate benefit of her trade, and to facilitate paying her debt to us. We should have little difficulty in arranging matters where our interests are so mutually to be served by common action to one end. But how is it to be done? On the whole, I believe we must see London rates higher than our – our 'prices' at least a bit higher, and Great Britain's a bit lower – and at the proper moment, a credit operation, secret at first, and only becoming public when £ is fairly close to par. My belief is growing that it will not be long before the job can be attempted. I'll give you more details on my return, and as Prosper said, 'We'll see what we'll see'.

If within ten years of our creation, the Federal Reserve System can have accomplished the restoration of the gold standard, our first decade will have justified itself.

After Strong had returned to New York, he set out his views on the return to gold and sterling once more in a long letter to the Secretary of the Treasury, Andrew Mellon, on 27 May. After outlining the theory of purchasing-power parity and its implications, he continued:[1]

At the present time it is probably true that British prices for goods internationally dealt in are as a whole, roughly, in the neighbourhood of 10 per cent above our prices and one of the preliminaries to the re-establishment of gold payment by Great Britain will be to facilitate a gradual readjustment of these price levels *before* monetary reform is undertaken. In other words, this means some small advance in prices here and possibly some small decline in their prices ... They will be to a certain extent fortuitous, but can be facilitated by cooperation between the Bank of England and the Federal Reserve System in the maintaining of lower interest rates in this country and higher interest rates in England so that we will become the world's borrowing market to a greater extent, and London to a lesser extent. The burden of this readjustment must fall more largely upon us than upon them. It will be difficult politically and socially for the British Government and the Bank of England to force a price liquidation in England beyond what they have already experienced in face of the fact that their trade is poor and they have over a million unemployed people receiving government aid. There will, however, be a period of time during which the Dawes program is being established in Germany and

---

[1] F.R.B.N.Y., Strong Papers, Strong to Mellon, 27 May 1924.

other debt adjustments are being effected within which cooperation between ourselves and the British can do much toward laying the price foundation required for the safe resumption of gold payment by the Bank of England.

Assuming that all debt adjustments can be effected upon a satisfactory basis and that price levels readjust to the point where the groundwork for the resumption of gold payment encourages belief in its success and permanence, there is still one important step which must be taken in most skilful fashion. Some large private credits must be opened in this country ... in order to steady the rate of exchange and gradually work it to a higher level corresponding to the international price parity, and hold it there, until the time arrives to actually announce a plan of resumption based upon such adequate credits in this country as will insure the final recovery of sterling to par ... (italics in the original).

In other words, Strong clearly saw the return to gold in Great Britain as a joint operation with the United States easing the necessary adjustments, and he saw the return as something that could be accomplished in the reasonably near future.

The reductions in New York rates by $\frac{1}{2}$ per cent on both 1 May and 12 June were certainly aimed in this direction, although the former saw domestic considerations as a more prominent determinant.[1] However, there were limits to this policy as there were suggestions that Strong was too much under Norman's influence; at the same time some Anglophobia was also evident.[2] Nevertheless, a further reduction of $\frac{1}{2}$ per cent was effected in August.

Norman, for his part, was attempting to raise rates in London,[3] but was having problems, for as he put it, 'it is necessary to find an excuse for raising it and at this moment no excuse is very apparent'.[4] However, he did not share Strong's urgency as to the need to return to parity; he only desired a statement of policy which was clear and final within the next few months.[5] Norman's rate problems were exemplified by the reaction to Walter Leaf's declaration in June in favour of an immediate rise in Bank Rate to 5 per cent and other measures including

[1]F.R.B.N.Y., Strong Papers, Strong to Norman, 3 June 1924; E. R. Wicker, *Federal Reserve Monetary Policy 1917–1933*. (New York, 1966), 83, 85, 89.
[2]Clarke, *Central Bank Cooperation*, 76n. The Anglophobia that existed in this instance recurs throughout the literature on Anglo-American financial relations. Thus Herbert Hoover in his *Memoirs* [vol. III (London, 1952), 9] referred acidly to Governor Strong as 'a mental annex to Europe'; a Roosevelt message to Secretary Hull at the World Economic Conference referred to 'banker-dominated cabinets' (Roosevelt to Hull, 20 June 1933, *Foreign Relations of the United States: Diplomatic Papers, 1933*, vol. I, 650); and Professor Sayers found American distrust of British methods an important factor in the Second World War [*Financial Policy 1939–1945* (London, 1956), 378–81].
[3]F.R.B.N.Y., Strong Papers, Strong to Jay, 4 April 1924.
[4]F.R.B.N.Y., Strong Papers, Norman to Strong, 16 June 1924.
[5]F.R.B.N.Y., Strong Papers, Norman to Strong, 16 June 1924.

an explicit announcement of a policy for returning to gold.[1] As Leaf himself put it, 'I am the most unpopular man in the City on account of it.'[2] This declaration may have been a trial balloon, for Leaf told the Chamberlain Committee of discussions with the Governor about rates,[3] but the adverse reaction is of interest if only because the City expected some rise in rates in the autumn to control foreign lending.[4] However, the Governor was able to secure some stiffening of rates through an agreement whereby the clearing banks increased their rates on discount market fixtures.[5] This increase seems to have occurred at the instigation of the Bank of England, for as Norman cabled Strong, 'In order to facilitate the programme we discussed and to avoid immediate increase in our rate we intend to maintain market rate of discount about $\frac{1}{2}\%$ higher than in recent months as you may have noticed.'[6]

However, as Norman attempted to increase his rates, Strong appears to have become more sceptical as to the effects of that alone. As he wrote to Norman on 9 July:[7]

Your reliance upon an advance in bank rate to help the exchange has always struck me as somewhat open to question and based upon past experience in a free gold market. Aside from its possible influence upon prices, are not the direct results of importance, usually but three : (1) A transfer of balances to London. (2) Discount bills elsewhere (New York). (3) Reduced foreign loans in London.

As to (1), I apprehend that so long as you are not paying gold and sterling fluctuates over so wide a range, the risks of exchange loss will deter this movement and London balances will remain at a minimum, at least so far as American houses are concerned.

As to (2), the total cannot be very large in any event, and as to all bills owned by American banks, which are drawn in sterling, they will not be 'carried' in London with American funds, to any great extent, again on account of exchange risks.

As to (3), undoubtedly our market becomes more attractive for foreign loans than it was, but your bankers are too reluctant to forego the business to make this market any permanent relief, and investment funds here will likely demand higher returns still than in the English market. Opportunity for safe and profitable investment here is still the chief factor.

[1]See for example, 'The Past Month', *Bankers' Magazine*, cxviii (965), August 1924;
    'Finance and Investment', *The Nation and Athenaeum*, 28 June and 5 July 1924.
[2]Pigou Papers, op. cit., Evidence of Mr Leaf, 3.
[3]Ibid., 3, 13.
[4]'Finance and Investment'. *The Nation and Athenaeum*, 28 June 1924.
[5]'Finance and Investment', *The Nation and Athenaeum*, 8 November 1924; *The Economist*, 3 January 1925, 4.
[6]F.R.B.N.Y., Norman to Strong, no. 95, 19 July 1924.
[7]F.R.B.N.Y., Strong Papers, Strong to Norman, 9 July 1924.

So on the whole I do not look for any great results until something more fundamental is undertaken than simply an increase in your rate.

In the same letter he also questioned the effects of a higher Bank Rate on prices except in a rather uncertain fashion over a fairly long period and again emphasised the need for speed in taking advantage of the existing favourable conditions for the consolidation of sterling's position even if the formal return to gold was a matter of months or years. Later in the summer his scepticism went even further and he began to question the strategy which he had outlined to Secretary Mellon in May. He noted the parallelism of American and British price developments during the summer, despite the differences in policy in London and New York, and suggested:[1]

I have a feeling that our studies have not yet proved conclusively whether a change in relative price levels in your country and ours must be relied upon as the major cause of a return of sterling to parity; or whether we may not have cause and effect reversed and that some thorough-going plan for restoring sterling to par must be relied upon as the means for a readjustment of price levels to purchasing-power parity upon the basis of par of exchange.

Thus Strong's views were moving in the direction of the necessity of an act of *force majeure* to restore sterling to par. In a sense his views paralleled Norman's presentation to the Chamberlain–Bradbury Committee, but they involved much more drastic action and in many ways a reversal of Norman's priorities. In late August the Bank of England was still uncertain as to its future policy and future price behaviour, although it saw the need for some decision as the embargo legislation neared the date of renewal and as the fiduciary issue of currency notes threatened the limit set by the Treasury Minute of 1919.[2] However, events in October 1924 and thereafter were to move the two viewpoints together in the direction of Strong's scepticism.

The Pace Quickens, October 1924–January 1925

The defeat of the first Labour Government in the House of Commons on 8 October and the ensuing General Election removed the decision which Norman had expected on gold policy from the realm of immediate possibility.[3] Norman expressed his uncertainty to Strong in the middle of the election campaign as follows:[4]

As a matter of fact our sudden and unexpected political upheaval has

[1]F.R.B.N.Y., Strong Papers, Strong to Lubbock, 10 September 1924.
[2]F.R.B.N.Y., Strong Papers, Lubbock to Strong, 25 August 1924.
[3]Clay, *Lord Norman*, 149–50.
[4]F.R.B.N.Y., Strong Papers, Norman to Strong, 16 October 1924.

come at the very moment when we had planned and expected to obtain an official decision about future gold policy ... As things are, I cannot say how or when our next Government will decide – we must 'wait and see'.

As a matter of fact, I can only suppose that the decision will be to declare for a free gold market here either at the end of 1925 or at the end of a somewhat later year, say, 1927.

In the interim, Norman thought that 'it would be neither necessary nor wise for us to take any strong measures'. However, once the policy of the next Government was settled, Norman noted, 'we must get together and devise a plan which will probably need to include some sort of a credit for steadying or holding the rate of exchange when we get into the eighties'. He also indicated his views on the difficulties of preventing sterling prices rising in sympathy with dollar prices, particularly if raw material prices led the price increase, but he did not go as far as Strong had in September as to the implications of this for policy. This would have to await the election results.

The election on 29 October and its resulting overwhelming Conservative majority seems to have revised expectations considerably. The change appears most clearly in Strong's first letter to Norman after the election, that of 4 November:[1]

Your political 'upheaval', as I view it, appears to make plans for a strong policy as to the exchange and a return to gold payment much easier than would have been the case had not the conservative party had such a sweeping victory and gained such a large majority in Parliament as to indicate the possibility of the new cabinet continuing in power for some time. I frankly did not look for any such development and it has made me wonder whether your natural conservatism in dealing with the problem may not now be somewhat modified ...

So we must also consider the subject of the relative price levels, concerning which I have always felt that a great deal of nonsense has been written. We may not adequately take into consideration that changes of price are not always a *cause* of a change in the exchange rate; in fact, it may at times be the case that changes in rates of exchange are themselves the chief influence upon the relation of international prices. I am inclined to the view that the latter is the case under present conditions when no movement of 'inflation' or 'deflation' is under way ...

I cannot feel that the shock to your business establishment would be any greater as a result of an advance in sterling from 4.50 to 4.87, than that already experienced in recent months in the advance from below 4.30 to 4.50, or the greater shock resulting from the fluctuations which occured when sterling advanced to above 4.70 and then declined to below 4.30.

In a general way the situation appears to me to be somewhat as follows:

1. Your program has been facilitated by the movements of our respective money markets, which has [sic] caused some return flow of funds to

[1]F.R.B.N.Y., Strong Papers, Strong to Norman, 4 November 1924.

London and has diverted borrowings from the London market to the New York market.

2. The outlook is improved by the adoption of the Dawes Plan, which should eliminate reparation payments, certainly for the next few years, as a seriously disturbing element in the exchange market.

3. Your election gives a greater political certainty than you have enjoyed for some years, and presumably the new cabinet will be sympathetic to a gold program.

4. If business improves, some action will be forced upon you as to currency notes.

5. You must either return to gold payments before the end of next year, or secure legislation extending the period of the embargo.

6. A continuance of lower money rates in New York than in London cannot be expected to continue indefinitely and may end some time next year.

7. It is illusory to expect price readjustments of themselves to effect a recovery of sterling. Sterling cannot return to par and gold payment cannot be resumed without an act of 'force majeure' ... (italics in the original).

Norman reacted to the change in circumstances in a somewhat similar manner, for on 4 November he was asking his Committee of Treasury to consider the possibility of obtaining a credit in America to steady the exchange if it approached parity.[1] Strong was, at about the same time, putting the possibilities of a credit of $200 million to the Governors' Conference of the Federal Reserve System.[2] Thus on both sides of the Atlantic, and seemingly on the foreign exchanges which rose strongly from the time of the election,[3] thinking was moving towards a more speedy restoration of the gold standard in England. In these circumstances, Norman first visited the new Chancellor, Winston Churchill, on 7 November, the date of the new Government's formation.

According to Norman's most recent biographer, the Governor, who still privately wished that Snowden had remained Chancellor, 'found Churchill in the receptive and responsive mood of a backward pupil who was willing to be taught'.[4] Certainly Churchill does not seem to have entered the Treasury with any rigid or sophisticated ideas on financial policy or technical matters other than free trade.[5] However, Churchill appears to have accepted this ignorance and to have approached all problems with an open mind, with the result that, although he depended heavily on his advisers, he required extensive justifications for every step he had to take, and every step he believed that

[1] Clay, *Lord Norman*, 151.

[2] Chandler, *Benjamin Strong*, 308.

[3] Sterling stood at $4.49\frac{11}{16}$ on 31 October, $4.63\frac{7}{16}$ on 30 November and $4.72\frac{3}{4}$ on 31 December.

[4] Boyle, *Montagu Norman*, 179.

[5] K. Middlemas and J. Barnes, *Baldwin: A Biography* (London 1969), 281.

he might take.[1] As Boyle remarks, Churchill 'would clearly have to be carried' to any decision on gold policy.[2] Events were to prove that he was often something of a burden.

No records seem to exist of the discussion on gold policy during his first month in office, but as P. J. Grigg, Churchill's Secretary 'for the more mundane problems of finance and administration', notes, he 'was certainly told soon after his arrival that the Act under which gold payments were suspended would expire with the year 1925, and that he would, therefore, have to face before very long the choice between going back to gold or legislating to stay off it for another period of years'.[3] By 4 December, however, Norman was writing to Niemeyer of his expected journey to New York at the end of the month, and of his plans concerning a credit which 'should probably exceed $300,000,000' to support a return to a free gold market;[4] and by 12 December, Churchill was writing to Stanley Baldwin, the Prime Minister:[5]

The Governor of the Bank will, I hope, have told you this weekend about the imminence of our attempt to reestablish the gold standard, in connection with which he is now going to America. *It will be easy to attain the gold standard, and indeed almost impossible to avoid taking the decision,* but to keep it will require a most strict policy of debt repayment and a high standard of credit. To reach it and have to abandon it would be disastrous.   (italics added)

Thus it would seem that by mid-December 1924, both Norman and Churchill had decided in a very general way to consider, at a minimum, a return to gold in the near future. In some ways, Churchill's letter indicates something more definite.

Norman arrived in New York on 28 December, accompanied by Sir Alan Anderson, the Deputy Governor-elect. In the ensuing fortnight he canvassed several people – J. P. Morgan and Governor Strong in detail; Secretary Mellon, Governor Crissinger and Vice-Governor Platt in principle – about the return to gold, its timing, expectations of economic trends and policy and possibilities of American support. Throughout the emphasis was exploratory, as Norman had made clear at the outset 'that they were not commissioned either by the Government or by the Bank of England to conduct definite negotiations which would result in the resumption of specie payment and the establishment of a free gold market in England, because their Government had not yet, in fact, made any decision on that subject'.[6] Those whom he consulted

[1]Leith-Ross, *Money Talks*, 88, 118.
[2]Boyle, *Montagu Norman*, 179.
[3]Grigg, *Prejudice and Judgement*, 174, 180.
[4]T172/1500A, Norman to Niemeyer, 4 December 1924.
[5]Chartwell Papers, File 18/2, Churchill to Baldwin, 12 December 1924.
[6]F.R.B.N.Y., Strong Papers, Memorandum, 11 January 1925.

'were unhesitating in expressing the view that the time for deciding upon a resumption of gold payment by England had arrived'. Strong expressed this view and assured him that Federal Reserve policy 'would be directed towards stability of prices so far as it was possible for us to influence prices'. However, he warned Norman 'that there were three factors in the situation which might operate at times so seriously to their disadvantage that there was in fact a real hazard to be reckoned with before final resumption was attempted'. First, Strong believed that the volume of new foreign issues in New York in 1924 had been unusual and had resulted from a particular set of conditions which might not be repeated. Any reduction in the volume of lending by New York might strain the sterling exchange. Second, he emphasised that the volume of war and related debt payments to the United States was large and likely to increase and that these payments would have to be provided in some fashion. Third, Strong continued,

there must be a plain recognition of the fact that in a new country such as ours, with an enthusiastic, energetic, and optimistic population, where enterprise at times was highly stimulated and the returns upon capital much greater than in other countries, there would be times when speculative tendencies would make it necessary for the Federal Reserve Banks to exercise restraint by increased discount rates, and possibly rather high money rates in the market. Should such times arise, *domestic considerations would likely outweigh foreign sympathies*, and the protection of our own economic situation, forcing us to higher rates, might force them to maintain still higher rates, with some resulting hardship to business, etc.

(italics added)

Though these matters were noted and discussed at considerable length, they were probably outweighed by Norman's expectations of the results of not returning to the gold standard. As Strong's memorandum put it in the paragraph immediately following that quoted above:

But Mr Norman's feelings, which in fact, are shared by me, indicated that the alternative—failure of resumption of gold payment—being a confession by the British Government that it was impossible to resume, would be followed by a long period of unsettled conditions too serious really to contemplate. It would mean violent fluctuations in the exchanges, with probably progressive deterioration of the values of foreign currencies vis-a-vis the dollar; it would provide an incentive to all of those who were advancing novel ideas for nostrums and expedients other than the gold standard to sell their wares; and incentive to governments at times to undertake various types of paper money expedients and inflation; it might, indeed, result in the United States draining the world of gold with the effect that, after some attempt at some other mechanism for the regulation of credit and prices, some kind of monetary crisis would finally result in ultimate restoration of gold to its former position, but only after a period of hardship and suffering, and possibly some social and political disorder.

Given these considerations, the Americans were willing to provide credit facilities for $500 million–$200 million from the Federal Reserve System to the Bank of England and $300 million from J. P. Morgan and Co. and their associates to the British Government – to be used as a cushion after the return to gold.

These general understandings and general arrangements were made clear to and were approved by the Directors of the Federal Reserve Bank of New York, the Federal Reserve Board and the Federal Reserve Open Market Committee early in January.[1] Thus in America, by 11 January 1925, the way was clear for a return to gold. Norman's next task was to obtain a favourable decision at home.

On 6 January, while he was in New York, Norman cabled Cecil Lubbock, the Bank's Deputy Governor, as to the general strategy:[2]

After consultation as arranged following plan is suggested in principle:

1. Prohibition of export of gold should terminate 31st December and free market should be re-established subject to arrangement of necessary details.

2. No announcement should be made before March nor until the revolving credit below mentioned shall have been arranged.

3. In order to maintain exchange and to ensure general confidence in all events revolving credit aggregating $500 million should be arranged forthwith in New York for use of British Government in connection with and in order to moderate export of gold.

4. Use of revolving credit and export of gold which require progressive increases in Bank of England rate.

The cable then went on to outline the details of the proposed credit arrangements and to authorise the communication in confidence of the plan to the Chancellor. This cable was followed by a further explanatory cable which discussed general attitudes in America and commented on particular features of the proposals. In it Norman noted that 'free exports [of gold] might with advantage be established long before 31st December perhaps after announcement in March and arrangement of revolving credits', that the total of $500 million was 'strongly recommended', and that the object of the credit operation was 'simply to give control of Market as far as possible to Central Banks.'[3] These cables in a very real sense triggered off discussion and the discussions of future months stemmed largely from them.

The London reaction was immediate, and largely centred around procedures and timing. Replying on 10 January, Lubbock in a cable drafted

[1]Chandler, *Benjamin Strong*, 313–16.
[2]F.R.B.N.Y., Norman to Lubbock, no. 15, 6 January 1925.
[3]F.R.B.N.Y., Norman to Lubbock, no. 16, 6 January 1925.

mainly by Sir Charles Addis, with Lord Revelstoke concurring immediately and Sir Robert Kinderseley somewhat later, argued:[1]

(1) . . . Much doubt is felt as to the wisdom of obtaining a credit in any form especially any credit not exclusively arranged with Central Banks and some of us would feel reluctant to recommend such a course to British Government.
(2) The restoration of the gold standard should follow and not precede the conditions of trade appropriate to the maintenance of a stable exchange.
(3) With reference to actual date to be now fixed it would be a mistake to anticipate a return to the free export of gold before conditions warrant it. The risk would be too great and the consequences of failure too grave for us to recommend it. We ought to be satisfied that the exchange situation is such as to afford reasonable grounds for believing that the parity of exchange having once been reached could be maintained by the natural play of the market force of supply and demand without resort to any artificial aids such as exists [sic] but I think it would be unsafe to rely on its permanence until it has been tested by a period of comparatively stable exchange.

The cable went on to suggest that if the conditions alluded to in (3) existed before 31 December they would be willing to lift the embargo, but that for the present they were only in favour of a statement of intent by the Chancellor at a comparatively early stage. Opposition in the Treasury existed for basically similar reasons. Niemeyer had said as much before Norman's departure for New York, and at this time he objected once again to 'the cushion' as he called it, as did Sir Warren Fisher.[2] There was also potential opposition to the ideas of credit in the Chamberlain–Bradbury Committee from Gaspard Farrer who had made his views known before Norman's departure for America.[3] Thus upon his return to London, Norman would have to argue for his New York proposals, and to some extent modify them.

Throughout January the discussions continued, largely in the Bank, with Norman reporting the tone to Strong as 'a general approval in principle but a strange opposition in detail'.[4] The Chamberlain–Bradbury Committee also resumed sittings for discussion purposes. By 26 January it had another Draft Report for the Governor's consideration before he gave further evidence on 28 January. This draft reflected the rise in the exchange, the change in expectations and Norman's New York conversations.[5] In general, it followed the final *Report* of the

---

[1] F.R.B.N.Y., Lubbock to Norman, nos. 54, 55 and 57, 10 and 12 January 1925.
[2] T172/1500A, Niemeyer to Norman, 8 December 1924; T175/9, Niemeyer to Lubbock, 9 January 1925; T172/1500A, Fisher to Niemeyer, 12 January 1925.
[3] T160/197/F7528/01/2, Farrer to Young, 20 December 1924.
[4] F.R.B.N.Y., Strong Papers, Norman to Strong, 24 January 1924.
[5] T160/197/F7528/01/3, Committee on the Currency and Bank of England Note Issues, Fourth Draft Report, 26 January 1925; Pigou Papers, op. cit., Evidence of the Governor of the Bank of England and Sir Charles Addis, 1.

Committee with very minor alterations. It recommended that the gold export prohibition not be renewed; that this be announced by the Government in the near future; and that in the interim between the announcement and the expiry of the prohibition the Bank of England be given a general license to export gold which should be freely used when sterling was below the gold export point.[1] It was satisfied that this policy could be carried out without foreign assistance but saw an American credit as useful for confidence purposes against speculation. However, the Committee believed that this credit, if used, should be treated by the Bank as equivalent to losses of its own gold reserves in its effects upon domestic credit.[2] The Committee estimated that the restoration of parity would require an adjustment of about 6 per cent in the general price level, or about $1\frac{1}{2}$ per cent more than would be necessary to maintain the existing rate of exchange of about $4.79, and argued that the sacrifices necessary to achieve parity were 'comparatively small'.[3] With opinion in this state, the Governor and Sir Charles Addis appeared before the Committee on 28 January.

Norman opened his evidence by referring to the discussions that had taken place at the Bank during the previous few days and by explaining that opinion was somewhat divided on the matter and that Addis had come along to the Committee 'in order that you might be informed of all the aspects of the question'.[4] Norman then went on to outline the bases for the change in his views since his previous appearance before the Committee, to note that the rise in the dollar exchange had 'certainly modified or altered my views to the extent that while I was then greatly in favour of a return to gold at an early date, but a date which I could not be brave enough to define then, I am now greatly in favour of a return during this year'.[5] He then reconstructed the results of his New York discussions, mentioning the advantages in the existing political situation and American stability – the possibility of a stock exchange boom being 'a minor question' which might change discount rates $\frac{1}{2}$ to 1 per cent – and emphasising the conjecture of circumstances that made 1925 more favourable for resumption than any time likely in the future.[6] After a review of the international movement towards gold with specific references to South

[1]T160/197/F7528/01/3, Fourth Draft Report, 6–7.
[2]Ibid., 7–8.
[3]Ibid., 5–6. These estimates suggest that the calculations were done using wholesale prices in a purchasing-power parity framework, for they reflect the January 1925 situation in this respect.
[4]Pigou Papers, op. cit., Evidence of the Governor of the Bank of England and Sir Charles Addis, 1.
[5]Ibid., 2–3.
[6]Ibid., 4, 5.

Africa, Australia, Sweden, Holland and Switzerland, he proceeded to
suggest that the announcement of the non-renewal of the embargo
should not come until after the March change in the American Congress and the arrangements of the credits which he proceeded to outline,
i.e. in April, with general licence for gold exports taking effect the day
of the announcement.[1] He emphasised that the chief purpose of the
credit was to make clear to speculators the determination of the Authorities to maintain the position which they would be taking up and the
uselessness of any attempts to break the sterling–dollar exchange.[2] Thus
to Norman the chief purpose of the credits would be to create what
Niemeyer would later refer to as the shop window effect.[3] The credit,
he said, was unconditional. Its amount would be difficult to change as
changes would probably induce the Americans to reconsider their position and he wished to 'start with confidence in the operation on the
part of our American friends'.[4] The Governor did not expect American
speculative balances in London to prove troublesome after resumption
as their size was normal and resumption would probably induce an
increase in such balances.[5] In fact, he expected that it was 'very likely'
that he would face an influx of gold after resumption.[6]

Addis, on the other hand, while agreeing with Norman's ultimate
goals could not 'share the argument for urgency'.[7] He did not think
that conditions in the United Kingdom had changed materially in the
previous six months; he was unsure as to relative price levels; and he
believed that a return to gold should follow the achievement of parity
on the exchange market.[8] Referring to Norman's proposals as 'this
adventure', he argued that the credits, if used, would make the restoration of an equilibrium position more difficult for they would have to be
repaid. They would also induce pressures for credit ease in periods of
gold loss.[9] He was prepared to return to gold payments on 1 January
1926, 'God willing ... bar earthquakes', and argued that a sufficiently
tight monetary policy would make such a return possible in the underlying sense without the use of credits.[10] Such a commitment could be
made public if desired. However, he was opposed to the use of such
devices as Norman proposed in all circumstances.

After a few more comments from the Governor, largely about the
stability of American foreign lending which Norman believed existed
and about the difficulties of preventing British overlending without the

[1] Ibid., 5–7, 11. [2] Ibid., 7–8.
[3] T172/1500A, Niemeyer to Norman, 16 March 1925 and enclosure called 'The Cushion'.
[4] Pigou Papers, op. cit., Evidence of the Governor of the Bank of England and Sir Charles Addis, 10–11.
[5] Ibid., 31–2. [6] Ibid., 39.
[7] Ibid., 18. [8] Ibid., 16–22.
[9] Ibid., 18–19. [10] Ibid., 22.

gold standard and the clear signal the exchanges provided in such circumstances, the hearings of the Committee ended.[1] After the hearings the Committee prepared its final *Report* which largely followed the Fourth Draft with only minor amendments by Professor Pigou in the section on the necessity for price adjustments which replaced specific estimates[2] with the phrase 'a fall in the final price level here of a significant, though not very large, amount', and with the excision of a discussion of foreign lending.[3] In this form, the *Report*, which concurred with the final hearings of the Committee in its minimisation of any problems of adjustment, went to the Chancellor on 5 February.

The Treasury Discussions and the Decision to Return, February–March 1925

At this point, discussions moved to the Treasury, for although there were still differences to be resolved at the Bank,[4] the basis for the expected decision had yet to be laid at the Treasury. There is some doubt as to who initiated the Treasury discussions,[5] but they certainly began in earnest with the circulation of a memorandum from the Chancellor to Norman, Niemeyer, Bradbury and Hawtrey which the Treasury files call 'Mr. Churchill's Exercise' and of which Lord Bradbury remarked, 'The writer of the memorandum appears to have his spiritual home in the Keynes–McKenna sanctuary but some of the trimmings of his mantle have been furnished by the "Daily Express" '.[6]

Churchill opened his memorandum as follows:[7]

If we are to take the very important step of removing the embargo on Gold export, it is essential that we should be prepared to answer any

---

[1] Ibid., 28–39.

[2] These estimates followed the Fourth Draft Report and suggested that a fall of about 6 per cent in the general price level would be necessary to make the return to gold at $4.86 a success.

[3] T160/197/F7528/01/3, Pigou to Young, undated. The revisions occur in what were paragraphs 19 and 20 of the published *Report*.

[4] F.R.B.N.Y., Norman to Strong, no. 67, 13 February 1925.

[5] In T172/1499B, Niemeyer's memorandum is undated but appears before the Churchill memorandum mentioned below. In T175/9, the Niemeyer memorandum, 'The Gold Export Prohibition', is dated 2 February 1925, i.e. after the Churchill Minute.

[6] T172/1499B, 'Mr Churchill's Exercise', 29 January 1925. This document appears in full in Appendix 5.

[7] There is no evidence that Keynes had any direct involvement in the drafting of this memorandum in either the Keynes or the Churchill Papers. However, the document certainly shows that Churchill was familiar with Keynes' views, probably through Beaverbrook as Bradbury suggested. See K. Young, *Churchill and Beaverbrook: A Study in Friendship and Politics* (London, 1966), 74.

criticisms which may be subsequently made upon our policy. I should like to have set out in writing the counter case to the following argument:

He then proceeded to question the return to the gold standard on several grounds:

(1) 'A Gold Reserve and the Gold Standard are in fact survivals of rudimentary and transitional stages in the evolution of finance and credit.' Domestic credit and stability, Churchill suggested, were independent of the gold standard as the greater British than American stability of the previous three years indicated. British credit internationally could be successfully upheld through financial policy and healthy trade.

(2) 'We are now invited to restore the Gold Standard. The United States seems singularly anxious to help us to do this.' He questioned whether British and American interests were parallel for the cost of maintaining the value of gold would then have to be shared by Britain.

(3) He then suggested an alternative course of action, the renunciation of attempts to re-establish the gold standard and the shipping of £100 million from the Bank of England's gold reserves to pay war debts. Such a course, he argued, would reduce the debt burden, congest the United States with gold and induce a rise in American prices which would be assisted by shipments of Empire gold production. The rise in American prices and the greater American lending that resulted would raise the value of sterling, reduce the cost of further debt payments and improve trade.

(4) He then moved to the wider effects of the proposed return to gold:

The whole question of a return to the Gold Standard must not be dealt with only upon its financial and currency aspects. The merchant, the manufacturer, the workman and the consumer have interests which, though largely common, do not by any means exactly coincide either with each other or with the financial and currency interests. The maintenance of cheap money is a matter of high consequence.

A rise in Bank Rate, he suggested, would administer 'a very serious check' to trade and employment and would leave the Government open to the accusation that it had 'favoured the special interests of finance at the expense of the special interests of production'. Such a risk would have to be offset by 'very plain and solid advantages'.

(5) Moreover, he suggested, there was no necessity for urgency. Legislation was renewable.[1] If the management of the previous few

---

[1] Given the views of businessmen and several bankers before the Chamberlain–Bradbury Committee, it is probably correct to say that, so long as respectable reasons were given, the political difficulties in prolonging the gold export prohibi-

years had been successful why not continue it, particularly when previous management had taken place against a backdrop of three elections, four Governments, five Chancellors and 'the advent of a Socialist
Administration to power for the first time'; whereas, the present prospect
was for three or four years of political stability.

(6)   Finally, he suggested, that if the United States was so in favour
of restoration, the Government should hold out in favour of better
terms, particularly when some papers suggested that the conditions
surrounding restoration would mean a decline in the position of London.

At this point, Churchill concluded:

> In setting down these ideas and questionings I do not wish it to be inferred
> that I have arrived at any conclusions adverse to the re-establishment of
> the Gold Standard. On the contrary I am ready and anxious to be
> convinced as far as my limited comprehension of these extremely technical
> matters will permit. But I expect to receive good and effective answers to
> the kind of case which I have, largely as an exercise, indicated in this note.

This memorandum, along with others that arise later, although possibly a statement of belief, most probably represents a manifestation of
Churchill's style of decision-making. This style, which has been noted
by several observers,[1] usually meant that Churchill would test and
probe his advisers' arguments in favour of the course of action they
proposed – often by putting the opposition case very strongly or by
even making accusations of incompetence. However, 'it was *seldom,
if ever,* that he would reject the tested and sustained positions adopted
by his technical advisers' (italics added).[2] Given this pattern of behaviour, it seems unlikely, as one commentator has recently suggested,[3]
that Churchill was opposed to the return to gold until his opposition
'was broken' by the weight of orthodox Treasury and Bank of England
opinion. Granted, he may have had some doubts, which were reinforced
by a visit from Beaverbrook and Keynes' article 'The Return Towards
Gold'[4] early in February, but he generally appears to have accepted
the advice of his advisers on the gold standard and defended it through-

tion would not have been too great – provided the Authorities acted *early* enough.
Certainly, if the Committee had written a stronger report along the line of its
third draft, the Authorities would have had no shortage of legitimate support.

[1]Lord Salter, *Slave of the Lamp: A Public Servant's Notebook* (London, 1967), 248–50;
Leith-Ross, *Money Talks*, 118; Grigg, *Prejudice and Judgement*, 175–6; Sir J. Wheeler-
Bennet, *Action this Day: Working with Churchill* (London, 1968), 27–8, 185–7, 191–2,
233; Sir Harold Macmillan, *Winds of Change 1914-1939* (London, 1966), 204–5.
[2]Ibid., 205.
[3]R. Skidelsky, 'Gold Standard and Churchill: the Truth', *The Times Business News*, 17
March 1969.
[4]*The Nation*, 21 February 1925. It also appears in J. M. Keynes, *Essays in Persuasion*
(London, 1931), 225–36.

out the life of the 1924 Conservative Government.[1] In the case of his 'Exercise' this long-standing tactic worked very successfully, for it brought forth a series of replies which revealed most of the pattern of expectations which characterised the Chancellor's senior advisers.

Niemeyer submitted two replies, one referring to Churchill's memorandum by paragraphs and another on these and more general matters to which he appended an unsigned copy of the Chamberlain–Bradbury Committee's *Report*.[2] The latter memorandum began by referring to the gold standard decision as 'probably the most important financial decision of the present decade' and by noting that the decision would incur criticism no matter which way it went. Niemeyer then proceeded to note the repeated declarations in favour of a return to gold by previous 'Governments of all political shades' and the current expectations in Europe and America of a forthcoming decision to return. These expectations, Niemeyer noted, were one of the factors – the others being the attraction of higher interest rates, the movement of American and British prices together, the return of refugee capital that had fled in the inflation scare of the autumn of 1923 and the rise in American foreign lending – which had pushed sterling towards parity. To continue the export prohibition would disappoint these expectations and would not continue the present state of affairs:

It would reverberate throughout a world which has not forgotten the uneasy moments of the winter of 1923; and would be the more convinced that we never meant business about the gold standard because our nerve had failed when the stage was set. The immediate consequence would be a considerable withdrawal of balances and investment (both foreign *and British*) from London; a heavy drop in Exchange; and, to counteract that tendency, a substantial increase in Bank rate. We might very easily reap all the disadvantages which some fear from a return to gold without any of the advantages.

With the engine thus reversed, no one could foretell when conditions, political, psychological, economic, would be such that the opportunity would occur again. It would certainly be a long time. (italics in the original)

He then proceeded to point out that the supporters of managed currency were few, that they had advocated a rise in Bank Rate some months previously, and that the overwhelming majority of opinion preferred restoration. The only point under discussion at present was the timing of the restoration or 'whether sacrifices should be made for its restoration and what the extent of those sacrifices should be'.

[1] See the letters to *The Times Business News* concerning the Skidelsky article mentioned above (p. 66 n. 3) in the issues of 24, 27 and 28 March 1969 and see below p. 96.

[2] T172/1499B, 'The Gold Export Prohibition', 'Commentary', 2 February 1925. These are reprinted in full in Appendix 5.

Niemeyer then proceeded to outline the work and the evolution of attitudes within the Chamberlain–Bradbury Committee, noting its decision at the outset to consider the question of the restoration of the gold standard. He noted its advice in favour of a restoration at an early date, and repeated its arguments on prices, the underlying balance of trade, the threat posed to the sterling bill by widespread restoration elsewhere and the relative ease of returning – 'this *may* involve a temporary increase in Bank rate' (italics in the original). He also mentioned the favourable conjuncture of circumstances then existing in politics, American stability and aid, concerted action with other countries and an easier spring restoration aided by the seasonal strength of sterling.

At this point he began to consider objections to a return to gold. He admitted that the United States had an interest in the gold standard and was anxious to see gold maintain its value, but he pointed out that Britain was a large holder of gold and that the Empire was a major gold producer with similar interests. He noted that the appreciation of sterling would increase the real value of British foreign investment (largely denominated in sterling) and increase the real value of war debts owed to the British Government. The restoration of the gold standard would stabilise the exchanges which was in the interests of British export trade, particularly if the major Dominions returned to gold with Germany and America, and which would prevent the replacement of the sterling bill by a bill denominated in a stable currency. The strengthening of the sterling bill would improve the position of London *vis-à-vis* New York which had deteriorated as a result of the war. The stabilisation of sterling, he argued, would probably force the Latin countries of Europe to stabilise and devalue their currencies, 'a great step in the restoration of Europe for trade and commerce'. He did not see any conflict between finance and industry on the disadvantages of dear money; the difference was 'rather between the long view and the short view. Bankers on the whole take longer views than manufacturers. But the view is of what is good for trade and industry as a whole, on which after all the banks entirely depend, not of what may enable the Bank to bleed its trader.' Finally he turned to the effects of restoration on trade where the most serious arguments against the gold standard, in his opinion, lay. He continued:

… No one would advocate such a return if he believed that in the long run the effect on trade would be adverse.

In fact everyone upholds the gold standard, because they believe it to be proved by experience to be best for trade. If it is agreed that we must have the gold standard, is it not better to get over any discomforts at once and then proceed on an even keel rather than have the dislocation (if dislocation there be) still before us?

No one believes that unemployment can be cured by the dole, and palliatives like road digging. Every party – not least Labour – has preached that unemployment can only be dealt with by radical measures directed to the economic restoration of trade ... On a long view – and it is only such views that can produce fundamental cures – the gold standard is in direct succession to the main steps towards economic reconstruction ... and is likely to do more for British trade than all the efforts of the Unemployment Committee.

Norman's reply was much more direct and much less 'analytical'.[1] It consisted of a number of statements referring to specific sections of the Churchill argument. He agreed with Churchill on the importance of financial policy and economic conditions in national credit, but argued that 'good faith' of which gold was the guarantee and liquid reserves of which only gold was internationally acceptable were also necessary and important. He argued that a gold reserve and the gold standard were as necessary, and as dangerous to do without, as a police force and a tax collector. He asserted that there was no alternative gold 'in the opinion of educated and reasonable men', and continued:

The only practical question is the Date.

The pound sterling on which paper Notes are based has advanced greatly because the date of free Gold is believed to be at hand.

'The financial reputation of Great Britain' is such that the world believes 1925 means 1925 and Gold in 1925 by Act of Parliament means Gold in 1925 in fact. Any other course means a declining pound.

He argued that Britain could not object to the American interest in stabilisation on gold, as she had insisted on the same gold standard in the European stabilisations which she had assisted. He accepted that Britain could ship £100 million in gold to America for war debt payment, but he argued that the Americans could successfully sterilise it. In Britain, on the other hand,

the result of so reducing our Gold Reserves would be psychological as well as financial: our Note-circulation would probably be discredited at home (as happened e.g. in Germany): specie payment would have to be formally suspended: Exchange would fall ... and fall: and the world-centre would shift permanently and completely from London to New York.

(ellipsis in original)

The Governor then turned to the question of the general interest that had been raised by Churchill:

In connection with a golden 1925, the merchant, manufacturer, workman, etc., should be considered (but not consulted any more than about the design of battleships).

[1] T172/1499B, 2 February 1925. Reprinted in full in Appendix 5.

Cheap money is important because 9 people out of 10 think so: more for psychological than for fundamental reasons ... The cry of 'cheap money' is the Industrialists' big stick and should be treated accordingly. The restoration of Free Gold *will* require a high Bank Rate: the Government cannot avoid a decision for or against Restoration: the Chancellor will surely be charged with a sin of omission or of commission. In the former case (Gold) he will be abused by the ignorant, the gamblers and the antiquated Industrialists; in the latter case (not Gold) he will be abused by the instructed and by posterity.

Plain and solid advantages can be shown to exist which justify – and seem to require – this sacrifice by the Chancellor. He could hardly assume office with Free Gold in one country and watch half-a-dozen others attain Free Gold ... without his own. (italics and final ellipsis in the original)

He admitted that there would be no urgency for a decision if the Act did not expire, but 'the National Credit of this country presupposes that measure of good faith which has gradually induced the whole world to believe that when an Act expires, it expires'. The prolongation of the Act would 'shatter' the exchanges and not help trade and industry. The managed finance of the previous three years had 'a golden 1925' as its goal and even its success depended on international confidence which allowed the Treasury to borrow foreign balances in London. In any case, he argued, a high Bank Rate would be necessary to reduce foreign lending, whether the U.K. returned to gold or not, as 'the present method of so-called persuasion' could not be successful for very long. The Governor concluded by emphasising that the gold standard was 'the best "Governor" that can be devised for a world that is still human rather than divine'; that the redistribution of the gold sterilised in America would present difficulties in future years and produce infla- tionary pressures which, however, would be a lesser evil than inflation of the recent European variety; and that London's relative weakness as a financial centre resulted from the war not from 'a golden 1925' and would be reduced by the gold standard and its experience.

Lord Bradbury's reply was pitched at a more general level, in many ways, than the previous two.[1] While admitting the possibilities of other systems of international settlement, either generally or among like- minded groups of countries, he believed that for the foreseeable future gold would be the ultimate means of settlement. He admitted that 'managed pounds' rather than golden pounds were feasible, for the goal of management just differed from that under a gold standard while the methods remained the same. He emphasised that 'the scientific advocates of the "managed pound" ' were not inflationists as were the normal opponents of the gold standard. However, he thought that the substitution of 'managed pounds' for golden pounds would not

[1] T172/1499B, 'The Gold Standard', 5 February 1925. Reprinted in full in Appendix 5.

eliminate the credit cycle in some form. Such a substitution could only reduce disturbances which would otherwise result from fluctuations in the value of gold, and it would only do that 'if the index on which you work contains a smaller margin of error than the amount by which the real value of gold fluctuates'. To secure this advantage, Bradbury thought, the statistics would need substantial improvement. Turning then to the present decision on the restoration of gold, Lord Bradbury admitted that there would be great force in the argument for waiting for a rise in American prices if there was a reasonable probability of this happening and if the gap between American and British prices was appreciable. However, as the difference was 'not more than 2% or 3%' there was little advantage and possibly serious disadvantages in waiting, particularly as the lack of any announcement of resumption would cause a depreciation of sterling, a rise in sterling prices and a restriction of credit if only on managed currency grounds. Lord Bradbury then concluded:

It is not unlikely that such restriction would be far more severe than that which would be occasioned by a restoration of the free gold market, more particularly if the latter operations should take place at a time when dollar prices are rising in America. Indeed I should not be at all surprised if very shortly after the restoration of the free gold market a period of cheap money and easy credit becomes necessary to repel an influx of unwanted gold.

Finally, there was a long rather involved reply from R. G. Hawtrey.[1] Hawtrey emphasised that the success of managed money had so far occurred during a period of recovery from a slump when cheap money was necessary, and he wondered what reactions there would be to a period of credit restriction that had not been foreshadowed by gold exports. He also emphasised that 'stabilisation of internal prices is only one of the two primary characteristics of a good currency', the other being 'stabilisation of the foreign exchanges'. He continued by arguing that unstable exchanges were particularly damaging to a country such as Britain which acted as a financial centre, lending short to finance the trade of third countries, for the forward exchange market found it more difficult to arrange coverage when, with stable exchanges in the third countries, the exchange risk would be one-sided. The restoration

---

[1]T172/1499B, 'The Gold Standard', 2 February 1925. The Genoa Resolutions concerning currency, which are referred to both in Hawtrey's reply and elsewhere in this study, grew out of the Genoa Conference of 1922. The resolutions contained detailed proposals for an international convention based on the gold exchange standard and the control of credit to prevent fluctuations in the purchasing power of gold, thus making adherence to an international gold standard and price stability possible. The resolutions are discussed in detail by R. G. Hawtrey, who provided the basic ideas for them, in *Monetary Reconstruction*, 2nd ed. (London, 1926), 122–38

of the sterling bill's predominance, he believed, was in both the national and the international interest. Stability could be achieved technically through stabilisation on sterling, but he argued that this would only be satisfactory if there was no risk of war and the blocking of exchange reserves of those countries which stabilised on sterling. As they would be unlikely to do so, Hawtrey concluded that the only method of international exchange stability was gold, particularly as in other countries the gold standard was an accomplished fact.

Hawtrey then continued to examine the case for a return to gold at the present time, and by the United Kingdom. To him, the fundamental objection to a return to gold was the 'influence of America on the Commodity value or purchasing power of gold'. The present rising trend of American prices was favourable for a return to gold because it did not necessitate deflation in Britain, but, he argued, the attendant risk of an American deflation once Britain had returned might produce a particularly cruel dilemma at present levels of unemployment, for 'in present conditions, with unemployment still severe, it would be better to let sterling lapse than to raise bank rate to a deterrent level'. However, he considered that such a dilemma was unlikely for he expected that the American expansion would continue for some time and communicate itself to Britain through a rise in prices and encourage British trade. 'When the turn of the tide comes', he continued, 'we shall be able to stand a rise in bank rate without trouble'. He also expected American prosperity and foreign lending to prevent any deterioration in the British international position resulting from British overlending or other causes. He admitted that there was, as Keynes had pointed out, a risk of excessive American expansion, but he suggested that this possibility was 'remote', and that if it materialised gold could be demonetised without any previous preparation. Hawtrey then moved on to discuss the Genoa Resolutions and their provision for co-operation to maintain the gold standard and the purchasing power of gold. These held out the promise of 'the best of both worlds – stable prices and stable exchanges'. They would prevent a general return to gold from being deflationary by encouraging economy of gold for monetary purposes and agreement to hold the purchasing power of gold stable. However, he did not really tie them into the current discussions of policy except to suggest an agreement with the Federal Reserve System that it would not contract credit unless a serious inflation threatened the United States and that the United States would not unload her gold reserves on Britain or vice versa.

In fact, Hawtrey made few suggestions as to immediate policy except that 'no *active* measures at all need be taken' (italics in the original). He hoped that the exchange would come to par 'of itself', and if it didn't he opposed credit contraction. If it went to par, but there was a subsequent reaction which resulted not from 'a credit expansion here', but rather from 'an adverse balance of payments' or 'a contraction in America', the Authorities should let 'large quantities' of gold go and suspend the fiduciary issue limit of the Bank of England. If these measures were unsuccessful, as 'it would be inadvisable to raise bank rate to a deterrent level or to contract credit to any serious extent', Hawtrey suggested that 'it would be better to let sterling fall to a discount'.

By 6 February, Churchill had read his advisers' replies to 'Mr Churchill's Exercise' and the Chamberlain–Bradbury Committee's *Report*, noting that the former were 'very able' and that the latter provided 'a solid foundation of argument and authority justifying the action proposed'.[1] However, he still had points that he wished to raise with Niemeyer and the Governor and he desired more information. In particular, he noted the results of a conversation with Mr Goodenough of Barclay's Bank. Goodenough favoured a return to gold but 'would deprecate decision being "rushed" '. He argued that the pound should be brought to par and held there for some months, perhaps with American support, before a return was attempted. The intervening uncertainty would be no problem as traders could cover their requirements in the forward market. Any announcement in March or even August would be 'precipitate'. Churchill also commented on Reginald McKenna's recent speech to his shareholders which had seemingly supported the gold standard and which had been used as support for the end the Treasury civil servants desired.[2] As he put it:

I read his speech as being a deliberately weak defense of the Gold policy, the only argument for which might in short be stated as a vulgar superstition. I have private confirmation of the opinions I derived from reading his speech. He is personally opposed to the gold policy and regards it as unnecessary and unwise.

On 6 February, Churchill also wrote to Sir Austen Chamberlain, enclosing a copy of the Chamberlain–Bradbury *Report* and asking for his comments. At this point, Churchill noted that 'the matter is one of considerable urgency, and decision on the question of the Gold Standard cannot long be delayed'.[3]

The reactions to these two notes were fairly rapid. Niemeyer, replied to Goodenough's proposals by pointing out that using a cushion to support the exchange before losing gold and raising Bank Rate implied that they would try 'to maintain an artificial exchange with limited

---

[1] T172/1499B, Churchill to Niemeyer, 6 February 1925.
[2] The speech referred to appears in Midland Bank Limited, *Monthly Review*, January–February 1925, esp. 4–5.
[3] Chartwell Papers, File 18/10, Churchill to Chamberlain, 6 February 1925.

means', and that this would encourage speculation and withdrawals of funds, exhaust the credit (if one was available for this purpose), push sterling to $4.00 or less, and require a Bank Rate of 11 per cent or more 'to stop the rot'.[1] He accepted that traders could cover themselves in the forward market, but argued that this merely passed the uncertainty on to bankers and brokers who would object. Moreover, forward cover only affected goods bought and sold; it did not cover the manufacturer who did not know the price of future goods in the market. He concluded by asking what Goodenough would do if sterling failed to rise to par before December or if sterling fell below $4.79 owing to doubt and subsequent profit taking.

Chamberlain's reply to Churchill's request was equally emphatic.[2] He reported that he had read the *Report* with 'profound interest' and 'complete agreement'. After noting his agreements with the Committee's interpretation of its feelings in the autumn of 1924 and its reaction to recent developments on the exchange, he continued:

I feel sure that, if you make your announcement with *decisive confidence* on your own part, the operation will now be found, all things considered, an easy one, and that to delay your decision much longer would be to expose you to a serious risk of a renewed fall in sterling. All the world is now expecting us to return to the gold standard, and has become convinced that we can do it. If we do not do it, we shall not stay where we were, but inevitably *start a retrograde movement*.   (italics in the original)

Thus he pressed for an immediate announcement of the decision to allow the embargo to lapse and a general licence to export.

On the same day as Chamberlain's letter, an article by Philip Snowden, the former Chancellor, appeared in *The Observer*.[3] In it Snowden referred to the recent rise in the exchange, the forthcoming expiry of the Act enabling the embargo on gold exports and the general expectation of a decision to return to gold at $4.86. He argued that a return to gold was necessary although the maintenance of gold might present some difficulties. These difficulties would be 'small compared with the evils from which the world is suffering as a result of unstable and fluctuating currencies'. The return to gold did not require prior ratification from the trade balance, because 'a stable currency is one of the essentials of a healthy state of trade'. The necessary risks of returning had to be taken, although they could be reduced through co-operation with the United States. This article gave some indication of the breadth of political support for a return to gold which probably made the ultimate decision easier.

---

[1]T172/1499B, Niemeyer to Churchill.
[2]T172/1499B, Chamberlain to Churchill, 8 February 1925.   [3]8 February 1925

However, discussion continued unabated for over a month. During February, Niemeyer, whom Churchill refused to allow to leave him, reported to Leith-Ross, who had gone to a meeting in Geneva in his place, 'Gold is excessively active and very troublesome. None of the witch-doctors see eye to eye and Winston cannot make up his mind from day to day whether he is a gold bug or a pure inflationist'.[1] The discussions covered much the same ground as before, and thus generally need not be outlined in detail. However, one particular exchange is of interest in that it crystallises the position that the return to gold held in the official pattern of expectations. The exchange occurred over Keynes' article in *The Nation*, 'The Return Towards Gold'.[2] Niemeyer accepted Keynes as 'a serious critic of monetary policy' and he attempted to answer many of the issues raised in the article. He agreed with Keynes that Bank Rate should rise to prevent excessive foreign lending and that under existing conditions such a rise would not harm trade and employment.[3] However, he disagreed with Keynes' plea for a managed currency and his proposals for a well managed return to gold, if the latter was the ultimate policy. Niemeyer did not expect American prices to rise by themselves by enough to produce parity, and he did not believe that even if they did rise by the requisite amount parity would result, and he pointed to the situation eighteen months previously when prices had been equal and the exchange remained below par. He agreed with Keynes that there were dangers in being linked to the United States, but he argued that the dangers of not being so linked were greater given Britain's position as a trading nation and a financial centre, particularly at a time when other countries were returning to gold. He also noted that there would be risks from the United States under any currency system. In conclusion he noted that, 'Mr. Keynes seems to me to contemplate the main alleged disadvantages of a gold policy (rise of bank rate, etc.) while depriving himself in the interests of an unexplored theory of "Managed Currency", of all the advantages.'

Churchill, on reading the article and Niemeyer's comments, reacted somewhat differently. After a few short comments on particular points of Niemeyer's, he fastened on Keynes' reference to 'the paradox of unemployment amidst dearth' and continued:[4]

The Treasury have never, it seems to me, faced the profound significance of what Mr Keynes calls 'the paradox of unemployment amidst dearth.' The

---

[1]Leith-Ross, *Money Talks*, 91–2.
[2]21 February 1925. It also appears in J. M. Keynes, *Essays in Persuasion*, 225–36.
[3]T172/1499B, Niemeyer to Churchill, 21 February 1925.
[4]T172/1499B, Churchill to Niemeyer, 22 February 1925. Churchill echoed this note to Niemeyer just over three years later in a minute to P. J. Grigg which also throws some light in the tactics underlying Mr Churchill's Exercise (above, p. 66).
    But the complacency of the Treasury and the Bank and their indifference to

Governor shows himself perfectly happy in the spectacle of Britain possessing the finest credit in the world simultaneously with a million and a quarter unemployed ... The community lacks goods, and a million and a quarter people lack work. It is certainly one of the highest functions of national finance and credit to bridge the gulf between the two. This is the only country in the world where this condition exists. The Treasury and the Bank of England policy has been the only policy consistently pursued. It is a terrible responsibility for those who have shaped it, unless they can be sure that there is no connection between the unique British phenomenon of chronic unemployment and the long, resolute consistency of a particular financial policy. I do not know whether France with her financial embarrassments can be said to be worse off than England with her unemployment. At any rate while that unemployment exists, no one is entitled to plume himself on the financial or credit policy which we have pursued.

It may be of course that you will argue that the unemployment would have been much greater but for the financial policy pursued; that there is not sufficient demand for commodities either internally or externally to require the services of this million and a quarter people; that there is nothing for them but to hang like a millstone round the neck of industry and on the public revenue until they become permanently demoralised. You may be right, but if so, it is one of the most sombre conclusions ever reached. On the other hand I do not pretend to see even 'through a glass darkly' how the financial and credit policy of the country could be handled so as to bridge the gap between a dearth of goods and a surplus of labour; and well I realise the danger of experiment to that end. The seas of history are full of famous wrecks. Still if I could see a way, I would far rather follow it than any other. I would rather see Finance less proud and Industry more content.

You and the Governor have managed this affair. Taken together I expect you know more about it than anyone else in the world. At any rate alone in the world you have had an opportunity over a definite period of years of seeing your policy carried out. That it is a great policy, greatly pursued, I have no doubt. But the fact that this island with its enormous resources is unable to maintain its population is surely a cause for the deepest heartsearching.

Forgive me adding to your labours by these Sunday morning reflections.

Niemeyer took up these remarks, and his reply is worth quoting at length.[1] After pointing out that some unemployment arose from factors

all other aspects of our national problem make it a duty to put the opposite case sometimes. They have caused an immense amount of misery and impoverishment by their rough and pedantic handling of the problem. In ruined homes, in demoralised workmen, in discouraged industry, in embarrassed finances, in inflated debt and cruel taxation we have paid the price. As the ship goes through the seas its smoke and smells drift to leeward. One always hopes one will make the port in good time when the discomforts of the voyage will soon be forgotten.
Chartwell Papers, File 18/75, Churchill to Grigg, 2 July 1928.
[1]T172/1499B, Niemeyer to Churchill.

such as 'maladjustment of labour supplies' and European transit conditions and tariffs which reduced trade, he continued:

I doubt whether credit policy is even a chief cause, and I at any rate would not advocate, still less be 'happy' with a credit policy which I thought would produce unemployment . . .
You can by inflation (a most vicious form of subsidy) enable temporarily, spending power to cope with large quantities of products. But unless you increase the dose continually, there comes a time when having destroyed the credit of the country you can inflate no more, money having ceased to be acceptable as value. Even before this, as your inflated spending creates demand, you have had claims for increased wages, strikes, lock outs etc. I assume it to be admitted that with Germany and Russia before us we do not think plenty can be found on this path.
If that be admitted, economic employment can only be given to the extent to which commodities can be produced at a price which existing uninflated wealth can pay for them. As the result of war there has been a great decrease in wealth, and there is consequently less effective demand. The only permanent remedy is to recreate the losses of war – really, not merely by manufacturing paper – and what we have to do for this purpose is (1) to stabilise our currency in relation to the main trading currencies of the world, (2) to reconstruct the broken parts of Europe and (3) to encourage thrift and the accumulation of capital for industry. These methods and not doles and palliatives are going to remedy unemployment (at least to the extent to which it was remedied in pre war days). We are now trying to put the finishing touch to (1). We have done what we can for (2) League Loans, Dawes etc. We do all we can for (3) especially by repaying debt and by encouraging a belief that currency will not lose its value. Other methods may give for a year or so a hectic prosperity (particularly if as in France there are largely devastated regions to mend) but they won't give a permanent cure . . .
The above is necessarily put in a doctrinaire way. In practice we have to go now slow, now fast. But the root idea I am convinced is right, and the only way to enable this small island bound to buy and sell largely abroad . . . ultimately to support its population.

This idea of the gold standard policy as an employment policy had come up before, and according to P. J. Grigg it was of some importance in the ultimate decision. Certainly this is a part of the drift of the famous dinner party of 17 March which Grigg reports and which has been used by some observers to refute parts of Keynes' *Economic Consequences of Mr. Churchill.*[1] Certainly after the event, the gold standard and resulting trends in unemployment were something that Churchill returned to in his discussions with his advisers.[2]

---

[1]Grigg, *Prejudice and Judgement*, 183. The date of the party is taken from Keynes' appointments diary for 1925 which is part of the Keynes Papers.
[2]See for example T175/11, Churchill to Niemeyer, 20 April 1927.

This 'confession of faith' by Niemeyer was, in many ways, the last important pre-restoration decision document. Discussions continued after late February on specific questions of detail raised by the Chancellor – such as the size of foreign speculative balances in London – but the general discussion of overall policy did not recur except at the dinner party of 17 March attended by Grigg, Churchill, McKenna, Keynes, Niemeyer and Bradbury which has been so extensively cited in the literature.[1] The general issues may have come up in Churchill's discussions with Norman, after the latter's return from holiday early in March – the time at which Norman had expected official consideration of the return to gold to occur.[2] However, we have very little knowledge of what occurred at these meetings.[3] We only know their result.

The decision[4] finally came on 20 March. Norman noted the final meetings laconically in his diary entries for 19 and 20 March:[5]

Chancellor for lunch in Downing St. Gold return to be announced April 6th or 8th. Cushion to be meanwhile arranged by Bank. I warn him of 6% Bank rate next month.

Prime Minister, Chancellor, Austen Chamberlain, Bradbury, Niemeyer at 2.30. Free gold statement to be in Budget about April 28th ...

Sir Otto Niemeyer noted the latter meeting more completely:[6]

Note of Government Decisions

On Friday, the 20th of March, the Prime Minister discussed the question of monetary policy with the Chancellor of the Exchequer, the Secretary of State for Foreign Affairs, the Governor of the Bank of England, Lord Bradbury and Sir Otto Niemeyer. The following conclusions were reached:

1. That the return to the gold standard should be announced as part of the Budget speech.

2. The announcement to take the form of a statement that the power to

---

[1]Grigg, *Prejudice and Judgement*, 182–4.

[2]F.R.B.N.Y., Norman to Strong, no. 71, 24 February 1925; Strong Papers, Norman to Strong, 9 March 1925.

[3]Boyle, *Montagu Norman*, 188–9. The quote given to Boyle was also given to the author by the late Mr Randolph Churchill. See also 'Mr Churchill's Success', *The Banker*, 1 (6), June 1926, 393.

[4]The decision never went to the Cabinet except as a part of the Budget preview. The leading figures throughout, other than Churchill, were Baldwin and Chamberlain. Churchill made reports as to the progress of implementation to Baldwin, as one suspects did Norman. The parallels with the 1957 Bank Rate decision are also of interest. (Chartwell Papers, File 18/8, Churchill to Baldwin, 17 April 1925; Boyle, *Montagu Norman*, 162, 177–8; R. A. Chapman, *Decision Making*, [London, 1969], Ch. 4.).

[5]Boyle, *Montagu Norman*, 189.

[6]T172/1499B, Note by Niemeyer. The undertaking by the Governor with regard to Bank Rate was valid for only one week (T172/1499B, Norman to Niemeyer, 21 March 1925).

prohibit exports will not be renewed after December next, and further, that the licences for the export of gold would be given freely, either from the date of this statement or very shortly afterwards: this point to be further discussed with the Bank.

3. That the Bank rate should not be put up contemporaneously with the Budget statement.

4. That it was desirable to make arrangements for obtaining a credit in America as an extra precaution and that the Governor of the Bank should make enquiries in America accordingly. It was clearly understood that such a credit was not to be used until (1) substantial exports of gold had taken place, and (2) Bank rate had been put up accordingly. The intention of the American credit was that it should be for show and not for use.

5. The Chancellor of the Exchequer undertook to see the Clearing Banks on Monday, the 23rd March, and to endeavour to obtain from them an understanding that they would use every effort in terms satisfactory to the Chancellor to discourage the use of gold for internal circulation in this country. It was recognised that unless satisfactory assurances could be obtained from the Bankers, it would be necessary to introduce legislation on this point before any announcement with regard to the gold standard was made.

Implementing the Decision, March–April 1925

From this point onwards, the attention of the Authorities was to be directed to the details of implementation of the basic decisions of the 20th. These details are best considered under three headings: the arrangement of the cushion, the conditions attached to the cushion by the Federal Reserve Bank of New York, and the agreements with the clearing bankers concerning the internal circulation of gold. We shall examine each of these briefly before turning to a general summary and consideration of the factors influencing the decision to return to gold.

As noted above,[1] one of Governor Norman's intentions in his New York trip was to obtain a cushion to maintain the exchange if that became necessary. The credit, he noted, 'should probably exceed $300,000,000' and would not be used 'until a sufficiently large amount of gold has been shipped to America and a sufficiently high rate had been in operation here'.[2] At this early proposal stage, Niemeyer's reaction was very cool.[3] Niemeyer noted that the Treasury had a 'nest egg' in New York of about $100 million and held Dominion bonds whose coupons were payable in dollars or sterling at par which would probably fetch $50 million. He also noted that legally the Treasury did not have the power to issue fresh obligations of the sort needed and

[1]See above, p. 58.
[2]T172/1500A, Norman to Niemeyer, 4 December 1924.
[3]T172/1500A, Niemeyer to Norman, 8 December 1924.

that, as he put it, 'we should have to legislate and explain our fears'. If the Americans were so interested in gold, he continued, 'ought not the U.S. . . . to co-operate without requiring us to go to the pawnshop?' Basically he disliked the idea of pegging the exchange and summed up his attitude in the following: 'Either the emergency will not arise – because either the gold shipment will be enough to save it or you will be allowed to put up your Bank rate high enough – or if it does the cushion will not save us.'

The proposal for the cushion was certainly one of the grounds for the opposition in January to the proposals set out by Norman in his cables from New York. Sir Warren Fisher disliked it because 'neither the gold standard nor anything else is worth having on sufferance of another country', and because it would advertise a lack of faith.[1] Niemeyer continued to dislike it for his previous reasons and for the implication of conditions on its use in Norman's cable, particularly, the one stating that use of the credit would 'require progressive increases in Bank of England rate'.[2] The discussion of these objections continued throughout January, as both Norman's cables to Strong and Addis' evidence to the Chamberlain-Bradbury Committee indicate.[3] The Treasury also remained unsure as to the need for the loan, the availability of the power to borrow and the size of the loan if needed.[4]

The critics in the Bank may have been won over in February by the news that 'in the event of a free Market . . . [a certain country] may decide to withdraw in gold London balances of £20/40,000,000'.[5] However, the Treasury remained unconvinced and Niemeyer summed up the current thinking in a long note to Norman on 16 March which began with the general observation that time increased his dislike for the scheme.[6] If the Bank was prepared to lose up to £100 million in gold before using the cushion, he questioned the usefulness of the idea, for if that much support wouldn't succeed a cushion wouldn't. He admitted that he could see the advantages of having the cushion 'in the shop window to impress speculative holders of sterling', but he feared that political pressure might force its actual use. He still expressed a preference for bonding the debt interest on American war loans and

[1] T172/1500A, Fisher to Niemeyer, 12 January 1925.
[2] T175/9, Niemeyer to Lubbock, 9 January 1925.
[3] See above, p. 61.
[4] T172/1500A, Niemeyer to Phillips and Graham-Harrison, 22 January 1925; Phillips to Graham-Harrison, 23 January 1925; Graham Harrison to Niemeyer, 24 January 1925; Niemeyer to Norman, 25 January and 10 February 1925; Norman to Niemeyer, 27 January, 10 and 26 February 1925; Rowe-Dutton to Niemeyer, 19 February 1925; Leith-Ross to Niemeyer, 13 March 1925.
[5] F.R.B.N.Y., Norman to Strong, no. 71, 23 February 1925.
[6] T172/1500A, Niemeyer to Norman, 16 March 1925 and enclosure called 'The Cushion'.

using the freed Treasury resources if support proved necessary, and he was prepared to use any pledged securities or securities borrowed for the purpose on a deposit scheme. If, however, the cushion was adopted as policy, he expressed a preference for a smaller sum, for as much as possible to be borrowed by the Bank, and for any commissions on Treasury credits to be waived to save Parliamentary criticism.[1]

As we have seen, the cushion was accepted in principle at the meeting of 20 March, but the details were left vague. The Governor put the proposal of a smaller credit raised solely by the Bank from Morgans and the Federal Reserve to Strong soon thereafter,[2] but the latter, after consulting J. P. Morgan, expressed a preference for the larger sum and one central bank and one Government market credit, if only to avoid adverse American comment and to make the two transactions appear separate as the Federal Reserve could not lend to foreign governments. Strong, was, however, prepared, if necessary, to accept a smaller total with the sum from the Federal Reserve System remaining unchanged to avoid the need for new negotiations with all the Banks in the System.[3] Norman agreed to this suggestion and the total was reduced to $300 million from the $500 million originally proposed.[4] The upshot was that the Treasury's part of the credits was reduced by $200 million. From that point on there remained only the arrangement of the timing of the loans, as this would depend on the enabling legislation which would guarantee the Bank's borrowing in New York and allow the Treasury to borrow. Initially there was some discussion of the possibility of putting the gold standard arrangements in the Finance Bill, but as that would not become law until July and as the gap between announcement and legislation was distasteful to all concerned, a special bill for resumption and the necessary borrowing was conceded.[5] From that point, there were no problems, and the Treasury and Bank arranged terms and passed the necessary formal letters without incident.[6]

In January 1925 Strong proposed for Norman's consideration, four conditions which would surround the credits: (1) continuity in the management of the Bank for two years (the period of the credit), (2)

[1] Ibid., See also T172/1500A, Niemeyer to Churchill, 20 March 1925.

[2] T172/1500A, Norman to Strong, nos 87 and 88, 21 March 1925.

[3] T172/1500A, Strong to Norman, nos 48 and 49, 24 March, 1925; J. P. Morgan to E. C. Grenfell, no. 2076, 25 March 1925.

[4] T172/1500A, Norman to Strong, no. 91, 26 March 1925.

[5] T172/1500A, Norman to Strong, nos 91, 93 and 100, 26 and 30 March, and 2 April 1925; Strong to Norman, no 52, 27 March 1925; Niemeyer to Churchill, 30 March 1925; Churchill to Niemeyer, 31 March 1925; Norman to Niemeyer, 30 March 1925.

[6] T172/1500A, Norman to Strong, 8 April 1925; T160/227/F8508, Churchill to J. P. Morgan and Co., 28 April 1925; E. C. Grenfell and Co. to Churchill, 28 April 1925.

the necessity for Bank of England approval of any change in the fiduciary limit for the currency note issue, (3) control by the Federal Reserve of the credit used at any particular time, and (4) no British Government barriers to gold exports if these were necessary to repay the credits.[1] The first was purely a matter for the Bank which Norman accepted in February,[2] but the other three required the co-operation of the Treasury for their realisation. The Treasury agreed to the third, which merely ensured that the Federal Reserve retained control of its own market, before the return to gold,[3] and the fourth gained formal acceptance when a Treasury Minute passed under the Gold Standard Act 1925 received approval in May.[4] However, the second condition proved impossible to realise in anything but a nominal sense. The Governor proposed the second condition to the Treasury the day after the settlement of 'the date for a public announcement of the golden age', as Norman put it.[5] However, the Treasury objected to the proposal as it would mean that, given the Treasury Minute of 1919, the removal of gold from the currency note account would imply contraction and as the Bank would not only have to approve of any change in the limit but also to initiate any proposals for change.[6] There were also objections because such a condition would have to be made public and might thus bring further controversy.[7] The Bank then waived this requirement from the Treasury and Strong accepted the Bank's suggestion that it be dropped.[8] However, to put Strong's mind at rest, Norman arranged to have a sentence added to the Chamberlain–Bradbury Report:[9] 'As from the date of the announcement [of resumption of gold payment] until such time as the arrangements governing the fiduciary issue can be put on a permanent basis, the existing limitation

---

[1] F.R.B.N.Y., Strong Papers, Strong to Norman, 15 January 1925.
[2] F.R.B.N.Y., Strong Papers, Norman to Strong, 13 February 1925.
[3] T172/1499B, Niemeyer to Norman, 15 April 1925.
[4] T160/227/F8508, Treasury Minute, 14 May 1925.
[5] T172/1499B, Norman to Niemeyer, 21 March 1925.
[6] T172/1500A, Niemeyer to Chancellor, Note on Norman's letter of 21 March 1925.
[7] T172/1500A, Norman to Strong, no. 92, 27 March 1925.
[8] Ibid., T172/1500A, Norman to Niemeyer, 30 March 1925; Strong to Norman, no. 53, 27 March 1925.
[9] S. V. O. Clarke (*Central Bank Cooperation*, 84) argues that 'no such recommendation was included in the Committee's report'. However, a comparison of the draft copy sent to Strong by Norman with the *Report* as published reveals that the quoted sentence was missing from paragraph 34. Norman wrote to Strong on 20 April that he was still attempting to obtain the inclusion of a sentence of this sort. It was finally added 'after consultation with the Governor and Lord Bradbury', by Niemeyer with the concurrence of Committee members (F.R.B.N.Y., Strong Papers, Norman to Strong, 15 and 20 April 1925; T160/197/F7528, Niemeyer to Pigou, 17 and 23 April 1925).

of that issue should be strictly maintained.'¹ The Government's acceptance of the *Report* in toto with the inclusion of this sentence proved acceptable to Strong.² Thus Strong's conditions of January were generally met.

Finally the Chancellor, to carry out the decisions of 20 March, had to arrange with the clearing banks an undertaking to prevent the internal circulation of gold coin. The Chancellor met the bankers twice after 20 March and attempted to persuade them not to ask for gold coin in exchange for Bank of England notes or currency notes for themselves or their customers and not to hold gold themselves for reserve purposes.³ The Treasury wanted to avoid the necessity for legislation on this point which it believed would be psychologically unfortunate and controversial, but it wanted to avoid the risk of an internal drain 'in time of crisis (due to a Socialist government)', or resulting from 'demands from the London agents of foreign powers, from the public which is affected by irresponsible newspaper suggestion and from "sound currency" fanatics'.⁴ However, Reginald McKenna of the Midland Bank opposed such an undertaking at first and wanted legislation suspending gold payment in coin, and the bankers believed that to prevent the internal circulation of coin would be extremely difficult if such circulation remained legal.⁵ They were prepared, however, not to hold gold themselves, and after further discussion they agreed for two years from the date of the gold standard legislation's passage not to acquire or hold coin or bullion on behalf of customers resident in the United Kingdom or themselves and to hold all gold that came their way in the course of business.⁶ However, to cover themselves against backsliders, the Treasury redrafted the relevant section of the Chamberlain–Bradbury *Report* to allow for legislation resulting from its acceptance if that became necessary, and to make compliance by the banks more likely they included in the Gold Standard Act 1925 a provision that made notes convertible into bullion in amounts of approximately 400 fine ounces at a time and that suspended the free convertibility of gold at the Mint.⁷

With the settling of these final details and successful arrangements

¹Committee on the Currency and Bank of England Note Issues, *Report*, para. 34.
²F.R.B.N.Y., Strong Papers, Strong to Norman, 30 April 1925.
³T176/22, Note of a Meeting between the Chancellor of the Exchequer and Representatives of the Clearing Banks, 23 March 1925; Note of a Second Meeting on 26 March 1925 between the Chancellor of the Exchequer and the Bankers.
⁴Ibid., Niemeyer to Churchill, 25 February 1925.
⁵Ibid., Niemeyer to Churchill, 6 April 1925.
⁶T176/22, R. Holland-Martin to Niemeyer, 23 April and 1 May 1925.
⁷Committee on the Currency and Bank of England Note Issues, *Report*, para. 45; T160/197/F7528, Niemeyer to Pigou 17 and 23 April 1925; Gold Standard Act 1925, 15 and 16, Geo. 5, c. 29, Section 1.

with several other countries for a co-ordinated return to gold on the
same day,[1] the United Kingdom returned to gold at the pre-war parity
at 4.5 p.m. on 28 April 1925. Before examining the wisdom of the
decision, it would be wise to look at the considerations that seem to
have proved influential in the final event and the expectations of the
Authorities as to the effects of the return, for many of these were dashed
by events after the restoration.

A Summary of the Discussions

In dealing in summary with the arguments employed at the time of
the return to gold it is probably best to look at them under four heads:
the consideration of alternative policies, the consideration of timing, the
consideration of adjustment mechanisms and difficulties, and the consideration of the underlying British international position.

In the discussions prior to the return devaluation never received
serious consideration. The Chamberlain–Bradbury Committee dismissed
it in all the various drafts of their report, out of hand at first and as
unnecessary, given the rise of the dollar exchange, later.[2] In the
Treasury and Bank of England discussions it was not mentioned as a
possibility until after the event and after the publication of Keynes'
Economic Consequences of Mr. Churchill and Sir Josiah Stamp's critical
Addendum to the Coal Court of Inquiry.[3] At that point, the devaluation alternative was rejected by Niemeyer and Bradbury largely for
balance sheet reasons, as it would involve either the writing down of the
value of Britain's international assets or the increasing of the value of
her liabilities.[4] In addition, in the discussions there were hints that

---

[1]Australia, the Netherlands, the Netherlands East Indies and South Africa all
agreed to move with the U.K. Switzerland refused to follow the U.K., as her
authorities wanted to wait until 'they have had time to witness the results of action
taken elsewhere, and particularly in Great Britain'. (T172/1499B, Norman to
Niemeyer, 20 April 1925. The other correspondence concerning co-ordinating
discussions also appears in this file.) In the case of New Zealand, her exchange rate
vis-à-vis the dollar moved with sterling and the New Zealand authorities agreed to
follow British practice and issue licences for gold exports. However, in practice
New Zealand returned more to a sterling exchange standard than a gold standard.
See G. R. Hawke, 'New Zealand and the Return to Gold in 1925', *Australian
Economic History Review*, XI (1), March 1971. (I also would like to thank Dr Hawke
for earlier correspondence on this point.)

[2]T160/197/F7528/01/1–3, Committee on the Currency and Bank of England Note
Issues, Second Draft of Report, para. 5; Third Draft Report, para. 5; Fourth
Draft Report, Section 5; *Report*, para. 7.

[3]Court of Inquiry concerning the Coal Mining Industry Dispute, 1925, *Report*,
Cmd. 2478 (London, 1925), 21ff.

[4]T176/16, Niemeyer to Chancellor, 4 August 1925; Bradbury, 'The Coal Crisis and
the Gold Standard', 4 August 1925. The Bradbury memorandum also appeared in

depreciation would involve a rise in food prices and a resulting rise in the cost of living and in wages – the converse being true for appreciation.[1] On the other hand, the managed money alternative received somewhat more discussion as it had received considerable publicity through Keynes and McKenna. The Chamberlain–Bradbury Committee, citing 'the overwhelming majority of opinion' presented to them by witnesses, rejected it as not being a 'practical present-day policy for this country'.[2] Even Keynes accepted this decision on their part as 'intelligible'.[3] As noted previously, in discussions with the Chancellor, only Bradbury and Hawtrey attempted to meet the argument of the Keynes–McKenna school, and both rejected it: Bradbury because he did not believe it was a practicable alternative as an international system for a world of stable exchanges and because he did not believe it would offer greater stability; Hawtrey because he did not believe that the system with its unstable exchanges[4] was in the British interest and because, to a certain extent, he believed that he could achieve the same ends with a Genoa-type gold standard.[5] The Treasury summed up its reasons for accepting gold in its Memorandum which accompanied the Gold Standard Bill:[6]

Whatever its imperfections, gold has for centuries commanded the confidence of the civilised world and has continued to command it. If the gold standard fails to give complete stability, its adoption is nevertheless the most simple and direct method of obtaining a high degree of stability. It is not proved that any other standard would give even as good results. All countries which have successfully restored stability and confidence in their currencies after the disturbances of the last ten years have done so on a gold basis.

This last sentence leads to the final factor against management without

the *Financial News* of 12 August 1925. If one reckons in sterling, the value of international assets denominated in sterling would be unaffected by depreciation; whereas, those denominated in foreign currencies (including under this head equities whose dividends would be based on profits earned in foreign countries) and dollar liabilities would rise. If one reckons in dollars, the position would be reversed and dollar liabilities would not rise. Bradbury made the distinction between these bases for reckoning successfully, but Niemeyer did not and thus did some double counting.

[1] Ibid.
[2] *Report*, para. 8.
[3] J. M. Keynes, 'Notes and Memoranda. The Committee on the Currency', 300.
[4] If one interprets Keynes sympathetically, the exchanges would not be all that unstable, particularly if other major countries' stabilisation policies were successful. Keynes, *Tract on Monetary Reform*, 189–94.
[5] T172/1499B, Bradbury, 'The Gold Standard', 5 February 1925; Hawtrey, 'The Gold Standard', 2 February 1925.
[6] T172/1499B. Gold Standard Bill, Memorandum, 28 April 1925, 5.

gold (management with gold along Genoa lines being acceptable to some observers[1]), the spectre of inflation. As Bradbury put it, 'the gold standard was knave proof'.[2] In the course of the discussions, Niemeyer often made management synonymous with inflation and frequently alluded to European experience as proof of the evils of that.[3] This fear of inflation, accompanied as it was by an underlying fear of considerable economic instability in both inflationary and deflationary directions, was the product of the War and early post-war periods. To a generation which, at worst, had experienced short slumps amidst the gently rising prices of 1896–1913, the wide swings in prices and activity after the beginnings of 'management' in 1914 – and especially during 1918–23 – and the inflationary experiences of Germany, Austria, Russia and the Latin Countries were hardly effective advertisements for management without the 'discipline' of gold. The resulting distaste for 'management' took the form in many circles of outright opposition to management in any form and, along with the lack of analysis of the origins of financial problems after 1914 – or, for that matter, of the reasons for gold's pre-1914 success – prevented any rational exploration of alternatives to gold in 1925 and minimised the possibilities of change from the pre-war order.[4] Almost everyone was prepared to accept as much the lesser of evils the moderate price fluctuations which might result from changes in the value of gold, and for some the Genoa proposals, 'a matter for the future', offered the possibility of mitigating these.[5] Thus the managed money alternative was, in the conditions of 1924–5, a non-starter which received little consideration outside academic circles.[6]

In fact, in 1925 the most important considerations were not rate

[1]Particularly Bradbury, Hawtrey and Norman.
[2]Grigg, *Prejudice and Judgement*, 183.
[3]T172/1499B, Niemeyer. 'The Gold Export Prohibition', 2 February 1925; 'Commentary', 2 February 1925; reply to Churchill's note of 22 February 1925; 'Notes on Gold Standard', 29 April 1925. In this connection, see also H. Withers, *Bankers and Credit* (London, 1924), 265; M. T. Rankin, *Monetary Opinions and Policy 1924–34* (London, 1935), 15.
[4]See for example Withers, *Bankers and Credit*, 1–3, 11, 34–7; E. Cannan, *An Economist's Protest* (London, 1927), 352–3, 406–7. See also the excellent discussion in D. Winch, *Economics and Policy* (London, 1970), 89–90. In this connection Addis' comment to Strong, '[L]et us be thankful we have escaped the managed currency people.', is most indicative. F.R.B.N.Y., Strong Papers, Addis to Strong, 14 April 1925.
[5]T172/1499B, Gold Standard Bill, Memorandum, 28 April 1925, 5. A conference of Central Banks along the lines suggested at Genoa was under discussion at the time of the official decision to return to gold. T172/1499B, F.B.I. to Churchill, 17 March 1925, 3; Niemeyer to Churchill, 20 March 1925; T172/1500A, Norman to Strong, No. 87, 21 March 1925; Strong to Norman, no. 48, 24 March 1925. The proposal never came to anything.
[6]On this point see Macmillan Committee, *Evidence*, Q. 6075, 6078.

choice or management criteria but rather matters of timing. Here, as we have seen in our examination of the Chamberlain–Bradbury Committee and the Treasury and Bank discussions, there was some controversy. Much of the debate turned on the importance of expectations, the best season of the year for such a change in policy and the parallel movements abroad towards gold, although the adjustment mechanisms and the difficulties anticipated also played some part. As we have seen, most of the participants laid considerable stress on the importance of the market's expectation that a return to gold would be likely in 1925 and on the difficulties that would arise if that expectation was disappointed.[1] This fear of a reversal in the trend of the exchange if the decision was delayed appears to have been justified, to some extent, for speculation did exist in the autumn of 1924 and in early 1925. Robert Z. Aliber, in a thorough study of the events after the autumn of 1924 found that as spot rates appreciated the premium on forward sterling increased or the discount on forward sterling decreased in a manner that would confirm the overtracking hypothesis that speculators were attempting to run their gains.[2] Throughout this period, sterling became increasingly overvalued on the basis of price indices, a fact which would also indicate a speculative movement to some extent.[3] This speculative improvement in the exchange left the Authorities facing a dilemma: they could either ratify the speculative anticipations and stabilise or they could delay stabilisation and face the prospect of a fall in the sterling exchange, as the speculative balances which Keynes estimated at approximately £100 million were withdrawn. If the Authorities were to ratify the speculation, most observers argued that the spring, a period of seasonal strength for sterling, was clearly the easiest period for a decision.[4] In 1925 the parallel movements of currencies abroad to stability and to gold was also of some moment, particularly as South Africa had announced a return for the summer of 1925 and Australia had privately decided the same and only held off in response to British promises of a

---

[1]Above, pp. 67, 69, 71.
[2]R. Z. Aliber, 'Speculation in the Foreign Exchanges', esp. 194–7.
[3]This is not to deny that there were other influences favouring sterling in the autumn and winter of 1924–5. See Clarke, *Central Bank Cooperation*, 83–5. If the Bank of England and the Treasury had really wished to inhibit the rise in the exchange during this period, they could have purchased the currencies offered for sterling and used the proceeds for such purposes as war debt repayments. In fact, the Treasury did purchase about $90 million for war debt repayments during this period. See T160/418/F6779/2, Treasury Exchange Transactions in the U.S.A., General Memoranda. However, there is no indication that these purchases were designed to inhibit the appreciation of sterling. Rather they appear to have resulted from a desire to avoid the need for such purchases after the return to gold.
[4]T176/16, Niemeyer to Churchill, 4 August 1925; T172/1499B, Niemeyer, 'Commentary', 2 February 1925; Niemeyer to Churchill, 6 February 1925.

G

decision.[1] Thus, to a considerable extent, external pressures and seasonal factors indicated that a decision was likely in 1925. However, official expectations as to the size of the adjustments necessary to make the return to pre-war par a success and the speed and ease of operation of the adjustment mechanism also heightened the pressure towards decision.

Official thinking about the size of the price adjustments necessary for the achievement of parity was very much conditioned by the actual rate of exchange at any moment, for only the additional price adjustment necessary to hold the exchange above the existing rate was often considered as the adjustment resulting from the return to gold. The Chamberlain–Bradbury Committee's *Report* expressed this view when it noted:[2]

The discrepancy between British and American gold prices which existed in September has not, however, disappeared, though it has been reduced. We must still be prepared to face a fall in the final price level here of a significant, though not very large amount, unless it should happen that a corresponding rise takes place in America, if the rate of exchange is to be restored to and held at the pre-war parity.

In present conditions, however, this argument against immediate action has not, in our opinion, great weight. For the adjustment of price levels required to restore and maintain pre-war parity needs to be only some $1\frac{1}{2}$ per cent larger than that required to hold the exchange at its present rate. If the adjustment of price levels necessary to this end is long deferred, the exchange will inevitably fall back to the rate justified by the comparative price levels—or below it, since the psychological causes which have operated to force it up will tend to operate in the other direction—and a period of fluctuating values is likely to ensue ... But if ... we are prepared to face any price adjustment which may be necessary to maintain the present exchange rate, there is nothing to be said for refusing to accept the very small ($1\frac{1}{2}$ per cent) extra adjustment involved in the re-establishment of an effective gold standard.

Even if those concerned accepted the need for a price adjustment greater than the minimal additional one suggested by the Committee, the amount of the adjustment required was generally underplayed. Throughout the discussions of 1924 and 1925 purchasing-power parity calcula-

---

[1]Committee on the Currency and Bank of England Note Issues, *Report*, para. 21. This represents a change from earlier drafts; for example the second – T160/197/ F7528/01/2, Second Draft of Report, para. 19 (ii) and (iii). See also T160/463/ F8362/1, Telegram, Governor General of Australia to Colonial Secretary, 8 January, 18 February and 10 March 1925; Colonial Secretary to Governor General of Australia, 22 January, 27 February; T17/1499B, Telegram, S. M. Bruce to Baldwin, 9 April 1925.

[2]Para, 19–20.

tions found extensive use. During his visit to London in 1924, Governor Strong summed up the extent of their use as follows:[1]

> As to monetary matters, one finds at the extreme 'left' Keynes, ... et al, in the middle Hawtrey, Cannan and others of rather better standing in the City than the former,—and the extreme 'Right' led by our stalwart Addis who thinks English prices must come down further if they are to regain their trade. All but Norman seem to have adopted the 'purchasing power parity' doctrine,—and think that a 12% increase in our price level will *cause* a 12% increase in the £ (to par with us) whereupon we could lose gold to much of the world and our troubles (and theirs) would be over. But there are other factors which I find Norman appreciates better than most,—and first of all is the [Dawes] 'report'. (italics in the original)

In fact Norman appears to have regarded purchasing-power parity calculations with suspicion. As he told the Chamberlain–Bradbury Committee.[2]

> Personally I would not know where to turn for such a calculation and I am not sure I would really believe such calculations if they were made because they are very experimental, these calculations, don't you think? ... The only way I should try and make a shot at it would be to ask a certain number of people in whose opinions I have confidence, add them together and divide and on the whole I should trust the result.

Within the Treasury, there was considerable, although largely formal, apparent distrust of such calculations, in the sense that on almost every occasion they found use there occurred a qualifying statement to the effect that 'overmuch importance should not ... be attached to any arguments based on precise interpretations of these figures'.[3] Nevertheless, purchasing-power parity calculations entered the gold standard discussions in the Treasury at almost every point and had a powerful influence on implicit thinking about the nature of the stabilisation problem throughout the period. When such calculations found use, however, the invariable tendency, both inside and outside the Treasury, was to use wholesale prices for both Britain and the United States.[4]

[1]F.R.B.N.Y., Strong Papers, Strong to Jay, 11 April 1924.
[2]Pigou Papers, op. cit., Evidence of Norman, June 1924, 19–20. See also Norman's January 1925 evidence to the Committee, 16; F.R.B.N.Y., Strong Papers, Norman to Strong, 16 October 1924.
[3]T172/1499B, Niemeyer, 'Notes on Gold Standard', 29 April 1925; Bradbury, 'The Gold Standard', 5 February 1925; Gold Standard Bill, Memorandum, 2–3. Committee on the Currency and Bank of England Note Issues, *Report*, para. 15. See also Churchill's speech to the Commons on the Gold Standard Bill, 183 H.C. Deb. 5 s. columns 677–8.
[4]See for example, Committee on the Currency and Bank of England Note Issues. *Report*, para. 15; Gold Standard Bill, Memorandum, 2–3. R. G. Hawtrey's memorandum 'The Gold Standard and Purchasing Power Parity' of 27 April (T163/130/G1942) was perhaps the most cautious of all in using such calculations, in that it

Such indices tended to move with the exchange as they contained a heavy emphasis on staple commodities in international trade with world prices that moved, as far as Britain was concerned, with the exchange rate.[1] In addition, those using the calculations made no attempt to adjust the figures for any deterioration in Britain's underlying international economic position in the period since 1913, the normal base year for such calculations. Thus the use of this very influential method of measuring over and undervaluations invariably tended to underestimate the extent of any adjustment problems involved in returning to gold at $4.86.

But, even though those concerned with policy formation tended to underplay the adjustment required, in that they probably understated the difference in relative prices and costs between Britain and America, they did recognise the need for some degree of adjustment. However, they were very imprecise as to the time period involved in the adjustment and as to its exact details. Two basic schools of thought seem to have existed in the spring of 1925 as before, those who expected inflation abroad and those who expected deflation at home. Professor Sayers, largely on the basis of the Chamberlain–Bradbury Committee's *Report* and P. J. Grigg's report of the supposedly fateful dinner party, denies that the former group which gambled on a rise in American prices existed or was influential in the final decision.[2] The Chamberlain–Bradbury *Report* did mention the possibility of American prices rising to ease the adjustment process, but it did not put too much stress on the possibility. However, the Memorandum that accompanied the Gold Standard Bill clearly entertained a reasonable probability that American prices would rise when it noted :[3]

This best opinion inclines to the view that allowing for the imperfection of the indexes any variation from purchasing power parity, if it exists at all, is very small.

If this view is correct, it is far from certain that any serious drop in prices will be required here, even supposing any gap, if there is a gap, is not bridged by a *rise* of prices in America ... Without making any prophecies and disregarding very short-term fluctuations it may be said that the balance of instructed opinion anticipates a rise rather than a fall in gold prices.

(italics in the original)

allowed for some changes in the American position since 1913 and for the possible influences of speculation and of British underlending abroad during the embargo on overseas loans. However, he dismissed these factors as not having any great influence on the situation and concluded, 'on the whole there seems to be very little reason to suppose that sterling is overvalued'.

[1]Keynes, *Tract on Monetary Reform*, 91; *The Economic Consequences of Mr Churchill*, 11.
[2]Sayers, 'The Return to Gold', 320.
[3]T172/1499B, Gold Standard Bill, Memorandum, 3–4.

Earlier Treasury discussions had also contained some indication that a rise in prices in America was expected. Bradbury's reply to 'Mr. Churchill's Exercise' concluded on the expectation that 'very shortly after the restoration of the free gold market', a period of cheap money to repel gold imports – presumably caused by a rise in prices abroad – would be necessary;[1] and Hawtrey's advocacy of the gold standard in the near future rested entirely on an expectation of rising American prices as he ruled out deflation as a means of adjustment at existing levels of unemployment.[2] Both Norman and Niemeyer, on the other hand, expected relatively stable American prices,[3] although the Governor did mention the danger of gold inflation in many countries in the near future and Niemeyer did include the reference from the Gold Standard Bill Memorandum quoted above in his final pre-debate note to the Chancellor.[4] Thus, while Professor Sayers may be right to some extent, I suspect that, judging from references made to the subject prior to the event, the expectation of some assistance from rising American prices in the easing of the adjustment to gold played a significant role in the presentation of the problem and in the final decision.

Such an expectation, and perhaps a desire to improve the presentation of the policy both to the Chancellor and to the public, might also explain the analyses of the problems of adjustment presented before the return to gold which, if anything, were generally brief and euphemistic. The Governor expected that the return to gold would require a high Bank Rate and some sacrifice, but generally went no further as to how any necessary adjustments would come about.[5] Similarly, Niemeyer referred to the 'discomforts' of return and the 'extra sacrifice' required to restore gold, and he occasionally went further and noted that the return to gold would require reductions in British costs in the short run, but he was not much more specific as to the mechanism.[6] Bradbury and Hawtrey paid very little attention to the adjustment mechanism associated with the return as they both expected the problems to be largely removed by rising American prices. True the former in his comments at that notorious dinner party indicated that there would

[1] T172/1499B, Bradbury, 'The Gold Standard', 5 February 1925.
[2] T172/1499B, Hawtrey, 'The Gold Standard', 2 February 1925.
[3] T172/1499B, Niemeyer, 'The Gold Export Prohibition', 2 February 1925, Section 7, Niemeyer to Churchill, 21 February 1925; Norman to Churchill, 2 February 1925, para. 3.
[4] Ibid., para. 7; Niemeyer, 'Notes on Gold Standard', 29 April 1925. See also Churchill's speech to the Commons on the Gold Standard Bill 183 H. C. Deb. 5 s. column 675.
[5] T172/1499B, Norman to Churchill 2 February 1925, para. 5; F.R.B.N.Y., Norman to Strong, no. 71, 24 February 1925; Strong Papers, Norman to Strong, 26 May 1925.
[6] T172/1499B, Niemeyer, 'The Gold Export Prohibition', 2 February 1925, sections 6 and 11; 'Notes on Gold Standard', 29 April 1925, section 7.

have to be 'reductions of costs in particular industries' and that over time 'some contraction of the basic industries would have to be faced', but he did not go further and the context of his remarks seems to indicate that these changes would occur over the longer term and resulted from Britain's loss of her industrial lead rather than from the restoration of the gold standard.[1] The Chamberlain–Bradbury *Report* was equally vague.[2] True, the Chancellor had heard Keynes' and McKenna's discussion of the ten per cent overvaluation of sterling at $4.86, the ensuing references to the need for deflation after restoration with its social dislocation surrounding attempts to reduce wages and costs, and the final comments of McKenna that restoration 'will be hell'.[3] However, with Treasury and Bank opinion so heavily on the other side, it would be difficult to put too much weight on Churchill's exposure to contrary opinions. Perhaps the best explanation for the lack of attention paid to the problems of adjustment came from R. H. Brand several years later when he suggested that, given the reductions in costs that had occurred since 1920, 'It was not apparent that it was going to be so frightfully difficult to get them down another ten per cent.'[4] This faith, plus the belief that the longer term results of the return to gold would increase British trade and employment, probably go far to explain the lack of consideration of the adjustment mechanism and its operation in the pre and early post gold standard restoration periods. Even in the summer of 1925 when both Bradbury and Niemeyer in their discussions of the coal position did indicate that the return to gold did involve reductions in wages and other costs, the emphasis still remained on the 'temporary' nature of the problem of adjustment,[5] even if American prices did not rise to ease its achievement.[6]

Similar to the lack of attention paid to the need for and the mechanism of adjustment in 1925 was the lack of attention paid to the international position of the United Kingdom and the effects of the restoration of the gold standard thereon.[7] Throughout the period of

[1] Grigg, *Prejudice and Judgement*, 183.
[2] Committee on the Currency and Bank of England Note Issues, *Report*, para. 32.
[3] Grigg, *Prejudice and Judgement*, 184.
[4] Keynes Papers, Macmillan Committee, Notes of Discussions, 23 October 1930, 22. See also, ibid., 20 February 1930, 22 for a similar statement by Bradbury.
[5] T175/16, Niemeyer to Churchill, 4 August 1925, 5.
[6] T176/16, Bradbury, 'The Coal Crisis and the Gold Standard', 4 August 1925.
[7] This lack of attention is even more striking when one realises that all of the discussions were dollar-centred and ignored the effects of sterling's appreciation *vis-à-vis* other European currencies. See below pp. 105–6. Even more remarkable is the general lack of attention paid to the effects of the 1925 decision on the international financial system. It was generally assumed that a British return to gold would be a 'good thing' for the international economy and would aid the revival of trade. However, analysis did not go much further other than in Bradbury's and Hawtrey's replies to Mr Churchill's Exercise which discussed the international economic

intense discussion of the subject after January 1925, there was no discussion of the effects of the appreciation of sterling upon the trade account. In fact, the only formal references to this area of the balance of payments came in Keynes' evidence to the Chamberlain–Bradbury Committee in the summer of 1924 when he noted the adverse effects of the appreciation of sterling on this particular area.[1] Similarly, there were no discussions of the effects of the appreciation on the invisibles position, except for the passing references to the effects of appreciation in improving the balance sheet position of the United Kingdom.[2] There was one study after the event which slightly inflated the Board of Trade's estimates of the 1924 invisibles position, but it certainly did not aid in the ultimate decision process.[3] In fact, the only statement of the position that seems to have appeared before the event came from the Chamberlain–Bradbury Report,[4] which, after noting that Britain's international financial position was 'in some respects less satisfactory than it was before the war', and after pointing out that certain special influences – post-war industrial stagnation and trade dislocation and unsettled war debts except in favour of Britain's creditors – had reduced British exports, concluded, rather unhelpfully, that:[5]

our existing volume of exports, visible and invisible, together with the income we derive from foreign investments is still undoubtedly sufficient to meet our foreign debts and pay for our necessary imports, and even to supply a moderate balance for new foreign investment.

In these circumstances a free gold market could readily be established and maintained at the pre-war parity, *provided that by control of credit we adjusted the internal purchasing power of the pound to its exchange parity, and restricted our foreign investments to our normal export surplus.*

(italics added)

Such discussion as occurred before 28 April centred on the capital account of the balance of payments, particularly on the interactions of

implications of managed pounds versus golden (or possibly Genoa-golden) pounds. This benign neglect of the international implications of British international financial decisions was also characteristic of both the Cunliffe and Chamberlain–Bradbury Committees.

[1] Pigou Papers, op. cit., Evidence of J. M. Keynes, 14. The F.B.I. Statement also noted the effects on exports to the Chamberlain-Bradbury Committee, 3.

[2] T172/1499B, Niemeyer, 'The Gold Export Prohibition', 2 February 1925, Section 9; 'Notes on Gold Standard', 29 April 1925. T176/16, Bradbury, 'The Coal Crisis and the Gold Standard', 4 August 1925, 2.

[3] T172/1499B, R. G. Hawtrey, 'Balance of Payments of the United Kingdom', undated.

[4] The Committee on Industry and Trade's *Survey of Overseas Markets* (London, 1925), contained a full discussion of Britain's international position in its introduction dated 12 March 1925. However, there is no evidence that it had any influence on the Treasury's deliberations.

[5] Committee on the Currency and Bank of England Note Issues, *Report*, para. 12–13.

American lending and the export of capital from Britain. Here, the emphasis was generally on the stability of American foreign lending which it was thought would strengthen the sterling–dollar exchange as it was transferred abroad and reduce the demands on the London market.[1] When British lending was discussed, the emphasis was placed on the difficulties of preventing overlending without the clear indicators of gold outflows and increases in Bank Rate and on the ease of correcting overlending on the gold standard, although there were occasional references to the elements of habit and established connections which made London borrowing more than a matter of price.[2] Discussions of the short-term position centred on the foreign balances placed in London, and here the discussants generally emphasised that the volume of balances placed for speculation or for higher interest earnings was 'relatively small', that the existing balances would probably grow with stabilisation, and that changes in Bank Rate could handle any short-term problems.[3] The only disturbing possibility in the short-term position might have been an American stock exchange boom and Norman, despite Strong's warning of January 1925, regarded this as a 'minor question' which again could be handled by a change in Bank Rate of $\frac{1}{2}$–1 per cent.[4] In fact, throughout the discussions of the balance of payments, particularly of the capital account, the discussants repeatedly assumed that after adjustment to gold standard conditions had occurred changes in Bank Rate could handle any potential problems without difficulty. The process of adjustment to the higher parity, its effects on the balance of payments and the time period required to effect adjustment received no consideration.

The Decision, the Discussions and the Chancellor

Given the facts and opinions which appear to have gone into the decision, it is possible to sort out the influences which appear to have moved Churchill to decide on gold at $4.86 in 1925. The Chancellor appears to have agreed in the end to the decision for four reasons.

---

[1] T172/1499B, Hawtrey, 'The Gold Standard and the Balance of Payments', 2 March 1925 as amended by Niemeyer, 1–4; Niemeyer to Churchill, 10 March 1925; Pigou Papers, op. cit., Evidence of the Governor of the Bank of England and Sir Charles Addis, January 1925, 32.

[2] T172/1499B, Hawtrey, 'The Gold Standard and the Balance of Payments', 2 March 1925, 5–6; Pigou Papers, op. cit., Evidence of the Governor of the Bank of England and Sir Charles Addis, 33–4; Committee on the Currency and Bank of England Note Issues, *Report*, para. 34–6.

[3] T172/1499B, Hawtrey, 'The Gold Standard and the Balance of Payments', 2 March 1925, 7–8; Niemeyer to Churchill, 29 April 1925; Pigou Papers, op. cit., Evidence of the Governor of the Bank of England and Sir Charles Addis, 31.

[4] Ibid., 4–5; above p. 59.

First, any decision not to return to gold, particularly after the appreciation of sterling after October 1924, carried great political costs, given the general unanimity of informed business, financial and political opinion on the matter.[1] As Sir Frederick Leith-Ross put it, one reason Churchill decided for gold was 'because he knew that if he adopted this course Niemeyer would give him irrefutable arguments to support it, whereas if he refused to adopt it he would be faced with criticisms from the City authorities against which he would not have any effective answer'.[2] In this Churchill was correct, for opposition to the decision was certainly limited. One director of the Bank of England, Mr Vincent Vickers, resigned in protest; a few economists, bankers and press barons, such as Keynes, McKenna and Beaverbrook, attacked the decision; and only a very few members of Parliament, notably Sir Robert Horne, I.C.I.'s Alfred Mond and Mr Robert Boothby, spoke against it. Second, the rise in the dollar exchange after the election of the Conservative government, coupled with the determination of the Bank and permanent officials of the Treasury to attempt to hold on to any appreciation, meant that, as most of Churchill's advisers pointed out, the additional adjustments necessary to achieve parity were relatively small, perhaps even smaller than those necessary to hold sterling at $4.80 given the expectations and elements of speculation that existed at the time.[3] Given these propensities, a decision not to go back to gold in 1925 could have been made and announced in the summer or early autumn of 1924, but not after the Conservative's electoral success revised expectations. Third, the evidence presented to the Chancellor eased the path towards a decision in favour of gold, for it emphasised the benefits of restoration, largely in terms of employment and trade which were both politically important, and minimised the problems both of adjustment to the new parity and of management at the new parity after the period of adjustment. This minimisation depended, to a considerable extent, on an expectation of inflationary developments abroad. It also depended on a concentration on the dollar exchange and a complete refusal to consider possible paths of development on the Continent, particularly the exchange rates likely to be chosen in the process of future stabilisations and the recovery of Germany from her post-war difficulties. After 1925, the low rates for stabilisation chosen by France and Belgium were often referred to as sources of difficulty, despite the fact that the possibilities of stabilising at such rates which reflected exchange conditions more

[1] For a good sample of opinion see the selections of contemporary clippings T172/ 1499B and T160/197/F7528/03.
[2] Leith-Ross, *Money Talks*, 92.
[3] Thus, for example, the March 1925 rise in Bank Rate would have come whether Britain intended to return to gold in April or not, merely because the Bank would have held to $4.80.

than price conditions had been foreseen as early as 1922.[1] True, Churchill was aware of Keynes' arguments against restoration in the early spring of 1925, but Keynes' was very much a voice in the wilderness, and a somewhat ambiguous one at that, given his inflationary expectations and his failure to distinguish clearly between the short and the long run. Finally, much of the public antagonism to such a decision had disappeared, partially because the unique connection between the gold standard and deflation had apparently ceased to hold with the managed money school's advocacy and acceptance of the March 1925 rise in Bank Rate, and with the rise in the exchange after October 1924, which had occurred without any outward and visible signs of deflation.[2] Even the Federation of British Industry, one of Keynes' chief sources of support on previous occasions, accepted that other considerations might make restoration necessary and that on a longer view such a decision 'would be greatly to the benefit of British industry' even though it might necessitate some short-term deflation.[3] To these considerations, Churchill certainly added an element of faith in the policy's success as his private disillusioned reactions to the results and his subsequent bitterness towards Norman indicate.[4]

More generally, the decision to return to gold at pre-war par was more or less inevitable, particularly after the rise in the dollar exchange. Successive Governments had committed themselves to such a policy goal; the overwhelming majority of opinion accepted it; the specialists in the Bank, the Treasury and the Chamberlain–Bradbury Committee accepted it and were prepared to force the necessary adjustments. Economic analysis, as such, played a minimal role in the decision. Public as well as official economic discussion was profoundly anti-empirical. '[T]here was an obvious confidence that the assumptions underlying the arguments were sufficiently realistic to justify the practical inferences drawn from them.'[5] This meant that arguments went untested and unrefined by any serious confrontation with reality, that the long and

[1] T. E. Gregory, *The First Year of the Gold Standard* (London, 1926), Ch. 1.

[2] Hume, 'Gold Standard', 242; J. M. Keynes, 'The Bank Rate', *The Nation and Athenaeum*, 7 March 1925.

[3] T172/1499B, R. T. Nugent to Churchill, 17 March 1925. Mr G. W. McDonald of University College, Cambridge has informed me that the F.B.I.s archives suggest that there was considerable F.B.I. opposition to the decision and substantial lobbying of Conservative members of Parliament after the announcement.

[4] See for example Grigg, *Prejudice and Judgement*, 193; Boyle, *Montagu Norman*, 190–1, 263; above, p. 75, n. 4. However, significantly, this bitterness was private and did not occur in Cabinet or in Churchill's published work, see, for example, Cab. 24/178, 22/87, C.P. 55(26) The Gold Standard, 10 February 1926; Cab. 24/202, 22/229, C.P. 53(29), Unemployment, 23 February 1929, covering memorandum and 4–7.

[5] K. Hancock, 'Unemployment and the Economists in the 1920s', *Economica*, N.S., XXVIII (108), November 1960, 320.

the short run tended to get mixed up and that, most important, the Authorities never had to present a hard, factual case for the course of action proposed. On all sides, the 1925 discussions never really got much beyond general theoretical arguments, overlaid with emotion and supported by a few well-chosen statistics. There was no need to go further. Official economic analysis and analysts such as Professor Pigou merely played a priestly role, justifying decisions taken for more deep-seated reasons.[1] Pigou, with characteristic honesty, admitted as much in his evidence before the Macmillan Committee :[2]

Prior to that it had been the decided policy of all Governments to go back to gold and, as a matter of practice, it was felt that nothing else could be done. No politician at the time advocated not going back to the gold system ... The real practical alternative in my view was to go back now or later. It may have been wrong. Of course one might be apt to say that it was wrong because gold is not so sacred as it was, but this was very soon after an inflation, and my impression of the general atmosphere was that it was quite impossible then to have done anything else ... If you did narrow the issue to that the argument for returning now was this : You have to take the plunge, the water is not terribly cold now; it is a gamble whether it will be colder later on. Get it over ... I thought the politician would make the plunge anyway.

The deep-seated reasons which provided the motivation to take the plunge had their roots in banking and financial attitudes towards gold, debt repayment and good faith, which were essentially moral, and in a deep faith in the apparent mechanisms of the pre-war gold standard.[3]

[1] C. P. Kindleberger, *Economic Growth in France and Britain 1860–1960* (Cambridge, 1964), 266–7.
[2] Macmillan Committee, *Evidence*, Q. 6075–6084.
[3] Brown, *International Gold Standard*, I, 279. See also R. G. Hawtrey's statement of 1920 in R. G. Hawtrey, 'The Return to Gold in 1925', *Bankers' Magazine*, CCIX (1505), August 1969, 65; and Sidney Pollard's harsher comments in *The Gold Standard and Employment Policies between the Wars* (London, 1970), 17–18, 22–3.

4. THE IMPLICATIONS OF $4.86

Before one can assess the consequences of the return to gold at $4.86, one must first have a set of criteria for the evaluation of exchange rate choices. In purely theoretical terms, the notion of a unique, policy-free, equilibrium rate of exchange which implies equilibrium in the balance of payments is, as Professor Joan Robinson has indicated, a chimera.[1] For given market supply and demand conditions there are an infinite number of 'equilibrium' rates which correspond to varying mixes of monetary, trade, fiscal and other policies.[2] Thus a much more useful approach to the problem of exchange rate choice in 1925 would be one which took account of the international and domestic policy goals of the Authorities in 1925 and looked at the choice of $4.86 as one which would or would not generate sufficient foreign exchange earnings to allow their successful realisation.

The Goals of Policy

As the Authorities, either in or after 1925, never really adopted this approach and never set out their policy goals in relation to the exchange rate policy under discussion, one is forced to search for what appear to have been their implicit goals. In this light, the evidence suggests that an 'appropriate' exchange rate would have allowed 'full employment' at, say, the pre-war average of 95.3 per cent of the labour force,[3] a surplus on current account sufficient to allow unrestricted overseas lending and the maintenance of Imperial commitments, and the maintenance of free trade

[1] J. Robinson, 'The Foreign Exchanges', *Essays in the Theory of Employment* (London, 1937), 208.
[2] B. Balassa and D. M. Schydlowsky, 'Effective Tariffs, Domestic Cost of Foreign Exchange, and the Equilibrium Exchange Rate', *Journal of Political Economy*, LXXVI (3), May/June 1968, 357, 359.
[3] W. Galenson and A. Zellner, 'International Comparison of Unemployment Rates', National Bureau of Economic Research, Special Conference Series, *The Measurement and Behaviour of Unemployment* (Princeton, 1957), Table 2, 459.

with the minimal pre-1931 exceptions.[1] The implicit pre-war employment standard existed in some of the pre-gold standard discussions and in the frequent post-1925 Treasury pressure for moderation in the Bank's policies.[2] It also found use in much of the political debate of the period and in Keynes' many discussions of post-1925 policy.[3] The goal of unrestricted foreign lending hung heavily over much of the discussion that led up to the return to gold and it lay at the roots of the official hostility after 1925 to such controls on overseas lending as proved expedient. In this respect, the *Report* of the Overseas Loans Sub-Committee of the Committee of Civil Research is instructive.[4] The goal of free trade never became completely explicit other than in the practice of the Authorities. However, during the Macmillan Committee's drafting discussions, when the alternatives of devaluation and protection were discussed with specific reference to British policy, a standard of judgement in the minds of two of those intimately involved in the 1925 decision became clear:[5]

Lord Bradbury: I am afraid of tampering with Free Trade, and I am also afraid of tampering with the gold standard. If I had to choose between tampering with the gold standard as a remedy and Protection, I should be solid for tampering with the gold standard. I should much prefer it to Protection.
Mr. Bevin: I agree.
Mr. Lubbock: I should be very sorry to think that the choice of one of these was the dilemma.
Lord Bradbury: So should I.

When to these specific goals one adds the desire to keep London as an international financial centre of the first rank, if not the premier financial centre, something that repeatedly appeared in the policy discussions of the period,[6] it becomes clear that the overall goal of the Authorities might be accurately summarised as the maintenance, as far as

[1]To these one might add a desire for a stabilised (and by implication stable) international economic system which would have allowed the growth of trade and investment. As this would have probably come with any stable rate, at least to some extent, the analysis below excludes this matter. It also excludes any specification of the trade-offs between goals.
[2]Below, Chapter 7.
[3]See for example Keynes Papers, Macmillan Committee, Notes of Discussions, 28 February 1930, 4.
[4]Cab. 58/9, Committee of Civil Research, Overseas Loans Sub-Committee, *Report*, 16 October 1925. The membership of this sub-committee included: Bradbury, Norman, J. C. Stamp, Niemeyer, S. J. Chapman, C. H. Kisch, and Henry Lambert.
[5]Keynes Papers, Macmillan Committee, Notes of Discussions, 7 November 1930, 29.
[6]T172/1499B, Niemeyer, 'The Gold Export Prohibition', 2 February 1925, Section 9; Norman to Churchill, 2 February 1925, para. 7; Hawtrey, 'The Gold Standard', 2 February 1925, 1–2, 9–10; Gold Standard Bill, Memorandum, 28 April 1925, 4.

possible, of the pre-1914 position. Whether the return to gold at the pre-war par was consistent with this overall goal is the basic question.

Any attempt to evaluate the 1925 decision on this basis must compare the overall goal with the international position of the British economy in 1924–5 as compared to that of a typical pre-war year. Such a comparison must take into account not only the basic trade, invisibles and capital positions but also the availability and effectiveness of the policy instruments available to the Authorities. Here our earlier discussion in Chapter 2 of the international position of the British economy in 1924 becomes extremely relevant. That discussion suggested that, despite the virtual elimination of Germany as a major competitor, British trade performance in 1924 as compared to 1913 was worse than world performance, even marginally worse than overall European performance *including* that of Germany. It also suggested that British imports, despite the depreciated exchange, had grown faster than world imports and faster than British exports; that the British invisibles position was weaker than pre-war; that British overseas lending had fallen from 1913 levels; and that the evolution of the international pattern of multilateral settlements probably made Britain's position potentially more difficult. At the same time as these underlying changes occurred, the movement towards a decentralised international financial system, suggested by the rise of New York as an international financial centre, increased the possibilities of strain on the exchange position and of conflicts between domestic and international policy goals, while the evolution of financial instruments and institutions made the traditional instruments of policy less effective. Given these underlying changes and given the policy goals of the Authorities, the basic criterion for an evaluation of the exchange rate chosen in 1925 could be summed up as follows: as the international position of Great Britain was, in many respects, weaker than before 1914, any exchange rate policy which did not improve her trading, competitive and policy-making position *vis-à-vis* that of a typical pre-war year was unwise. Given this criterion, the long-standing debate as to whether sterling was overvalued in 1925 takes on its relevance.

Was Sterling Overvalued at $4.86?

Most observers since Keynes have accepted that in 1925 sterling was overvalued by at least 10 per cent at the pre-war parity of $4.86.[1] However, there has been a significant undercurrent of opinion that has rejected or seriously questioned Keynes' overvaluation argument, its most important advocates being Professors Youngson, Morgan and

---

[1]W. Ashworth, *An Economic History of England 1870–1939* (London, 1960), 387; Pollard, *The Development of the British Economy* 217–20; Kindleberger, *Economic Growth*, 207.

Gregory.[1] In many senses, the traditional argument as to whether sterling was overvalued or not on a purchasing-power parity basis is rather irrelevant to the point at issue, for it would seem that with the changes that had occurred in the international position of the United Kingdom since 1913, the base year for most comparisons, any exchange rate that did not markedly undervalue sterling on such a basis would, given the goals of the Authorities, probably have been unfortunate. However, given the heat generated by the debate, both at the time and occasionally since, a re-examination of the statistics and the issues is worthwhile.

A standard method for testing an exchange rate for overvaluation involves the use of purchasing-power parity calculations, which played some role in the decision. Stated in its comparative form, the theory of purchasing-power parity 'asserts that the equilibrium exchange rate roughly moves parallel with the ratio of the movements in the two countries of the price levels over time'.[2] If, so the argument runs, comparing two countries from a base year in which the exchange rate was in 'equilibrium', the price level has doubled in country A and trebled in country B, then the 'equilibrium' exchange rate (units of A's currency per unit of B's) will have changed in the ratio of $\frac{2}{3}$. So stated, the theory appears to be extremely simple to use as a guide to the appropriate exchange rate between two currencies, but this apparent simplicity hides two basic problems: which are the relevant price levels for comparisons and which additional assumptions underlying the basic statement of the theory are relevant to the particular case at hand.

The choice of the appropriate price level for comparisons boils down to a decision as to which is the most appropriate price index for international comparisons of competitiveness. The traditional choice has been an index of wholesale prices, and this index found considerable use during the period under consideration, largely as a result of its ready availability.[3]

However, such an index, particularly in an open economy, consists largely of price observations for the staple commodities of international trade. For these commodities, and for an index heavily weighted with such goods, prices in domestic currency will reflect changes in foreign exchange rates reasonably accurately. Thus any comparison based on such prices would tell one very little about the implications of exchange rate choices or existing exchange levels as it would contain very few

[1] A. J. Youngson, *The British Economy 1920–1957* (London, 1960), 230–8; Gregory, *First Year*, 53–4; Morgan, *Studies*, 367. Professor Gregory's views on this point have since wavered somewhat. Sir T. E. Gregory, 'The "Norman Conquest" Reconsidered', *Lloyds Bank Review*, October 1957, 15; 'Lord Norman, A New Interpretation', *Lloyds Bank Review*, April 1968, 39.

[2] G. Haberler, 'A Survey of International Trade Theory', *Special Papers in International Economics No. 1*, rev. ed. (Princeton, 1961), 48.

[3] Keynes, *Treatise on Money*, I, 67, 73.

quotations that reflected domestic costs.[1] Thus one begins a search for alternatives. An index of export prices seems, at first glance, to be a useful possibility and as such it has found use in one discussion of the 1925 decision.[2] However, export prices may also prove poor indicators of the implications of exchange rate choices, for although they do contain elements of domestic costs they relate only to goods exported. If goods are in perfect competition internationally, differences in relative prices between countries will not be reflected in indices of export prices but rather in market shares. Even where goods are in imperfect competition internationally, in the short period firms may continue to export at the world price and absorb increased production costs by reducing profit margins. Firms may also reduce their selling effort while continuing to accept orders at the world price, and thus reduced competitiveness would again appear as a loss in market share rather than an increase in relative price.[3] The imperfections of export prices as short run indices of international competitive conditions are apparent in the 1967 devaluation of sterling when British firms raised their export prices in sterling by more than the cost increases implicit in the devaluation and the associated increases in taxation would warrant in order to reconstitute profit margins that had been previously squeezed by high relative British costs, whereas, foreign exporters raised their sterling selling prices by less than the depreciation of sterling by reducing profit margins to maintain markets. Other attempts to choose an appropriate price index have involved the use of more domestically oriented indices of relative costs, particularly the one implicit in the cost of living or retail price index.[4] However, as this is a highly sectional index, usually heavily weighted towards the consumption patterns of working people, it may be inappropriate as a guide to the costs faced by producers of export or import-competing goods and services. However, it has the advantages of being relatively immune to divergent structural changes between countries over time and of being representative of a large class of expenditures. Another possible index is the national income implicit price deflator. Such an index, although subject to divergent structural changes over time when two countries are compared, is a composite index reflecting changes in the prices of various goods and services in the economy. In use such deflators for two countries have proved to be 'fairly good rivals of consumer prices' in purchasing-power parity calculations.[5] However, even here, service prices provide a source of difficulty, for these are not equalised by trade and tend to reflect international

[1] Ibid., 73–5; Keynes, *Tract on Monetary Reform*, 87–106.
[2] Morgan, *Studies*, 361–7.　　　　　　　[3] Maizels, *Industrial Growth*, 202–4.
[4] This was the index used by Keynes, *The Economic Consequences of Mr Churchill*, 11.
[5] A. N. McLeod, 'A Critique of the Fluctuating-Exchange-Rate Policy in Canada', *The Bulletin*, no. 34–5, April–June 1965, 62.

TABLE 4. *Selected indices of purchasing-power parity for the sterling–dollar exchange, 1923–27* (U.S. price index as a percentage of U.K.)

Basis of comparison	1923	1924	1925	1927
Sterling exchange as a percentage of par	94.0	90.8	99.2	99.9
Wholesale Prices — 1913 = 100 U.S. and U.K. — Federal Reserve	96.8	90.1	100	n.a.
Wholesale prices — 1913 = 100 U.S. — Bureau of Labor U.K. — Board of Trade	97.0	90.3	99.1	100.0
Export prices — 1913 = 100 U.S. and U.K. — Federal Reserve	103.4	98.8	104.1	n.a.
Retail prices — July 1914 = 100 U.S. — Bureau of Labor U.K. — Ministry of Labour	97.5	97.3	99.2	103.1
Retail prices — July 1914 = 100 U.S. — Massachusetts U.K. — Ministry of Labour	89.8	89.2	91.1	93.2
Retail prices — July 1914 = 100 U.S. — League of Nations U.K. — Ministry of Labour	93.6	93.7	95.5	97.6
Implicit G.N.P. deflator 1907–11 = 100 U.S. — Kuznets U.K. — Peacock and Wiseman	n.a.	88	89	90
Reference Indices Unemployment — 1912–14 = 100 U.S. — L.C.E.S.	42.9	89.3	57.1	58.9
U.K. — Trade Union	393.7	282.2	365.8	n.a.
— Unemployment Insurance	407.6	358.9	393.7	337.9
Unit wage costs — 1913 = 100 U.S.	176.6	173.4	164.1	157.5
U.K.	n.a.	168.0	167.2	162.2

n.a. = not available.

Sources: 1. E. H. Phelps Brown and M. H. Browne, *A Century of Pay* (London, 1968), Appendix III and Table 19.
2. Federal Reserve Board, *Federal Reserve Bulletin*.
3. League of Nations, *International Statistical Year-Book, 1929* (Geneva, 1930), Table 109.
4. London and Cambridge Economic Service, *The British Economy, Key Statistics, 1900–66* (London, n.d.), Tables E and O.
5. B. R. Mitchell and P. Deane, *Abstract of British Historical Statistics* (Cambridge, 1962), Labour Force 3.
6. A. T. Peacock and J. Wiseman, *The Growth of Public Expenditure in the United Kingdom* (London, 1961), Table A3.
7. U.S. Department of Commerce, *Historical Statistics of the United States from Colonial Times to 1957* (Washington, 1960), Series E113, F1-5.

H

differences in wages and manufacturing productivity.[1] Thus the evidence would indicate that for purchasing-power parity calculations, most indices contain problems, but that in many respects consumer prices and national income deflators might provide useful indices of relative domestic costs for exchange rate calculations.

However, even if the indices chosen are relatively appropriate, a second problem still faces the analyst, the problem of structural changes. Over the period of years normally chosen for purchasing-power parity calculations other things do not remain equal or change in the two countries concerned in offsetting directions. Changes in tastes, technology, tariffs, international investment and trading positions, and internal relationships in the economies concerned can occur and undermine any direct comparisons of costs, prices, competitiveness and balance in a nation's international accounts, particularly when such balance depends on much more than the trading position for which purchasing-power parity calculations are most relevant.[2] However, such indices, if used cautiously, can be 'of considerable diagnostic value' in discussions of exchange rate choice. Nevertheless, after major international changes such as those involved in a world war and its aftermath such calculations require considerable additional evidence to support their use; and one must never forget that the appropriate exchange rate in relation to any one currency depends on the exchange rates prevailing (or likely to prevail) in third countries as well.

Putting this last point to one side for the moment, despite its implications, Table 4 presents a variety of estimates of purchasing-power parities for the sterling–dollar exchange between 1923 and 1927. The estimates used are all annual averages, as quotations for individual months are not available for some series and are subject to random influences such as bad harvests for others. The estimates include those most commonly used in the debates of the period and since, as well as others added at this time. The indices of unemployment and unit wage costs in manufacturing appear at the bottom as indicators of more general economic conditions.

The figures presented in Table 4, although conflicting, are illuminating. Using indices of wholesale prices, those most frequently employed in 1925, sterling was not overvalued at the time of the return to gold. However, the same indices indicate that sterling was slightly undervalued in 1927, a situation that seems difficult to believe and which no one has subsequently suggested.[3] The export price indices indicate that sterling

[1] B. Balassa, 'The Purchasing-Power Parity Doctrine: A Reappraisal', *Journal of Political Economy*, LXXII (6), December 1964, 593.

[2] Haberler, 'Survey', 49–50.

[3] However, Professor Gustav Cassel, the high priest of purchasing–power parity calculations, did suggest that sterling was undervalued in late 1925 by as much as

was significantly undervalued in 1923 and 1924 and slightly under-valued in 1925. Unfortunately the Federal Reserve Board ceased publication of the export price indices at the end of 1925 so that later comparisons are impossible. The retail price indices conflict. The Massachusetts index, the index of retail prices for the United States regularly quoted at the time in the *Federal Reserve Bulletin* and used by Keynes in his discussions of the return to gold, when used with the U.K. Ministry of Labour cost of living index suggests that sterling was significantly overvalued in 1925 and thereafter and slightly overvalued in 1924. The fact that this index only applied to one state led Professor Gregory to challenge Keynes' use of the Massachusetts index and to use the more general Bureau of Labor index to argue that the difficulties of the British position stemmed from the transition from an undervalued exchange to parity.[1] Significantly, however, Professor Gregory did not proceed to argue that sterling was slightly undervalued thereafter on the basis of the same index, despite several opportunities to do so. The League of Nations' index of American retail prices follows the Massachusetts index in indicating that sterling was overvalued in 1925, although by a lesser amount than the use of the later index would indicate. The more general implicit G.N.P. deflators indicate that sterling was overvalued throughout the period covered by the series in Table 4. This overvaluation occurred, despite the effect on the service component of the U.S. index of the faster rise in American money wages during the period after 1913.

On balance, these estimates must be regarded as conflicting. However, given the differing behaviour of the series for unemployment and unit wage costs in the two countries, the deterioration in Britain's international financial position and the transformation of America's international position, including the tariff increases of 1921, one would incline towards the position that an exchange rate which did not undervalue sterling *vis-à-vis* the dollar was probably too high. As even the most optimistic indices for purchasing-power parity calculations hardly did that, and as the most pessimistic indices suggested an overvaluation of as much as 10 per cent, one would incline towards the view that given official policy goals sterling was significantly overvalued at the exchange rate chosen in 1925. An exchange rate at least 10 per cent lower than $4.86 would probably have been somewhat more appropriate for sterling.

The overvaluation of sterling implicit in the purchasing-power parity and related indices for the sterling–dollar exchange becomes more striking if the position of sterling *vis-à-vis* other European currencies enters into consideration. Niemeyer's expectation that the stabilisation

6 per cent. 'Credit and Currency Restoration', *The Times Annual Financial and Commercial Review*, 9 February 1926.
[1] Gregory, *The First Year*, 51.

of sterling might encourage other European stabilisations was, to some extent, reasonable, but his implicit expectation that they would do so in a manner which would not affect the viability of certain exchange rates chosen for sterling was not.[1] The German stabilisation of 1923–4 with its undervaluation of the mark suggested a route that other European countries might conceivably choose to follow in their stabilisation policies.[2] Given the possibility of undervaluations occurring elsewhere and given the existing uncertainty as to European rates of stabilisation, there was a strong case for waiting somewhat longer before fixing a par value for sterling. The unsettled conditions in France and Belgium could not continue for ever, no matter what the British decided to do, and a year's wait might have clarified and stabilised the stituation sufficiently to allow a more co-ordinated return to gold at mutually convenient exchange rates. However, throughout the discussions surrounding the return to gold, no one really considered the implications or probabilities of European exchange rate choices affecting sterling, although after the event these same rate choices found use as one explanation of the problems that beset the British economy after 1925.[3] Those entrusted with advising the Chancellor on the return to gold did not even pay attention to the implications of the German stabilisation that antedated the giving of that advice or the effects of the almost certain revival of German competition on sterling's prospects. The concentration on the dollar as the only gold currency excluded that, as did the tendency to regard 1925 as a return to gold at pre-war par rather than as a choice of an exchange rate which carried multilateral implications. The results of this dollar-centred, gold-centred view were, to say the least, unfortunate.

The Balance of Payments and $4.86

The overvaluation of sterling resulting from the announcement of 28 April had implications for the balance of trade and the balance on

---

[1]T179/1499B, Niemeyer, 'The Gold Export Prohibition', 2 February 1925, Section 9. The approach taken by Keynes to the French franc was a plausible means to stabilisation with important consequences for Britain: J. M. Keynes, 'An open letter to the French Minister of Finance (whoever he is or may be)', *Essays in Persuasion*, 105–113.

[2]Using unit wage costs as a rough index of competitiveness, taking 1913= 100, German costs in 1925 were 147·7 as compared with 167·2 for the U.K. and 164·1 for the U.S. at a time when the three countries' exchange rates bore the same par value relationship to each other as in 1913. (Brown and Browne, *Century of Pay*, Appendix III and Table 19). For another, albeit rough, index of competitiveness, see the estimates of export unit values below, p. 120. The possibility of undervaluation had certainly been discussed in reference to exchange choices before 1925.

[3]See, for example, Macmillan Committee, *Evidence*, Q.3350 and following; Youngson, *The British Economy*, 237.

invisibles which weakened Britain's international position still further.[1] It would have tended to reduce exports and increase imports by amounts dependent on the relevant cost conditions, supply and demand elasticities and businessmen's reactions. Although the statistical difficulties are legion,[2] the evidence from the numerous attempts to measure the various relevant elasticities for both the interwar and later periods suggests that the price mechanism is a powerful force in international trade and that any overvaluation of sterling would have led to a significant deterioration on trade account.[3] Appendix 1 provides a rough indication of the implications of the overvaluation of sterling on Britain's balance of trade.

On the income from invisibles, the overvaluation of sterling would also have had significant effects (all references being to incomes in sterling unless explicitly otherwise noted). Income from shipping would have tended to deteriorate as British prices and/or costs would have been above those of competitors, who could have increased their share of the market through greater price competition or greater selling effort. British income from overseas fixed interest investment would have remained largely unchanged, as most British foreign investment of this type was denominated in sterling, although the costs of servicing such investments would have risen for foreigners in terms of their own currencies if their Governments had not appreciated their exchange rates with sterling. This might have increased the incidence of bad debts and thus reduced sterling investment incomes somewhat, but this was unlikely so long as international conditions remained prosperous. British incomes from overseas equities would have been reduced, as dividends were determined by profits and economic conditions in overseas countries. On Government account, the overvaluation of sterling would have reduced the sterling costs of servicing Britain's war debts, but have left the value of war debt payments to the U.K. unchanged as these were denominated in sterling. Overvaluation, however, would have reduced the sterling value of reparation receipts as these were denominated in gold. It would also have tended to reduce the sterling costs of other

---

[1]An overvaluation of sterling might also affect capital flows by encouraging direct investment abroad in more prosperous and more profitable economies, by reducing direct investment in Britain, and, through high interest rates, by reducing British overseas fixed interest lending. However, these matters are not explored here.

[2]G. H. Orcutt, 'Measurements of Price Elasticities in International Trade', *The Review of Economics and Statistics*, xxxii (2), May 1950; F. Machlup, 'Elasticity Pessimism in International Trade', *Economia Internazionale*, iii (1), February 1950.

[3]See, for example, A. C. Harberger, 'Some Evidence on the International Price Mechanism', *Journal of Political Economy*, lxv (6), December 1957; R. E. Zelder, 'Estimates of Elasticities of Demand for Exports of the United Kingdom and the United States 1921–1938', *Manchester School*, xxvi (1), January 1958; A. Maizels, *Industrial Growth*, 211–16; M. FG. Scott, *A Study of United Kingdom Imports* (Cambridge, 1936), 49; and the literature cited therein.

British official overseas commitments. The 1925 decision would have tended to reduce the income from banking and insurance commissions and the like, for these were largely percentage commissions. For the foreigner, exchange overvaluation would have meant that he needed less insurance in sterling to cover a foreign currency risk of a given size, a smaller sterling bill to finance a trade transaction of a given size, or a smaller sterling loan to finance a foreign project of a given size. Therefore, with a given volume of such business in terms of foreign currencies, sterling proceeds would have been smaller. Of course, a stable exchange might have increased the volume of business, but this increase in business and the resulting rise in British incomes would have resulted from the act of stabilisation or from a growth in the volume of risks requiring insurance, trade requiring finance and investment projects requiring foreign funds and not from an overvaluation of the sterling exchange. The income from miscellaneous invisibles probably would also have fallen as a result of overevaluation. Recent research[1] has suggested that earnings from tourism are very sensitive to changes in exchange rates, although the effects in the 1920s, when many tourists visiting Britain were determined to visit the mother country and therefore perhaps less price conscious, may have reduced the impact of sterling's overvaluation. Emigrants' remittances would probably have fallen in terms of sterling because they largely originated outside the U.K. and thus depended on external conditions for their determination. Overvaluation would also have reduced sterling receipts from royalties, although it would have left royalty payments from the U.K. unchanged – such payments largely being set in the national currency of the licensee.

Thus the effects of sterling's overvaluation in 1925 would have been mixed. However, there is little indication that the improvement in the Government's debt servicing and overseas activities position would have offset the losses on trade, shipping, short-interest and commissions, miscellaneous invisibles and non-sterling denominated fixed interest and equity investment incomes. Thus, from a balance of payments point of view, overvaluation hardly made sense, despite the fact that exchange stabilisation probably did.

The additional deterioration in Britain's international position suggested by the above considerations would have had repercussions on the domestic economy. The rise in imports and the decline in exports, assuming that the Authorities did nothing to offset them, would have had multiplier effects, which although they would have improved the balance of payments position – and thus offset some of the effects of the appreciation – to some extent, would have reduced domestic incomes and employment. These short-term depressive effects would have tended to

[1] A. S. Gerakis, 'Effects of Exchange-Rate Devaluations and Revaluations on Receipts from Tourism', *I.M.F. Staff Papers*, xii (3), November 1965.

be cumulative to some extent, for an uncompetitive economy would have shared less in the overall growth of the world economy and would have been hurt more by any decline in world incomes, as it would have tended to become a high cost, marginal supplier – last engaged, first dismissed. Insofar as the consequences of these effects affected the climate of enterprise in Britain, the overvaluation would have had even more serious long-term implications in that it might reduce future investment and hence reduce future growth prospects and future competitiveness.[1] These effects on future progress would have been independent of any others that might have followed from an effort by the Treasury and/or the Bank to improve Britain's international position by domestic deflation.

The Problems of Adjustment

As previous discussions have indicated, those advising the Chancellor to return to gold had generally admitted that this act of policy would leave sterling somewhat overvalued and that some adjustments in relative costs would be necessary, if only to prevent deterioration in the balance of payments. They were unsure as to the amount of adjustment required, but as they generally judged the necessary amount through a comparison of British and American wholesale price indices they were naturally convinced that it was relatively slight. As to the means of adjustment, their attitudes were vague and conflicting, but, aside from some expansion of exports, domestic activity and employment which they believed would accompany the resulting European stability and recovery, they recognised that either their competitors' prices and costs would have to rise or British prices and costs would have to fall. Some combination of these two routes was also possible. Generally speaking, none of Churchill's advisers contemplated the possibility of having to reduce British prices and costs more quickly than those of her competitors.[2]

As to possible means of adjustment if British prices and costs proved to be those which required absolute reduction as relief from foreign inflation proved insufficient or unavailable, the Chancellor's advisers admitted that some deflation operating along the lines outlined by the Cunliffe and subsequent official committees would be necessary.[3]

[1]Maizels, *Industrial Growth*, 217–24.
[2]T172/1499B, Hawtrey, 'The Gold Standard', 2 February 1925, 4–6. Here Hawtrey considers the possibilities of a fall in American prices resulting from credit contraction and argues that if this occurred the U.K. should be prepared to let gold go and, if necessary, ultimately 'it would be better to let sterling relapse than to raise bank rate to a deterrent level'. However, such a development he considered unlikely.
[3]Cunliffe Committee, *First Interim Report*, para. 4–5; T172/1499B, R. G. Hawtrey, 'How does a gold standard work in regulating credit', undated. Other possible

Through a high Bank Rate and restrictive credit policies domestic activity would be depressed by an amount sufficient to produce a volume of unemployment large enough to allow reduction in money wages to be successfully carried through by employers. Thus the Authorities were expecting the Bank Rate mechanism to carry a heavier burden than it had been asked to carry in the pre-war period. True, in particular pre-war years, money wages had fallen by 1–2 per cent,[1] and a sufficiently severe Bank Rate policy might be expected to produce that result. However, if the necessary adjustment involved was in the range of 5–10 per cent or more, pre-war experience provided no examples. The only available example of reductions in money wages of this order came from the period of the post-war slump of 1920–2. Between their peak in January 1921 and their nadir in December 1922 average weekly money wages rates fell by 38 per cent – while the cost of living fell by over 50 per cent.[2] However, these reductions occurred in the course of a world slump coupled with an unusually severe aggregate domestic economic policy of which a high Bank Rate was only one aspect. Moreover, a large proportion of these reductions were accomplished under sliding scale agreements through which money wages were related to the cost of living.[3] After the experiences of 1921–2 such agreements naturally became somewhat less popular and this change meant that this 'easy' route could be less relied on in future,[4] even if the cause of the fall in the

means of adjustment were not discussed. Appendix 1 gives an indication of some of the available possibilities. There is no indication that anyone examined at the time the distributional implications of a general fall in wages and prices in conditions where there was a large national debt. Any policy which resulted in such a price fall in such conditions would imply higher real interest receipts for bondholders, large capital gains for bondholders upon repayment of the capital sums involved and higher real tax needs to service the debt at a lower price level. Such discussions were common in the literature of the period (see, for example, Keynes, *Tract on Monetary Reform*, Chs 1 and 2) and the basic problem was alluded to by the F.B.I. in its evidence to the Cunliffe Committee (above p. 21).

[1]Mitchell and Deane, Wages and Standard of Living, 3.
[2]Routh, *Occupation and Pay*, 114.
[3]Ibid., 115. Additional wage reductions in some industries came only after large and bitter industrial disputes.
[4]The appreciation of the exchange rate involved in the return to gold in Britain in 1925 would have an affect on the cost of living which was relatively small when compared with the relative cost changes necessary to make gold at $4.86 a success. A change in the exchange rate would have its major cost-of-living effect through food prices, although the fall in raw material prices would also affect the cost of other goods. As food, including all further processing and margins accounted for about one third of consumers' expenditure (probably more for working class homes whose pre-war consumption patterns served as the basis for the official index), a 10 per cent appreciation of the exchange rate would, *ceteris paribus*, probably have no more than a 4 per cent effect on the cost of living. In this connection it is interesting to note that between October 1924 and June 1925 food

cost of living was an international slump.[1] Further reductions would depend more on great industrial disputes such as those in coal and engineering in 1921–2 and on unemployment levels. However, in future even reductions of this sort might become more difficult to achieve, for real wages in the unsheltered trades, those which would be first affected by the overvaluation of sterling, had fallen in the post-1920 slump to levels below those of 1914 and workers in these trades would be extremely resistant to the further reductions in money and real wages which the successful restoration of gold at an overvalued exchange required. Thus the task which the Authorities set themselves in 1925 was potentially very difficult. If American prices failed to rise as expected by an amount sufficient to remove a large part of the overvaluation of sterling or if third countries stabilised at relatively low exchange rates, the burden for official financial policy would be particularly great. If the calculations of the Authorities as to the overvaluation of sterling were inaccurate in a conservative direction, as previous discussions have suggested, the necessary reductions in British wages were of an order of magnitude which would be difficult to achieve without great industrial disputes, social strife and unemployment. If the prices of Britain's competitors fell, of course the reductions would have to be greater, provided that the increase in British productivity was not above that of her competitors, which it was not.[2] However, any difficulties that arose after 1925 in this respect would be less the result of any fall in foreign prices and costs than of the basic decisions of 1925, for these implied that the economy would be subject to considerable stress largely as a result of a deliberate act of national economic policy.

The discussion of the previous paragraphs suggests that the overvaluation of sterling in 1925 impaired Britain's international economic position, already weakened by the war and its aftermath, and left British society open to the possibility of great internal social and political strains resulting from efforts to make a go of attempts to successfully adjust to $4.86. It suggests as well that some deliberate undervaluation of sterling on a purchasing-power parity basis to offset the unfavourable longer-term effects of the war would have been advisable. This would have been true even if other European countries had not, sensibly and thoughtfully in many respects,[3] undervalued their currencies when they devalued and returned to gold. The addition of British overvaluation,

---

prices fell by 6.7 per cent, while the working class cost of living index fell by 3.9 per cent. (L.C.E.S., *Key Statistics* Tables B and E; Pigou, *Aspects of British Economic History*, Statistical Appendix, Section III, Table 1.)

[1] A. G. Pool, *Wage Policy in Relation to Industrial Fluctuations*, (London, 1938), 256–7.
[2] Aldcroft, 'Economic Growth in Britain in the Inter-War Years: A Reassessment', 313–14; Phelps Brown and Browne, *Century of Pay*, Fig. 36.
[3] On the French revaluation see Moreau, *Souvenirs*, 177, 182–3.

plus undervaluations elsewhere, to a difficult underlying internal economic position laid the basis for many of the peculiarly British problems of the later 1920s. A lower exchange rate in 1925, although it certainly would not have solved all the problems of the British economy of the 1920s, certainly would have provided a better basis on which to solve those problems which centred around the transition of the industrial structure from the nineteenth to the twentieth century. A lower parity, as Clay suggests,[1] might have had to have been supported at some time by credit restriction, and industry and finance might still have been forced to adjust to external developments. Such a possibility exists under any system of fixed exchange rates irrespective of the particular exchange rate chosen. However, it was one thing to ask the British economy of 1925 to face an initial large adjustment resulting from overvaluation and to run the risk of additional adjustments as international conditions changed, and another to ask the same economy to accept only the risk of the latter, particularly when a more buoyant British economy, the world's largest importer and traditional lender, would have had important favourable repercussions elsewhere.

However, such more general considerations did not enter the minds of most observers in 1924–5. Gold at any rate other than $4.86 was unthinkable: gold at $4.86 at some cost to the economy was desirable. The tendency to simplify the decision to one of gold at a given rate or no gold at all, rather than to consider the possibility of gold at alternative rates of exchange, represents one of the most tragic aspects of the decision-making process. It meant that once gold as a system became official policy, the British economy had to adjust, or not adjust, as best it could to the new circumstances, for, throughout, policy thinking ruled out the possibility of gold plus deliberate exchange rate adjustment.[2] The resulting attempts at adjustment form a central theme for much of the economic history of the period after 1925, and for the chapters which follow.

[1]Clay, *Lord Norman,* 159.
[2]It also meant that much more of the responsibility of running the international economy was thrust on to the shoulders of other countries, for with her exchange rate markedly out of line with the rates of other countries, Britain had neither the potential resources nor the freedom to give much consideration to the needs of the international economy in framing her national policies.

5. 1925–1931: A GENERAL BACKGROUND

Before analysing official international monetary policy after 1925 in the context of the adjustment 'problem' presented by the return to gold at $4.86, it may prove useful to have a picture of the period 1925–31 as a backcloth against which specific official policy measures can be set. The discussion in this chapter attempts to do this from three points of view: that of the domestic economy; that of the balance of payments and Britain's position in the international economy; and that of the Bank of England, the body responsible for day-to-day exchange management.

The Domestic Economy

Given the balance of payments implications, outlined in the last chapter, of the decision to return to gold at pre-war par, it would seem probable on *a priori* grounds that British economic performance during the period of the interwar gold standard period would be constrained by external developments. This suspicion is strengthened by the figures presented in Tables 5 and 6. There it is apparent that only during 1927–9 did exports provide a significant stimulus to economic activity. In 1926, 1930 and 1931 exports provided a strongly deflationary impulse to economic activity, while in 1924 and 1925 they made very little difference. At the same time, imports drawn in by rising domestic incomes and, at the beginning and end of the period by a deteriorating competitive position, served to moderate domestic expansion in every year but two.

Now given the relatively weak expansionary impulses emanating from overseas in most years up to 1929, the next appropriate question is exactly how did Britain manage to achieve as respectable an overall performance as she did between 1924 and 1929, when Gross Domestic Product at constant prices rose at an average annual rate of 2.8 per cent. Excluding 1925, when, as in 1930, heavy stockbuilding provided a stimulus to economic activity,[1] the summary figures in Tables 5 and 6

[1] At 1958 prices, the rise in stocks in 1925 was £361 million, which provides a contrast to the fall of £16 million in the previous year. In 1930, stocks rose by £324 million. In both 1925 and 1930, some of this stockbuilding was probably unintended.

TABLE 5. *Changes in exports and imports of goods and services, current external balance and gross domestic capital formation as compared with changes in G.D.P., 1924–31 (£ million at 1958 prices)*

Change from previous year	1924	1925	1926	1927	1928	1929	1930	1931
Exports of goods and services	+29	−4	−221	+364	+64	+108	−534	−584
Imports of goods and services	+357	+67	+87	+68	−90	+163	−80	+89
Current balance	−328	−71	−308	+296	+154	−55	−454	−673
Gross fixed capital formation	+200	+198	−111	+217	+25	+52	−28	−37
Gross domestic product	+258	+745	−714	+942	+281	+292	−95	−867
Change in exports as a percentage of G.D.P. in later years	0.27	0.03	2.06	3.12	0.54	0.88	4.40	5.18
Change in imports as a percentage of G.D.P. in later years	3.34	0.59	0.81	0.58	0.75	1.33	0.66	0.79
Change in current balance as a percentage of G.D.P. in later years	3.07	0.62	2.87	2.53	1.29	0.45	3.74	5.97
Change in gross fixed capital formation as a percentage of G.D.P. in later years	1.87	1.73	1.04	1.86	0.21	0.43	0.23	0.33
Percentage change in G.D.P.	+2.5	+7.0	−6.2	+8.9	+2.4	+2.4	−0.8	−7.1

+ = increase; − = decrease.

Source: London and Cambridge Economic Service, *Key Statistics 1900–66*, Table B.

TABLE 6. *Indices of business activity* (1924 = 100)

	1924	1925	1926	1927	1928	1929	1930	1931
Economist index of business activity	100	101½	91½	108½	107½	112	106½	98[a]
Exports of manufactures (volume)	100	102	94½	104½	108	109½	86	62[a]
Employment:								
All trades	100	100¾	99¾	105	105	107	102¾	98½[a]
Heavy trades	100	89½	57	87	82	84½	77½	66[a]
General industries	100	103	101	107½	108	109½	101½	95½[a]
Distributive trades	100	103	104	108½	109½	112½	112½	114½[a]
Industrial production	100	103.9	98.4	113.4	110.2	115.8	110.8	103.7
Gross domestic product[b]	100	107.0	100.3	109.1	111.7	114.5	113.6	105.5
Consumers' expenditure[b]	100	102.3	101.8	105.9	107.6	109.9	111.5	112.6
Public authorities current expenditure[b]	100	104.3	106.9	108.6	110.7	113.5	116.3	119.3
Exports of goods and services[b]	100	99.9	93.0	104.4	106.4	109.7	93.0	74.7
Imports of goods and services[b]	100	102.1	104.7	106.7	104.0	108.9	106.5	109.2
Gross domestic capital formation:[b]	100	115.0	106.5	122.2	124.1	128.0	125.9	123.1
public[b]	100	129.5	147.7	160.2	140.7	139.7	154.4	164.7
private[b]	100	110.5	93.9	−110.5	119.0	124.4	117.1	110.3
dwellings[b]	100	125.1	157.4	172.2	134.4	152.6	142.3	149.2
Unemployment	100	108.5	122.6	96.3	107.7	107.6	169.6	232.7

[a] First nine months.
[b] At constant prices.

Sources: *The Economist*, 'Supplement: An Index of Business Activity', 21 October 1933.
The Economist, 'Trade Supplement', 29 June 1935.
K. S. Lomax, 'Production and Productivity Movements in the United Kingdom since 1900', *Journal of the Royal Statistical Society*, Ser. A, CXXII (2), 1959, Table I.
London and Cambridge Economic Service, *Key Statistics 1900–66*, Tables B, E, and J.

provide much of the answer. They indicate that rising levels of public authorities' current expenditure provided part of the basic floor for levels of income during the period. In addition, except in 1928-9 when private fixed capital formation took up the slack resulting from the fall in local authority housebuilding, rising public sector investment provided another relatively stable base for the economy, as did private housebuilding.[1] Added to these impulses were the high levels of public utility investment, particularly that connected with electricity, and of investment associated with the newer industries such as motor vehicles and electrical engineering which, fortunately, were affected mildly, if at all, by the slump after 1929.[2]

In many respects, therefore, British growth after 1924 had at its roots in most years a large number of what might be called 'autonomous' impulses. Investment in industries producing goods resulting from recent innovations, plus the making up of previous deficiencies and the adjustment to new concentrations of population as in the case of housing and other social capital, sustained the 1924-9 expansion, with help towards the end from exports, and provided a floor for the economy after 1929. The industries producing new goods were much less dependent upon export markets for their success, although, as we shall see,[3] their export performance generally surpassed that of more traditional industries in the years after 1924. The export sector, rather than being an engine of growth between 1924 and 1929, merely allowed domestic expansion to proceed relatively unimpeded. That the external sector could even allow the growth that did occur, with its rising level of imports, depended on an expanding international economy as events after 1929 tellingly indicated.[4] That declining exports broke the British 'sloom' of the 1920s is

[1]C. H. Feinstein, *Domestic Capital Formation in the United Kingdom 1920-1938* (Cambridge, 1965), 41-3, 47; H. W. Richardson and D. H. Aldcroft, *Building in the British Economy between the Wars* (London, 1969), Chs 2, 10, 12.

[2]If one defines growth industries as those for which gross fixed investment between 1924 and 1929 in relation to their initial capital stock exceeded the average relationship for manufacturing, one gets almost a roll-call of the newer industries and of industries committed to domestic, rather than international, expansion. After 1929, investment in many of these industries declined by less than the national average for manufacturing. Feinstein, *Domestic Capital Formation*, Tables 8.00-8.54.

[3]In manufacturing, these industries accounted for 52.9 per cent of gross investment between 1924 and 1929; in 1930-1 they accounted for 55.2 per cent. Their shares of output and employment were lower. See also A. E. Kahn, *Great Britain in the World Economy* (London, 1946) Ch. VII; below, p. 123.

[4]Adjusting U.K. export volume in 1924 for the effects of overvaluation (see Appendix 1), the 1929 volume of 109 (unadjusted 1924 = 100) represents an increase of almost 22 per cent. During the same period, world exports (including the U.K.) rose by 32 per cent. For a more complete discussion of the relationships between U.K. exports and world demand see Maizels, *Growth and Trade*, Ch. 8; T. C. Chang,

clear from the figures presented in Tables 5 and 6, as is the moderating effect of other influences.[1]

The relatively strong underlying growth trend in the domestic economy, in conjunction with other factors,[2] carried with it implications for the level of money wages and the problems of relative cost adjustment implicit in the decision to return to gold at $4.86. For although the return to gold at an overvalued exchange rate, combined with the maintenance of free trade, carried with it difficult marketing prospects for producers of export and import competing goods, and although falling prices carried with them rising real wages, it proved impossible to reduce money wages by that 'extra' 10 per cent. To some extent, domestic buoyancy must be considered as part of the explanation for the stickiness of money wages, for until 1930–1 high rates of unemployment were in particular industries and particular areas, and employment and demand conditions were such as to make a sustained attempt to reduce money wages unnecessary and unwise. Therefore, as wages in the unsheltered trades had lagged behind those in more domestically orientated industries before 1924–5 and as any reduction in money wages in the unsheltered trades affected by the overvaluation of sterling would imply a reduction in real wages for those concerned, any direct and successful attack on money wage rates in these trades was impossible, as the events of 1926 indicated. This high level of wages, plus moderate levels of social insurance, helped to keep consumers' expenditure buoyant and to stabilise domestic economic activity, particularly after 1929, but it meant that the 'adjustments' of 1925 were never faced during the period of the interwar gold standard.[3]

The Balance of Payments and Britain's International Economic Position

Against this backcloth of domestic developments, one can now set the overall balance of payments position of Britain after 1925. Table 7 presents estimates for the components of the balance between 1924 and 1931. Although these estimates, which are explained in detail in Appendix 2, are not strictly comparable with those for the post-1945 period, they appear in a similar format.

Cyclical Movements in the Balance of Payments (Cambridge, 1951), Ch. VII.
[1] D. H. Robertson, *Money*, 4th ed. (London, 1948), 184; E. H. Phelps Brown and G. L. S. Shackle, 'British Economic Fluctuations 1924–38', *Oxford Economic Papers* (2), May 1939, 113–19, 125.
[2] The fall in money wages after 1920, the existence of unemployment insurance and a tendency before 1929, and to a lesser extent thereafter, for unemployment to be concentrated in certain industries.
[3] Between 1929 and 1931, consumers' expenditure in the United States fell by 9 per cent in constant prices; in Britain it rose by 2.5 per cent, L.C.E.S., *Key Statistics*, Tables, B and O.

TABLE 7. *Balance of payments of the United Kingdom, 1924-31 (£ million)*

	1924	1925	1926	1927	1928	1929	1930	1931
Current account								
Visible trade								
Retained imports (c.i.f.)	−1137	−1167	−1116	−1095	−1075	−1111	−958	−797
Exports of U.K. produce (f.o.b.)	+801	+773	+653	+709	+724	+729	+571	+391
Net	−336	−394	−463	−386	−351	−382	−387	−406
Invisibles								
Shipping (net)	+140	+124	+120	+140	+130	+130	+105	+80
Investment income (net)	+220	+250	+250	+250	+250	+250	+220	+170
Short interest and commissions (net)	+60	+60	+60	+60	+65	+65	+55	+30
Other invisibles (net)	+15	+15	+15	+15	+15	+15	+15	+10
Government transactions (net)	−25	−11	−4	+4	+15	+24	+19	+14
Net	+410	+438	+449	+467	+475	+484	+414	+304
Current balance	+74	+44	−14	+81	+124	+102	+27	−102
Long-term capital account								
New issues	−134	−88	−112	−139	−143	−96	−98	−41
Repayments	n.a.	n.a.	+27	+34	+35	+49	+39	+27
Other long-term capital movements	n.a.	n.a.	n.a.	n.a.	n.a.	n.a.	+−0	+15
Balance on long-term capital account	−134	−88	−85	−105	−108	−47	−19	+1
Balance on current and long-term capital transactions	−60	−44	−99	−24	+16	+55	+8	−101
Monetary movements								
Change in short-term liabilities	n.a.	n.a.	n.a.	n.a.	+136	−84	−26	−293
Change in acceptances on foreign account	n.a.	n.a.	n.a.	n.a.	−61	+25	+15	+35
Change in gold reserves	+15	+15	−7	−1	−3	+8	−2	−45
Change in foreign exchange reserves	0	−5	−16	−21	+22	0	−5	+9
Change in central bank and other official assistance	0	0	0	0	0	0	+7	+102
Balance of monetary movements	+15	+10	−23	−22	+94	−51	−11	−192
Balancing item	+45	+34	+122	+46	−110	−4	+3	+293

Source: Appendix 2.

n.a. = not available and assumed o.

Because sterling was overvalued at $4.86, one of the prime determinants of Britain's trade performance and balance of payments outcome in the years after 1925 was her competitive position in exports and import-competing goods. Two possible indices of this competitiveness appear in

TABLE 8.   *Unit wage costs in industry in four countries, 1925–31* (1925 = 100)

Country	1925	1926	1927	1928	1929	1930	1931
U.K.	100	100	97	97	95	92	90
Germany	100	102	101	106	112	113	108
U.S.	100	98	96	93	90	88	79
Sweden	100	90	87	88	80	72	70

Source: E. H. Phelps Brown and M. H. Browne, *A Century of Pay*, Appendix III.

Tables 8 and 9. These suggest that, as a general rule, Britain's overall international competitive position changed very little in terms of unit export values, although there was some variation among competing countries, while in terms of unit wage costs her competitive position deteriorated in comparison with all countries noted, except Germany where Britain's 1925 competitive disadvantage had disappeared by 1929.[1] Thus, throughout the years after 1925, British exporters and producers of import-competing goods laboured under a competitive disadvantage which at best changed relatively little and at worst increased.

Additional evidence confirming the competitive disadvantage of British exports in the years after 1925 comes from Maizels' study of exports of manufactures which uses 1913 and 1929 as benchmark years.[2] Between these two dates, Britain's share of world trade in manufactures fell from 30.2 to 23.0 per cent.[3] The decline in Britain's share of this trade occurred in all major commodity groups and in most major markets, not just in her traditional industries.[4] On the basis of the area and commodity patterns of Britain's 1913 trade, world market growth would have led one to expect an increase in British exports of manufactures between 1913 and 1929 of $730 million at 1913 prices; whereas, such

[1] Above, p. 106. The French franc was undervalued in terms of unit wage costs throughout the period after 1925. Brown and Browne, *Century of Pay*, 229–32.

[2] Maizels, *Growth and Trade*, Ch. VIII.

[3] Ibid., Table 8.1. If one includes figures for the Netherlands in 1929, which are unavailable for 1913, Britains' share becomes 22·4 per cent.

[4] Ibid., Table 8.4.

I

exports actually fell by $140 million.[1] This suggests that losses in market shares rather than the area and commodity pattern of Britain's pre-war trade lay at the root of Britain's export performance in the world economy of the late 1920s. It also implies that price competitiveness was an important factor, particularly as Maizels' estimate that, comparing 1929 with 1913, Britain's unit values for manufactures exports rose by 13 per cent more than those of her competitors.[2] Although changes in the quality and composition of British exports of manufactures relative to

TABLE 9.   *Indices of export unit values, (in current dollars) 1925-31* (U.K. = 100)

Country	1925	1926	1927	1928	1929	1930	1931
U.K.	100	100	100	100	100	100	100
Belgium	72	69	65	69	72	72	75
France	73	63	67	64	64	64	63
Germany	73	77	81	83	83	82	86
Netherlands	83	81	82	83	84	80	79
Sweden	91	99	96	97	97	95	94
Switzerland	90	88	90	94	95	95	102
U.S.	84	82	81	84	84	79	74
Competitors' average	81	80	80	82	83	81	82

Source: A. Maddison, 'Growth and Fluctuations in the World Economy, 1870–1960,' *Banca Nazionale del Lavoro Quarterly Review,* June 1962, Table 29.

those from other countries might explain some of the additional price rise, it is most unlikely that the improvement in Britain's relative position in this respect was so marked as to remove the suspicion that she became less competitive over the period. The heavy losses suffered by British exporters of manufactures from import substitution in both industrial and semi-industrial markets strengthens this suspicion, although with their heavy concentration in semi-industrial markets in 1913 in comparison with competitors – 40 per cent as against 10–15 per cent – they were more prone to such losses.[3] The export losses resulting from a lack of competitiveness had important domestic repercussions, for even in the relatively depressed late 1920s, exports accounted for 37 per cent of manufacturing output (as compared with 45 per cent in 1913) and demand declines in this area, especially of this magnitude, could have

[1]Ibid., Table 8.5.
[2]Ibid., Table 8.6. These relative price relationships differ from those in Table 9 as a result of differences in weighting and coverage. In this connection, the continuous marked improvement in Japan's competitive position was to pose a substantial threat to Britain's hold on Far Eastern markets. Ibid., 207; Fig. 8.3.
[3]Ibid., 231, Table 8.13.

powerful cumulative effects on industrial profits and hence possibly on investment and innovation.[1]

Throughout the period after 1925, Britain's export performance was poor by international standards, as Table 10 suggests.[2] Despite the expansive international environment between 1925 and 1929, which most of her competitors exploited, the volume of British exports in 1929 barely surpassed the level which European exports (including those of the U.K.) were to reach in the midst of the slump in 1931. After 1929,

TABLE 10. *U.K. export and import volumes and volumes of competitors' exports, 1924–31 (1924 = 100)*

	1924	1925	1926	1927	1928	1929	1930	1931
U.K. exports	100	100	90	102	106	109	90	68
U.K. imports	100	103	107	110	107	113	112	115
Exports								
World[a]	100	108	111	120	126	132	123	113
W. Europe[a]	100	106	109	121	128	134	122	107
Germany	100	83	98	101	115	128	122	111
France	100	104	113	123	124	124	111	94
Belgium[b]	–	100	105	133	148	147	127	130
Sweden	100	105	107	131	130	152	140	114
Netherlands	100	107	113	126	133	135	128	120
U.S.	100	106	113	122	126	130	107	91

[a] Including U.K.

[b] 1925 = 100.

Source: A. Maddison, 'Growth and Fluctuations in the World Economy, 1870–1960', Tables 25 and 27.

the decline in the volume of world trade fell very heavily on British exporters with the result that the volume of British exports in 1931 reached its second lowest peacetime level of this century, the lowest being 1921. At the same time, the volume of imports continued to rise.

Of course, volume indices do not tell the whole story. Trends in the terms of trade and the general level of prices are also important in the evolution of the balance of trade. However, it is impossible to sort out the effects of price level and terms of trade changes on a partial equilibrium basis and conclude that the balance of trade would have been different by £x million if the terms of trade or the price level had remained unchanged and all other things had developed in exactly the

[1] Ibid., Table 8.11.

[2] If one allows for effects on exports of the appreciation of sterling during 1924–5, Britain's post-1925 performance is somewhat more respectable, but nevertheless it remains below that of her competitors. See above, p. 116, n. 4.

same way, if only because changes in price levels and the terms of trade will affect income levels, income distributions and expenditure pattern thus reacting back on the balance of payments.[1] However, one can poke around behind the outcome and, without implying causality, give some idea of orders of magnitude. Some of the results of such hypothetical poking for the years 1923–31 appear below (all sums in £ million).

Year	Actual trade balance at current prices	Volume	Hypothetical change in the actual trade balance due to changes in: Price level	Terms of trade
1924	−336			
1929	−382	−93	+52	−16
1931	−406	−333	+60	+168

The overall outcome of price and volume changes over the period indicates that Britain became increasingly dependent on invisible earnings to meet a growing trade deficit. Whereas in 1913 and 1924 British export earnings had covered 80 and 70 per cent of British import requirements, between 1925 and 1929 (excluding 1926 and 1927 when the coal stoppage and its aftermath had extensive effects on visible trade) exports hovered between 66 and 67 per cent of import requirements before falling to 49 per cent in 1931. In the light of these figures, it is of some interest that the trade position only really began to excite comment in 1930 and 1931.[3]

An examination of British trade by classes indicates the underlying trends[4] more clearly. Taking 1924 as a base, the volume of food, drink and tobacco imports had risen by 2.9 per cent on average by 1928/9, thus keeping roughly in line with the 2 per cent rise in population over the same period. By 1931, such imports, further stimulated by the fall in prices and the shift to necessities in a period of depression had increased further to 14.3 per cent above their 1924 level. On the other hand, raw material imports rose by less than industrial production or domestic

[1]Kindleberger, *The Terms of Trade*, 276–9.
[2]Hypothetical Volume Change = value of current exports and imports at 1924 prices.
Hypothetical Price Level Change = value of 1924 trade balance at average (unweighted) of export and import prices.
Hypothetical Terms of Trade Change = (1924 value of exports times terms of trade) – (1924 value of imports).
[3]See E. C. Snow, 'The Relative Importance of Export Trade', *Journal of the Royal Statistical Society*, xciv (3), 1931, 396; 'The Balance of Trade', *Journal of the Royal Statistical Society*, xcv (1), 1932, 77, 80, 91–2; C. G. Clark, 'Statistical Studies Relating to the Present Economic Position of Great Britain', *Economic Journal*, xli (163), September 1931; H. W. Macrosty, 'The Overseas Trade of the United Kingdom 1924–1931', *Journal of the Royal Statistical Society*, xcv (4), 1932.
[4]Ibid., Appendix Tables I and II.

output between 1924 and 1928/9, largely as a result of the stagnation in textiles and the classification of some non-ferrous metals and petroleum as manufactures.[1] With the decline in output after 1929, raw material imports fell off to a level below that of 1924. The difficulties of the textile trades, plus the reductions in stocks that falling prices encouraged, were important determinants of a decline that exceeded that in industrial production.

TABLE 11.   *Changes in the volume of selected British manufactured exports and imports, 1924–31*

	Percentage change from 1924	
	1928/9 (average)	1931
Exports		
Vehicles	+95.3	+26.4
Other textile materials	+30.7	−12.1
Chemicals	+24.1	−5.1
Machinery	+24.0	−28.2
Electrical goods	+22.6	−21.7
Non-ferrous metals and manufactures	+18.9	−33.5
Iron and steel	+14.3	−45.2
Cottons	−9.9	−50.4
Woollens	−20.4	−53.9
Imports		
Electrical goods	+100.0	+163.3
Cottons	+97.0	+96.2
Machinery	+80.0	+53.8
Paper goods	+50.0	+59.4
Pottery and glass	+44.0	+37.6
Iron and steel	+38.7	+26.8
Other textile materials	+26.4	+16.6
Woollens	+25.0	+57.0
Non-ferrous metals and manufactures	+22.4	+29.3

Source: H. W. Macrosty, 'The Overseas Trade of the United Kingdom, 1924–31', *Journal of the Royal Statistical Society*, xcv (4), 1932, Appendix Tables I and II.

On the other side of the trade balance, one's attention naturally centres on exports of manufactures and raw materials which made up 90 per cent of Britain's exports by value in both 1924 and 1928/9. Coal dominated raw material exports, representing almost 70 per cent of such exports in 1924. After 1924, coal exports so declined that in 1928/9 they stood at 88 per cent of their 1924 volume, while by 1931 they had fallen further to 69 per cent of their 1924 volume. In the case of coal, the impact

[1]Ibid., 637.

of sterling's overvaluation after 1925, plus the combined effects of a relatively slow rate of growth of productivity and technological and structural changes in consuming markets, meant that British costs stood well above those of her competitors in a fiercely competitive market.[1] This poor performance by the dominant element in the raw materials class meant that as a group such exports remained below 1924 levels, except for a brief surge to 1 per cent above them in 1929.

The position of manufactures was much more complex. Table 11 summarises the major changes in both exports and imports by commodity groups. Between 1924 and 1928/9, the major export gains occurred in the newer commodity groups – vehicles (including locomotives, ships and aircraft), electrical goods, chemicals and machinery. In the older groups, such growth as did occur took place in the more finished, less homogeneous products in any range. In iron and steel, for example, the volume of exports of crude iron and steel fell by 15.5 per cent between 1924 and 1928/9; whereas, that of rolling mill and more finished products rose by 6 and 22 per cent respectively.[2] The traditional export leaders, cotton textiles and woollens, suffered heavily from foreign competition and foreign tariffs, particularly in Far Eastern markets, and never really surpassed their 1924 levels.[3] However, after 1929, falling foreign incomes, relatively high British prices and rising foreign tariffs combined to almost completely destroy the export position. Except in vehicles, chemicals and rayons, all of the gains of 1924–9 disappeared and in some trades such as textiles, exports reached levels that had not been seen since the nineteenth century.[4]

On the other side of the balance in manufactures, imports rose in every year of the period with electrical goods and machinery leading the way. In older lines, imports also rose as domestic producers became less competitive: in iron and steel, British domestic prices for merchant bars and structural shapes were the highest in Europe.[5] In these conditions, the British market for iron and steel was relatively unprotected against competitive imports in areas other than those where restrictive agreements existed.[6] Imported rolling mill and more finished steel products entered the British market in such quantities that Britain, a net importer

---

[1]Board of Trade, *Statistical Tables Relating to British and Foreign Trade and Industry (1924–1930)*, Part II, Cmd. 3849 (London, 1931), 10, 49; I. Svennilson, *Growth and Stagnation in the European Economy* (Geneva, 1954), 104–11; Macrosty, 'Overseas Trade', 635–6; League of Nations, *The Course and Phases of the World Economic Depression* (Geneva, 1931), 59–60; Kahn, *Britain in the World Economy*, 84–8.
[2]Board of Trade, *Statistical Tables*, II, 62–3.
[3]Kahn, *Britain in the World Economy*, 94–8.
[4]For piece goods since 1864, for thread since 1880, for twist and yarn since 1865. Mitchell and Deane, *Abstract*, Textiles 4.
[5]Svennilson, *Growth and Stagnation*, Chart 28.
[6]Ibid., 128.

of only iron and crude steel in 1924, became a net importer of more sophisticated rolling mill products in the years after 1925. A similar process occurred in textiles as cheaper cottons and light Continental woollens found their places in the British market as did rayons. Many of the new imports were semi-manufactures, but, as the continued high level of manufactured imports after 1929 helps indicate, a large proportion probably consisted of finished consumption goods. Thus manufactured imports, which were 32.5 per cent higher in volume in 1928/9 than in 1924, were 5 per cent above their 1929 volume in 1931.

The changes in Britain's trade position in the years after 1924 indicate to some extent how Britain had become a marginal supplier in many export markets – last engaged, first dismissed. Throughout the period, her exports continued to move increasingly into more sheltered markets where imperfections – tariff preferences, transportation preferences and traditional commercial ties – worked to her advantage, even to some extent in the 1920s.[1] Thus up to 1929, the proportion of her exports moving to the Empire and South America rose, as did exports to most areas in Asia outside of India, China and Japan, where Japanese (and in the Indian case, domestic) competition made itself felt. At the same time, her imports came increasingly from industrial countries, especially in Europe where the post-war recovery brought about a considerable substitution of European goods for those previously imported from North America. However, British imports from some overseas areas also rose, but these were predominantly foodstuffs and raw materials. This shifting of her export trade pattern left Britain particularly exposed to an international slump as the import capacities of her growing overseas markets depended heavily on export earnings from primary products and new overseas investment, both of which were strongly cyclical, and as import demands in these markets concentrated on relatively simple capital goods which were also strongly cyclical. In the years after 1929, both of these cyclical factors made themselves strongly felt.[2]

As a result of her disappointing post-1924 export performance and the rising level of imports, Britain became increasingly dependent on her invisible earnings to cover her growing trade deficit and allow new net foreign investment. Until 1929, the rise in invisible earnings more than offset the deterioration on trade account – £74 million as against £46

[1] G. D. A. MacDougall, 'British and American Exports: A Study Suggested by the Theory of Comparative Costs', Part II, *Economic Journal*, LXII (247), September 1952, 500ff. This trend had started in the 1870s. For one explanation see Kindleberger, *Economic Growth*, 271–7.

[2] The heaviest falls in the value of exports occurred in what were to become the overseas sterling area countries and the rest of the world outside Europe where Britain's 1931 exports were roughly half those of 1929 (Europe 62 per cent). L.C.E.S., *Key Statistics*, Table K. As for the commodities affected, Table 9 tells most of the story. See also Clark, 'Statistical Studies', 347.

million. However, the improved invisibles position depended almost completely on rising overseas investment income and on war debt and reparation payments which transformed the Government account.[1] Shipping earnings, on the other hand, fell as freight rates declined and as Britain's share of the available traffic fell slightly.[2] Short-interest and commissions remained almost stagnant. Given that a large proportion of overseas investment income came from cyclically sensitive equities[3] and given that the whole edifice of war debts and reparations was rarely without uncertainties, the payments position had its precarious elements, as the events of 1929–31 demonstrated. During that period, income from invisibles fell by £180 million while the trade balance declined by £24 million, even if one includes the post September 1931 rise in the trade deficit resulting from the initial effects of sterling's depreciation and fears of protection.[4] Thus, given the unstable nature of invisible earnings, the post-1925 current account depended on the trade account for its underlying strength. However, the trade account had been weakened by the effects of 1925 and never really recovered.

The overall balance of payments figures for the years 1924–31 were the outcome of the developments in trade and invisibles, plus those in long-term foreign lending. The 'best guess' estimates presented in Table 7 suggest that up to 1927 Britain became progressively less liquid internationally, as her cumulative balances on current and long-term capital accounts ran to −£227 million. This estimate perhaps overstates the deterioration as it excludes some repayments and foreign subscriptions to overseas issues. However, even if these averaged out at levels suggested by the figures for the latter part of the period – £32–£35 million, depending on whether one includes the high 1929 figure, and £5 million respectively – the overall cumulative deficit remains in excess of £150 million.[5] The estimate also leaves out any movements in outstanding securities, which *The Economist* in October 1929 suggested could exceed gross new issues, and ignores any direct investments in either direction.[6]

[1] *The Economist*, 'War Debts and Reparations Supplement', 23 January 1932, 12.
[2] Mitchell and Deane, *Abstract*, Transport 4; Board of Trade, *Statistical Tables Relating to British and Foreign Trade and Industry (1924–1930)*, I, Cmd. 3737 (London, 1930), 218, 234.
[3] R.I.I.A., *Problem of International Investment*, 148–50.
[4] During the first nine months of 1931, the trade deficit was £329.4 million as compared with £344.6 million for the same period in 1930. In addition, as suggested below (p. 246) the depreciation of sterling after 1931 would have aided the invisible balance, even in the short run.
[5] If one adds in the rise in official reserves of over £30 million, the deterioration in the private position exceeds £180 million (here we are ignoring the change in the value of Britain's gold reserves resulting from appreciation in 1924–5).
[6] 26 October 1929, 753. J. H. Dunning, *American Investment in British Industry* (London, 1958), 37ff., provides some indication of the extent of American direct investment

Thus the estimate incompletely reflects the changes that were occurring in London's international balance sheet position, but it hardly suggests that London became more liquid. Moreover, it compares roughly with the contemporary estimates of Keynes and Gregory who put the deterioration in London's short-term liquidity position at between £130 and £200 million.[1] It was from this weakened position that the Authorities faced the stresses and strains of 1928–31.

At the beginning of this latter period, the overall liquidity position appears to have improved marginally. Both 1928 and 1929 brought small surpluses on the current and long-term capital account which allowed an improvement in the liquidity position of as much as £70 million, if one trusts the incomplete official figures.[2] Thereafter, improvements were minimal, and in 1931 a large current and long-term capital account deficit, plus a massive outflow of short-term funds and an immobilisation of considerable short-term assets in Central Europe left the Authorities unable to maintain the 1925 sterling parity.

During the difficult years between 1928 and 1931, the Authorities' policy problems were heightened by unfavourable changes in Britain's pattern of international settlements which also had significant effects on the character of the foreign balances in the London market and on the Authorities' policy position. During the period after 1925, as before, Britain depended on her surpluses on trade and invisibles with the Empire and Asia to settle her deficits with Europe and America and to allow her to undertake new foreign lending. In addition, the willingness of what might be called the proto-sterling area countries to hold their foreign exchange and, in many cases, some or all of their commercial bank reserves in London meant that Britain's need to attract short-term funds from Europe or America to finance an overall deficit on her part or other monetary movements was reduced. Up to 1928/9, this system worked successfully and, as Britain reduced her large post-war dollar area deficit somewhat, one might even argue that Britain's settlements position improved slightly in the early years after 1925.[3] However, as declining raw material prices, declining new overseas lending and, eventually, declining raw material demands from the advanced countries entering the depression affected the balance of payments position of these

in the U.K. during the period. C. Wilson, *The History of Unilever: A Study in Economic Growth and Economic Change* (London, 1954), I, 285ff. gives an indication of the overseas direct investment of one U.K. company during the period.

[1] J. M. Keynes, 'The British Balance of Trade 1925–27', *Economic Journal*, XXXVII (148), December 1927, 562; Gregory, *First Year of the Gold Standard*, 77–9.

[2] This improvement was not large enough to offset the pressures on London resulting from the attraction of short-term funds to the United States and elsewhere, which made policy formulation so difficult at the time. See below, pp. 136–8.

[3] Kahn, *Britain in the World Economy*, Ch. XII.

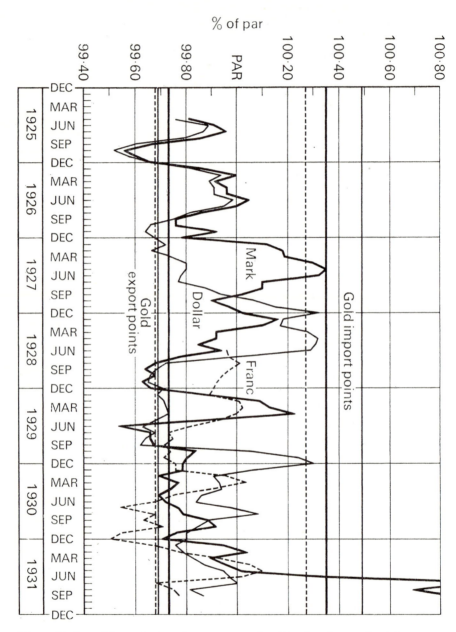

Fig. 1. Major gold standard exchange rates and gold points for sterling May 1925–September 1931. SOURCES: London and Cambridge Economic Service, *Bulletin;* O. Morgenstern, *International Financial Transactions and Business Cycles* (Princeton, 1959), table 34.

countries, they moved into deficit with Europe and America. Thus the pattern of settlements broke down. Initially, this breakdown did not affect London too severely as the countries concerned let gold go and as this gold's arrival in the London market allowed Britain to meet the heavy Continental demands for gold in 1929 and 1930 at less cost to the reserves than would otherwise have been the case. However, once the overseas sterling countries turned to running down their sterling exchange reserves and/or began borrowing in London to help meet balance of payments deficits,[1] the pressure on London became particularly intense, for she had to replace a large part of these funds by actively attracting balances from centres which did not 'automatically' hold funds in London. At the same time, as deflationary measures in the overseas areas reduced imports, they also weakened the current account of the British balance of payments thus further heightening the pressure on London.

Thus in 1931, not only did Britain face a deficit on her balance of payments which would have subjected London to considerable strain, but she also faced the prospect that those areas of the world which normally would have helped to finance that deficit 'automatically' were themselves in deficit and further weakening London's position by running down their sterling balances. Thus, even without the international liquidity crisis, 1931 would not have seen a repetition of 1926 when Britain ran a deficit on current and long-term capital account of £99 million and yet gained £23 million in reserves. The conjuncture of circumstances was simply not that favourable.[2]

The Bank of England's View of Developments

With our knowledge of the behaviour of the domestic economy and the trends in the balance of payments, we can now turn to an examination of the Bank of England's overall view of these developments. This discussion, for which Figures 1 and 2 provide useful points of reference, will serve

[1]Balogh, *Studies*, 150; Williams, 'London and the 1931 Financial Crisis', *Economic History Review*, 2nd Ser., xv (3), April 1963, 521.
[2]In 1926, there had been an excess supply of dollars and capital flights from European countries such as France which eased the British situation. In contrast, in 1931 there was an excess demand for dollars of a larger amount and those countries which had experienced a capital flight in 1926 were now drawing down their London balances. (H. B. Lary and Associates, *The United States in the World Economy* [Washington, 1943], Appendix Table II; Below p. 140). In addition, the 1926 deficit could be regarded as temporary; whereas, the 1931 deficit, which even the Board of Trade (before the depreciation of sterling) expected to exceed £80 million, could only be regarded as the first of a series which would increase as world depression deepened. (Cab. 58/18, Balance of Trade, Memorandum by the Board of Trade, 21 September 1931.) See also D. E. Moggridge, 'The 1931 Financial Crisis: A New View', *The Banker*, cxx (534), August 1970, 833-5, 839.

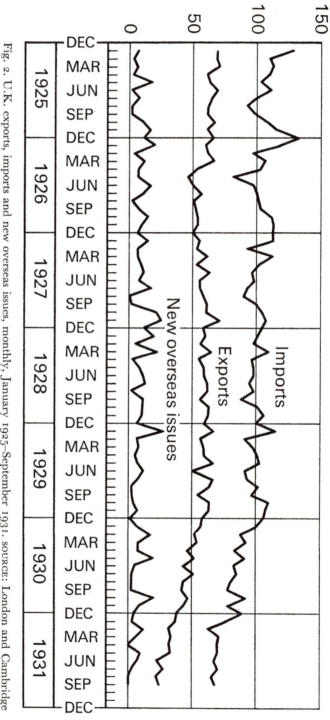

Fig. 2. U.K. exports, imports and new overseas issues, monthly, January 1925–September 1931. SOURCE: London and Cambridge Economic Service, *Bulletin.*

as the final piece of background material for the detailed discussions in later chapters of specific policy instruments used by the Authorities over the entire period.

At the time of the decision to return to gold in March 1925, Norman had expected that a high Bank Rate would be necessary to aid the adjustment to the new exchange parity, and, although he agreed that Bank Rate would not rise with the Budget announcement of restoration, he only believed that this commitment would be operative for the first week of the 'golden age'.[1] A month after the announcement Norman wrote to Strong reaffirming these expectations and mentioning that a successful restoration would require high interest rates and a contraction of credit.[2] Although the first few weeks of the gold standard went 'according to plan' except in so far as the transition to gold 'caused not only less alarm but even less interest than could have been expected', the 'plan' soon came unstuck.[3] American funds flowed into London, attracted by favourable interest rates,[4] there was some accumulation of central bank exchange reserves in stabilised sterling, and the market quickly tended towards lower interest rates and higher Colonial issues than Norman considered appropriate,[5] despite some offsetting official security sales. As a response, Norman considered a $\frac{1}{2}$ per cent reduction in Bank Rate as early as May, but held off, probably awaiting developments in both the domestic situation and the exchanges, particularly the latter.[6] However Norman was under Treasury pressure to reduce interest rates, particularly in the light of the coal situation and the increase in the Bank's gold holdings, and he did so once the coal situation was settled for the time being.[7] Nevertheless, despite the narrowing of interest differentials in London's favour and further official security sales, Norman still had difficulty in controlling short-term rates in the London market, which, with the embargo on overseas loans, controls on Empire borrowing and central bank accumulations of exchange balances, remained flush with short-term funds. On 1 October he reduced Bank Rate by another $\frac{1}{2}$ per cent despite some gold losses and the beginnings of an outflow of funds to New York.[8] He then continued to keep Bank

[1] The phrase is Norman's. T172/1499B, Norman to Niemeyer, 21 March 1925.
[2] F.R.B.N.Y., Strong Papers, Norman to Strong, 26 May 1925.
[3] Ibid., Norman to Strong, 8 May 1925.
[4] The covered interest arbitrage differential between the two discount markets was 0.75 per cent per annum in London's favour. F.R.B.N.Y., Norman to Strong, no. 41, 22 May 1925; Strong to Norman, nos 90, 91 and 96, 21, 23 and 29 May 1925.
[5] F.R.B.N.Y., Strong Papers, Norman to Strong, 26 May 1925; Annual Report of the Netherlands Bank, *Federal Reserve Bulletin*, XII (8), August 1926, 592–3.
[6] T176/13, Norman to Niemeyer, 24 July 1925.
[7] T176/13, Niemeyer to Norman, 21 July 1925; F.R.B.N.Y., Strong Papers, Strong to Case, 1 August 1925.
[8] Ibid., Strong to Jay, no. 6, 1 August 1925; Clay, *Lord Norman*, 219; F.R.B.N.Y.,

Rate at 4 per cent, despite autumnal gold losses, the beginnings of speculation on the New York Stock Exchange and the removal of the embargo on overseas loans in November,[1] awaiting a sufficiently large loss of gold or a change in American interest rates to force his hand and make the ensuing change in Bank Rate politically acceptable.[2] This wait lasted until December before the Treasury's inability to market sufficient Treasury bills for several weeks as a result of market uncertainty as to future rates and the lack of the public excuse for higher rates resulting from any likely rise in New York rates forced him to move to 5 per cent.[3] The rise in Bank Rate reversed interest differentials sharply in London's favour and allowed the Bank to ride out the rest of the year with reduced gold losses, despite an unusually large end-of-year trade deficit and revived overseas lending.

Despite internal industrial problems and a very large trade deficit, 1926 was a relatively quiet year for the Bank. Sterling recovered from its late 1925 low and by early February Norman was beginning to worry about his ability to maintain a 5 per cent Bank Rate, particularly as he expected to gain market gold and as the only factor keeping market rates higher was the seasonal pressure created by Government tax collections which increased public deposits at the Bank and which the Bank did not offset.[4] However, uncertainty as to the coal position meant that Norman attempted to maintain 5 per cent and renewed the 1925 credits for another year.[5] The General Strike passed without incident, from an exchange point of view, despite its adverse effects on the trade position, largely as a result of the inflow of refugee capital from France during the last months before its adoption of stabilisation measures,[6] and the Bank

Norman to Strong, no. 16, 19 September 1925; no. 56, 15 October 1925; *Federal Reserve Bulletin*, xii (6), June 1926, 377–8.

[1] This had been designed partially to regain control of the money market and perhaps, partially to provide an excuse for an increase in Bank Rate. See below, p. 209. F.R.B.N.Y., Norman to Strong, no. 65, 22 October 1925.

[2] The crucial floor for the gold reserves was the level of 28 April 1925. F.R.B.N.Y., Norman to Strong, nos 56 and 61, 15 and 22 October 1925; Strong Papers, Norman to Strong, 23 November 1925.

[3] F.R.B.N.Y., Strong Papers, Anderson to Strong, 27 November 1925; Norman to Strong, nos 25, 28 and 30, 30 November, 1 and 2 December 1925. Even under these circumstances, the Chancellor objected to the increase (below, pp. 162–3).

[4] F.R.B.N.Y., Norman to Strong, no. 14, 2 February 1926.

[5] T160/227/F8508, Niemeyer to Churchill, 10 February 1926; Clay, *Lord Norman*, 225.

[6] The franc fell from an average of 128·7 to the pound in January 1926 to 197·7 to the pound in July. As covered interest arbitrage margins on a discount basis with New York were in London's favour but under the required ½ per cent per annum necessary to attract fresh funds from February to October (with the exception of April), it is unlikely that the exchange position received much assistance during the period of the General Strike from the American end. P. Einzig, *The Theory of Forward Exchange* (London, 1937), 172–3; H. G. Grubel, *Forward Exchange, Speculation and the International Flow of Capital* (Stanford, 1966), 66–8.

gained gold until September. After September, however, the Bank had to deal with the effects of the usual seasonal strain in the dollar exchange, heightened to some extent by the beginnings of industrial restocking after the strikes of earlier months, and by the efforts of the Reichsbank to reduce capital inflows by ceasing to peg the mark on the dollar and allowing private arbitrage in gold, which meant London was subject to a drain to Berlin.[1] However, Norman managed to ride out the autumn at 5 per cent, despite difficulties in placing Treasury bills in November. In many respects, in fact, 1926 represented the most uneventful year of the interwar gold standard period for the Bank.

From the Bank's point of view 1927 opened inauspiciously. The exchange position remained, in Norman's words, 'weaker than one would wish to see at this time of the year', and in January and February he was loath to lower Bank Rate, despite the desirability of doing so on domestic grounds[2] and the Bank's inability to make 5 per cent effective in the money market in the season of tax collections. Foreign lending remained high as did imports. In March, however, Norman regained some control of the money market, and, with the repayment to the Bank of a French loan of 1916 and the rise in the dollar exchange, he felt able to reduce Bank Rate to $4\frac{1}{2}$ per cent on 21 April and to allow the 1925 credit arrangements in New York to lapse. However, in May the situation deteriorated dramatically with heavy gold purchases in London by the Bank of France.

As these purchases and the discussions surrounding them throw considerable light on the Bank's position in the years after 1925, it is worthwhile exploring the incident in some detail. To fully understand the episode, however, one must first backtrack somewhat. Following the successful July 1926 measures directed at the stabilisation of the internal financial situation, the French Authorities were still undecided as to the appropriate rate of stabilisation for the franc.[3] After 7 August 1926, however, the Bank of France could acquire gold, silver and foreign exchange at a premium and it used this power to moderate the appreciation of the franc until the *de facto* stabilisation of December 1926 at f.124 to £1. The French economy, however, continued to attract funds as confident nationals repatriated balances and as foreigners bought francs for investment and speculation.[4] The repayment of the 1916 loan from the Bank of England to the Bank of France before maturity and the regaining of the gold pledged as security by the Bank

[1]Clay, *Lord Norman,* 223–4; Clarke, *Central Bank Cooperation,* 113–15.
[2]F.R.B.N.Y., Norman to Strong, 15 February 1927; Clay, *Lord Norman,* 235.
[3]Moreau, *Souvenirs,* 9 and 18 August 1926.
[4]F.R.B.N.Y., Confidential Minutes of Meeting of 27 May 1927 (present: Moreau, Rist, Quesnay, Norman, Siepmann), 5.

of France only served to heighten bullishness.[1] By the end of May 1927, the Bank of France's foreign exchange holdings (largely in sterling), which, given the Bank's commitment to peg the exchange, reflected these trends, stood $720 million above the level of November 1926.[2]

This heavy inflow of foreign balances represented a threat to the domestic market control of the Bank of France, which moved to minimise it through a parallel shift of Government debt from the Bank to the market.[3] However, such shifting had its limits and Moreau, the Governor of the Bank of France, feared excessive currency issues and inflation.[4] He also feared that the influx of funds would give heart to those who wished to restore the franc to its pre-war parity, a repetition of the British experience he wished to avoid.[5] To reduce the influx, Moreau decided to use his strong position in London to force an increase in Bank Rate, a tightening of market rates, a reduction in the credit which London extended to the Continent and a general tightening of European monetary conditions which would reduce the volume of funds available for franc speculation.[6] He asked the Bank of England to acquire gold worth £30 million on a set schedule and also sold sterling for dollars.[7] Simultaneously in New York, for similar reasons, he asked for $100 million in gold, in this case assisting the open-market operations of the Federal Reserve.[8] This programme, given the Bank's gold position and likely arrivals of open market gold, caused considerable alarm in London:

[1] This loan was granted in 1916 and 1917 and renegotiated in 1923. In 1927 the French attempted to alter the terms of repayment again to allow for a possible stabilisation of the franc, but the Bank of England declined the suggestion with the result that the French repaid the debt in full with accumulated London balances in April 1927. The Bank of England's intransigence to the proposed renegotiation did not endear Norman further to Moreau, the Governor of the Bank of France, who suspected Norman's motives. E. Moreau, *Souvenirs*, 29 July 1926, 19 October 1926, 23, 26 and 28 February 1927, 21–3 March 1927 and 24 April 1927, Clay, *Lord Norman*, 227–8; T160/153/F5904.

[2] Ibid., 227–8; Clarke, *Central Bank Cooperation*, 111.

[3] League of Nations, *International Currency Experience* (Princeton, 1944), 76.

[4] Moreau, *Souvenirs*, 25 and 28 April 1927, 9 May 1927.

[5] Ibid., 20 February 1927, 25 and 29 April 1927, 10 and 12 May 1927; T160/430/ F12317/1, Siepmann, 'The French Franc', 30 November 1926; Siepmann to Leith-Ross, 30 November 1926; T176/29, Conversation with M. Quesnay on French Monetary Policy, June 1927.

[6] In addition to these effects, the policy would provide Moreau with additional gold reserves for any subsequent *de jure* stabilisation and, given the position of sterling, increase the quality of his international assets. Moreau, *Souvenirs*, 12, 13 and 21 May 1927, F.R.B.N.Y., Rist to Harrison, 17 May 1927; Moreau to Harrison, no. 96, 16 May 1927.

[7] Moreau, *Souvenirs*, 13, 16 and 18 May 1927.

[8] Ibid., 18 May 1927; F.R.B.N.Y., Moreau to Harrison, no. 99, 17 May 1927; Harrison to Moreau, nos 94 and 97, 16 and 17 May 1927; Strong to Moreau, 26 May 1927.

Norman believed that the 'havoc' resulting from these 'capricious' demands 'would menace the gold standard'.[1] When Moreau realised this, he agreed to suspend his programme pending a meeting with Norman in Paris on 27 May.[2]

At this meeting Norman gave his brilliant and often-quoted exposition of his operating position at the time and attempted to encourage Moreau to make the majority of the adjustments required.[3] Neither banker gave ground. However, Moreau seems to have increased his understanding of Norman's position and this plus a combination of British Treasury pressure over war debts, increases in London bill rates and a reduction in the flow of funds to Paris eventually produced agreement.[4] The arrangements, evolved during Quesnay's early June visit to London, attacked the problem under three heads: the Bank of England would provide Moreau with £30 million in gold or dollars (of which £3 million had already been provided) in the next six months; the Bank of France would discriminate against sterling in the foreign exchange market; the Bank of France's balances would not exceed £50 million, the level at which they would stand after these operations.[5] Ultimately the Bank of England transferred approximately £25 million to the Bank of France through a combination of open market gold purchases, borrowing from the Federal Reserve and sales from its dollar reserves, but the interesting fact about the whole incident is that it indicates the very tenuous nature of London's gold standard and policy-making position *well after* the return to gold.[6]

The famous July 1927 meeting of central bankers, which put the finishing touches on the scheme for the conversion of the Bank of France's sterling balances, also marked the beginning of a more relaxed period for the conduct of monetary policy by the Bank.[7] The reduction in the discount rates of the Federal Reserve Banks which followed this meeting relieved any remaining pressures on the sterling

---

[1] F.R.B.N.Y., Strong Papers, Norman to Strong, 22 May 1927; Norman to Strong, nos 38 and 40, 24 and 26 May 1927.

[2] F.R.B.N.Y., Moreau to Strong, no. 13, 25 May 1927.

[3] Moreau, *Souvenirs*, 27 May 1927; F.R.B.N.Y., Confidential Minutes of Meeting of 27 May 1927.

[4] Moreau, *Souvenirs*, 30 and 31 May 1927, 7 and 13 June 1927; F.R.N.B.Y., Moreau to Strong, no. 16, 31 May 1927; T176/29, Leith-Ross to Churchill, 9 and 13 June 1927; Conversation with M. Quesnay of the Bank of France in regard to Reparations and Inter-Allied Debts, 9 June 1927.

[5] F.R.B.N.Y., Moreau to Strong, no. 23, 8 June 1927; Norman to Strong, no. 50, 4 June 1927; Moreau, *Souvenirs*, 8 June 1927.

[6] The remaining French balances were a source of worry to the Authorities for the rest of the period under consideration. See below p. 164.

[7] No record of the meeting exists. For some indication of the subjects discussed see Ibid., 9 and 16 July 1927; Chandler, *Benjamin Strong*, 311; Clay, *Lord Norman*, 236–7; F.R.B.N.Y., Norman to Lubbock, no. 9/27, 8 July 1927.

K

exchange. Sterling rose strongly, despite the season of the year, as American foreign lending increased[1] and as London's covered interest advantage widened significantly. The Bank was quickly able to liquidate the summer's Federal Reserve support and accumulate dollars on its own account. December brought gold imports from New York, the first since the war, largely for advertising purposes.[2] It was with sterling in the unusual position of being above par on the major gold standard exchanges that the Bank entered 1928.

With the beginning of 1928, the Bank began its almost two-year struggle with the exchange effects of the rising tide of speculation in New York. Although the full effects of New York conditions in the exchange market were not felt until the second half of 1928, an examination of London–New York covered interest arbitrage differentials gives some indication of the developing pressures.[3] By April, Norman was sufficiently worried to offer to forego interest earnings on $50 million of his dollar balances by transferring them from the market to the Federal Reserve Bank of New York in order to help the American Authorities stem the tide of speculation.[4] The offer was not taken up. On several other occasions Norman sold dollars, without purchasing offsetting securities to increase his control of the London market while at the same time assisting any Federal Reserve efforts to control speculation.[5] However, these offers and efforts were mere drops in the bucket, and the growing speculative tide, plus rising American interest rates, increasingly drew funds from London – and from the Continent through London – and threatened the Bank's reserves from early August.

In the course of the rest of 1928 the Bank was under considerable pressure in the form of reserve losses, at first to New York and subsequently to both Berlin and Paris.[6] These losses totalled £46.5 million, of which

[1]New capital issues for foreigners which had averaged $99 million per month in 1926 and the first seven months of 1927 rose to $131 per month on average in the eleven months after July 1927. Federal Reserve Board, *Banking and Monetary Statistics*, Table 137.

[2]F.R.B.N.Y., Norman to Harrison, no. 234/27, 7 December 1927; T176/22, Norman to Holland-Martin, 8 December 1927; Leith-Ross to Grigg, 9 December 1927.

[3]Using averages for the last five months of 1927 and the first six months of 1928, the covered interest arbitrage differential in favour of London for bill rate arbitrage fell from 0.51 per cent per annum to 0.02 per cent per annum, while that in favour of New York for London bill rate–New York time rate arbitrage rose from 0.56 per cent per annum to 1.06 per cent per annum. A high level of capital exports from New York probably offset unfavourable interest rate developments for the better part of the half year, but not after June.

[4]F.R.B.N.Y., Case to Norman no. 98/28, 25 April 1926; Norman to Harrison, no. 81/28, 30 April 1928; Strong Papers, Case to Strong, 30 April 1928.

[5]Below, pp. 186–7.

[6]The Paris reserve losses were not private arbitrage transactions but rather Bank of France purchases designed to restore the Bank's reserve proportion and under-

£26.5 million came from the Bank's hidden foreign exchange reserves. Norman realised that any measures the Bank could take short of raising Bank Rate were 'like spitting against the wind if . . . [New York] call money continues round 8 per cent', but the Bank, afraid that a rise in its rates would produce a general rise in European rates and increase the difficulties of domestic industry, was prepared to lose a considerable proportion of its reserves before taking action, although Norman realised 'that sooner or later it will suck our vitals' if New York rates remained high.[1] Norman was prepared to await the turn of the year before taking any steps to raise Bank Rate and to allow more time to gain information for any future decisions.[2]

The turn of the year brought no relief. There was increased uncertainty about the future course of American monetary policy as a result of the struggle between the Federal Reserve Bank of New York and the rest of the Federal Reserve System over the choice between higher rates and direct intervention in particular markets as means to reduce speculation which had replaced the earlier 'disposition to do nothing'.[3] Norman moved increasingly towards the position that a rise in Bank Rate was inevitable, particularly as exchange and gold losses were inevitable in the early part of the year and as Federal Reserve support for sterling would prove 'merely a temporary expedient', particularly as the Federal Reserve's lack of earning assets available to offset such support would make such operations expansionary in New York.[4] A visit to New York proved extremely disappointing in that he found no possibilities of the speculation-breaking rise in American discount rates which he believed necessary.[5] As a result, Norman became extremely pessimistic as to the future of the gold standard.[6] But the increase in Bank Rate to $5\frac{1}{2}$ per cent forced during his absence by an inability to place Treasury bills and continued reserve losses, while it did not prove immediately or strikingly effective, eased matters, to a limited extent, from mid-February.[7] This

taken in conjunction with the Bank of England. F.R.B.N.Y., Norman to Harrison, no. 227/28, 13 November 1928.

F.R.B.N.Y., Norman to Harrison, no. 166/28, 6 September 1928; Lubbock to Harrison, 3 August 1928; Norman to Harrison, 2 November 1928.

F.R.B.N.Y., Norman to Harrison, no. 249/28, 6 December 1928.

Clarke, *Central Bank Cooperation*, 150–8, Wicker, *Federal Reserve Monetary Policy*, Ch. 9–10; Friedman and Schwartz, *Monetary History*, 254–68; F.R.B.N.Y., Harrison to Lubbock, no. 201/28, 31 August 1928.

F.R.B.N.Y., Norman to Harrison, nos 6 and 15/29, 4 and 15 January 1929; Harrison to Norman, no. 15/29, 16 January 1929.

F.R.B.N.Y., Norman to Lubbock, no. 41/29, 7 February 1929; Wicker, *Federal Reserve Monetary Policy*, 134; Clay, *Lord Norman*, 248–9; Clarke, *Central Bank Cooperation*, 152.

F.R.B.N.Y., Norman to Lubbock, no. 41/29, 7 February 1929; Harrison Collection, Memorandum of 11 February 1929.

F.R.B.N.Y., Lubbock to Norman, no. 28/29, 31 January 1929.

rise in Bank Rate, coupled with the January fall in the Reichsbank' rate and increasing uncertainty as to the outcome of the Paris conference on reparations, reduced the pressures on sterling from Berlin. However rising European interest rates and deteriorating reserve positions in several European central banks gave Norman cause for alarm – alarm heightened by French financial pressures on Berlin after the breakdown of the Paris conference.[1]

The middle part of the year brought increased pressures upon the British position rather than relief. The reflux of funds into Germany after the reparations scare brought the mark exchange to the gold export point in London and sterling fell again in New York. In addition, the franc exchange began to deteriorate. Initially, Norman did nothing as he attributed the weakness in sterling partially to election and reparation uncertainties, as well as New York rates, and he expected the next month to clarify the situation.[2] The weakness in the sterling exchanges may also have resulted, to some extent, from the deterioration in trade balance, noted in Figure 2, which reflected a decline in exports and a high level of imports. The situation was not helped by Harrison's June admission of defeat in his attempts to raise American discount rates to curb speculation, and Norman increasingly expected he would have to raise Bank Rate to $6\frac{1}{2}$ per cent.[3] June and July brought gold losses, some of them perhaps the result of a shifting of Bank of France balances from London to New York, but, perhaps as a result of political pressures, the Bank kept Bank Rate unchanged.[4]

However, the rise in the Federal Reserve Bank of New York's discount rate to 6 per cent on 9 August, just after Norman's return from a second trip to America, increased the pressures on London. This unexpected increase disrupted London markets, requiring assurances as to short-term Bank Rate policy to settle them.[5] In the short run, a change in Bank Rate was constrained by political considerations, in particular the reparations discussions at the Hague. Thus Norman supported the dollar exchange with owned and borrowed dollars, and allowed gold to flow to Germany and France until the end of the Hague negotiations and the Hatry collapse left him politically free to raise Bank Rate to $6\frac{1}{2}$

---

[1]F.R.B.N.Y., Norman to Harrison, nos 47, 67, 75 and 78/29, 18 February, 14, 25 and 28 March 1929; Norman to Harrison, 12 April 1929; Clarke, *Central Bank Cooperation*, 165; Clay, *Lord Norman*, 251; H. Schacht, *My First Seventy-Six Years*, 238; *The End of Reparations* (London, 1931), 89.

[2]F.R.B.N.Y., Norman to Harrison, no. 126/29, 24 May 1929.

[3]F.R.B.N.Y., Harrison to Norman, no. 181/29, 10 June 1929; Norman to Harrison, no. 152/29, 14 June 1929; Clay, *Lord Norman*, 252–3.

[4]Below, pp. 163–4; Clarke, *Central Bank Cooperation*, 167–8.

[5]Clay, *Lord Norman*, 253; F.R.B.N.Y., Norman to Harrison, no. 202/29, 9 August 1929; Bank of England to F.R.B.N.Y., no. 206/29, 13 August 1929.

per cent.[1] The rise in Bank Rate proved effective in the exchange markets, and the collapse of the speculative boom in New York brought a further easing of the pressure on London. From November, funds began returning to Europe from New York, a factor which constrained sterling's improvement *vis-à-vis* Continental currencies, but meant an end to severe pressure for the time being.[2] The Bank made no open attempt to maintain a high level of short-term rates and allowed market rates to lead Bank Rate downwards.[3] In December, the dollar exchange was sufficiently favourable to London that the Bank received its first post-war arbitrage gold shipments from New York.[4]

The problems of international depression and exchange pressures became the major preoccupations of the Bank as 1930 progressed. In the early part of the year, the Berlin exchange remained weak, and, with the fall in London rates, there was some reflux of funds to New York and some shift in bill finance from New York to London.[5] In the late spring, the American position eased, but the mark exchange remained weak. Late May brought the beginnings of a major gold movement to Paris, to which the uncertainty as to the exact gold export point from mid-June onwards proved only a minor impediment. This weakness in the Continental exchanges caused serious concern at the Bank[6] and in August the Bank attempted to reduce the weakness somewhat through operations with its dollar exchange reserves with some slight success. However, the autumn brought the usual seasonal pressures on sterling, heightened by the effects of uncertainty as to the future of Germany and reparations payments, by the first signs of distrust of sterling and by the backwash of a financial crisis in France.[7] To meet these, the Bank lost both gold and dollars, and received supplementary assistance from both New York and Paris. As the autumn pressures developed, there was an increasing feeling, in both London and New York, that the British Authorities would have to take fundamental deflationary measures to meet the deterioration in the exchange position.[8]

---

[1]F.R.B.N.Y., Norman to Harrison, no. 250/29, 7 September 1929; Below, p. 164.
[2]F.R.B.N.Y., Case to Harvey, no. 355/29, 12 December 1929.
[3]F.R.B.N.Y., Norman to Harrison, no. 299/29, 28 October 1929; Harvey to Harrison no. 335/29, 11 December 1929. However, see below, p. 190.
[4]F.R.B.N.Y., Bank of England to Crane, no. 336/29, 11 December 1929.
[5]F.R.B.N.Y., Norman to Harrison, no. 98/30, 12 April 1930; Harrison to Norman, no. 94/30, 10 April 1930. Between 31 March and 31 May, 1930 the short-term British liabilities of New York banks rose by $100 million. Federal Reserve Board, *Banking and Monetary Statistics*, Table 161. At this time there was also a minor revival in stock market activity in New York.
[6]Below, p. 240; F.R.B.N.Y., Harvey to Harrison, nos 135 and 153/30, 18 June and 17 July 1930; Norman to Harrison, no. 171/30, 22 August 1930.
[7]Clay, *Lord Norman*, 369.
[8]Ibid., 369; Clarke, *Central Bank Cooperation*, 176; F.R.B.N.Y., Record of Certain

1930 ended with all the exchanges relatively weak and with only the dollar exchange clearly above the gold export point.

The new year brought no reduction in uncertainty for the Bank. The gold drain to the Continent, especially to France, continued unabated, encouraged somewhat by changes in the Bank of France's gold import regulations which removed uncertainty as to the gold export point from London; the dollar exchange remained weak; and the forward exchanges fell below the gold export point, an indication of the lack of confidence that existed in the future of sterling.[1] Opinion in London increasingly moved towards the view that only 'radical measures' could remedy the underlying situation.[2] Between March and June the exchange position eased somewhat and the Bank gained foreign reserves. True, after May, the spreading European financial crisis occupied much of the Bank's time, but it did not impair the reserve position of the Bank, except insofar as the Bank granted assistance to crisis-swept European central banks.[3] In fact, up to July, the Bank had withstood successfully the strains of a developing current account deficit, a moderate withdrawal of short-term funds, perhaps totalling £65 million and the beginnings of a European liquidity crisis.[4] Its reserves were not large by previous standards, but they were largely unchanged from six months earlier. A large portion was to disappear, directly or indirectly, in the crisis which broke on London on 15 July and which is discussed in Chapter 8.

Having completed our sketch of background conditions we can now turn to a more detailed examination of the policies followed by the Bank in its efforts to manage sterling on gold at $4.86.

Conversations in London and Paris, November 11–December 17 1930. Conversation with Dr Sprague, December 5 1930; Below, pp. 240–1.

[1]Clay, *Lord Norman*, 371; *The Economist*, 7 and 20 February 1931; Einzig, *Theory of Forward Exchange*, 260.

[2]T160/430/F12317/2, S. D. Waley, Notes of a Conversation between Leith-Ross, Siepmann and Sprague, 30 January 1931; Leith-Ross, Talk with Hopkins and the Governor on Gold Movements, 17 February 1931; F.R.B.N.Y., Norman to Harrison, no. 40/31, 12 February 1931; Clay, *Lord Norman*, 372.

[3]Ibid., 375–83; Clarke, *Central Bank Cooperation*, 185–201.

[4]Williams, 'London and the 1931 Financial Crisis', 528.

6. AGGREGATE FINANCIAL POLICY, 1925–1931

Any analysis of the role of official policy in the non-adjustment of the British economy to $4.86 must necessarily begin with an examination of official use of the instruments of financial policy. At the time of the decision to return to gold, these instruments, in particular the Bank Rate mechanism, were expected to bear the brunt of any 'residual' adjustment burdens that existed, after allowing for expected favourable developments abroad, and to successfully manage the exchange thereafter.

As Chapter 5 has indicated, the favourable external developments expected by the Chancellor's advisers to ease the adjustment to $4.86 did not materialise. Except for a relatively unexpected expansion in the volume of world trade to 1929, events generally turned out in the direction opposite to that forecast. Given this outcome, the burden for the traditional instruments of financial policy was particularly great–probably greater than any required during the nineteenth century gold standard period. The induced effects of the appreciation of the sterling exchange to $4.86, by depressing exports and increasing imports, had moderated the balance of payments effects of the appreciation and had reduced domestic demand. From November 1924 the British economy entered a period of recession that was to last over a year and a half, a recession that originated largely in the external sector.[1] However, if the Authorities were to make a successful adjustment to $4.86 using the traditional instruments of financial policy, the deflation resulting from the induced effects of the appreciation of sterling during 1924–5 would have to be supplemented by additional domestic deflation, if the deflation–wage reductions method of adjustment was to be successful. It is from this point that any discussion of official 'adjustment' policy must begin.

---

[1]Although world import demand grew by 7.8 per cent in 1925, British exports, by volume, were below those of 1924; whereas, British imports rose by 2.6 per cent. The deterioration in Britain's external position in 1924 and 1925, at constant prices, amounted to almost 40 per cent of the change in Gross Domestic Product in those two years or $3\frac{1}{2}$ per cent of G.D.P. in 1925. See also A. F. Burns and W. C. Mitchell, *Measuring Business Cycles* (New York, 1946), Table 16.

The Treasury

Given the more general goal of a balanced (or a surplus) budget, two main preoccupations dominated Treasury policy in the 1920s: the determination to reduce 'the problem of the public debt' and the desire to control, and if possible to reduce, public spending to allow reductions in taxation. The former concern generally took priority, despite periodic economy campaigns, partially because the reduction and conversion to lower rates of interest of the national debt was seen as the means of achieving the latter goal, particularly as the other major element in expenditure, the social services, was largely a function of the level of employment.

The war had increased the nominal value of the public debt from £706.2 million on 31 March 1914 to £7,875.6 million on 31 March 1920 and had considerably shortened its maturity structure.[1] This change in the size and the composition of the debt, in addition to its effects on Government expenditure[2] forced the Authorities to be in the market continually, taking in old issues and putting out new. The shortness of the debt introduced complications into the budgetary process as interest rates fluctuated with monetary policy,[3] and it made Treasury policy peculiarly dependent on the market, as market expectations of future interest rates affected the success of particular placements. These management problems, particularly the memory of the ever-present threat in 1920 of being unable to meet day-to-day revenue needs at short-term,[4] plus the dictates of classical political economy which emphasised that sound public debt policy required long-term or perpetual issues, provided the impetus towards funding throughout the interwar period. Between March 1920 and March 1925, in addition to reducing the total debt outstanding by £209.8 million (foreign debt reduction £108.5 million), the funding policy successfully reduced the proportion of the debt in the floating debt and converted a large portion to periods beyond fifteen years. However, as its 1925 evidence to the Colwyn Committee on National Debt and Taxation indicated, the Treasury was determined still to reduce further the floating debt as circumstances allowed and to fund maturing debt if at all possible.[5] This determination provided the foundation for debt management policy after 1925.

---

[1]Pember and Boyle, *British Government Securities*, 385, 397.

[2]Interest charges in 1919–20 financial years exceeded total Government expenditure in 1914 by over 70 per cent. Mitchell and Deane, *Abstract*, Public Finance 4.

[3]A change in interest rates from 4.25 per cent to 6.45 per cent on the 1925 volume of Treasury bills outstanding would have altered interest payments by £12 million or 1.5 per cent of total central Government expenditure. Committee on National Debt and Taxation, *Report*, Cmd. 2800 (London, 1927), para. 184.

[4]Sayers, *Financial Policy 1939–1945*, 148; Clay, *Lord Norman*, 177ff.; Morgan, *Studies*, 114–15.

[5]T160/194/F7380/02, Ways and Means Advances, Treasury Bills, October 1924;

Between 1925 and 1929 the national debt fell slightly, by £45 million, and between 1929 and 1931 by a further £38 million. If, however, one excludes the Government's external war debts which fell throughout the period, one finds that 'internal' debt fell in the two periods by £8.1 and £19.9 million respectively.[1] However, these changes give no indication of the changes in private sector holdings by U.K. residents. If one removes public sector and non-resident holdings of 'internal' debt, as shown in Appendix 3, Table 17, one finds that private sector holdings by U.K. residents probably fell throughout the period, with most of the fall occurring between 1925 and 1929. However, as the margin of error is fairly large, the best assumption seems to be that resident private sector holdings of the national debt remained roughly constant between 1925 and 1931.

However, within a roughly constant total, changes in the maturity structure could affect decisions concerning and preferences for other assets. In Appendix 3, estimates of the maturity structure of official and foreign holdings of 'internal' U.K. debt are made which take one a long way in analysing the net effects of debt management policy on private sector portfolios.

Generally speaking changes in overseas and known official debt holdings do not appear to have greatly affected the private sector's share of various maturities, except in the classes under five years (including floating debt) and 15–25 years where movements in official holdings served to heighten the effects of funding and in other securities where official funds took up most of the increase in the outstanding debt. In 1930–1 changes in official holdings of Treasury bills mitigated the overall decline in their supply, as far as the private sector was concerned,[2] but this was exceptional. Thus the upshot of the changes in official and overseas holdings during the period after 1925 was that, although total private sector resident holdings of the national debt remained roughly constant, their composition changed considerably. Between 1925 and 1929, although private sector holdings of Treasury bills rose from £426.7 to £484.5 million,[3] the market became less liquid

Hawtrey to Niemeyer, 23 October 1924; Committee on National Debt and Taxation, *Minutes of Evidence* (London, 1927), Niemeyer, Q. 8689–90; Bradbury, Evidence in chief, para. 7 and 9, Q.9221, 9223. For later expressions of the same attitude see T175/46, Hopkins, Conversion Loan and Paying off Treasury Bills, 1930; Macmillan Committee, *Evidence*, Q. 5433.

[1] Pember and Boyle, *British Government Securities*, 407, 415, 419.

[2] In 1929–30 market Treasury bills fell by £79.8 million, whereas in 1930–1 there was some reversal of the trend, for, although the total supply fell by £19.1 million, official holdings fell by £68.4 million, thus partially restoring the previous position. T175/46, Treasury Bill Figures; Pember and Boyle, *British Government Securities*, 494–5; H.M. Treasury, Issue Department: Bank of England, Treasury Bills and Securities to 28 February 1935.

[3] T175/46, Treasury Bill Figures, undated.

in all other respects as it came to hold a smaller proportion of its portfolio in short maturities. After 1929, the supply of market Treasury bills fell sharply, by 16.5 per cent in 1929–30,[1] and, even with the decline in known official holdings in 1930–1, this meant that the market's supply had fallen by over 6 per cent in two years. The period after 1929 also saw a continuation of previous trends in areas other than the floating debt. Thus overall the events of the period 1925–31 saw private sector holdings of debt under five years fall by roughly £550 million, its holdings between five and fifteen years remain roughly unchanged, and its holdings above fifteen years rise by roughly £500 million. Thus the private sectors' holdings of the national debt became progressively less liquid.[2] Throughout the period, the national debt as a proportion of the value of fixed assets remained roughly unchanged at about $\frac{2}{5}$ having risen from $\frac{1}{40}$ in 1914 to $\frac{1}{4}$ in 1920 before being carried up to the 1925–31 level by falling prices.[3] The overall balance between Government debt and fixed assets thus remained roughly constant, only the maturity distribution of the former changed greatly.

Before a discussion of the effects of changes in the size or maturity structure of private holdings of the national debt is possible, a general discussion of Bank of England monetary policy is necessary. However, at this point, the general trends in Treasury policy are clear. Through debt policy, the Treasury after 1925 successfully managed to increase the average maturity of the debt outstanding from between 15 and 25 years to over 25 years while keeping the total in private sector hands roughly constant. At the same time, the policy of balanced or slight surplus central government budgets that made this debt management policy possible was an additional background factor to the monetary policy of the period after 1925.

The total supply fell by 15.9 per cent.
[2]This illiquidity was heightened by changes in the security holdings of the clearing banks. Between March 1925 and March 1929, the benchmark years for most debt calculations in this study, clearing bank holdings of bills and investments, both of which would tend to be predominantly in Government issues and the maturity of which would largely be, on *a priori* grounds, under five years, fell by £40 million or by less than the fall in private holdings. Between March 1929 and March 1931, they rose by over £100 million, thus substantially increasing the portfolio pressure on the rest of the private sector.
For the period 1930–1, this suggestion of illiquidity has been challenged by the suggestion that war loan 1924–47 offered investors a relatively risk free, high yield investment. This issue had been available until 1928 and on 31 March 1929 the total outstanding was £2.2 billion. However, it was subject to some considerable price fluctuations, the 1930–1 range being $105\frac{3}{16}$–$90\frac{1}{2}$. See U.K. Hicks, *The Finance of British Government 1920–1936* (London, 1938), 355–6.
[3]Morgan, *Studies*, 155; Mitchell and Deane, *Abstract*, National Income and Expenditure, 7.

The Bank of England

At the time of the decision to return to the gold standard, the Governor expected that a high Bank Rate and a period of tight money would be necessary to aid the adjustment to $4.86. Although this expectation continued to exist for a short time after 28 April, Norman's correspondence with Strong and his comments to others as recorded by Clay, with occasional exceptions, suggests that the more abstract idea of adjustment reverted to the back of the Governor's mind and that the day-to-day problems of exchange management took pride of place.[1] Thus the most appropriate context for a discussion of the Bank's aggregate management of the gold standard after 1925 appears to be the more general one of management goals and criteria in relation to the gold standard rather than that of adjustment.

Throughout the period after 1925, the Bank recognised its primary duty as being the maintenance of the international exchange value of the pound. As Sir Ernest Harvey, the Deputy Governor of the Bank, put it to the Macmillan Committee:[2]

The principal duty of the Central Bank is to maintain in the general interest of the community the stability of the national monetary unit ... Now in a gold standard world, the maintenance of the stability of the national monetary unit means, I take it, the maintenance of its stability in relation to gold as the common international denominator.

All other matters were subsidiary to that aim.[3] Given this overriding goal, the Bank took 'the total effect of all foreign influence' as the determining factor in the formulation of policy, although it admitted that it also considered such factors as prices and employment.[4] In giving attention to the foreign influence, the Bank looked at more than the foreign exchange value of sterling, for it also considered the size of the gold reserve, the season of the year, the size of prospective future gold demands and the condition of the money market – its rates and the general character and volume of its funds – in the determination of policy.[5] Even this list is not exhaustive, for as Norman put it to the Macmillan Committee: 'I cannot say that there are hard and fast facts which would guide me in all circumstances.'[6] However, the general thrust of the Bank's evidence confirms the central tendency of its post-1925 aggregate policy, its emphasis on the short term. Throughout the period, the central concern of the Bank lay with particular markets,

[1]Above, p. 131.; below, p. 164.
[2]Macmillan Committee, *Evidence*, Q. 3.
[3]Ibid.
[4]Ibid., Q. 348, 349, 350, 3322, 3451.
[5]Ibid., Q. 338, 348, 7512.
[6]Ibid., Q. 3485.

particularly those for gold, foreign exchange, securities and money.[1] Within these or related markets, the Bank did not normally concern itself with actual statistics of volumes of funds or general trends: it did not worry ostensibly about the balance of payments, the volume of acceptances outstanding, the volume of foreign funds in London, or even the note holdings of the clearing banks in a statistical sense, if only because it did not have or try to develop the statistics.[2] Rather it normally focused its attention on particular rates or particular signs of stress available to it from its market relationships – discount market borrowing or gold losses for example – and used these as indicators of the feel of the market.[3] The Bank also used the Governor's extensive circle of contacts to extract qualitative estimates of trends in these and other markets.[4] It appears throughout this period to have had a deep aversion to quantitative estimates or statistics, despite the beginnings of a statistical section under W. W. Stewart in 1928.[5] In considering the effects of any policy change, the Bank similarly did not normally go beyond these markets. Throughout its evidence to the Macmillan Committee, the Bank's emphasis lay not on generalised relationships or criteria but rather on particular circumstances in particular markets. Anything beyond these seemed outside the Bank's ken or its defined area of responsibility, although if particular pressures of circumstances brought them to the Bank's attention it might take them into consideration.[6] It was within this short-term, rather limited context that the Bank attempted, using the methods of 'backing and filling' or 'successive approximation' that are characteristic of central banking,[7] to pursue its overriding policy goal, the maintenance of the sterling parity.

In any discussion of the Bank's conduct of monetary policy after 1925, this combination of an overriding goal and an official concentration on limited markets suggests a similar emphasis in analysis. In this context, perhaps the most useful approach lies in an extension of the type of analysis used in discussions of 'rules of the game'.[8] Such rules represented attempts to set out general principles of 'good' national behaviour in an international system of adjustment and implied that adherence to

[1]Clay, *Lord Norman*, 161–6; D. Williams, 'Montagu Norman and Banking Policy in the Nineteen Twenties', *Yorkshire Bulletin of Economic and Social Research*, XI(1), July 1959, 39–46.
[2]Keynes Papers, Macmillan Committee, Notes of Discussions, 5 December 1930, 26ff.
[3]Macmillan Committee, *Evidence*, Q. 3450–1.
[4]Clay, *Lord Norman*, 276–82.
[5]Macmillan Committee, *Evidence*, Q. 9173–5.
[6]Clay, *Lord Norman*, 165–6; Williams, 'Montagu Norman and Banking Policy', 41.
[7]Above, p. 40; Canada, Royal Commission on Banking and Finance, *Report* (Ottawa 1964), 324.
[8]League of Nations; *International Currency Experience*, 66ff; Bloomfield, *Monetary Policy*, Ch. V.; M. Michaely, *Balance-of-Payments Adjustment Policies* (New York, 1968), esp. Chs 1 and 2.

such rules would improve the efficiency of the system.[1] At this point the concern is not really whether the Bank followed or broke any specific rules of the game – if only because the interwar 'rules' hardly touched on the case of a country with over a million unemployed and an overvalued exchange rate – rather the concern is with the Bank's goal of exchange maintenance and its use of aggregate policies to this end.

Ideally such an analysis would begin with the plotting of several policy variables against exchange variations. However, as the number of relevant exchanges is too large for any coherent diagrammatic presentation and as changes in the stock of international reserves serves as an equally good index of changes in the balance of payments position in an overall sense, the analysis begins with movements in the Bank's stock of international reserve assets, both owned and borrowed.[2] It then moves on to consider the Bank's policy responses to changes in its reserve position, particularly changes in Bank Rate, that barometer for many domestic interest rates and for expectations, and changes in the Bank's holdings of securities or open market operations. Finally, the analysis considers some results of such policy changes on several domestic variables, particularly the behaviour of the banking system and short-term money markets. The variables chosen and their sources appear in Table 12 in the form of seasonally unadjusted quarterly averages for the interwar gold standard period. Table 13 presents a summary of the directions of change for each variable from the average of the previous quarter. Figure 3 provides a rough guide to conditions abroad by comparing Bank Rate with the discount rates of central banks in Paris, Berlin and New York during the period.

On the basis of the Bank's reserves of gold and foreign exchange, the Authorities gained reserves in eighteen quarters and lost them in eight quarters between the second quarter of 1925 and the third quarter of 1931. In the eighteen quarters that brought reserve gains, the average gain was £6.5 million of which £4.2 million came in the form of gold. Remembering that gains in foreign exchange were normally

[1] The search for such 'rules' still continues. For recent examples see A. I. Bloomfield 'Rules of the Game of International Adjustment ?', Whittlessey and Wilson, *Essays in Money and Banking*; J. M. Fleming, 'Guidelines for Balance of Payments Adjustment under the Par-Value System', *Essays in International Finance No. 67*, May 1968; O.E.C.D., *The Balance of Payments Adjustment Process* (Paris 1966); essays by Fellner and Machlup in W. Fellner, F. Machlup, R. Triffin, et al., *Maintaining and Restoring Balance in International Payments* (Princeton, 1966).

[2] A chart of movements in the three major exchanges, with the relevant average gold points appears, however, in Figure 1. Ideally the use of the Bank of England's gross international reserves as a guide to international pressures should be supplemented by an indication of its known liabilities, particularly as its official French sterling liabilities were a cause for concern from 1927 onwards. See below, pp. 164 and 240.

TABLE 12. *Monetary Indicators, 1925–31 (£ millions, quarterly averages)*

Indicator	1925				1926				1927				1928			
	I	II	III	IV	I	II	III	IV	I	II	III	IV	I	II	III	IV
Gold reserve	153.8[a]	154.2[a]	160.3	147.2	143.5	146.9	152.3	151.5	149.5	151.4	150.0	149.7	155.5	161.4	172.3	160.7
Exchange reserve	n[d]	0.1	1.9	4.8	8.2	10.2	15.4	18.7	23.8	28.9	32.7	40.6	43.6	45.0	40.2	27.3
Total reserves	153.8	154.3	162.2	152.0	151.7	157.1	167.1	170.2	173.3	180.3	182.7	190.3	199.1	206.4	212.5	188.0
Central bank assistance										2.7	6.3					
Bank Rate (%)	4.29	5.00	4.69	4.31	5.00	5.00	5.00	5.00	4.61	4.50	4.50	4.50	4.50	4.50	4.50	4.50
Three months prime bill rate (%)	4.04	4.44	3.99	4.05	4.48	4.32	4.42	4.60	4.23	4.09	4.33	4.32	4.16	3.94	4.15	4.37
Bank of England – Banking Department:																
Total securities	106.9	99.5	98.0	101.0	101.6	97.1	93.0	92.0	92.4	82.3	85.9	88.6	81.3	75.9	67.1	73.7
Discounts and advances	15.7	14.0	11.7	16.8	19.0	17.0	14.3	16.3	16.2	17.5	14.8	15.0	13.4	10.2	12.1	12.8
Clearing banks:																
Cash reserves	184.3	194.4	183.9	196.8	183.4	192.3	186.1	194.8	183.9	198.2	184.4	195.2	178.9	186.3	184.2	202.8
Short-term assets	337.0	304.2	352.9	346.1	318.8	308.8	344.7	343.2	340.6	328.4	352.8	382.3	367.2	359.6	397.8	395.4
Investments	325.4	309.5	292.8	294.0	287.7	279.3	283.2	287.7	278.2	270.5	270.8	270.7	277.7	269.5	275.0	279.1
Advances	810.9	831.4	822.5	821.8	846.1	855.2	856.7	874.2	889.5	899.7	904.3	903.2	915.3	923.7	921.6	933.7
Deposits	1607.0	1594.6	1596.9	1612.2	1585.1	1587.9	1612.2	1650.3	1634.6	1648.1	1632.5	1699.2	1677.6	1687.2	1714.6	1756.6
Currency outside banks	275.6	282.2	280.0	277.1	267.8	277.4	273.1	269.7	259.8	269.7	270.8	272.5	262.0	272.8	271.3	264.0
Proxy money supply[b]	1882.6	1876.8	1876.9	1889.3	1852.9	1865.3	1885.3	1920.0	1894.4	1917.9	1923.3	1971.5	1931.6	1960.0	1985.9	2020.6
Clearing bank reserve ratio (%)	11.5	12.2	11.5	12.2	11.6	12.1	11.5	11.8	11.3	12.0	11.2	11.5	10.7	11.0	10.7	11.5
Clearing bank short-term asset ratio (%)	21.0	19.1	22.1	21.5	20.1	19.4	21.4	20.8	20.8	19.9	21.3	22.5	21.9	21.3	23.2	22.5

Year and quarter

Indicator	1929				1930				1931		
	I	II	III	IV	I	II	III	IV	I	II	III
Gold reserve	152.0	159.3	141.4	134.2	151.1	159.0	154.7	155.6	141.6	150.9	140.8
Exchange reserve	17.9	20.5	24.6	22.2	16.9	15.2	24.2	25.0	28.3	31.4	21.5
Total reserves	169.9	179.8	166.0	156.4	168.0	174.2	178.9	180.6	169.9	182.3	162.3
Central bank assistance			1.6	1.1				6.3	3.9		60.0[c]
Bank Rate (%)	5.10	5.50	5.56	5.81	4.45	3.17	3.00	3.00	3.00	2.74	4.11
Three months prime bill rate (%)	4.90	5.25	5.48	5.41	3.56	2.32	2.22	2.19	2.47	2.30	3.87
Bank of England – Banking Department:											
Total securities	66.6	62.3	88.9	86.2	64.1	65.1	71.1	68.6	64.5	59.9	74.8
Discounts and advances	13.7	10.9	9.6	9.7	9.3	7.7	8.0	8.9	9.7	8.6	10.5
Clearing banks:											
Cash reserves	186.4	185.8	178.1	198.6	176.3	189.9	183.7	202.5	190.6	181.8	179.1
Short-term assets	364.7	350.0	377.9	369.4	348.9	381.4	418.5	441.1	415.2	360.8	377.7
Investments	278.4	276.7	275.5	269.5	265.9	268.4	288.7	303.1	331.5	295.6	301.8
Advances	960.4	970.1	966.8	958.6	958.9	947.5	922.1	905.3	902.3	932.6	910.8
Deposits	1744.0	1730.5	1734.6	1743.1	1689.5	1732.3	1750.2	1791.3	1746.3	1696.6	1680.7
Currency outside banks	253.2	260.9	261.6	255.4	246.3	257.4	259.4	256.0	249.2	257.6	262.7
Proxy money supply[b]	1997.2	1991.4	1996.2	1998.5	1935.8	1989.7	2009.6	2047.3	1995.5	1953.6	1943.4
Clearing bank reserve ratio (%)	10.7	10.7	10.3	11.4	10.4	11.0	10.5	11.3	10.9	10.7	10.7
Clearing bank short-term asset ratio (%)	20.9	20.2	21.8	21.2	20.7	22.0	23.9	24.6	23.8	21.3	22.5

[a] The gold reserves are as they appeared in the Bank's weekly return and are thus not adjusted, as in Table 7, for the appreciation of sterling before 28 April 1925.

[b] Currency outside banks + Clearing bank deposits.

[c] Some double counting here as the loans were taken into the Bank's foreign exchange reserves.

[d] n = less than £100,000.

Sources: Bank of England.

Bank of England, *Statistical Summary*.

Board of Governors of the Federal Reserve System, *Banking and Monetary Statistics* (Washington, 1943), Table 172.

Committee on Finance and Industry, *Report*, Appendices I and II.

B. R. Mitchell and P. Deane, *Abstract of British Historical Statistics*, Banking and Insurance 9.

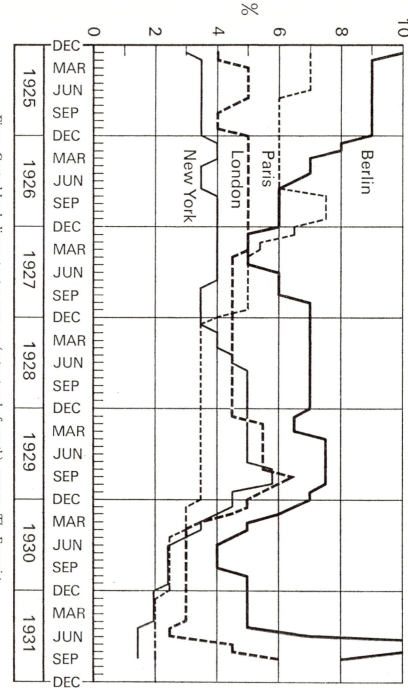

Fig. 3. Central bank discount rates, 1925-31 (rate at end of month). SOURCE: *The Economist.*

offset within the class of Other Securities where they were held,[1] these reserve gains were normally offset by sales of Bank of England securities of £3.9 million and market debt repayments of £1.1 million. In these eighteen gain quarters, total reserves and Bank of England securities moved in opposite directions on thirteen occasions, four of the five movements in parallel directions occurring in quarters when the Bank lost gold reserves but gained more than enough exchange reserves to offset this loss; the market repaid indebtedness to the Bank in eleven of the eighteen gaining quarters. In the eight quarters that brought overall reserves losses, the average fall in the reserves was £13.4 million of which £10.8 million was gold. Remembering again that the Bank normally offset changes in exchange holdings within the class of Other Securities, these quarters saw the Bank increase its total holdings of securities by £4.7 million and the market increase its debt to the Bank by £1.1 million, thus offsetting all but £5.0 million of the reserve loss. In these eight quarters, the Bank bought securities in addition to those internally offsetting the dollar loss on five occasions and the market increased its indebtedness on all but two occasions.[2] Thus the Bank tended largely to offset reserve gains and only partially offset reserve losses (actually reinforcing them when they occurred in the first quarter), and changes in the market's indebtedness to the Bank tended to reinforce the Bank's behaviour in their effects on the cash base. On a total reserve basis, Bank Rate increased in five of those quarters in which reserves fell, decreased in one[3] and remained unchanged in two on an average basis. The quarters of reserve gain saw seven decreases in Bank Rate, two increases[3] and nine occasions when the rate remained unchanged. The rate for three months prime bills rose in all but one of the quarters of total reserve loss and it fell in twelve of the quarters of

[1] The Bank normally sterilised its foreign exchange operations' effects on the domestic credit base through offsetting purchases of Other Securitiess in its balance sheet, so as to hide these operations from the general public and, it seems, the Treasury, For a more complete discussion of the technique and the rationale behind it, see below, p. 185.

[2] If one takes the reserve loss periods by season of the year, the results appear as appear as follows:

(£ million)

Quarter	No. of incidents	Average Reserve loss	(of which Gold)	Average change in banking department securities	Average change in market indebtedness
4th	3	14.8	10.6	+2.3	+1.5
1st	3	9.7	8.8	−3.5	+1.3
3rd	2	16.9	14.0	+20.8	−0.3

[3] Both of these cases represent statistical freaks resulting from the averaging process.

L

TABLE 13. *Changes in selected indicators, 1925–31*

Indicator	1925 II	III	IV	1926 I	II	III	IV	1927 I	II	III	IV	1928 I	II	III	IV	1929 I	II	III	IV	1930 I	II	III	IV	1931 I	II	III
Gold reserves	+	+	−	−	+	+	−	−	+	+	−	+	+	+	−	−	+	+	−	+	+	−	+	−	+	−
Exchange reserves	+	+	+	+	+	+	+	+	+	+	+	+	+	−	−	+	+	+	−	−	−	+	+	+	+	−
Total reserves	+	+	−	−	+	+	+	+	+	+	+	+	+	+	+	+	+	+	−	+	+	+	+	+	−	+
Central bank assistance				+				+	−	−		+	+	+				+		−			+	+	−	+
Bank Rate	+		−	+						+	−					+	+	+	+	−	−	−	+	−	−	−
Three months prime bill rate	+	+	+	+	−	−		−	+	−	−	−	−	−	+	+	+	+	+	−	−	−	+	+	−	+
Bank of England securities	−	−	−	+	−	−	+	+	−	+	−	−	−	−	−	+	+	+	+	−	−	−	+	+	−	+
Discounts and advances	−	−	−	+	−	−	−	+	−	+	−	+	−	+	+	+	−	−	+	−	+	+	−	+	−	+
Total securities and discounts and advances	−	−	−	+	−	−	−	+	−	+	−	−	−	+	+	+	−	−	+	−	+	+	−	+	−	+
Clearing bank cash reserves	−	−	+	−	+	+	+	−	+	−	+	−	+	+	+	−	−	+	+	+	+	+	+	−	+	+
Clearing bank short assets	−	+	−	−	−	−	−	−	−	+	+	+	−	−	+	−	+	−	−	+	+	+	−	+	−	+
Clearing bank investments	−	−	+	+	+	+	+	+	+	+	−	−	+	+	+	−	−	−	−	+	+	+	+	+	+	+
Clearing bank advances	+	−	−	+	+	+	+	+	+	+	+	+	+	+	+	+	+	−	−	+	−	−	−	−	+	−
Clearing bank deposits	−	+	+	−	+	+	+	−	+	−	+	−	+	+	+	−	+	+	+	−	+	+	+	−	+	−
Currency outside banks	+	+	−	−	−	+	−	−	+	−	+	−	+	−	+	+	+	+	−	+	+	+	−	−	+	+
Proxy money supply	−	+	+	−	+	+	+	−	+	+	+	−	+	+	+	−	+	+	+	−	+	+	+	−	+	−

+ means increase from previous quarter; − means decrease from previous quarter.

Source: Table 12.

eserve gain. The differential between Bank Rate and the bill rate tended o narrow by eight points in periods of reserve loss and widen by three points in periods of reserve gain. Thus interest rates tended to move in an equilibrating direction on most occasions, although the Bank was less inclined to lower Bank Rate in periods of reserve gain than it was to raise t in periods of reserve loss. Throughout the period, the evidence suggests that the Bank's policies tended to operate in a direction that would damp down economic activity[1] in that it was generally unwilling to allow reserve gains to greatly affect the cash base or interest rates but willing to allow reserve losses to affect the same variables.

In terms of the pressures faced by the Bank, the period after 1925 seems to divide itself into two equal parts as it did in the narrative and balance of payments sections of Chapter 5. In the first thirteen quarters to mid-1928, the Bank only lost reserves in a total sense on one occasion, a period of two quarters covering late 1925 and early 1926. During this period it lost gold in six quarters, lost foreign exchange in none and had central bank assistance outstanding in two quarters. After mid-1928, on the other hand, the Bank lost reserves in an overall sense in six quarters, lost gold in seven quarters, sold foreign exchange in seven and had assistance from other central banks outstanding in five quarters. Whereas, before mid-1928, the Bank gained both gold and foreign exchange in seven quarters, after that date it managed to do so in only three. This greater pressure was communicated to the financial system as Bank Rate rose, on an average basis, in five quarters instead of two, as bill rates rose in seven quarters instead of six, as clearing bank reserves fell in nine quarters instead of six, as clearing bank deposits fell in five quarters instead of three, and as the money supply proxy fell in seven quarters instead of five, the majority of these last falls occurring after 1929. To the trends in the banking system resulting from changes in reserves and the Bank's response thereto the discussion now turns.

With the clearing banks' figures, one is faced with a heavily seasonal pattern in the behaviour of the relevant statistical series as there was window dressing over and above the normal levels in the June and December balance sheets, as there was a seasonal pattern in the availability of commercial and Treasury bills and as there was a seasonal pattern for tax payments. In Table 12 the statistics reflect these seasonal

---

The one decrease occurred in a quarter where Bank Rate moved downwards at the start and upwards at the end. The two increases reflect changes in Bank Rate which occurred in the previous quarter but which were operative for the first time for a full quarter.

[1] On a quarterly average basis, reserves rose by £8.0 million while Banking Department assets fell by £37.3 million over the whole period.

swings fairly clearly. The banking statistics for the period are also rendered much less useful in some respects by the fact that the banks tended to increase their window dressing in normal months when it was profitable for them to do so owing to heavy demands for industrial accommodation or favourable investment opportunities.[1] However, even with these limitations in the statistics, certain trends for the period after 1925 emerge fairly clearly.

Throughout the period after 1925, the banks worked with levels of cash reserves which were constant or gently falling. In Table 12, this stability is extremely noticeable, as is the tendency for seasonal increases in reserves to be constrained and decreases to be accentuated in the period after 1928. However, the effects of this stability in the cash base were minimised for a considerable period after 1925 by the fall in the average ratio of cash to deposits for the system of about 1 per cent. This fall reflected the movement by the Midland Bank, and to a lesser extent by Barclays, to lower working reserve ratios.[2] However, 1929 saw the completion of this process of adjustment to post-amalgamation conditions for the banks concerned, and thereafter given changes in Bank of England policy had potentially greater effects on the banks. Nevertheless, the reduction in reserve ratios prior to 1929 allowed the banking system to build an increased structure of deposits on the relatively stable reserve base. The overall growth of deposits was constrained in 1925, but thereafter it was fairly continuous until the end of 1928. In 1929 the growth was halted by official restraint, although the effects of this restraint were reduced by some decline in reserve ratios. Although the growth of deposits resumed briefly in 1930, the expansion soon gave way to a renewed fall so that by the third quarter of 1931 bank deposits stood at the level of the first quarter of 1928.

The deposit growth of 1925–9 was accompanied by a relatively stable ratio of short-term assets to deposits and a falling investments ratio. Thus clearing bank advances, after moving irregularly in 1925 were able to rise with two very slight interruptions to the second quarter of 1929. Thereafter, however, they ceased to grow and, with two interruptions, they fell until the end of the period as banks reacted to increased reserve pressures and industrial uncertainty by increasing their short-term assets and investments as advances fell due or as reserves rose.

Thus, up to the end of 1928, the effects of gold movements and general monetary policy on the domestic economy were relatively limited, at best creating slight restraining pressures on an expansion originating elsewhere. Interest rates were relatively high in historical terms, but the availability of bank finance at these high rates does not appear to have

[1] Balogh, *Studies*, 54; R. S. Sayers, *Modern Banking*, 2nd ed. (Oxford, 1947), 40.
[2] Balogh, *Studies*, 43; E. Nevin, 'Monetary Policy Again', *Bulletin of the Oxford University Institute of Statistics*, xiv (8), August 1952, 287.

been greatly impaired, except perhaps in the sense that a greater expansion of the monetary base might have allowed even more bank lending. Thereafter, the position was somewhat reversed and, as the banking system became relatively more open to pressures resulting from gold movements and monetary policy, finance appears to have become less readily available. After rising with Bank Rate in 1929, interest rates on bank advances fell, although the normal lending minimum of, probably, 5 per cent which became operative as Bank Rate fell meant that the relatively low rates of 1930–1 were probably not passed fully on to industry.[1] As business conditions became less favourable and bank advances even less liquid than they had been previously,[2] the banks moved to increase their liquidity, encouraged by favourable shifts in relative interest rates between securities and advances, by increasing their holding of short-term assets and Government Securities. Thus, despite lower interest rates for a large part of the time – at the short end of the market at least – the years after 1928 saw monetary policy as being more restrictive than did those immediately following the return to gold.

The Overall Impact of Bank and Treasury Policy

When the trends in Treasury debt management policy are combined with those of monetary policy, the impression of two somewhat contrasting periods in the years after 1925 is heightened. Up to late 1928 or early 1929, relatively high, in an historical sense, but relatively stable short-term interest rates and the Treasury's funding policy appear to have had perhaps a restraining influence on the development of economic activity. Throughout the period, portfolio holders could hold increased bank deposits, a roughly constant total of commercial and Treasury bills and a roughly constant amount of currency. Under these conditions, they appear to have been willing, given the relatively favourable business conditions, to hold an increasing proportion of their portfolio of Government securities at slightly longer maturities and to hold increasing quantities of new private sector issues at slightly falling yields. Equities became increasingly attractive to investors as their rise in price and fall in yield in Table 14 indicate. Such securities provided investors with a hedge in portfolios which were becoming increasingly laden with long-

[1]Generally speaking, the advances rate was fixed at Bank Rate plus 1 per cent with a minimum. However, it is difficult to sort out exactly what was the minimum rate on advances before the Bank Rate clause became operative. Sayers, 'Bank Rate in the Twentieth Century', 61, 78; Balogh, Studies, 75; Macmillan Committee, Evidence, Q. 3435–9, 7597.

[2]See Norman's comment in Moreau, Souvenirs, 330. See also E. Nevin and E. W. Davis, The London Clearing Banks, (London, 1970), 176, 178.

TABLE 14.   *Selected assets, prices and yields, 1925–31*

Year	Average bank deposits (£m)	Commercial bills taxed (£m)	Market Treasury bills— 31 March (£m)	Average currency outside banks (£m)	Total domestic new issues (£m)	Total new issues (£m)	Average Bank Rate (%)	Average three months prime bill rate (%)	Average 2½ per cent Consols (%)	Average new debenture yield (%)	Ordinary shares Price (1958 = 100)	Ordinary shares Dividend yield (%)
1925	1603	633	427	279	132	220	4.57	4.13	4.44	6.43	41	n.a.
1926	1609	493	436	272	140	253	5.00	4.45	4.55	6.48	43	6.91
1927	1659	508	501	268	176	315	4.65	4.24	4.56	6.21	46	6.12
1928	1709	563	458	268	219	362	4.50	4.16	4.47	6.10	53	5.60
1929	1738	520	485	258	159	254	5.49	5.26	4.60	6.10	52	6.13
1930	1741	440	405	255	127	236	3.40	2.57	4.48	5.96	42	7.26
1931	1709[a]	328	454	257[a]	43	89	3.28[a]	2.88[a]	4.31	6.33	43	8.03

n.a. = not available.
[a] First nine months.

Sources: Table 12.
T175/46, Treasury Bill Figures, Undated.
T. Balogh, *Studies in Financial Organisation* (Cambridge, 1947), Table XXXIX
A. T. K. Grant, *A Study of the Capital Market in Britain from 1919–36*, 2nd ed. (London, 1967), 64.
London and Cambridge Economic Service, *The British Economy, Key Statistics*, Table M.
Midland Bank Review.

term Governments. The falling yields on new debenture issues of the private sector relative to those on Governments also suggests that the diversification extended in this direction.

However, share prices began to fall away early in 1929, before the decline in industrial production or the spectacular break in share prices in New York. High interest rates and increased uncertainty resulted in a fall in new issues for domestic purposes, despite the informal controls that existed on some types of overseas lending.[1] After the break in the New York stock exchange boom and the late autumn reductions in Bank Rate, short interest rates fell away from their previous peak, in many cases more quickly than Bank Rate, as the volume of Treasury and commercial bills fell more rapidly than the demand, but longer term yields remained high. These higher yields continued until the end of the period under consideration, particularly on private sector issues as the business outlook worsened and uncertainty increased, despite the continued existence of informal controls on some types of overseas lending. During this period, the volume of bank deposits was constant or falling and the supply of both commercial and Treasury bills fell. Funding, which continued unabated, probably added a further destabilising element to the already difficult situation. It meant that the private sector, in difficult conditions, was asked to unbalance portfolios more than previously and in the opposite direction than the pressures created by the contemporary financial situation really required. Deteriorating industrial conditions and general uncertainty were already restraining private sector capital issues and the high long-term interest rates necessary to induce portfolio holders to hold increasing volumes of longer term securities and fewer liquid assets as a result of official funding certainly did nothing to ease the situation. Moreover, uncertainty and high interest rates affected equities most severely, for their attractiveness as a hedge in portfolios to fixed interest securities fell with the level of activity and prices, and new equity issues declined even more than total home issues as yields reached twentieth century peaks.[2] At the same time, the pattern of asset yields and the pressures on the banking system to restrain, or even to reduce or reverse, deposit growth removed another source of industrial finance while further reducing the supply of short-term securities outside the banking and the public sectors. Thus the whole pattern of post-1928 financial policy was generally more deflationary than previously.[3] Prior to 1929, pressure existed, but

[1]Below, p. 212.
[2]A. T. K. Grant, *A Study of the Capital Market in Britain*, 135.
[3]The one bright spot in this picture lay in housebuilding, where, although interest rates remained high, falling housebuilding costs and increased building society deposits meant that both the availability of funds and the cost of houses were moving in directions that would stimulate demand and reduce the impact of the

industry remained somewhat insulated from its effects as funds remained available – at a price. Thereafter, funds became less available and, as the United Kingdom moved into depression, although short-term interest rates fell away from their 1929 peaks, longer term interest rates remained high or moved even higher, as the private sector became increasingly illiquid in conditions of uncertainty. Industry faced a funds famine. Monetary and debt management policy certainly did not cause the slump, but they did nothing to ease the passage of the domestic economy through difficult times in the period before Britain left gold.

slump. Richardson and Aldcroft, *Building in the British Economy between the Wars,* Statistical Appendix to Ch. 2, Table 7; Ch. 9.

7. THE PRESSURES ON THE BANK'S POLICY POSITION—THE ORIGINS OF MORAL SUASION AND POLICY INNOVATIONS

In the previous discussion of the Bank's aggregate policy, the Bank of England's evidence to the Macmillan Committee, with its concentration on the sterling exchange and a selection of short-term markets, served as a guide. In that discussion, the slightly deflationary bias of the Bank's policy came out clearly, as in previous chapters did the incomplete nature of the post-1925 adjustments to the situation of overvaluation. However, an examination of the Bank's public statements as to its policy goals and of its aggregate policies does not exhaust the list of post-1925 policy possibilities. For the Bank's policy position in the years after 1925 was much more complex than its public pronouncements would suggest. To fully understand the range of responses to the post-1925 world one must go somewhat more deeply into the policy-making environment and the limitations experienced by the Bank on its freedom of action.

Legally, of course, the Bank of England was a private company. By the time of Bagehot, however, the Bank had come to accept wider public responsibilities and these were well defined before the outbreak of war in 1914.[1] But despite this wider perspective, the Bank and the public still set great store by the Bank's formal independence. The Macmillan Committee, in Keynes' words, accurately set out the general contemporary opinion on the subject.[2]

The major objectives of a sound monetary policy ... cannot be attained except by the constant excercise of knowledge, judgement and authority, by individuals placed in a position of unchallengeable independence with great resources and every technical device at their disposition ... The managing authority should be the Bank of England ... an excellent instrument for the purpose; independent of political influences, yet functioning solely in the public interest ... entrenched in the centre of the struggle for profit and with access to the arcana of the market, yet aloof and untinged by the motives of private gain.

[1]Fetter, *Development of British Monetary Orthodoxy*, Ch. IX.
[2]Macmillan Committee, *Report*, para, 280–1. The attribution to Keynes is that of Sir Theodore Gregory, 'The "Norman Conquest" Reconsidered', 4.

During the 1920s the tide of opinion ran very strongly in favour of the independence of central banks from political pressures,[1] and civil servants stressed the Bank's independence time and again to their political superiors. The strongest statement of principle came, characteristically, from Sir Otto Niemeyer in the course of one of the Treasury's two surveys of opinion after 1925 on the Bank–Treasury relationship at times of changes in Bank Rate:[2]

There never has been, either in my time or previously, any 'consultation' between the Bank of England and the Treasury in any shape or form with regard to changes in bank rate. In pre-war days a change in bank rate was no more regarded as the business of the Treasury than the colour which the Bank painted its front door; and while a change is obviously of different importance now, it is both by law and custom a matter for the Bank of England. . .

As far as regards 'information', my recollection is clear that neither I or any Minister under whom I served was directly informed by the Bank in advance that the rate would be put up. What usually happened was that we were aware from the general facts of the situation that a change in rate might be necessary; but I do not recollect anything more.

The others questioned in these surveys, Lord Chalmers, Lord Bradbury and Sir Basil Blackett, corroborated Niemeyer's statement, and Blackett recalled the reversion to the pre-war practice of no prior information and no consultation after the *abnormal* period of the war (during which the Bank Act had been suspended and the Treasury's desire for cheap war finance had been dominant) at the Treasury's request in 1920.[3] Lord Bradbury summed up the peacetime situation by noting that:[4]

anything which savoured of interference (or even undue curiosity) was to be avoided. I don't remember a Chancellor of the Exchequer 'refusing to be told' but such an attitude would be quite in accordance with the feeling.

During the 1920s, what the Bank told the Treasury, outside the sphere defined by legislation and custom, was largely its decision, and this meant that in areas beyond changes in Bank Rate that the Treasury did not learn of the Bank's holdings of over $200 million in New York during the discussions surrounding the Currency and Bank Notes Act

[1] C. H. Kisch and W. A. Elkin, *Central Banks*, (London, 1928), 17; Clay, *Lord Norman*, 282–4.

[2] T176/13, Relations between the Treasury and the Bank of England, Testimony of former Permanent Secretaries and Controllers of Finance, Niemeyer to Phillips, 18 February 1929.

[3] Ibid., Blackett to Phillips, 17 February 1929. See also Cockayne's comments to the Cunliffe Committee (T185/2, 506, 529) as to the respective roles of Treasury and the Bank in exchange management.

[4] Ibid., Bradbury to Phillips, 18 February 1929.

1928.[1] After the Act came into force, the Treasury did learn of some of the Bank's exchange holdings, but not all, when these were carried in Other Securities in the Issue Department, the holdings of which were communicated monthly to the Treasury under the terms of the Act from November 1928.[2] However, the 1928 Act did not cover the Banking Department's holdings of foreign exchange, with the result that the Treasury only knew of the up to £13.5 million in foreign exchange carried in the Issue Department, while the Bank's total holdings fluctuated between £13 and £28 million during the rest of the gold standard period. This lack of knowledge on the part of the Treasury certainly affected the Treasury's appreciation of certain situations.[3]

However, despite these comments from Treasury officials and this example of Bank behaviour, it would be a delusion to see the Bank of the 1920s as a completely independent agent or the Treasury as not attempting to influence the Bank as to the means it believed appropriate to the achievement of the agreed end, the maintenance of the gold standard. True, the Treasury generally did not carry its pressures or express its doubts outside informal channels, and it always maintained in its answers to Parliamentary questions the complete independence of the Bank.[4] The Cabinet in its one gold standard period discussion of a change in Bank Rate, before the public announcement of the increase of 1 per cent to $5\frac{1}{2}$ per cent on 7 February 1929, concluded that 'His Majesty's Government has no responsibility for the movement of Bank Rate and does not control the policy of the Bank of England.'[5] It thus affirmed the tradition of non-intervention in a formal sense. Nevertheless, within the formal facade of non-interference and independence, the opportunities for informal pressures were extensive. The Governor, or when he was absent his Deputy, called frequently at the Treasury, and members of the Treasury did the reverse in the performance of their duties with regard to Treasury Bills and Government loans.[6] Thus the Treasury normally knew the Bank's opinions as to current developments[7] and opportunities existed for mutual influence. It was

[1]F.R.B.N.Y., Strong Papers, Memorandum on the Currency and Bank Note Bill, 24 May 1928; below, p. 183.

[2]T160/511/F8759/01, Lubbock to Hopkins, 23 July 1928; Hopkins to Norman and Lubbock, 3 August 1928.

[3]H.M. Treasury, Issue Department: Bank of England, Treasury Bills and Securities to 28 February 1935; Bank of England, Economic Intelligence Department, Holdings of Foreign Exchange, weekly, 1924–31. For the effect on Treasury policy appreciations see T176/13, Leith-Ross to Hopkins, 9 March 1929.

[4]T176/13, Relations between the Treasury and the Bank of England, Control of Bank Rate, Extracts from Parliamentary Questions.

[5]Cab. 23/60, Cabinet Conclusions, 5(29), 7 February 1929, Conclusion 1.

[6]Clay, Lord Norman, 295–6.

[7]T176/13, Niemeyer to Churchill, 4 March 1925; Niemeyer to Phillips, 18 February 1929.

in this informal, day-to-day context that Churchill in 1925 secured an undertaking as to the use of Bank Rate at the time of the return to gold,[1] that Niemeyer sounded out the Governor as to a reduction in July 1925,[2] that Churchill instructed Sir Richard Hopkins to approach the Deputy Governor in August 1928 and 'exert every effort to prevent the Bank again restricting credit and adding further to the burdens of industry',[3] and that Sir Warren Fisher, Sir Richard Hopkins and the Chancellor tried on various occasions to urge restraint in increasing Bank Rate in 1929.[4] In fact, in almost every instance of pressure on sterling in the course of the interwar gold standard, the Treasury appears to have made its views known against an increase in existing rates.[5] Such increases in Bank Rate were generally assumed to be linked with increased unemployment and industrial difficulties. Changes in Bank Rate were also held to have a substantial influence on public expectations :[6]

owing to its associations ... because all the newspapers begin to howl and tell all the traders that they are ruined ... The traders do not know ... whether it is a signal that they are going to be ruined, or not, because if it were to be the beginning of a long period squeeze the Bank would ostensibly do the same thing.

As unemployment and industrial conditions were highly charged political issues during the period, such representations were politically perfectly natural.

The political nature of Bank Rate changes was most clearly shown in the reactions to increases by the Chancellors of the Exchequer of the period. Churchill appears to have been upset by the three increases in rate that occurred during his tenure of office, and, as noted above, on other occasions he did not hesitate to intervene through his civil servants in the direction of lower rates. The first increase, in March 1925, passed with comments to the senior civil servant on duty in the Finance Division, Frederick Leith-Ross,[7] but the second, December 1925, and the third, February 1929, saw Churchill being much more direct in his complaints. On the second occasion, Churchill telephoned the Governor. He told the Governor, according to Frederick Leith-Ross,[8]

[1] T172/1499B, Niemeyer, Notes on Government Decisions, 20 March 1925.
[2] T176/13, Niemeyer to Norman, 21 July 1925.
[3] Chartwell Papers 18/75, Churchill to Hopkins, 14 August 1928.
[4] T176/13, Leith-Ross to Hopkins, 9 March 1929 and attached note by Hopkins, 18 March 1929; Clay, *Lord Norman*, 297.
[5] The one exception appears to have occurred during the 1931 crisis, when Bank Rate rose twice before sterling left gold.
[6] Keynes Papers, Macmillan Committee, Notes of Discussions, 5 December 1930, 20.
[7] Leith-Ross, *Money Talks*, 95–6.
[8] T176/13, Leith-Ross, Memorandum, 3 December 1925; Clay, *Lord Norman*, 293
   Grigg, *Prejudice and Judgement*, 193.

that if the rate were raised he would have to inform the House that it had been done without his being consulted and against his views. It was not fair to the Exchequer that action should be taken which affected all its affairs without an opportunity being given to him to consider it. He expressed an earnest request that action should be deferred, at any rate for a week, to enable this to be done.

The Governor rejected his request; Churchill did not carry out his threat; and the Treasury civil servants undertook their first survey of opinion among previous Permanent Secretaries and Controllers of Finance to convince the Chancellor that the Governor's refusal was justified.[1] On the third occasion, Sir Richard Hopkins informed Churchill of the proposed change on Wednesday evening, and Churchill immediately telephoned the Deputy Governor, told Lubbock to come and see him and delivered a strong protest.[2] As noted above, the Cabinet also considered this particular rate change and emphasised the Bank's independence. Again Bank Rate was increased and another survey of past Treasury practice was initiated to influence the Chancellor.[3] Despite these rebuffs, Churchill always defended the Bank's independence in public:[4] his successor was, on occasion to be less discreet.

Excluding the crisis rises of July and September 1931, the only rise faced by Snowden as Chancellor occurred in September 1929. At this point the Bank was labouring under considerable external pressure resulting from high interest rates in New York and Germany, movements of French balances to New York, and seasonal demands for funds in Paris, as it had been for several months. The rise in Bank Rate to $5\frac{1}{2}$ per cent in February had been partially effective but for some months Norman had seen the need for further increase.[5] In July the Chancellor, sensing the trend of events, took an unprecedented step and used his Mansion House speech as the vehicle for a public statement against a rise in Bank Rate and in favour of restrictions on overseas lending to ease the position.[6] These remarks caused a considerable stir in the City and at the Bank where a rise in Bank Rate was considered inevitable.[7] Throughout the Conference at the Hague, the Governor

[1] T176/13, Leith-Ross to Bradbury and Chalmers, 4 December 1925.
[2] T176/13, Note by Hopkins, 19 February 1929; Lubbock to Hopkins, 9 February 1929.
[3] T176/13, Phillips to Bradbury, Blackett and Niemeyer, 16 February 1929.
[4] T176/13, Relations between the Treasury and the Bank of England, Control of Bank Rate, Extracts from Parliamentary Questions.
[5] F.R.B.N.Y., Norman to Harrison, no. 75/29, 25 March 1929; Norman to Harrison 12 April 1929; Norman to Harrison, nos 126 and 152/29, 24 May and 14 June 1929.
[6] The speech appears in full in *The Bankers' Magazine*, cxxvii (1026), September 1929, 411–9 (especially 416).   [7] T176/13, Harvey to Hopkins, 26 July 1929.

held his hand on Bank Rate for fear of weakening Snowden's bargaining position, but thereafter he believed himself free to move, if only he could find an excuse as he was still under informal pressure from the Chancellor.[1] The Hatry collapse eventually provided an excuse in September and Bank Rate rose without incident, but the increase was, in many respects, the result of several months' hard work by the Governor.

These pressures on the use of that most orthodox instrument of monetary control, although not necessarily in the direction of actual reductions in rates, had their effect on the conduct of policy. At the time of the return to gold Norman had expected 'a gradual contraction of credit and, internationally speaking, a high rate of interest',[2] but at a very early stage political considerations moved him towards ease in 1925. As Norman put the policy of ease to Strong in November, 'nothing else could have taken the wind out of the sales [*sic*] of McKenna and Co. as this has done or do more to silence criticism of the gold standard'.[3] Thereafter each movement in Bank Rate seemed to be a highly political act, and the Bank on most occasions attempted to find a clear external excuse for action which would silence criticism, as reserve movements by themselves were not always sufficient. Thus in November–December 1925, despite heavy losses of gold and difficulties in placing Treasury Bills in the market, owing to expectations of a rise in rates, Norman delayed raising Bank Rate for several weeks while awaiting a rise in the New York rate which he could use as an excuse and follow.[4] From that point onwards, the emphasis in his correspondence with Strong and other central bank Governors was on his determination to generally maintain rates if possible, to give way to pressures for reductions slowly and to avoid increases. From 1927 onwards the existence of a large overhang of short-term French funds in London strengthened the desire for Bank Rate stability, despite a period of favourable exchanges, as the Bank attempted to increase the size of its reserves.[5] Throughout the entire period the thrust of Bank thinking was towards stable rates, with reductions only on occasions of relatively great safety and increases only as a last resort. This thrust lies at the root of Bank Rate's amazing stability between 1925 and 1931 when it

[1]Clay, *Lord Norman*, 253; T176/13, Hopkins to Grigg, 6 and 19 August 1929.
[2]F.R.B.N.Y., Strong Papers, Norman to Strong, 26 May 1925.
[3]F.R.B.N.Y., Strong Papers, Norman to Strong, 23 November 1925. See also Keynes Papers, Beaverbrook to Keynes, 11 August 1925.
[4]Above, p. 132.
[5]See, for example, F.R.B.N.Y., Norman to Harrison, 6 November 1926. Strong Papers, Norman to Strong, 11 October 1927; Lubbock to Harrison, 3 August 1928, Macmillan Committee, *Evidence*, Q. 7597; T176/13, Hopkins to Grigg, 19 August 1929.

moved only half as often as it had in the period 1907–13 and remained unchanged for periods of over a year on three occasions, something that had not occurred since the 1890s.[1] The level of rates was historically high[2] but by no means sufficient for adjustment as we have seen. The Bank, knowing the pressures that existed against rate increases, tended to keep Bank Rate steady to avoid at least part of the odium of future increases. The resulting rates were never high enough to effect adjustment or low enough to avoid criticism and the Bank ended up, in a sense, falling between two stools.

Given the inhibitions and the limitations that existed on the use of Bank Rate policy after 1925, the Bank of England found its freedom to use open-market operations affected also, for the Bank could not determine the rate of interest and the volume of funds in the market simultaneously. As a result, both the Bank and, to a lesser extent, the Treasury were faced with a dilemma. As previous discussions have suggested, the British balance of payments after 1925, even given the historically high rates of unemployment and interest, was not particularly healthy at the par of exchange chosen. Thus the existing aggregate policies did not offer in general much prospect of reserve gains, particularly in the case of gold, while they offered a reasonable probability of reserve losses. Moreover, they could not be used with any great degree of flexibility, given the 'frictions' involved in the use of Bank Rate. In the light of these restrictions on the use of the traditional instruments of monetary policy, the Authorities began, almost simultaneously with the return to gold, to develop policy instruments which would in varying degrees serve as substitutes for Bank Rate in controlling the international payments of the British economy and even allow reserve gains on occasion. As the brief introductory examination of the operation of the pre-war gold standard has indicated, such supplements were not new to the U.K. in principle or in practice, but their extensive use in the interwar period had no precedent, except perhaps in the experiences of the war itself.

As our earlier discussion of methods of balance-of-payments adjustment indicated, the possible supplementary means of intervention are fairly extensive and may occur on almost any sector of a country's international payments. However, during the interwar gold standard period, policy preferences, traditional attitudes and limitations of analysis limited the number of possible course of action. The tradition of free trade, which in many respects was stronger than that of the gold standard,[3] at least in Treasury and City preferences, ruled out direct intervention on trade account to reduce imports, particularly as this course would require

[1] Calculations from Mitchell and Deane, *Abstract*, Banking and Insurance, 9.
[2] Above, p. 4.
[3] Above, p. 99.

legislation and explanation. The same tradition and the same need for explanation, plus desires to keep expenditure down and administrative complexities, probably ruled out intervention on the invisibles account which was in surplus. With the Government account largely fixed by Imperial commitments and almost immune from analysis along these lines, adjustments in this area were also ruled out. Thus, almost by default in an operational sense, the Authorities were left with only the possibility of influencing the capital and official settlements accounts of the balance of payments.

From the point of view of the Bank of England, which carried most of the operational responsibility for such matters, and from the point of view of the Treasury and the Government, which directly or indirectly carried ultimate political responsibility, intervention in these two areas carried several advantages. First, intervention by the Bank removed the Government from any apparent direct responsibility for such intervention in a world where official intervention was still looked on with disfavour and where the Bank's independence from political interference was a matter of faith.[1] The Treasury could encourage intervention by the Bank privately if it desired, but if challenged by hostile public reactions it could say that legally it had nothing to do with it and that, of course, it would not interfere with the policy of the Bank of England.[2] Second, intervention in these areas without legislation was simpler, for in the City and among sister central banks the Bank of England could often make its wishes felt effectively without great fuss and publicity. Also, as the Bank carried ultimate legal responsibility for the maintenance of the exchange and as it was constrained by Treasury pressures in other areas of operation, it had the maximum incentive to innovate and to ease its way along the golden path for which it had fought so effectively in 1924–5. However, given the lack of public official sanction that normally existed for its efforts,[3] the Bank's area of initiative was somewhat limited. Where it had a free hand legally, as in gold and foreign exchange policy, as we shall see, its secretiveness and the dangers of the public's misreading the changed situation limited its freedom of manoeuvre. Where it did not have a free hand legally, it depended on moral suasion, a policy instrument subject to severe limitations.

Moral suasion as an instrument of economic policy represents an 'attempt to coerce private economic activity via governmental exhortation in directions not already defined or dictated by *existing* statute

---

[1]See, for example, Cab. 58/9, Committee of Civil Research, Overseas Loans Sub-Committee, *Report*; Committee on Industry and Trade, *Final Report*, Cmd. 3282 (London, 1929). 49–50. Also, see above pp. 159–60.

[2]See, for example, T175/4, Leith-Ross to Churchill, 6 October 1928.

[3]The major exceptions occurred in 1925 and 1929. See below, p. 202.

law' (italics in the original).[1] Such attempts may be qualitative or quantitative in character, but they basically involve an encouragement to private business to undertake action which is unprofitable or relatively less profitable and which it would not normally undertake. The success of such suasion depends on several factors.[2] The number of units to be persuaded normally must be relatively small.[3] Here of course the London market in all its various guises is ideal, for channels of communication exist through various committees and associations and the number of firms to be persuaded is small relative to many other financial systems. The requests and the consequences of non-compliance must be both clear and credible. Here again smallness in numbers is an advantage in that deviations can be easily identified and the costs of compliance for any one firm kept down. The costs of non-compliance depend ultimately on the power of the Authorities in the market concerned with this 'polite blackmail'[4] and they may be increased by threats of legislation, although such threats may backfire and force the Authorities to legislate – something they may have hoped to avoid in the first place.[5] The occasions on which suasion finds use are also important. In a national emergency or when the national interest or the interests of those subject to suasion are clearly involved, suasion may become more effective, as public support for its ends may increase both the scope for altruism and the group penalties for non-compliance. Similarly its period of operation is of considerable importance, for pressures for the termination of suasion increase as the unprofitability of compliance becomes cumulative and self-restraint becomes more onerous. Finally, because suasion's success ultimately depends on contact and communication between individuals or groups of individuals, the personal relationships and beliefs of those involved become most important. In the former respect, Norman's dominant position in the City and his usefulness to its members were of great importance;[6] as in the latter respect were the City's unified

[1] J. T. Romans, 'Moral Suasion as an Instrument of Economic Policy', *American Economic Review.* LVI (5), December 1966, 1221.

[2] Ibid., J. Aschheim, *Techniques of Monetary Control* (Baltimore, 1965), 100–6; Canada, Royal Commission on Banking and Finance, *Report*, 425–6.

[3] However, the number to be persuaded need not always be small. Thus, since 1965, the Chancellor of the Exchequer's requests for voluntary restraint on investment, both direct and portfolio, in the four developed sterling area countries has, in the Chancellor's words, been quite successful as 'United Kingdom companies and institutions ... under growing pressure have continued to give loyal co-operation'. 799 H.C. Deb. 5s. column 1227. See also 'The U.K. exchange control: a short history', Bank of England, *Quarterly Bulletin*, VII (3), September 1967, 258–60.

[4] T175/4, Niemeyer to Churchill, 5 March 1925.

[5] See, for example, the negotiations with the clearing banks concerning gold holdings, T176/22; above, p. 83.

[6] Clay, *Lord Norman*, 278–9.

M

belief that *laissez faire* was the best policy and its almost universal anti-intellectualism in matters economic which blurred any ends–means considerations beyond the very simple and the very short-term.[1]

Within this atmosphere and this pattern of limitations, the Bank after 1925, deprived of part of its traditional armoury of policy instruments, attempted to operate. The pressures towards innovation were strong, as the Bank, the City and the Government had a deep commitment to the ultimate success of the policy of 1925, despite the practical obstacles to its realisation by traditional means. Future chapters will consider the Bank's post-1925 innovations and revivals of earlier practice in several directions, beginning with markets more directly under the Bank's control and moving outwards into the wider areas of moral suasion.

[1]S. G. Checkland, 'The Mind of the City 1870–1914', *Oxford Economic Papers*, N.S., IX (3). October 1957; L. E. Jones, *Georgian Afternoon* (London, 1958). 111–28; R. H. Brand, 'A Banker's Reflections on Economic Trends', *Economic Journal*, LXIII (252), December 1953, 763–4; P. Einzig, *In the Centre of Things* (London, 1960) 54–5.

8. BANK OF ENGLAND OPERATIONS IN GOLD AND FOREIGN EXCHANGE MARKETS

When Britain returned to gold in 1925, she implicitly set a range of possible fluctuations for sterling *vis-à-vis* foreign currencies. The range was effectively determined by the Bank of England's statutory buying and selling prices for gold,[1] and the costs of settling imbalances in payments by gold movements, for if it was profitable to do so arbitragists would take gold from the Bank of England in exchange for sterling, ship it to another gold standard centre, sell it to the central bank there and sell the resulting foreign currency proceeds for sterling or vice versa. The costs involved in such arbitrage – fees for brokerage, insurance, transport, interest on borrowed funds, assays, forward cover, etc. – determined its profitability at any given exchange rate. Generally speaking, in the short run, all costs other than interest and exchange cover (if used at all) were known fairly well in advance and were reasonably stable.[2] Changes in interest costs would cause some variation in the gold points, but these would be relatively small and, moreover, would involve variations in domestic financial policy to bring them about.[3]

In these underlying circumstances, the Authorities, if they wished to alter the range of exchange fluctuations that would affect the reserves without altering domestic interest rates, could operate in three basic ways: (1) they could attempt to alter the costs of moving gold from centre to centre by efforts to change the relatively fixed costs of the situation; (2) as London was the major gold market of the world, they could easily actively bid for new supplies coming into that market, rather than merely

---

[1]Statutory buying price 77s 9d per standard ounce; selling price 77s 10½d per standard ounce. Such prices were for gold $\frac{11}{12}$ fine. The equivalent open market prices for fine gold were 84s 10d and 84s 11½d respectively.

[2]However, they could vary between arbitragists depending on their positions in respective markets. Morgenstern, *International Financial Transactions*, 176–91; Einzig, *International Gold Movements*, Appendix I.

[3]A 1 per cent change over eight days would make a difference of 0.09 cents in the gold points for the dollar exchange. Ibid., 150.

acting as residual buyer or seller at the statutory prices; (3) they could intervene, within existing gold points through foreign exchange operations to increase or decrease the reserves. Of course, these methods could be used in combination.[1] Prior to 1914, the Bank had depended on (1) and (2). Thus it effectively lowered the gold export point by paying out light, but legal, coin and thus marginally reducing the gold content of the sovereign in foreign centres. On other occasions, through interest-free loans to importers, it effectively lowered the gold import point by removing one of the costs of arbitrage.[2] However, the Bank, unlike many other central banks, even in major gold standard countries, did not operate actively in foreign exchange markets.[3]

Such foreign exchange operations may substantially alter the day-to-day policy position of central banks. First, the accumulation of foreign exchange reserves does not require that the exchange rise as high as the gold import point. Thus foreign exchange operations may increase the gains to a central bank's reserve position that result from the pursuit of an interest rate policy which holds the exchange above the gold export point. Second, if movements in gold reserves trigger expectations of interest-rate changes that will reduce or limit that flow (for example, if a gold inflow produces expectations of an interest-rate decline), foreign exchange operations, if they are successfully hidden, can increase the short-term freedom of action of the Authorities with respect to domestic interest rates. On occasions when the Authorities wish to affect the international flow of short-term funds, yet do not want to alter domestic interest rates, the possession of hidden exchange reserves opens up the possibility of forward exchange operations as a device for further insulating the domestic economy from international pressures.[4]

If such gold and/or foreign exchange operations can be conducted on a co-operative basis by several central banks, the possibilities of effective insulation for a particular economy become even more extensive. Such co-operation can alter flows of gold by making it cheaper to take it from one centre than another, and can, to a considerable extent, minimise interest rate movements which would be domestically or internationally damaging.

All of these 'devices' can work in both directions. They do not solve fundamental problems that require readjustments of exchange parities; they merely make life more tolerable for the central banks concerned and allow policy-makers more time to make decisions.[5] In few cases has

---

[1]Below, pp. 172-3.
[2]Above, p. 8.
[3]Bloomfield, 'Short-Term Capital Movements', Ch. III.
[4]Below, p. 188.
[5]Naturally, this occurs at some cost to the Authorities, for if they increase market uncertainty they may reduce the prevalence of uncovered short-term capital

the distinction between these short-term devices and long-term fundamental problems been so clear as in the British economy after 1925.

The Bank and the Gold Market

Although the pre-war British tradition offered extensive examples of official intervention in the gold market to obviate or decrease the need to restrict domestic credit while increasing or preventing the depletion of official international reserves, the early post-war period saw an almost complete refusal to accept that such gold devices had formed a part of the normal pre-war system or to consider their use. The Cunliffe Committee, for example, in its highly stylised account of the working of the pre-war system, completely ignored the use of such devices, although, in another context, Lord Cunliffe remembered their use in the days before he became Governor.[1] In fact, England had been on the gold standard for over two years after 1925 before the subject of the Bank's active use of pre-war gold devices was seriously discussed, although before that date intervention had occurred in certain other forms.[2]

The major changes in the Bank's thinking concerning gold devices occurred in the course of 1927. During that year, the subject of gold movements increasingly preoccupied central bankers as they moved to prevent gold leaving Europe for New York, and to encourage each other to take gold from America rather than London, despite the lower shipping and interest costs of gold movements from the latter.[3] In August 1927, Norman, following up the results of the famous Long Island meeting of central bankers, wrote Strong :[4]

movements and hence require larger official efforts to achieve a given exchange
    rate movement.
[1]F.R.B.N.Y., Strong Papers, Cunliffe to Strong, 2 March 1917; Cunliffe Committee,
    First Interim Report, para. 2–7; Sayers, *Bank of England Operations*, 137–8.
[2]Below, pp. 174, 176.
[3]The reasons for this preoccupation were two: (1) the higher eastbound Atlantic
    freight rates and the high interest costs involved in shipping gold from America
    made such shipments less attractive, particularly when (2) the key position of
    sterling as the link currency between the United States and Europe meant that,
    in periods when European currencies were strong against the dollar, they were
    also strong against sterling and vice versa. Both of these factors, moreover, tended
    to increase the pressure on London's gold reserves. For London's relatively un-
    balanced dollar gold points position and a picture of the relationships involved
    see Figure 1 above and Morgenstern, *International Financial Transactions*, Table 34.
    F.R.B.N.Y., Strong Papers, Strong to Moreau, 19 May 1927; Schacht to Norman,
    21 May 1927; Strong to Norman, 25 August 1927; F.R.B.N.Y., Harrison to Gov-
    ernors of Federal Reserve Banks, 11 June 1927; Norman to Lubbock, nos 11 and
    14/27, 13 and 19 July 1927; Norman to Strong, no. 122/27, 9 August 1927;
    Moreau, *Souvenirs*, 9 and 15 July 1927.
[4]F.R.B.N.Y., Strong Papers, Norman to Strong, 29 August 1927.

As to gold purchases and prices in general, I now have some hope that the Bank of England will be allowed to pay more than 77s. 9d. for gold on this Market in case of undesirable competition : that would be a great help to us. There has of course always been a legal requirement that we should pay that price and legally we are free to pay more. *But I have only ascertained within the last few days* that 20 or 30 years ago, when there were heavy demands upon this Bank for sovereigns, it was the custom occasionally to pay above 77s. 9d. for bars. Of late, on the other hand (with no such demand for sovereigns as formerly), it has not been thought we would be wise to pay over the statutory price and the result of not having done so has doubtless tended to supply gold for the Central Banks of Europe. Before, however, I can speak definitely, I must wait to get the blessing of Addis and several others, who have strong views on gold purchases and prices.   (italics added)

These discussions appear to have proceeded successfully, for Clay records a Committee of Treasury decision favouring a more active policy in early October 1927 and Norman in a subsequent letter to Strong noted:[1] 'As I hinted to you in an earlier letter, we here will no longer be as chary as hitherto of occasionally paying over the minimum price of 77s. 9d. if it should seem wise to do so.'

There matters stood for over a year, for, although the matter came up again later that autumn when Norman and Strong discussed possible changes in American gold policy to keep gold from going to New York, the Bank seems to have adhered to its normal post-1925 policy of non-intervention.[2] Late in the summer of 1928, as rising American interest rates accompanied the speculative boom on Wall Street, the Bank was prepared to bid above 77s. 9d. 'as a last resort',[3] but it does not appear to have actually entered the market until 22 January 1929, when the buying price was 84s. $11\frac{3}{8}$d. per ounce of fine gold, more than a penny above the statutory minimum.[4] At this point, Lubbock, the Deputy Governor, informed Governor Harrison, Strong's successor as Governor of the Federal Reserve Bank of New York, that the Bank might repeat the operation and that between 1898 and 1913 more than half the bar gold bought by the Bank came at above the statutory minimum.[5] The London gold market found the purchase 'somewhat of a surprise',[6] but thereafter the operations became very common, over thirty such instances being noted in 1929 alone.[7] This regular bidding at above the statutory price con-

[1]Clay, *Lord Norman*, 237; F.R.B.N.Y., Strong Papers, Norman to Strong, 10 October 1927.

[2]F.R.B.N.Y., Strong Papers, Strong to Norman, 20 October 1927; Norman to Strong, 4 November 1927.

[3]F.R.B.N.Y., Strong Papers, Lubbock to Strong, 18 August 1928.

[4]F.R.B.N.Y., Lubbock to Harrison, no. 23/29, 24 January 1929.

[5]Ibid.

[6]S. Montagu & Co., *Weekly Bullion Letter,* 23 January 1929.

[7]In *The Economist* and S. Montagu & Co., *Weekly Bullion Letter.*

tinued right up to the end of the interwar gold standard, with one long interruption from March 1930 to March 1931, when heavy French and Continental demands plus the Bank's delivery of standard rather than fine gold bars made outside bids as high as 85s. o⅜d. profitable, and when French forward purchases of South African gold denuded the market of supplies.[1] On occasion such bidding was covert, as during the summer of 1931 when the Bank bought fine bars at above the statutory buying price for an 'unknown buyer' and then released the equivalent amount of sovereigns from earmark to swell the Issue Department's gold holding.[2] Thus the bidding for gold became as much a part of day-to-day policy as it had been before 1914, and it certainly aided the Bank in its struggle to obtain gold more quickly than it would have if it had worked through the more orthodox method of domestic credit restriction and high interest rates to adjust the exchanges, possibly adversely affecting home trade in the process. However, the Bank did not seem to increase its buying price in other ways such as free insurance or more direct means to induce dealers to ship gold directly to it as it had done before the war.[3]

The use of open-market bidding tactics was not the only means used by the Bank to alter gold flows to suit its purposes. Through moral suasion the Bank appears to have convinced British bullion brokers and arbitragists not to take the initiative in orders for export, thus effectively adding an extra commission to the expenses of those who wanted to take gold from London.[4] On occasion the Bank appears to have gone even further to discourage gold exports. For example, in September 1928 Norman gave Rothschilds his priorities for gold shipments, saying that they should come from the Bank only as a last resort and that they should go to Europe rather than America when they did occur.[5] Again, in the period April to July 1931, the Bank convinced brokers that they should neither initiate nor execute gold orders from America, although after July this policy was somewhat relaxed.[6] Thus the Bank certainly attempted to make the export of gold as expensive as possible and to make the market less responsive to export opportunities. Einzig estimates that such measures could affect the gold export point from London to

[1] Below, p. 175. The Bank of England's selling price which was equivalent to a market price of 84s. 11½d, set an effective maximum for its open market bids.
[2] The sovereigns would have been earmarked for an overseas central bank. By its bidding policy the Bank could substitute fine gold, which was more acceptable to overseas central banks, for the sovereigns and take the sovereigns into the Issue Department.
[3] F.R.B.N.Y., Norman to Strong, no. 223/27, 29 November 1927.
[4] Einzig, *International Gold Movements*, 21; Brown, *International Gold Standard*, II, 1014; Keynes, *Treatise on Money*, II, 326.
[5] Clay, *Lord Norman*, 238. The brokers could have some influence here, if only through their willingness to execute orders.
[6] Brown, *International Gold Standard*, II, 1014.

New York by as much as 1 cent,[1] and the number of violations of the conventional gold export point to New York recorded by Morgenstern gives some indication of the success of this, plus other, policy measures,[2] The Bank could operate effectively in such a manner because the number of London dealers and brokers was small, thus easing the communication problem; because most of the dealers, and particularly Rothschilds, who formed the centre of the London market, had other interests which the Bank's actions could affect; and because of the Bank's general position of power in the City.[3]

At this point, it is best to note one event in the interwar period where some observers mistakenly believed that the Bank was using gold devices.[4] The event referred to is the decision of the Bank to deliver standard rather than fine bars when called upon for gold for export after June 1930. After the return to gold in 1925, the Bank delivered fine bars when called upon for gold unles specifically asked otherwise.[5] In the vast majority of cases, exporters took such bars; whereas the Bank despite its active bidding for fine bars in the market after January 1929, bought most of its gold in sovereigns of standard fineness, 0.916 being the fineness of sovereigns compared to the 0.996 fineness of so-called fine bars.[6] For example, from 1 June 1929 to 31 May 1930 the Bank gained £39,199,100 net in sovereigns while it lost £45,281,000 net in fine bars.[7] As a result, by early 1930 the Bank was nearing the end of its stock of fine gold which had fallen from £70 million in May 1925 to £25 million in April 1930.[8] Late in 1929 the Bank saw that it was approaching the end of its stock of fine bars, but found it impossible for capacity reasons, to get the Mint to refine sovereigns into fine bars.[9] As a result, in January 1930 the Bank began negotiations with the Bank of France, the chief central bank whose regulations did not allow it to accept gold of less than 0.995 fineness. The outcome of these discussions was 'not very satisfactory, and practically amounted to a refusal to accept

---

[1]Einzig, *International Gold Movements*, 88.
[2]Morgenstern, *International Financial Transactions*, Chart 17. The classic example of this type of suasion occurred in 1925, when efforts to raise westbound Atlantic freight rates to levels comparable to eastbound rates were successful and resulted in a change in the gold export point from $4.8479 to $4.8431. T176/16, Niemeyer to Rincquesen, 8 May 1925; F.R.B.N.Y., Norman to Strong, no. 26, 6 May 1925; Strong to Norman, no. 80, 7 May 1925; Crane to Strong, 7 May 1925.
[3]Balogh, *Studies*, 213–4.
[4]Keynes, *Treatise on Money*, 11, 328; Einzig, *International Gold Movements*, 106.
[5]F.R.B.N.Y., B. S. Catterns, Memorandum on Gold, 17 December 1930, 2.
[6]S. Montagu & Co., *Weekly Bullion Letter*, 11 June 1930.
[7]Ibid.
[8]F.R.B.N.Y., Catterns, Memorandum on Gold 2.
[9]T160/281/F11789, Phillips to Johnson, 14 November 1929; Perry to Phillips, 15 and 29 November 1929; Catterns to Hopkins, 27 March 1930; Hopkins to Phillips, 27 March 1930.

coin [standard] bars'.[1] At this point the Bank, by arrangement with the Treasury, began to melt sovereigns into coin bars,[2] and on 6 June it began delivering these for export, thus offering exporters 'gold of exactly the same fineness as they would have received if our obligation to pay sovereigns had still been in force'.[3] This change effectively limited the Bank's gold losses to Paris, which still refused to accept coin bars, to £300,000 per day, the capacity of London's gold refiners.[4] It also lowered the gold export point from the Bank of England to Paris by an amount dependent on the charges for refining standard bars and the rate of interest at which funds were borrowed to carry out the transaction which was now lengthened as a result of the need to refine. Beyond the sum of £300,000 per day, the gold points, even in this lowered form, became meaningless and the London–Paris exchange rate on occasion went below the normal gold point adjusted for interest and refining charges of about 123.70, falling on one occasion below 123.60 (the normal gold export point was 123.90 – 123.92 at this time).[5] There matters stood for some time, although attempts to reach a settlement continued at the Bank for International Settlements. Eventually the Bank for International Settlements proved to be an effective source of a settlement, and on November 24–25 1930 the Committee for Transactions in Foreign Exchange and Gold met and resolved that 'the majority of the Committee felt that Central Banks should accept gold bars having a fineness varying between 900/1000 and 1000/1000'.[6] A later session of the Board of Directors of the B.I.S. effected a settlement on these lines which came into force in January 1931 thus bringing this period of conflict betwen central bank regulations and necessity to a conclusion.[7]

Finally, the Bank's gold policies were assisted and supported on occasion by the efforts of other central banks. Central banks desiring to rebuild or reconstitute their reserves of foreign exchange often shipped

[1] F.R.B.N.Y., Catterns to Crane, 18 January 1930; Bank of France, A Confidential Note to Central Banks, 10 July 1928; Catterns to Crane, 23 April 1930.

[2] The Treasury was involved because the Issue Department's profits, out of which any melting costs would be met, went to the Treasury. T160/281/F11789, Catterns to Sydney-Turner, 11 April 1930.

[3] F.R.B.N.Y., Harvey to Harrison, no. 129/30, 11 June 1930.

[4] F.R.B.N.Y., Moreau to Harrison, 13 June 1930.

[5] F.R.B.N.Y., Harvey to Crane, 4 July 1930; Einzig, *International Gold Movements*, 151–2. The absolute lower limit for sterling would have been the rate at which it became profitable to ship standard gold to Berlin, to exchange it for fine gold and to ship the fine gold to Paris (ibid., 103).

[6] F.R.B.N.Y., Summary of the Meeting of the Committee for Transactions in Foreign Exchange and Gold, 24 and 25 November 1930, 13.

[7] F.R.B.N.Y., Norman to Harrison, no. 9/31, 13 January 1931; Moret to Harrison, no. 2, 14 January 1931; Franck to Harrison, 24 January 1931; B.I.S. Annual Report for 1930, *Federal Reserve Bulletin*, xvii (7), July 1931, 377–8.

gold directly to the Bank of England rather than rebuild their reserves through open-market gold sales or exchange purchases both of which were less likely to benefit the Bank's reserve.[1] On occasion they also supported Bank of England policy by refraining from drawing gold from London, even when it proved to be the cheapest market for such transactions. For example, for a year or more after 1925, Schacht, the Governor of the Reichsbank, kept his sterling balances up to the level of the Dawes Loan's proceeds, and, despite the fact that London was the cheapest gold market, met his needs elsewhere.[2] He did so again after the 1927 Central Bankers' meeting on Long Island, this time by reducing his purchase price for gold to minimise the strain on London.[3] Similarly, one result of the 1927 confrontation with the Bank of France was an attempt by the Bank of France to limit the accumulation of claims on London, to limit its acquisitions of gold in London and to accumulate its stabilisation gold reserve in New York rather than London.[4] After the 1928 *de jure* stabilisation the Bank of France was not as solicitous in regard to London's position, but on occasion it attempted to divert French gold purchases to New York or to reduce London's gold losses.[5] Thus the central banks for a considerable part of the period attempted to minimise their demands for gold from London by fairly direct means. After 1928, as the system became subject to greater strains, such co-operation became less common, although as the discussion of support measures for sterling below will indicate it did not cease completely. The important difference was the form the support took, loans and credits which ultimately had to be repaid rather than unilateral support, for this meant that the burden of adjustment was increasingly shifted to the British side. It was with this decline in this unilateral central bank support that the Bank of England moved to the much more active gold market policy on its own account that was noted above.

The Bank and the Foreign Exchange Market

One of the Bank's most interesting interwar innovations lay in the development of a foreign exchange policy. Before 1914 such operations, at least in the spot market, were not uncommon among smaller central

---

[1] See, for example, Annual Report of the Netherlands Bank, *Federal Reserve Bulletin*, XII (8), August 1926. 592–3.
[2] Clarke, *Central Bank Cooperation*, 113; Brown, *International Gold Standard*, 636; H. Schacht, *The Stabilisation of the Mark* (London, 1927), 208.
[3] F.R.B.N.Y., Strong Papers, Schacht to Strong, 31 December 1927; Clay, *Lord Norman*, 236–7.   [4] Above, p. 135.
[5] F.R.B.N.Y., Moret to Harrison, no. 40, 30 April 1931; A Sproul, Record of Certain Conversations in London and Paris, Conversation with M. Cariguel, 19 November 1930. 3.

banks, and on occasion even extended to their larger cousins.[1] However, after the First World War, the holding of foreign exchange reserves and operations therein also became much more characteristic of the larger central banks.[2] In this field the Bank of England stands as one of the largely unknown innovators.

The existence of the Bank's post-war exchange operations has been officially known since 1931, when the Macmillan Committee's *Minutes of Evidence* and the large-scale intervention with borrowed funds by the Bank during the final futile defence of the gold standard made them patently clear. The former material was not picked up by most subsequent commentators, including the Committee itself, when it came in the course of Sir Ernest Harvey's evidence. Harvey admitted that the Bank held assets denominated in foreign currencies under other Securities in both the Issue and Banking Departments, that these holdings represented a considerable proportion of the assets in such classes, despite fluctuations, and that the Bank had used foreign exchange assets extensively in its 1928–9 defence of sterling.[3] The actual use of such assets in the market was noted by several observers both before and during the 1931 crisis.[4] More recently 'official' histories of the interwar period on both sides of the Atlantic have noted the operations, even indicating their extent on particular occasions, and the Bank of England has published, without commentary, a quarterly series of its exchange holdings for the period.[5] However, knowledge of the Bank's operations is far from complete.

Table 15 presents a monthly summary of the Bank of England's major holdings of foreign exchange – francs and dollars – for the period of the interwar gold standard. Changes in the Bank's gold reserve are included for reference. In the discussion that follows, particular emphasis will be placed on the Bank's dollar operations, as detailed information exists for these and as they represented the bulk of the Bank's holdings.[6] After brief reference to the Bank's pre-1925 foreign exchange experience, the discussion will concentrate on the sources and uses of reserves within the context of the pressures of 1925–31, with

[1] Bloomfield, 'Short-Term Capital Movements', Ch. II; Lindert, 'Key Currencies', Ch. 2.

[2] League of Nations, *International Currency Experience*, 30.

[3] Macmillan Committee, *Evidence*, Q. 137, 156–60, 300–2, 315, 7597; *Report*, para. 354–60. See also Hopkins' reply to Q. 5371.

[4] *The Economist*, 'Market Notes, 18 September 1926, 1, 8 and 9 August 1931; P. Einzig, *The Tragedy of the Pound*, (London 1931), 90–5.

[5] Clay, *Lord Norman*; Clarke, *Central Bank Cooperation*; Bank of England, *Quarterly Bulletin*, x (1), March 1970, Supplement,

[6] All until September 1928; all but a nominal amount until March 1931 when French franc holdings first exceeded £1 million.

TABLE 15. *Bank of England exchange balances and changes in gold holdings, April 1925–September 1931 (£ million)*

Year	End of	Total exchange	Gold change from previous month
1925	April	n	
	May	n	+1
	June	0.9	+n
	July	0.9	+7
	August	2.5	−1
	September	3.4	−3
	October	5.0	−10
	November	5.0	−4
	December	5.1	−2
1926	January	6.1	+n
	February	9.7	+n
	March	9.7	+2
	April	10.0	−n
	May	10.2	+3
	June	10.7	+1
	July	14.1	+2
	August	16.6	+2
	September	16.1	+1
	October	17.5	−3
	November	18.8	+n
	December	21.0	−2
1927	January	21.8	+n
	February	24.7	−n
	March	27.5	+n
	April	28.1	+3
	May	28.9	−2
	June	31.3	−n
	July	31.6	−n
	August	27.9	−1
	September	38.1	−n
	October	39.9	+1
	November	41.8	−2
	December	41.9	+3
1928	January	42.8	+4
	February	44.5	+1
	March	44.7	+1
	April	44.7	+2
	May	45.2	+2
	June	45.4	+9
	July	42.4	+4
	August	38.8	−n
	September	35.9	−3
	October	31.0	−7
	November	22.2	−4
	December	19.9	−5

TABLE 15—*continued*.

Year	End of	Total exchange	Gold change from previous month
1929	January	17.6	−1
	February	18.0	−2
	March	17.8	+2
	April	17.8	+3
	May	21.4	+6
	June	23.1	−3
	July	24.7	−10
	August	23.3	−13
	September	25.4	−4
	October	23.8	−1
	November	19.6	+4
	December	19.7	+11
1930	January	16.7	+4
	February	16.1	+1
	March	15.5	+4
	April	14.1	+8
	May	15.2	−6
	June	19.5	−n
	July	24.9	−5
	August	25.5	+2
	September	24.1	+1
	October	24.6	+3
	November	25.0	−3
	December	25.1	−9
1931	January	25.1	−7
	February	28.9	+1
	March	33.3	+3
	April	31.3	+3
	May	31.1	+5
	June	30.7	+12
	July	19.5	−31
	August	18.3	+1
	September	8.7	+2

Note: All figures are for the last Wednesday of each month.
  n = something but less than £500,000.

Sources: Bank of England, Economic Intelligence Department.
  Bank of England, *Quarterly Bulletin*, March 1970, Supplement.
  Bank of England, Weekly Return, gold bullion and coin in the Issue Department.
  Federal Reserve Bank of New York, Correspondence Files, C261 – Bank of England.

particular reference to the techniques used.[1] The 1931 crisis operations which represent the culmination of previous experience, are dealt with at the end of the discussion.

The Bank's interwar exchange operations had their origins in its wartime pegging, on the Treasury's behalf, of the dollar exchange,[2] in its intervention on the Treasury's behalf after the war to accumulate dollars for debt repayments;[3] and in the arrangements made between central banks, both during and after the war for, among other things, the opening of accounts and the purchase of bills. One of the earliest and most typical of this last type of arrangement was that of 1917 between the Bank and the Federal Reserve Bank of New York, the latter operating on behalf of the Federal Reserve System.[4] Between the end of the war and the return to gold, exchange operations by the Bank on its own account were minimal. The Bank did not even open a regular account on its own behalf in New York until September 1924 when it deposited $250,000 with the Federal Reserve.[5] However, at the time of the return to gold, Norman foresaw that foreign exchange operations by the Bank might have a useful role to play.[6]

Given the unexpectedly easy conditions following the return to gold, the possibility of the Bank accumulating exchange reserves occurred somewhat earlier than expected. When Norman first broached the idea of a ½ per cent reduction in Bank Rate to Strong in May 1925, Strong replied that he thought that the Bank should accumulate exchange reserves to support sterling in the autumn when sterling was seasonally weak,[7] Norman purchased some dollars on Treasury account, but found that he could not do so in any quantity without depressing the exchange.[8] However, as the Bank did begin to accumulate dollars, from non-market transactions, soon thereafter, this exchange of views could be taken as the beginning of the Bank's exchange operations. To the sources of funds through which the Bank fed its exchange reserves the discussion now turns.

Although all accretions to the reserves might well be regarded as

---

[1]This discussion will also include a brief treatment of foreign central bank support for sterling.

[2]Morgan, *Studies*, 356-9; Clay, *Lord Norman*, Ch. 4.

[3]T160/418/F6779/1, Rowe-Dutton, Purchases of American Exchange, 14 June 1927.

[4]Chandler, *Benjamin Strong*, 94-8.

[5]F.R.B.N.Y., Norman to Strong, 17 May and 17 September 1924.

[6]Clay, *Lord Norman*, 151. In fact the first draft of the Gold Standard Bill 1925 was called the Gold Exchange Standard Bill, T163/130/G1942.

[7]F.R.B.N.Y., Strong Papers, Norman to Strong, 8 and 26 May 1925; Norman to Strong, no. 41, 22 May 1925; Strong to Norman, no. 9, 23 May 1925.

[8]F.R.B.N.Y., Norman to Strong, no. 46, 25 May 1925; T160/418/F6779/1, Waley to Phillips, 26 January 1928. The Treasury purchases totalled $25 million in May and $8 million in June.

coming directly from the exchange market, particularly if one assumes that any inflow of funds would have occurred anyway and that the Bank would have tapped the exchange market for the equivalent sum, it is nevertheless rather useful to indicate the sources of flows into the Bank's exchange reserves. This is particularly true as approximately half the funds involved in the Bank's exchange operations came from non-open-market transactions and as such transactions dominated exchange reserve gains in particular years. Generally speaking, in addition to open market purchases normally conducted through the Anglo-International Bank or its American correspondents, the Bank's exchange reserves were fed by central bank transactions of various types.[1]

Direct central bank transactions predominated as a source of exchange gains, until the sustained rise in sterling in late 1927 brought the Bank heavily into the open market. Between the return to gold and the early autumn of 1927 such central transactions, as far as they can be identified, resulted in accruals of over £32 million. Throughout this early period, much of this took the form of diversifying portfolios. After the return to gold, many central banks which had previously held their exchange reserves in dollars partially converted them into stabilised sterling and the Bank of England gained the title to the resulting dollar balances in the process. The Annual Report of the Netherlands Bank for 1925 sets out this process of portfolio diversification most clearly:[2]

When, however, England had returned to the gold standard and we were thus assured once more that sterling would maintain the same value as gold in our accounting, there was every reason for sending to England also[3] part of our still excessive stock. There upon in the months from June to August, 1925, we sent 65,000,000 florins in gold to England, and besides transferred part of our large [dollar] balance in America to England.

Such portfolio-diversifying transactions in 1925 appear to have totalled approximately £5 million.

In 1926 and early 1927, although such diversification transactions continued – they totalled approximately £3.5 million in 1926 – a major new source of central bank funds appeared which resulted in accretions of almost £24 million to the Bank's dollar reserve. The source of these large accretions was the Commonwealth Bank of Australia which exchanged two types of assets, which increased the Bank of England's dollar balances, for sterling.[4] The largest segment, from the Bank's point

---

[1] All of the general comments which follow, unless otherwise noted, are based on information collected from the cable files, C261 – Bank of England, of the Federal Reserve Bank of New York.

[2] *Federal Reserve Bulletin*, XII (8), August 1926, 592. See also, Annual Report of the Swiss National Bank, ibid., XII (4), April 1926, 267–8.

[3] Previously, the Bank had sent gold to America to rebuild its exchange reserves.

[4] In addition to the sums discussed below, the Australian Authorities also transferred

of view, came from a series of gold shipments by the Commonwealth Bank to San Francisco whence the proceeds were transferred to the Bank of England's New York dollar reserves. Such shipments totalled £14.5 million. The remainder came from transfers of the proceeds of Australian government borrowing in New York into sterling. Such transfers as affected the Bank's dollar reserves directly, about £9.2 million, occurred in 1927, earlier and later borrowing proceeds going to the Treasury.

After 1927, the Bank also began to use open market purchases on a more extensive scale to increase its foreign exchange reserves. Previously, such purchases had been relatively limited, about £5 million in the period January–March 1926 and small amounts on other occasions. In the first two periods of heavy open market purchases during late 1927 and early 1928 accretions totalled £9 million. Thereafter, the Bank depended on both open market purchases and central bank transactions as open market conditions and foreign central banks' asset preferences allowed.[1] Thus in early 1929 and in the late summer of 1929 central bank transfers significantly reduced the reserve losses resulting from the Bank's support of sterling against the dollar, while in late 1929 the Bank used the open market. Similarly, in the spring of 1931, a transaction with the Bank of France added substantially to the Bank's previously nominal franc reserves at a time when exchange conditions prevented open market purchases.[2]

Given that a reasonable proportion of the exchange accretions resulted from what might be called gold exchange standard considerations,[3] the Bank of England in accepting such funds or similarly motivated

$97 million from the proceeds of loans in New York in 1925 and 1928 to the Treasury, which used the proceeds for war debt payments in the United States. T160/419/F6779/1–2, Waley to Phillips, 26 January 1928; Bewley to Waley, 15 December 1928.

[1] Annual Report of the Netherlands Bank, *Federal Reserve Bulletin,* xiv (9), September 1928, 650.

[2] F.R.B.N.Y., Lubbock to Norman, no. 31/29, 2 February 1929. The Reichsbank provided the active support in the late summer of 1929, for, although it was taking gold from London for arbitrage reasons, it desired 'that the Bank of England might not be led to adopt a discount policy which in turn would be undesirable for the German money market'. Annual Report of the Reichsbank, *Federal Reserve Bulletin,* xvi (5), May 1930, 299. Clay (*Lord Norman,* 371) is the only source of information available on the 1931 French transaction, for the Federal Reserve Bank of New York's archives only indicate Bank of England–Bank of France dollar transactions of about £500,000 during a period when the Bank of England's holdings of French francs rose from their conventional post-1928 level of £81–84 thousand to over £4.6 million. The rest could have come from operations through the B.I.S. or through Bank of France purchases of sterling, See below, p. 192.

[3] If one takes only transactions referring to central banks by name and excludes all others, even though the central bank concerned might be operating through a commercial bank, the total, excluding B.I.S. transactions, for the period May 1925 to June 1931 comes to £44 million.

gold movements did place itself at some risk. For as long as the balances of payments of the overseas countries concerned (including here overseas sterling countries holding sterling balances in London) moved out of phase with the U.K.'s the risk was minimal. If, however, as in 1929 and 1931, some of those countries which held exchange balances in London suffered from exchange pressures at the same time as the U.K., the additional reserves in the accounts of the Bank of England were somewhat illusory. On the basis of pre-war experience, the Bank could have expected that this phenomenon of simultaneous deficits in London and abroad would be highly unlikely for extended periods, given the cyclical behaviour of the U.K. trade balance. After 1920, however, the cyclical pattern of the U.K. trade balance changed to a form which closely parallelled those abroad, a factor which the 1929–31 experience makes patently clear.[1]

In its operations with these foreign exchange balances, the Bank was continuously preoccupied by the need for secrecy and discretion. That its efforts in this respect were generally successful, before the summer of 1931, is beyond doubt, as the paucity of press, and even Treasury, guesses as to the extent of its activities indicates. Norman summed up the Bank's attitude to outsiders knowing anything as to its foreign exchange operations to Harrison in August 1926, when there had been press rumours as to the destination of the proceeds of some of the early gold shipments to San Francisco by the Commonwealth Bank of Australia:[2]

I do not want them [the newspapers] to know or suspect that the Bank of England is thus acquiring and retaining the proceeds of this gold (among other sums) in the form of Dollar assets with your Reserve Bank. In that case we should risk to be accused of having larger reserves or gold holdings than we publish and we might also be accused of acquiring Dollars which were, or would be, useful to our Treasury.

This last reference to the Treasury highlights one of the most interesting and significant aspects of the Bank's exchange operations. The Bank, except for those sums in the Issue Department reported monthly to the Treasury after November 1928, normally did not tell even the Treasury of its exchange holdings or of their use in particular circumstances. For example, during the negotiations surrounding the Currency and Bank Notes Act 1928, the Bank did not tell the Treasury that its exchange holdings exceeded £45 million, although this sum equalled the reserve of the Banking Department – the normal index of British free reserves.[3] Similarly, when the Treasury discussed the exchange

---

[1]Mintz, *Trade Balances*, Ch. III.
[2]F.R.B.N.Y., Norman to Harrison, 23 August 1926.
[3]F.R.B.N.Y., Strong Papers, Memorandum on the Currency and Bank Note Bill, 24 May 1928.

N

situation in March 1929 and contemplated the reserves available for exchange support it only took account of the Issue Department's exchange holdings, or two-thirds of the total.[1]

This general tendency towards secrecy was understandable from the Bank's point of view and traditions. Except where the Bank acted as an agent for the Treasury, as in the case in the Issue Department after 1928 or the Exchange Equalisation Account after 1932, there was a belief that the Treasury had no right to knowledge of 'the affairs of the Bank'.[2] Such a distinction clearly existed in the 1920s as the discussions of the role of the Chancellor in Bank Rate changes indicated.[3] To this traditional distinction, one might add a practical consideration. Given the political and public pressure towards lower interest rates that existed throughout the interwar gold standard period, public or even wider official knowledge of the fact that the Bank held hidden reserves, at times as large as its published reserves, would have made execution of its even mildly deflationary policy impossible. Moreover, if changes in these reserves had been known, as regularly perhaps as changes in gold reserves, given the structure of expectations that existed as to the connection between gold movements and changes in Bank Rate, the Bank would have lost considerable flexibility in its operations, particularly during 1928-9.[4]

The Bank attempted to keep its operations secret in three ways.

[1] T176/13, Leith-Ross to Hopkins, 9 March 1929. Sir Ralph Hawtrey has informed me that the above statements and impressions culled from official documents correspond to his experience in the Treasury at the time. However, the Treasury, largely as a result of the experiences of 1931, eventually did learn of the existence of the Bank's hidden reserves, but then only in the vaguest way. See T175/17, Memorandum by Hopkins, April 1933.

[2] M. J. Artis, *Foundations of British Monetary Policy* (Oxford, 1965), 30; Select Committee on Nationalised Industries, Session 1969-70, *First Report: The Bank of England* (London, 1970), evidence of Professor R. S. Sayers, Q. 1762.

[3] Above, pp. 160-1. As with the disagreements over Bank Rate policy, the Bank's secrecy over its foreign exchange operations provides another example of the tensions that existed between the Bank and the Treasury over the conduct of policy. The same problem also arose over Snowden's behaviour at the Hague in 1929 (Boyle, *Montagu Norman*, 243-4; Clay, *Lord Norman*, 270-1) and over the timing and extent of the measures necessary to defend sterling during the Labour Government's part of the 1931 crisis (Clarke, *Central Bank Cooperation*, 207, 210 -11; Boyle, *Montagu Norman*, 266-7). During the National Government's segment of the same crisis, the Bank and the Ministers involved were prepared to consider a much wider range of measures – exchange control, emergency protection, requisition and sale of overseas securities – than had been the case in August. For the range of alternatives considered see Cab. 27/462, Committee on the Financial Situation.

[4] One would expect that the Bank would have found it impossible to lose almost £30 million in reserves, as it did between June and December 1928, and keep Bank Rate unchanged. If we convert to current prices and to dollars, this would be asking the E.E.A. to lose over $450 million without producing some change in policy.

First, in its market operations it deliberately disguised itself. Through a system of numbered accounts at the Federal Reserve Bank of New York it prevented banks paying funds in or receiving them from knowing their ultimate destination or origin.[1] Also, by operating through the Anglo-International Bank, itself a large dealer in dollars, it further reduced the possibilities of discovery. Second, the Bank hid the assets concerned from public view in its balance sheet. Other Securities in the Banking and Issue Departments proved to be the ideal place in this respect, and complete offsetting through compensating security purchases or sales normally meant that a connection between movements in these items and any suspected support was difficult to detect.[2] Finally, in its exchange operations before the summer of 1931, the Bank attempted to minimise discovery possibilities by not operating as an unlimited seller of exchange at a pegged rate. Moreover, the Bank did not operate on every day or in large amounts during any particular period of intervention.[3]

Given the above sources of funds and general operating characteristics, one must now turn to an examination of the Bank's uses of its exchange reserves. An examination of Table 15 indicates that prior to 1928, there were only two occasions when the Bank's exchange reserves fell. Thus most examples will concern operations after 1928. In discussing these operations, it is helpful to distinguish between those affecting the spot and those affecting the forward exchange rate, as well as to consider other possible uses of exchange. In each case, several variants of method and purpose must be considered.

Taking normal exchange support operations to prevent gold export first, and excluding the summer of 1931, the most active period for such operations was September 1926–September 1929. During this period, the Bank sold dollars in the open-market spot in ten months during which the average sterling–dollar exchange rate was \$4.8505 or below the average gold export point for London of \$4.85145.[4] These averages provide a rough indication of the tactics involved, for they suggest that the object of normal intervention on the dollar exchange was not to keep the exchange above the gold export point, but to keep gold from moving. This implies that the Bank was taking advantage of

---

[1] F.R.B.N.Y., Osborne to Crane, 24 February 1926.

[2] Clay, *Lord Norman*, 255. This normal policy of complete offsetting represented an innovation, in so far as it occurred automatically, for it meant that the Bank, unless it took other action, was insulating the economy from the impact effects of movements in the exchange reserves. As such, it set a precedent for the institutionalisation of insulation in the E.E.A.

[3] F.R.B.N.Y., Norman to Harrison, no. 205/28, 24 October 1928. For example between 14 August and 1 September 1928 the Bank's intervention occurred on ten occasions, averaging £390,000 on each; between 8 October and 26 October 1928 the Bank's intervention occurred on thirteen occasions and averaged £545,000.

[4] See Figure 1 above.

a peculiar characteristic of the New York, as compared to the Continental exchanges, the fact that fast steamers did not leave every day. Therefore, given irregular sailings sterling could be allowed to fall below the gold export point by the amount of the additional interest and/or transport costs involved in taking gold on slower boats or in waiting for a fast sailing without the Bank being involved in a loss of reserves. As speculation would prevent such movements, in that speculators could expect to make small profits in the movement of the exchange back to the gold point on days of sailings, support would be unnecessary on these occasions.[1] Thus the Bank's task centred on keeping the exchange above the gold export point on the days very close to a sailing. That the Bank understood this tactic is clear from its 1928–9 cables.[2]

As the Bank at times wanted to allow some gold to go to impress the domestic market with the seriousness of the situation, it occasionally adopted a variant of the above policy and only sold on selected days or in parts of a given day so that gold could move. Behind such considerations lay the decision of Norman in October 1928 to allow equal losses of gold and exchange.[3]

In addition to using its exchange resources for spot exchange support at the gold export point, the Bank also on occasion appears to have sold foreign exchange to reduce the funds in the domestic market, a tactic followed in a much more sophisticated form by the Bank of Italy in recent years.[4] Although such operations would serve to support the exchange rate, such support was purely incidental on the first occasion on which the Bank operated in this manner in the period March–July 1928, for sterling stood at $4.87–88. On this occasion the Bank's holdings of Government securities averaged £31.3 million – probably at a level where further sales would threaten its holdings for income purposes – while Other Securities averaged £45.3 million, only £2.5 million above

---

[1] A reworking of Einzig's calculations (*International Gold Movements*, 150) suggests that each additional day involved in holding gold, with interest rates at 6 per cent, represented a reduction of 0.07 cents in the gold export point to New York. Therefore, over two days without shipping movements, the exchange could fall by up to 0.14 cents before it became profitable to take gold for arbitrage purposes from the Bank. On £1 this represented a maximum return of 25.6 cents per annum, or 5 per cent, with very little risk. As exchange settlements could occur up to three days after the transaction occurred, speculation here might not even involve capital costs.

[2] F.R.B.N.Y., Lubbock to Harrison, no. 137/28, 3 August 1928; Norman to Harrison, nos 203 and 211/28, 23 and 30 October 1928; nos 214 and 218/29, 19 and 20 August 1929; Norman to McGarrah, no. 240/29, 2 September 1929.

[3] F.R.B.N.Y., Strong Papers, Lubbock to Strong, 31 August 1928; Norman to Harrison, nos 165 and 188/28, 5 September and 5 October 1928.

[4] S. I. Katz, 'External Surpluses, Capital Flows, and Credit Policy in the European Economic Community, 1958 to 1967', *Princeton Studies in International Finance No. 22*, 19ff.

the exchange holdings. During the period March–July, Other Securities fell by the amount of the exchange sales, about £8 million, thus confirming that Lubbock's plans for the July sales, 'to reduce surplus funds in the market here with a view to arresting downward tendency of rate', had probably been followed earlier.[1]

The Bank also appears to have used this same method to tighten the domestic market, to a more limited extent, in 1930. At that time sterling stood well above $4.86, but the Bank was having difficulties in keeping market rates in touch with Bank Rate owing to a shortage of bills.[2] On 20 March, the Bank reduced Bank Rate to $3\frac{1}{2}$ per cent, although New York rates remained unchanged. As there was some uncertainty as to future New York rates and American prospects,[3] the Bank appears to have attempted to make Bank Rate effective and to prevent any falling away of market rates, by using the squeeze resulting from tax payments, the final call for the conversion loan and the popularity of late June Treasury bills to tighten the market. Spot foreign exchange sales of approximately £2.6 million, not offset by bill purchases were only part of the process. Between 19 and 26 March Public Deposits rose by £6 million, Government Securities by £3 million and Other Securities fell by £3 million. Thus the market found itself short by £6 million at a time when it could least afford it. The rise in discounts and advances of £4 million the next week, and the temporary end of falling bill rates indicates the success of the measures, which were occasionally reinforced by small sales of spot exchange in early April, the total sums involved being about £1 million.

Of course the Bank did not need to restrict the use of such sales to periods when sterling was relatively strong. It could on occasion fail to offset exchange support sales to increase its pull on the market. Thus, for example, after July 1928 when the Bank remained under heavy pressure, it continued to offset only part of its exchange sales, so that of the £20 million equivalent sold from August to November 1928, only £7 million was offset.

A third use of foreign exchange operations arose out of the position of sterling *vis-à-vis* the dollar and Continental currencies. Throughout the period under consideration, sterling tended to be the currency through which one moved between, say, francs and dollars, or vice versa. Thus, in many instances, weakness against Continental currencies often coincided with strength against the dollar. Under such conditions, if sterling was strong against the dollar and weak against the franc to the extent of losing gold, sales of dollars might raise the dollar exchange sufficiently to make it profitable for bullion arbitragists to take gold from

[1] F.R.B.N.Y., Lubbock to Case, no. 126/28, 4 July 1928.
[2] Above, p. 144.
[3] Above, p. 139.

New York rather than London, or at least reduce losses from London through the effects of inter-currency arbitrage. The above process describes almost exactly how the Bank operated in August 1930 to stem the flow of gold to Paris and provides the rationale of £3.8 million equivalent in exchange sales at a time when sterling averaged between $4.865 and $4.870.[1] These sales were one of the reasons for the decline in gold losses to Paris and the flows of gold from New York to Paris during the period.

In addition, the Bank used its foreign exchange holdings to effect asset conversions for other central banks. These conversions might take the form of the reversal of previous overseas central bank support of sterling in periods of pressure, as did the repayments of $16.1 million and $11.2 million to the Federal Reserve Bank of New York in November 1929 and March 1931 respectively.[2] They might also represent exchanges of dollars or other foreign currencies for sterling, the classic case here being the payment of $25 million to the Bank of France in August 1927 as a part of efforts to allow the Bank of France to increase its dollar reserves (or readily available future gold reserves) and thus remove one source of the difficulties of June 1927.[3] Finally, they might represent exchanges of gold for dollars, a transaction which might, as in 1929, prevent gold going to the U.S.A. from Europe, but would not weaken the Bank's overall position.[4] All of these variations occurred during the period under consideration, the Bank's payments to named central banks totalling £14.3 million between May 1925 and early May 1931.[5]

However, the Bank's exchange operations on its own account were not confined to the spot market or to inter-bank exchanges. On occasion, prior to the summer of 1931, the Bank also intervened in the forward market. This intervention took various forms and occurred for several reasons, but before discussing it fully, a brief discussion of the significance and effects of such intervention is necessary.

The forward exchange market offers extensive opportunities for official intervention designed to prevent unwanted changes in official reserves and/or to alter the incentives to move short-term funds between centres. By altering the relationship between forward and spot exchange rates through purchases or sales of forward exchange, the Authorities,

---

[1]F.R.B.N.Y., Harvey to Harrison, no. 153/30, 17 July 1930; Harrison to Harvey, no. 179/30, 18 August 1930.
[2]For this support see below, p. 192.
[3]Above 135; F.R.B.N.Y., Strong Papers, Moreau to Strong, 19 August 1927; Rist to Strong, 14 September 1927; Norman to Strong, no. 122/27, 18 August 1927.
[4]Annual Report of the Netherlands Bank, *Federal Reserve Bulletin*, xv (9), September 1929, 624.
[5]This excludes the 1931 crisis support to Central Europe and transactions with the B.I.S.

assuming that they are able to prevent any resulting movements in short-term funds from influencing domestic interest rates, can alter the incentives for the shifting of short-term balances between money markets in a manner which will possibly affect the spot rate in the direction desired. To take an example, in November 1927 spot sterling averaged $4.8744; whereas three months forward dollars stood at an average premium of $\frac{23}{32}$ or of 0.76 cents. At the same time, the three months rates for bills differed by 1.09 per cent per annum, London rates being higher. Thus someone moving dollar funds into London could, after covering himself in the forward exchange market, make 0.47 per cent more per annum than he could in New York.[1] If in these circumstances, the Authorities by selling forward dollars could reduce the forward premium, they would increase the returns available to investors in London using dollars by the amount of the reduced premium. Of course, the Bank could work in the opposite direction if it desired.

In the period between May 1925 and May 1931 the Bank operated in both directions in the forward market. It only admitted operating in a direction which would increase the inflow of short-term funds into London once, in January 1931. At that point it sold $3.5 million forward to test the market, but concluded 'that the exchange position is too wide and deep to encourage further transactions of this kind'.[2] However, the pattern of payments from the Bank's New York dollar reserves suggests that the Bank also attempted to support sterling through forward exchange operations in 1929.

During the period from late October 1929 to late February 1930, the Bank's cables to the Federal Reserve Bank of New York reveal a series of exchange sales which totalled over $35 million. At this time spot sterling stood well above the gold export point (average rate $4.8724) and the Bank was gaining reserves.[3] The cables instructing the Federal Reserve to make payments reveal that the Bank knew of some of these sales as much as three weeks in advance, something hardly characteristic of spot transactions, and the clearing of the payments through the Anglo-International Bank makes it improbable that they reflected central bank co-operation.

The sales between 28 October and 8 November – about $8.5 million – reflect (a) periods three months earlier when spot sterling was above the

---

[1] Buy sterling at $4.8744, invest for three months at 1.09 per cent more than in New York, and sell forward sterling forward for dollars at $4.8668.

[2] F.R.B.N.Y., Norman to Harrison, no. 16/31, 21 January 1931. At that time, forward sterling stood below the gold export point on most major exchanges, a fact which suggested a lack of confidence in the future of sterling. *The Economist*, 'Market Notes', 7 February 1931; Einzig, *Theory of Forward Exchange*, 260.

[3] The reserve gains were limited by the payment of $16.1 million to the Federal Reserve in November to reverse support granted during the previous summer and by the series of transactions under discussion.

gold export point but forward rates for discount-acceptance and dis-count-time/call money[1] arbitrage were insufficiently favourable or strongly unfavourable to London; (b) periods two months earlier when spot sterling was weak and under support and forward sterling barely favoured covered interest arbitrage to London on a discount-acceptance basis and strongly favoured New York on a discount-time/call money basis; or (c) periods one month earlier when spot sterling was moving above the gold export point after a change in Bank Rate and official spot support and when discount-acceptance arbitrage favoured London, but discount-time/call money arbitrage strongly favoured New York. The pattern of payments leads one to accept possibility (b) as being the most plausible. On past experience, support would be unlikely in case (a) and in case (c) the January payments might be more plausible. Moreover, in late August and early September, Norman was working extremely hard to keep domestic interest rates stable,[2] and in such circumstances, forward sales of dollars would aid the process.

The heavy January and February payments are more difficult to account for, but again one notes that until well into November, the constellation of forward and spot rates and discount-time/call money rates favoured covered interest arbitrage to New York. One also notes that from September to November, London was able to keep the premium on forward dollars sufficiently low to manage some of the highest covered interest arbitrage differentials in favour of London of the gold standard period, but despite this differential the U.K. liabilities of New York banks refused to fall.[3] At the same time, with spot sterling strong, a tightening of domestic interest rates or even an attempt to make Bank Rate effective, would have seemed unnecessary to most domestic observers.[4] Moreover, the cheapening of forward cover would have

---

[1] In his correspondence with his London colleagues and his New York opposites, Norman had repeatedly emphasised that the call and time money rates in New York were the most significant international notes in that market. F.R.B.N.Y., Strong to Norman, no. 96, 29 May 1925; Norman to Strong, no. 72, 26 October 1925; no. 167/27, 13 September 1927; Norman to Harrison, no. 6/29, 4 January 1929; Norman to Lubbock, no. 41/29, 7 February 1929.
   The call money rate is a daily rate rather than a three months rate. Thus for the call rate to affect arbitrage flows, the operative rate would be the *expected* call rate over the next one to three months. As the call rate was associated with periods of stock market speculation in New York, and as by the late summer of 1929 call rates had been high for some months, one might well argue that arbitragists might operate on the assumption that the current call rate might be expected to operate for the future. On call rates and arbitrage, see C. A. E. Goodhart, *The New York Money Market and the Finance of Trade, 1900–1913* (Cambridge, 1969), 48–9.
[2] Above, p. 164.
[3] Federal Reserve Board, *Banking and Monetary Statistics*, Table 161.
[4] At that time, the Bank was experiencing some difficulty in keeping Bank Rate effective in the market. Clay, *Lord Norman*, 249, 360; *The Banker*, XII (47), December

increased the attraction of funds to London after the exchange rose above $4.87 in October and the demand for forward cover naturally became more insistent.[1] The cessation of these transactions one to three months after the removal of the covered interest differentials would also increase the probability of these operations representing forward exchange support for sterling, the Bank of England's first recorded efforts in this area.[2]

However, the 1929 forward support operations do not represent the Bank's first operations of any description in that market, for it had used the market in a different way somewhat earlier. In November 1926, when spot sterling was near the gold export point, the Bank instructed the Federal Reserve Bank of New York to sell spot dollars for sterling and to repurchase any dollars sold two to three months forward.[3] This operation suggests that the Bank was gaining its early experience in exchange intervention at almost no cost to the reserves, by taking advantage of an important relationship between spot and forward rates under gold standard conditions: the floor provided, under conditions of confidence in the parity, for the forward rate by the gold export point. Under such conditions, when the spot exchange nears the gold export point, forward sales of the currency defended spot will not drive the forward rate against the Authorities substantially and thus disturb interest differentials, because the existence of the floor noted above (which sets a minimum for probable future spot movements) and the demand for forward cover by businessmen with receipts due in foreign currency will inhibit the deterioration of the forward rate.[4]

In addition to the exchange operations on its own account discussed above, the Bank of England, on several occasions during the period, received assistance from foreign central banks in its defence of the sterling exchange. The Federal Reserve System, operating through the Federal Reserve Bank of New York, purchased sterling on three occasions (the sums involved on each occasion appearing after the date) – June

---

1929, 275; F.R.B.N.Y., Norman to Harrison, no. 299/29, 28 October 1929; Bank of England to Scott, no. 319/29, 20 November 1929; Harvey to Harrison, no. 335/29, 11 December 1929.

[1] Keynes, 'The British Balance of Trade', 559.

[2] Previously, official forward support for sterling has not been noted before the 1931 crisis. Einzig, *Theory of Forward Exchange*, 371; *Tragedy of the Pound*, 91–4.

[3] F.R.B.N.Y., Bank of England to F.R.B.N.Y., no. 22, 3 November 1926. The November sale represents the first sale announced in the cables as an exchange support operation. However, the Bank did dispose of dollars in September, when sterling was also weak. The exact amount of the September sales was repaid by the same bank three to five months later and could represent an earlier use of the same technique. However, the evidence is much less powerful.

[4] I am indebted to Mr S. V. O. Clarke for putting up with my earlier ruminations on this problem.

1927 (£12 million), August–September 1929 (£3.3 million) and October–December 1930 (£7.15 million).[1] The Bank of France also supported sterling in late 1930 and early 1931, although the sums involved are unknown.[2] The Federal Reserve support in 1927 took the form of sales of gold, earmarked in London, to the Bank of France in exchange for sterling and allowed the latter to reduce the value of its sterling assets;[3] whereas, the 1929 and 1930 support took the form of active exchange market purchases of sterling designed to prevent gold movements to New York.[4] The Bank of France support in 1930 involved purchases of sterling to prevent the complete disorganisation of the exchange market during the French liquidity crisis following the Ousric scandal, at a time when the Bank of France's unwillingness to accept standard gold made the gold export point from London somewhat indeterminate.[5] French support in early 1931 involved an exchange of francs for dollars, a few purchases of sterling, and an occasionally active sale of dollars designed to so affect the franc–dollar exchange as to alter the franc–sterling exchange through arbitrage.[6]

Generally speaking, the Bank's access to such foreign support appears to have become more difficult as time passed, particularly in the case of the Federal Reserve. In 1927, there appear to have been no questions asked. In 1929, however, Norman's gold standard pessimism had reached such a level that Harrison at one point suggested a gold guarantee for any Federal Reserve purchases of sterling. Norman's blunt reply – Of course sterling is repayable in gold. That is the gold standard.'–

---

[1] These sums have been calculated from file C261 of the Federal Reserve Bank of New York's archives.

[2] T160/430/F12317/1, Leith-Ross to Hopkins, 2 December 1930; F.R.B.N.Y., Sproul, Record of Certain Conversations in London and Paris, Conversation with M. Cariguel, 19 November 1930, 3; Clay, *Lord Norman*, 369, 371.

[3] Above, p. 135; F.R.B.N.Y., Norman to Strong, no. 57, 9 June 1927; Strong to Norman, nos 85 and 89, 10 and 11 June 1927.

[4] F.R.B.N.Y., Harrison Collection, Telephone Conversation with Governor Norman, 9 August 1929; Harrison to Norman, no. 221/29, 10 August 1929; Norman to Harrison, no. 205/29, 13 August 1929; Harrison to McGarrah, 14 August 1929; Harrison Collection, Meeting in Washington, 15 August 1929; Conversation with Governor Young, 16 and 19 August 1929; Harvey to Harrison, no. 230/30, 9 October 1930; Harrison to Harvey, no. 244/30, 10 October 1930; Clarke, *Central Bank Cooperation*, 175.

[5] *The Economist*, 8, 15 and 29 November 1930, 853–4, 890, 990; above, p. 175. For a discussion of the Bank of France's legal position in such cases, see Appendix 4.

[6] Clay, *Lord Norman*, 371; F.R.B.N.Y., Bank of England to F.R.B.N.Y., 126/31, 8 May 1931; Moret to Harrison, nos 40 and 41, 30 April and 4 May 1931. The purchases of sterling are not explicitly recorded but as dollar transactions between the Bank of England and the Bank of France through the Federal Reserve Bank of New York totalled approximately £500,000 and as the Bank of England's holdings of francs rose by £4.5 million, the possibility is open, although some transactions could have occurred through the B.I.S.

seems to have satisfied Harrison, but the change in tone was significant.[1] As the 1930 operation progressed, there was a much more general feeling in London and New York that such support should be limited.[2] As Dr Sprague, one of Norman's advisers, summed it up:[3]

Such purchases [of sterling by the Federal Reserve] merely postpone the setting in motion of the forces which will really correct the underlying situation. In this case they would foster the willingness of England to take her difficulties sitting down, instead of standing against them.

This growing unwillingness reached its apogee in 1931 with the existence of signed credit agreements and ultimately the refusal of further support.

The 1931 crisis represented the culmination of the Bank's experience in exchange market intervention. During a period of less than two months after 23 July, the Bank's sales of dollar exchange of $381.1 million spot and over $125 million forward were supplemented by Federal Reserve spot purchases of £9.5 million.[4] At the same time, the Bank's franc operations, both spot and forward, which are more difficult to sort out, appear to have amounted to approximately £53 million.[5] Additional gold losses totalled £34 million. Thus, of the total reserve losses in these estimates of £201.5 million, 83 per cent came in exchange operations.[6] It is in this sense that 1931 drew heavily on the Bank's knowledge of and experience in exchange operations.

The negotiations and politics of the period of eight weeks between the first exchange intervention and rise in Bank Rate to $3\frac{1}{2}$ per cent on 23 July and the suspension of the gold standard have been extensively discussed elsewhere, as have most of the Bank's exchange operations.[7]

[1] F.R.B.N.Y., Harrison to Norman, no. 224/29, 14 August 1929; Norman to Harrison, no. 209/29, 15 August 1929. Harrison appears to have taken no further steps to cover himself against possible exchange losses (Harrison Collection, Conversation with Governor Young, 16 August 1929).

[2] Clay, *Lord Norman*, 369; Clarke, *Central Bank Cooperation*, 176.

[3] F.R.B.N.Y., Sproul, Record of Certain Conversations in London and Paris, Conversation with Dr Sprague, 5 December 1930, 8.

[4] The spot transactions are those recorded in cables between the Bank of England and the Federal Reserve Bank of New York. The forward transactions were mentioned in F.R.B.N.Y., Crane to Harrison, 22 September 1931 (reporting a telephone conversation with Mr Lefeaux of the Bank of England) The forward transactions were unwound, in most cases, as they fell due after 21 September.

[5] The Bank of England's French credits totalled £65 million. In addition, on 22 July, the Bank held £4.1 million in francs in its exchange reserves. By 21 September, $61.4 million remained in the credit and $15.1 had been converted into dollars and used for dollar exchange support, F.R.B.N.Y., Harrison Collection, Conversations with Harvey, 6.30 and 8.35 a.m., 19 September 1931, plus cable files of the Federal Reserve Bank of New York.

[6] If this sum was converted to dollars at current prices, it would exceed $3 billion.

[7] Clay, *Lord Norman*, 383–90; Boyle *Montagu Norman*, 263–75; R. Bassett, *1931: Political Crisis* (London, 1958); Clarke, *Central Bank Cooperation*, 201–18. This last source contains a reasonably full discussion of the exchange operations.

The discussion below concentrates in a summary and rather critical way on the overall tactics of the period, and leaves the interested reader to follow the details in other sources.

The 1931 crisis operations as a whole should have represented an occasion on which the Bank applied its accumulated exchange intervention experience of previous years. However, given that the Authorities believed that a final defence of sterling was necessary and possible, which they did until very near the end,[1] they were remarkably inept. The exchange operations and their extent were widely known on a day-to-day basis, *The Times* of 24 August being accurate to within £1 million in announcing the virtual exhaustion of the central bank credits.[2] The Bank's choice of market operators contributed to this publicity, for the banks concerned were not normally large operators in the markets for dollars and francs and did not normally sell large amounts of spot and forward exchange at what were virtually pegged rates.[3] Towards the end of August the Bank appears to have realised this in the forward market, for it began to use the clearing banks in forward markets,[4] and in September they found use in spot markets as well. The clearing banks used were changed regularly in the hope that 'if by this means operations in London were given a more normal appearance ... some diminution in demand might result'.[5] The choice of an unreasonable peg, around $4.86 from August 15, probably decreased confidence and increased sales 'without accomplishing anything permanently constructive' rather than increasing confidence as Harvey, his Directors and his French opposites expected.[6] Market operators knew that the situation did not justify such high and relatively stable rates both spot and forward, and these, plus the gold gains by the Bank during most of August and early September heightened uncertainty because they were at such odds with market reality. This behaviour by the Bank is curious in the light of previous experience where intervention had always been kept to a minimum and had been designed largely to just prevent gold movements rather than peg the exchange well above the gold export point.[7]

---

[1]Cab. 27/462, Meeting of 14 September 1931, 10; Meeting of 17 September 1931, 1. Discussions on suspending gold convertibility appear to have started in earnest on 17 September. See T163/68/G3788.

[2]F.R.B.N.Y., Harrison to Harvey, no. 307/31, 24 August 1931.

[3]Einzig, *Tragedy of the Pound*, 90–2. The Bank's change in its agent for dollar exchange operations from the previously successful Anglo-International Bank to the British Overseas Bank from 24 July probably contributed to the lack of secrecy. The Anglo-International Bank appears to have taken over as agent for the Bank's franc exchange operations.

[4]Ibid., 90–1. F.R.B.N.Y., Harvey to Harrison, no. 334/31, 3 September 1931.

[5]Ibid.

[6]Harvey to Harrison, nos 402 and 411/31, 4 and 8 September 1931; Harrison to Harvey, no. 334/31, 3 September 1931; Harrison Papers, Conversation with Harvey, 16 September 1931.   [7]Above, pp. 185–6.

This technical ineptness was combined with a peculiar ineptness in timing. By mid-July, sterling had been under a cloud of some sort for over six months, the Authorities had been aware of the possibility and the high degree of probability of a German crisis for as long and they had realised the probable effects of a German crisis on London's position for over two years.[1] However, other than discussing the possibilities of credits, in a very desultory way, with the French in January and February and other than implicitly deciding that a programme of deflationary measures would be necessary at some time in the very near future, if not immediately, to deal with Britain's international economic position, official thinking had made no real preparations for action or for a crisis before the situation was 'boiling up' in mid-July.[2] At that point, as usual, they hesitated and decided to 'ride along for at least a week hoping that the conference called for London . . . will put Central Europe on a more permanent basis and clarify the situation'.[3] Thus it was late July before any solutions to the problems at hand were seriously considered and at that stage serious and careful thought was impaired by the need to act immediately.[4] Yet, even then, despite the need for action at that point, the Treasury and the Government were extremely dilatory over their handling of the crisis, largely it seems because of a belief that the situation could be held until after Parliament reassembled for *normal* business in October.[5] The publication of the May *Report,* whose effect Norman admitted would be 'devilish', with minimal official comment, the increase in the fiduciary issue and the cessation of exchange support early in August – this last measure being a further attempt by the Bank of England to impress the need for action upon the Treasury and the Government – all served to reduce confidence even further.[6] This meant that the Treasury and the Cabinet had even less time to consider the

[1] Above, p. 140. see T160/393/F11300/032; T176/13 Hopkins to Grigg, 19 August, 1929; T176/29, Leith-Ross to Niemeyer, 8 June, 1927.

[2] Clay, *Lord Norman,* 370; Moggridge, 'The 1931 Financial Crisis', 835–7; T160/430/F12317/2, Waley, Notes of a Conversation between Leith-Ross, Siepmann and Sprague, 30 January 1931; Gold Movements: Points for discussion with the French Treasury, 12 February 1931; Leith-Ross, Talk with Hopkins and Governor on Gold Movements, 17 February 1931; Royal Commission on Unemployment Insurance, *Evidence* (London, 1931), Q. 3294, Memorandum of Evidence by the Treasury, para. 4; 251 H.C. Deb. 5 s. columns, 1397, 1402–3. F.R.B.N.Y., Harrison Collection, Conversation with Norman, 15 July 1931.

[3] Ibid.; Skidelsky, *Politicians and the Slump* (London, 1967), 341–2.

[4] F.R.B.N.Y., Harrison Collection, Conversation with Norman, 29 July 1931.

[5] Ibid.; T175/51, Hopkins to Chancellor, 24 July 1931; 255 H.C. Deb. 5s. columns 2512–3.

[6] F.R.B.N.Y., Harrison Collection, Conversation with Norman, 29 July 1931; Conversation with Lacour-Gayet, 7 August 1931; Sproul, Conversation with Catterns, 5 August 1931; T160/430/F12317/2, Leith-Ross, Note of a Discussion with French Treasury Experts, 11 August 1931, 4.

economy measures that the Bank was pressing on them as preparation for a long-term loan.[1] The ensuing problems in gaining political acceptance of a programme suitable to the Bank and the City, the rumours thereof and the heavy exchange losses during the period meant that when the National Government came to power speed was of the essence, a fact that made a long-term credit almost impossible.[2] In the event, even obtaining short-term credits presented 'enormous difficulties'.[3] Moreover, Governor Norman for one believed that the programme underlying the credits was inadequate and that it would cause trouble in a year or so.[4] Throughout the crisis, in fact, the Authorities were never in a position to control events–they always appeared to be reacting to events and this did little to enhance the confidence so necessary in such conditions. By late August, it was probably too late to save sterling, even if it had been possible through very drastic measures previously, for even central banks were beginning to fear for the future and ask for gold guarantees for their sterling balances or withdraw them.[5] In fact, the 1931 crisis saw a refusal to apply much of the experience gained in previous exchange support and an exercise in how not to behave in a confidence crisis.

Gold and Foreign Exchange Operations, the Overall Results

The events of August and September 1931 conclude the examination of the Bank's foreign exchange and gold policies, although the former only represent the beginnings of peacetime exchange operations which have lasted to this day. In the period after 1925 the existence of the exchange reserves, an active gold policy and the willingness of foreign central banks, particularly the Federal Reserve and the Reichsbank, to support the Bank of England gave the Bank increased room for manoeuvre. Given that sterling was rarely above par on any of the major exchanges during the period and that the Authorities could thus not depend on attracting gold through arbitrage operations or even on holding gold coming into the London market, exchange and gold operations were instrumental in allowing official international reserves to rise in eighteen of the twenty-six quarters that composed the period.[6] This easing of the

[1] F.R.B.N.Y., Crane to Harrison, nos 4 and 7, 10 and 13 August 1931; Burgess to Crane, no. 10, 14 August 1931.
[2] T160/435/F12568/1, Note by Hopkins, 26 August 1931.
[3] T160/435/F12568/1, Hopkins to Fisher and Chanceller, 31 August 1931.
[4] F.R.B.N.Y., Harrison Collection, Conversation with Norman, 23 August 1931.
[5] F.R.B.N.Y., Crane to Harrison, no. 20, 3 September 1931; Harrison Papers, Conversation with Norman and Harvey, 2 October 1931; J. E. Crane, Report of European Trip, 1932, Conversation with Dr Bachman, 20 October 1932; Annual Report of the Swiss National Bank, *Federal Reserve Bulletin*, xviii (4), April 1932, 252; T160/439/F12712, Trip to Norman, 27 October 1931; Harvey to Waley, 18 February 1932.
[6] Above, p. 147.

reserve position allowed the Bank to be more solicitous towards domestic considerations. The form of the reserves allowed the Bank to prevent gold movements through selective sales and thus to allow the exchange to violate the gold points on eleven occasions with New York, six of which occurred during periods of exchange sales; while gold policy and central bank co-operation allowed the same to occur *vis-à-vis* Berlin on thirteen occasions (each occasion representing one month's average exchange rate).[1] The operations as well helped to stabilise Bank Rate and thus to free the Government from embarrassment. However, the operations, particularly in foreign exchange, had their limitations. Given the private and secret nature of the exchange operations, changes in dollar reserves removed any sense of urgency from particular periods of stress. True, their use might find the exchanges close to the gold export point, but that by itself might not create a sense of urgency outside the Bank, as the market was much more sensitive to gold movements as a determinant of expectations. Lubbock noted this problem late in August 1928 after the Bank had been selling dollars for some time to prevent gold losses.[2]

I think that what we have done so far is right: but our dollar selling has remained an absolute secret, and I am beginning to fear that our markets are beginning to build too firmly on the hope that gold will not move from us to you and that our rate will remain indefinitely where it is.

To some extent, this problem was solved later in 1928 and in 1929 when sales occurred only to limit gold shipments or to prevent them on a selective basis. These methods allowed the exchange to violate the gold points and allowed moderate amounts of gold to move, thus giving some public indication of pressure without excessive losses of gold, which would have been more difficult to retrieve and which would have resulted in pressure on the Authorities through the Treasury bill tender. In 1931, however, the Bank did not use either device and a sense of unreality prevailed, for although some market insiders knew the extent of market support which occasionally became public knowledge, others believed that sterling was stronger than it was in reality, partially one suspects because press reports were generally influenced by a desire not to 'sell sterling short'.[3]

The Bank's forward exchange operations, although rudimentary, allowed it in the early stages of its career as a market operator to gain experience relatively cheaply. Later, however, their purpose found extension in that they allowed the Bank, during parts of 1929, somewhat greater freedom with regard to domestic interest rates and international

[1] Above, Figure 1.
[2] F.R.B.N.Y., Lubbock to Strong, 31 August 1928.
[3] Einzig, *In the Centre of Things*, 82.

policy. In 1931, however, they probably did not achieve this aim to a similar extent, for in a liquidity crisis rates of interest are not of great importance. At that time forward support merely allowed cheaper covering for those with sterling obligations, perhaps marginally increased confidence, and cheapened speculation. More probably, the 1931 forward support consumed valuable foreign exchange and, in conjunction with the Bank's feeling that it had to maintain gold reserves to repay its New York and Paris borrowings, meant that the Bank tied up large reserves which could have found use for spot exchange support.[1]

Throughout the period after 1925, however, the Bank's ability to build up its stock of international reserves through gold market and foreign exchange operations without having to force the exchange to the gold import point through domestic deflation and its ability, to some extent at least, to control the timing and extent of public reserve losses certainly allowed some domestic insulation for the rigours of the full implications of 1925. In 1931, the owned and borrowed exchange reserves only prolonged the defence of sterling, while the Authorities' tactical ineptness helped to shorten it. At that time, even the most skilful defense would have only prolonged the agony for Britain, for sterling was in more fundamental disequilibrium than in 1925 and the world was much more sensitive to nuance and much more pessimistic in its outlook.[2] However, the whole experience, did prepare the way for the Bank's and the Treasury's experiences after 1931 with the Exchange Equalisation Account.[3]

[1]Cab. 23/268, Harvey to Snowden and MacDonald, 19 September 1931, in Appendix to Conclusions, 21 September 1931; Cab. 27/462, Meeting of 17 September 1931, 7; T163/68/G3788, Leith-Ross to Phillips, 18 September 1931 and Phillips comments thereon.

[2]Above Tables 8 and 9; Moggridge, 'The 1931 Financial Crisis; 833–5, 839.

[3]For a discussion of the origins and early experiences of the E.E.A. see 'The Exchange Equalisation Account: its origins and development' Bank of England, *Quarterly Bulletin*, VIII (4), December 1968.

9. THE USE OF MORAL SUASION IN CAPITAL MARKETS

Official intervention in long and short-term capital markets during the period of the interwar gold standard had as its main purpose an attempt to partially insulate the domestic economy from international payments pressures and their policy implications. As it evolved, the intervention provided classic examples of the scope and limitations of moral suasion. As well, this experience, which represented a distinct break from pre-war practice, provided a basis for the many later attempts at control which have remained important factors in British capital account transactions since 1931.

The basis for the policies of control lay in two characteristics of the London capital market: its propensity to lend much more at long term (and to some extent at short term) than the current account surplus, even allowing for capital inflows from abroad, and its organisation into a relatively small number of interdependent firms working from a small geographical area. The London capital market before 1914 had developed a body of practice and a set of institutions which made it an extremely efficient medium for channelling British funds abroad.[1] In the last years before 1914, the market's highly specialised firms successfully placed abroad at long term 9 per cent of the U.K.'s national income and over three-quarters of all new issues (by value) were for abroad.[2] After the war, the connections, traditions and issuing costs of the market made it internationally unique, but the deterioration in Britain's international economic position did not allow, except in an accounting sense, the same freedom of investment. The volume of foreign lending did decline in real terms and as a proportion of total new issues, but it remained substantial, totalling roughly £1,380 million over the period 1918–31 and £730 million between 1925 and 1931.[3] This later figure compares with a cumulative current account surplus of £262 million over the same

---

[1]A. K. Cairncross, *Home and Foreign Investment 1870–1913* (Cambridge, 1953), Ch. V; Balogh, *Studies*, Ch. 13–14.
[2]B. Thomas, 'The Historical Record of International Capital Movements, to 1913', 15.
[3]Midland Bank estimates.

O

period. True, the above lending estimates do not allow for repayments or foreign subscriptions, which would thus tend to overstate the problem, or transactions in outstanding securities, which would do the opposite, but the outlines are clear. Given this tendency towards lending more than the available current account surplus, the U.K., despite possible tendencies towards international financial intermediation,[1] was compelled to attract an increasing volume of short-term funds to minimise, prevent, or even reverse reserve losses. Such funds might be in London on a relatively permanent basis,[2] but, even if a small proportion was volatile and interest sensitive, the implications for monetary policy were clear: London would have to contain foreign lending or to hold, or at times increase, the volume of short-term funds deposited in the City. Given that, for long-term loans, London's issuing costs were below those abroad, to deter foreign borrowing interest rates in London would have to be well above those abroad to overcome traditional ties and to induce borrowing in New York, particularly in the case of Empire borrowers whose securities had trustee status.[3] At the same time, the Authorities' concern as to the level of domestic interest rates limited the scope for 'orthodox' monetary policies designed to reduce foreign lending at long term and increase British borrowing (and to some extent reduce British lending) at short term within the prevailing set of interest rate conventions. Thus the Bank, and to a lesser extent the Treasury, had to develop new methods for controlling long-term issues or for altering the conventional interest rate differentials between various markets so as to increase the rates relevant to international financial transactions which were effective for any given level of domestic interest rates.

In any attempts to alter traditional relationships, the nature of the London markets made them likely objects for the exercise of moral suasion by the Authorities. The Bank benefitted from the committees which the war and 'the growing cohesion of City interests'[4] had brought forward. These, in particular the Discount Market Committee, the Accepting Houses Committee and the extended Committee of the London Clearing Bankers, gave the Bank easy contact with the relevant City institutions and supplemented the day-to-day consultations with the inhabitants of the square mile for which Norman was famous. Given

[1]C. P. Kindleberger, 'Balance-of-Payments Deficits and the International Market for Liquidity', *Europe and the Dollar* (Cambridge, 1966); W. S. Salant, 'Capital Markets and the Balance of Payments of a Financial Center', Fellner, Machlup, Triffin, et al., *Maintaining and Restoring Balance*; Lindert, 'Key Currencies', 58–76.
[2]For example, those of central banks, colonial currency boards and overseas banks. See Williams, 'The Evolution of the Sterling System', 284ff.
[3]R.I.I.A., *Problem of International Investment*, 136–7; I. Mintz, *Deterioration in the Quality of Foreign Bonds Issued in the United States 1920–1930* (New York, 1951), 63ff.; below. p. 210.
[4]Clapham, *Bank of England*, II, 412.

the relatively small number of firms involved (22 acceptance houses of which 6 did the bulk of the foreign issues in London, 22 discount houses and 10 clearing banks) and the small geographical area in which they operated, contact was relatively frequent and easy.[1] In addition to these underlying advantages the Bank had access to a series of sanctions to make its desires effective. These are best discussed below in the context of its policies in particular markets.

The Long-Term Capital Market

Probably the most famous instances of the use of moral suasion during the period of the interwar gold standard occurred in the London market for long-term foreign capital. Norman had foreseen the need for 'the prevention of export of capital and foreign loans'[2] as part of the reconstruction policy prior to the return to gold, but had expected them to prove unnecessary after the return. However, as the situation evolved, controls of various sorts became much more than reconstruction devices and a pervasive feature of the post-war capital market.

During the war, the Authorities had attempted to prevent the export of capital in all forms with controls which grew more pervasive as the war progressed.[3] However, the end of the war brought pressures for the relaxation of the controls to which the Authorities succumbed to a considerable extent. Nevertheless, as there were pressures for loans to capital-starved Europe and to the Empire, and as the capital market faced domestic demands for the reconstruction of industry and for such officially encouraged programes as local authority housebuilding, the Authorities, with their own needs for continuous debt refinancing, tended to maintain some degree of control over overseas issues.[4]

In any attempts to operate controls the Bank had several advantages. Just before the war, the issuing houses had started to consult the Bank about new overseas issues and during the war consultations had occurred for all issues.[5] After the war, the habit of consultation continued and firms took any big foreign issue to the Governor to obtain his views, big issues being those over £1 million.[6] This process inevitably also brought many smaller issues into the net. On occasions when consultations occurred, the Governor had an opportunity to express his views on

---

[1] For a description of the City of this period see R. J. Truptil, *British Banks and the London Money Market* (London, 1936), Ch. II–IV.

[2] Clay, *Lord Norman*, 112.

[3] Morgan, *Studies*, 261–6; J. Atkin, 'Official Regulation of British Overseas Investment, 1914–1931', *Economic History Review*, 2nd Ser., XXIII (2), August 1970, 324–5.

[4] Ibid., 325–30.

[5] Keynes Papers, Macmillan Committee, Notes of Discussions, 28 November 1930, 20.

[6] Ibid., 21.

both the soundness and the general advisability of the issues concerned. This process of consultation gave him valuable information about forthcoming demands and allowed him to influence their timing.[1] Clay's biography of Norman provides several examples of the Governor's diary notes on such consultations.[2] On some occasions, his advice would be unambiguous and the Bank's wishes would be generally observed,[3] but often the advice was not sufficiently clear. As R. H. Brand put it:[4]

If he expressed a strong view we would [be mainly guided by it] but he would very likely say 'You must take your own line. This is my view. You must decide.' Then it is more difficult to know.

In these cases the advice merely became another factor in the merchant banker's decision to undertake an issue. Generally such consultation worked by itself, but on occasion Norman could draw on stronger resources. Speeches by the Chancellor, such as Churchill's Sheffield speech of November 1925 and Snowden's Mansion House appeal of 1929 could be used to enlist public support and to provide a justification for a certain course of action by the Bank.[5] The British Government could also, as in 1925, approach potential borrowing governments and ask them to rephase their borrowing or even to borrow elsewhere.[6] Action of this type would remove pressure at one source, the borrower, and could thus usefully supplement action taken in London. Finally, the Bank could issue general directives to such bodies as Bankers' Clearing House or the Committee of the Stock Exchange to favour or bar certain classes of issue.[7] Such methods were useful for a general class of loans, such as those to countries which had not funded their war debts or loans under twenty years, but lacked flexibility for particular cases or peculiar circumstances.

All of these avenues of suasion could be backed by sanctions of various types. The ultimate sanction was a refusal of permission to deal in the offending issue on the Stock Exchange, for this would largely destroy the marketability of the issue concerned.[8] Pressures to limit clearing bank participation in the issue would be almost as effective, as would well-timed press leaks as to the Bank's opposition. In addition, as the largest issuing

[1]Ibid., 20–22; Macmillan Committee, *Evidence*, Q. 391–5, 1352–68, 1584.
[2]Clay, *Lord Norman*, 144–5, 239–40.
[3]Macmillan Committee, *Evidence*, Q. 392, 395.
[4]Keynes Papers, Macmillan Committee, Notes of Discussions, 28 November 1930, 21.
[5]Below, p. 210; above, p. 163.
[6]Below, p. 207.
[7]Morgan, *Studies*, 265; Clay, *Lord Norman*, 368; T160/111/F4319/1, Blackett to Chancellor, 28 December 1921; Norman to Chairman of Bankers Clearing House 1 February 1922 and 14 January 1924; T175/4, Hopkins to Norman, 10 October 1928.
[8]C. Iversen, *Aspects of the Theory of International Capital Movements*, (London, 1935), 85.

houses combined an acceptance business with their issuing activities, they were dependent upon the willingness of the Bank to rediscount or take as collateral the bills they had accepted. If they incurred the Bank's displeasure, such facilities for their bills might disappear or be somewhat restricted, thus weakening one foundation of their business. Beyond that, the Bank and the Treasury both suggested agents to local authorities and other issuers of trustee securities and could use this influence to direct business away from the offending houses.[1] Thus the Authorities had several channels of influence to keep offenders in line. These channels were only useful on an individual basis: any show of strength by the issuing houses as a group would break the system of sanctions as their use on a large scale would damage the London market in a long-term sense.[2] However, such a mass revolt would probably end in a rise in Bank Rate, which, although it represented the policy step the Authorities had attempted to avoid through the use of suasion and was, therefore, counterproductive, would affect the issuing houses by reducing the volume of business and imposing capital losses on portfolios of unsold securities.[3] Nevertheless, the rise in Bank Rate represented less a sanction than an admission of failure.

To sort out the effects of the controls in their various forms a somewhat more extensive breakdown of the aggregate figures noted above is necessary. Table 16 presents a summary of all new issues for overseas purposes extracted from *The Economist* by Dr. J. Atkin, formerly of the London School of Economics.[4] The summary includes all issues to the public, except private placings and introductions, the key to inclusion being a mention in *The Economist*'s weekly list of new issues. The totals for such issues are rather less than those of the Midland Bank, but they provide a useful indication of trends and the availability of Dr Atkin's worksheets which list every issue in the series has eased the job of classification.

From the totals in the Table, both for the amounts and number of issues, certain suggestions as to policy immediately arise. First, the only loans that are, on average, above the £1 million consultation limit mentioned by R. H. Brand are those of governments – the company issues

---

[1]R.I.I.A., *Problem of International Investment*, 77.

[2]However, even one well-placed firm might break the system of suasion as did the Hong Kong and Shanghai Banking Corporation whose chairman, Sir Charles Addis, was a member of the Court and the Committee of Treasury of the Bank of England. See Atkin, 'Official Regulation of British Overseas Investment', 329–30.

[3]However, whether it would reduce the volume of business to the same extent as the suasive controls is another matter. If it did not, and if the increase in business (ex controls) increased profits by more than the capital losses resulting from the rise in Bank Rate, the issuing houses might prefer it.

[4]J. M. Atkin, 'British Overseas Investment, 1918–1931', University of London, unpublished Ph.D. dissertation, 1968.

TABLE 16. *New overseas issues by type of borrower, 1923-31*

| | Empire | | | | | | Foreign | | | | | | | Midland Bank estimate |
| | Government | | Municipal | | Company | | Government | | Municipal | | Company | | Total | Total |
Year	(£'000)	No. of issues	(£'000)	No. of issues	(£'000)	No. of issues	(£'000)	No. of issues	(£'000)	No. of issues	(£'000)	No. of issues	(£'000)	(£'000)
1923	64,406	16	4,788	10	18,430	72	26,461	7	—	—	18,491	30	137,376	136,176
1924	59,080	10	6,085	9	16,014	66	40,619	6	2,412	1	9,350	20	124,560	134,223
1925	30,648	10	2,625	11	27,262	142	—	—	1,350	1	14,970	30	77,055	87,708
1926	31,866	8	1,222	4	20,227	81	23,817	8	6,235	2	18,361	36	101,723	112,404
1927	55,697	13	5,135	7	38,851	77	11,027	6	7,186	6	30,546	34	148,422	138,671
1928	40,222	11	7,304	9	15,344	61	15,937	8	4,331	4	22,204	34	105,342	143,384
1929	26,366	5	3,859	3	30,881	70	3,650	2	472	1	22,469	35	81,697	94,347
1930	49,080	11	3,031	44	9,207	28	21,330	3	—	—	14,387	21	97,035	108,803
1931	30,571	5	—	—	7,983	26	1,740	1	—	—	5,658	11	45,952	46,078

Sources: J. Atkin, Worksheets compiled from *The Economist*.
Midland Bank Monthly Review.

average, even when the large railway issues are included, under one half that amount or just over £434,000 during the period 1923–31. Second, the relative stability of company issues is also extremely noticeable during the period until 1929 when deflationary conditions made such borrowing less likely. Finally, the relative volatility of foreign official issues, both in number and volume, in most years is immediately apparent, as are the sharp slumps in the annual figures for 1925 and 1929–31. (The figures are even more depressed for these years and for 1924 if officially 'approved' League of Nations and Reparations loans are excluded.) From these figures alone, rough indications of the timing and the direction of any official intervention in the long-term foreign capital market are immediately apparent. However, further details of their operation increase our understanding.

By January 1924, the Authorities had removed all general restrictions on overseas lending, other than loans to governments in default and to governments which had not funded their war debts.[1] However, the process of consultation continued, and Clay records Norman's April view that 'foreign loans [are] too frequent, too cheap, and poor reasons', plus his agreement with McKenna's view that 'our only remedy [is] a 5% rate which must be used if such loans continue on a large scale'.[2] The consultations must have resulted in more forceful advice from the Governor by mid-year, for after the Czech State Loan of 24 May there were no non-League of Nations, non-Reparations loans for foreign governments or municipalities until January 1926. At this point, loans to foreign governments totalled £16,015,000 and implied a rate of lending above that of 1923. Thus it would seem that the Bank became stricter on applications for foreign government new issues from mid-1924, a date that agrees with the R.I.I.A.'s informed estimate of the beginning of controls eighteen months before November 1925.[3]

However, the first stages of the controls were not widely appreciated, and in public circles there was still some discussion as to whether controls on new foreign issues might be necessary as a part of the policy for returning to gold. Thus, the Chamberlain–Bradbury Committee from its Third Draft Report onwards made specific references to the need to prevent excessive foreign lending, for as Bradbury put it, 'I believe there is a real risk that the success of the policy we recommend may be jeopardised by excessive foreign lending.'[4] In this regard, it is of

---

[1]Previously, controls had existed as to the term of overseas lending and, to a lesser extent after 1920, its destination. Atkin, 'Official Regulation of British Overseas Investment', 325–30.

[2]Clay, *Lord Norman*, 145.

[3]R.I.I.A., *Problem of International Investment*, 134.

[4]T160/197/F7528/01/2–3, Bradbury to Young, 11 September 1924; Third Draft Report, para. 25–30, Fourth Draft Report, section 11, *Report*, para. 36.

interest to note that the Committee made reference only to foreign lending rather than Empire and foreign lending, a distinction that was common at the time. The Authorities were advised that 'any tendency to weakness in the exchanges should be treated as a ground for discouraging foreign loans upon the London market and even for a general restriction of credit *in the event of other methods of discouragement not being effective*'.[1] (italics added) Thus even before the return to gold, many of those people who were influential in formulating Treasury policy believed informal or formal restrictions were preferable to orthodox instruments of credit control.

By the autumn of 1924, 'the Governor's polite blackmail against foreign issues' was in full operation, and after the Dawes Loan of October and the Greek Government League Loan of 13 December all foreign loans except a small League Loan to Danzig in April 1925 were kept from the market.[2] The Governor also appears to have worked to prevent some company issues in cases where the company was foreign rather than British owned,[3] but the results here were of less importance as the results for both 1924 and 1925 indicate.

These matters stood until the return to gold. After 28 April, however, events suggested further restrictions, for in early May Norman wrote to Niemeyer.[4]

I think that even if he cannot prevent it, the Chancellor should realise the present effects of the Colonial Stock Act in relation to gold. For instance Australasia has long been over-supplied with funds in London, a position which has been settled (in Gold through New York) to the extent of perhaps £11 millions in the last month or so. There remains probably as much more to be settled in one way or another sooner or later, together with the proceeds of any further Loans to and exports from Australia.

Owing to this position and to information of impending Australian Loans, I had last week asked the High-Commissioner to restrict the present New Zealand issue to £5 millions. I regret to say that, after taking counsel with his Government, my request was refused and the present issue is for no less than £7 millions.

Thus under the Colonial Stock Act, the indebtedness of London to Australasia, that is to another economic unit, already considerable, is increasing and is largely needed for the local expansion of credit and currency; it is an immediate menace to our Gold Reserves in practically the same way as would be the case with Foreign Loans, were we not able to turn them away under present conditions.

[1] T160/197/F7528/01/2, Third Draft Report, para. 30.
[2] T175/4, Niemeyer to Chancellor, 5 March 1925; Niemeyer, Memorandum, 29 November 1924. Most of the proceeds of the Dawes Loan remained in London until well after the return to gold (see above, p. 176).
[3] Clay, *Lord Norman*, 143.
[4] T176/17, Norman to Niemeyer, 11 May 1925.

The orthodox defence against overborrowing by an outside economic unit (Colonial or Foreign) is a high Bank Rate: at present the prospects of such a rate are being hastened more by the effects of the Colonial Stock Act than by the general tendency of the Exchanges.

Niemeyer passed the letter and a brief to the Chancellor on 13 May with the comment, 'I am not disposed to be over alarmed: but we want to go as slow with overseas loans as we can.'[1] In the brief Niemeyer noted that the U.K. was overlending abroad and that for this reason the Authorities had been attempting to check foreign loans. However, they had found Colonial loans whose economic effects were the same more difficult to deal with owing to sentiment and to their trustee status which made them more attractive to investors and to issuing houses. He argued that Colonial issues should be slowed down, but admitted that in the case of Dominion loans it was difficult to do much. At this point he was loath to advise asking the Colonial Secretary to take direct action, and thus he concluded that the Authorities 'must trust to such persuasion as the Governor can use in the City and to the repercussions of that persuasion on brokers and issuing houses'.

In the ensuing weeks the failure of four large loans which left £17 million with the underwriters effectively closed the market, but pressure for action continued and Niemeyer prepared for Churchill's approval draft telegrams for Dominion Governors-General which expressed the Authorities concern with Dominion demands for funds in London and noted that:[2]

They would welcome any action that you can take to diminish for the present your demands on London for loans. They would also be glad to receive as long notice as may be possible of any loans which it may be essential to place in order that these loans may be co-ordinated with other essential financial operations.

At the same time, the Bank was attempting through the Commonwealth Bank to moderate Australian demands for funds.[3]

However, Amery, the Colonial Secretary, to whom the draft telegram was passed for comment opposed any restrictions on the Dominions. As Sir Henry Lambert, Senior Crown Agent for the Colonies, put it:[4]

[1] T176/17, Niemeyer to Churchill, 13 May 1925. Niemeyer's distinction between the ease of dealing with the Colonies and the problems of dealing with the Dominions finds an echo in Sir Dennis Robertson's comments on controlling the use of the dollar pool after 1945: '[T]he little black children ... could be smacked on the head if they showed too great a propensity to spend dollars, while the grown-up white daughters, who were often pretty extravagant, could only be quietly reasoned with.' *Britain in the World Economy* (London, 1954), 39.

[2] T176/17, Niemeyer to Churchill, 22 and 27 May 1925.

[3] T176/17, Niemeyer to Lambert, 30 May 1925.

[4] T176/17, Lambert to Leith-Ross, 5 June 1925. On Amery's repeated battles with Churchill and the Treasury see, L. S. Amery, *My Political Life: War and Peace 1914–1929*, II (London, 1953), 299–300, 358, 503–6.

Owing to the needs of Empire development he is firmly opposed to a policy of restriction on borrowing and is prepared if necessary to make it a Cabinet matter. If therefore the Chancellor desires to pursue the question, he will no doubt take it up in the Cabinet.

The Treasury felt this attitude was unreasonable and suggested that the matter be dealt with privately and orally by the Chancellor.[1] Spurred on by a warning from Norman that 'present conditions require . . . your earnest consideration if (*merely* because of the amount shortly to be lent outside this country . . .) we are to avoid a high Bank Rate' (italics in original),[2] Churchill appears to have successfully persuaded Amery without recourse to the Cabinet, and the telegrams went off to the Dominions as drafted. However, probably as a *quid pro quo*, there was to be an investigation by the Committee of Civil Research which set up a Sub-Committee in June:[3]

To examine the question of our capacity to meet the demands for credit at home and abroad, having particular regard for the requirements of Empire development and the maintenance of our export trade, and to make recommendations.

The telegram had its effects and Dominion borrowing in London fell off considerably, particularly as the Authorities encouraged them to meet immediate needs through joint issues through a British house in London and New York. Thus, for example, Australia, instead of borrowing £20 million in London, placed only £5 million of its 25 July issue in London and raised the balance in New York.[4] However, the embargo on overseas government issues was becoming increasingly unpopular in London where it was regarded as 'a distinct "off-side" ' in the gold standard game, and there was a 'unanimous feeling' that it should go as soon as possible.[5] Such feelings of course reached the Treasury which in the summer still contemplated that the market would remain closed into 1926 and favoured total exclusion of foreign government loans and control of Empire issues, if only because any discrimination would damage the reputation of the London market.[6] The unpopularity resulted both from the loss of income for the City and from the ease of evading the spirit of the embargo through purchasing foreign securities

---

[1] T176/17, Leith-Ross to Fergusson, 8 June 1925.
[2] T176/17, Norman to Churchill, 9 June 1925.
[3] Cab. 58/1, Meeting of 18 June 1925, Conclusion 4. The membership of this Committee was as follows: Norman (Chairman) Bradbury, Niemeyer, Lambert, Sir S. C. Chapman and Sir J. C. Stamp. Sir C. H. Kisch became a member later and by the time the report was signed Bradbury had become Chairman.
[4] T176/17, Niemeyer to Churchill, 21 July 1925.
[5] *The Nation and Athenaeum*, 26 September 1925, 774; *The Bankers Magazine*, cxx (980), November 1925, 641.
[6] T176/17, Churchill to Niemeyer, 21 July 1925; Niemeyer to Churchill, 21 July 1925.

issued abroad and through issues for British concerns operating abroad.[1] The Bank also found that the policy had unfortunate side effects, for with the restrictions on foreign lending at long term and with expectations that the restrictions would not be permanent, potential lenders built up short-term balances, the short-term market was somewhat inundated with funds and the Bank's control of short-term interest rate was impaired with unfortunate exchange effects.[2] In these circumstances, Norman came under considerable pressure from his Directors to 'raise the loan embargo and let gold go until market conditions are reached which would in themselves produce a natural rise in bank rate'.[3] It was in these circumstances that the Overseas Loans Sub-Committee of the Committee of Civil Research finished its deliberations and signed its *Report* on 16 October.

The *Report* recommended that the embargo be lifted on 9 November 1925.[4] The Sub-Committee noted that evasion of the informal controls was becoming more frequent, and continued :[5]

The very natural discontent of those who have conformed to the restrictions – both lenders and borrowers – when they see others evading them is rapidly growing, and there is a strong body of public opinion which regards the restrictions themselves as being from a national point of view not only not beneficial, but actually harmful. Indeed, we are definitely assured by those most qualified to form an opinion that it is not practically possible much longer to maintain an embargo on overseas issues by present methods.

The alternatives as the Committee saw them were to remove the embargo completely or to make it effective by legislation. It regarded the latter as 'undesirable in itself' and subject to 'insuperable' practical difficulties, and it pointed to the wartime experience which had the advantages of censorship, Stock Exchange co-operation, patriotism and limited opportunities for profitable investment outside war industries, but which 'was notoriously difficult to administer and could only be made effective by inflicting hardships on individuals and at the cost of great friction'.[6] Besides being 'utterly unworkable' in normal times, the Committee believed that 'the effect upon the national credit of any such measures would be most damaging'.[7] It thus approached the other alternative,

[1]Cab. 58/9, Committee of Civil Research, Overseas Loans Sub-Committee, *Report,* para. 47; Macmillan Committee, *Evidence*, Q. 7597.
[2]F.R.B.N.Y., Norman to Strong, no. 56, 15 October 1925.
[3]F.R.B.N.Y., Strong to Norman, no. 93, 22 October 1925. This cable was written by Sir Charles Addis, a Director of the Bank.
[4]Cab. 58/9, Overseas Loans Sub-Committee, *Report*, para. 41. In the *Report* itself the date was omitted 'in view of the exceptional need for secrecy', but it appears in the second draft of 12 October 1925 in T176/17, Niemeyer Papers.
Ibid., para. 24–5.   [6]Ibid., para. 27.
Ibid., para. 28.

one which was 'consistent both with our traditions, with the general financial policy embodied in the gold standard, and as we have reason to know is strongly advocated in banking and industrial circles in this country'.[1] After placing the onus of proof on those who advocated the retention of the embargo, the Committee accepted that there was some margin for overseas investment in the balance of payments and in national savings, that 'the normal operation of the gold standard will supply a speedy, although perhaps drastic, corrective' if overlending occurred and that 'whatever inconvenience may arise must be faced as part of the price which has to be paid for restoring normal conditions'.[2]

The *Report* then went on to reject any tying of loans to purchase in the United Kingdom which 'would give rise to administrative difficulties even more formidable than those of an outright prohibition'.[3] It recommended that the preferential treatment given Dominion and Colonial securities under the Colonial Stock Act 1900, which gave such securities trustee status and thus enabled such securities to be issued in London at terms only slightly less favourable than those granted the British Government, be maintained but not extended.[4] Finally, it expressed its approval of attempts to issue securities jointly in London and New York and its hope that, if New York terms of borrowing so developed that rates for new issues were as or more favourable than those in London, Colonies and Dominions would use such joint issues rather than sever their London connections completely.[5]

There matters stood, except that the date of the embargo's removal was advanced from 9 to 3 November,[6] when the Chancellor announced that 'the old full freedom of the market will be restored' at a speech in Sheffield. The 'old full freedom' excluded countries that had not funded war debts or were in default, but these exceptions remained in the Governor's hands for interpretation and enforcement without any public statements to that effect.[7] The only limitation attached to the restoration came in the portion of his speech where Churchill noted:[8]

I trust with confidence to the corporate good sense of the City to manage its affairs with discretion; to pay regard not only to the capacities of the market, but to the position towards this country of would-be borrowers, and I hope that so far as possible, without impairing the freedom of the market, that preference will be given in the matter of credit to those issues

[1]Ibid., para. 30.
[2]Ibid., para. 30, 32, 39.
[3]Ibid., para. 42.
[4]Ibid., para. 44.
[5]Ibid., para. 55.
[6]Both dates were under consideration in late October. F.R.B.N.Y., Norman to Strong, no. 80, 30 October 1925.
[7]T176/17, Niemeyer to Churchill, November 1925.
[8]*The Times*, 5 November 1925.

which bring a high proportion of orders for goods immediately to the trade of this country.

This proviso gave some general guidance for the inevitable consultations that would come in the ensuing period and for any pressures that the Governor chose to exert.

The removal of the embargo did not lead to a rush of loans, if only because a badly priced Colonial loan failed leaving $97\frac{1}{2}$ per cent with the underwriters[1] and because the ensuing Bank Rate uncertainties made issuing houses, borrowers and investors wary. However, five Colonial issues found their way to market before the end of the year. Foreign issues waited until 1926.

Given the tone of the *Report* of the Overseas Loans Sub-Committee and given its signatories, who included Norman, Niemeyer and Bradbury, one would have thought that, for the moment, efforts to control new overseas issues by suasion were over. During 1926 and 1927 this appears to have been the case, for I can detect only one indication that there were active efforts to restrict such lending in London beyond the usual informal consultations.[2] Interest differentials made London more expensive than New York and helped to keep foreign issues from London, particularly when one adds the 2 per cent Stamp Duty on bearer bonds, the type most commonly issued by foreign governments, and the decline in issuing costs in the United States that resulted from competition between issuing houses.[3] During 1926 and 1927 this reduction in London's cost advantage, which had partially offset higher interest rates in the early 1920s, brought representations to the Treasury for the reduction or the removal of the 2 per cent duty.[4] This reduction in new

[1]T176/17, Norman to Amery, 10 November 1925 (copy sent to Niemeyer on 11 November 1925).

[2]The one suggestion I have found occurred in an unsigned note in *The Nation and Athenaeum* of 13 November 1926 (p. 205), which the marked copy of that issue in the Keynes Papers reveals to have been written by Keynes. This ran as follows:
The view, which we have expressed strongly in *The Nation* that there had better be no more Foreign Government Loans for the present, has, we understand, been accepted in responsible City circles. An exception will be made in favour of the Bulgarian loan, which is to appear shortly under the League of Nations. But other applicants will be quite definitely discouraged. Thus, in effect, probably by agreement rather than by open compulsion, the old semi-official embargo has been largely restored.

[3]R.I.I.A., *Problem of International Investment*, 173. High London interest rates also affected loans to the Empire by encouraging governments to borrow in their domestic markets. Atkin, 'British Overseas Investment', 172–4.

[4]T160/470/F10549/1, Vansittart to Secretary of the Treasury, 28 November 1927; Revelstoke to Chancellor, 26 March 1928 and enclosed Memorandum on the Stamp Duty of 2 per cent on Bearer Bonds and its effect on the issuing of Foreign loans in London. The Colwyn Committee had recommended that the tax go if it hindered foreign issues. Committee on National Debt and Taxation, *Report*, para.

issues resulting from cost considerations did not mean a fall in the outflow of funds of a comparable amount, for British investors purchased securities issued in lower cost foreign markets, often holding them abroad to avoid any payment of duty. One firm of brokers reported doing £7 million of such business in New York in the period 1924–7 and on many occasions new foreign issues in New York reserved substantial blocks of securities for European sales of this type.[1] However, the duty possibly did keep U.K. foreign lending below what it would otherwise have been during the period after 1925 and it lessened the need for further controls. The Authorities recognised that the 2 per cent duty was 'a serious obstacle to the issue of foreign loans', but they were at first, and to some extent always, unwilling to sacrifice the revenue, unwilling to make the 1929 pre-election Budget long and complex and of the belief that 'some slight check such as the stamp duty imposes on issues for abroad is rather useful at the present moment ... apart from revenue considerations'.[2]

From mid-1928, the rise in American interest rates, the increasing attractiveness of shares *via-à-vis* bonds and the relative shift in American asset preferences combined to make London more attractive than previously. The Authorities seem to have allowed the 1928 pattern to develop without too much interference, as they keep their watching brief on new issues and even lifted the embargo on loans to countries which had not funded war debts,[3] but after loans in February and March 1929 there were no foreign government loans for the rest of the year. There were no government issues of any kind, foreign or Imperial, after 27 July. Clay argues that Norman imposed no ban on foreign lending, but Snowden's Mansion House speech probably served to discourage loans.[4] In November 1933, the Treasury noted:[5]

562–5. At the time of its writing its *Report*, 1926, the Committee did not believe that the tax was impairing London's competitive position.

[1] T160/470/F10549/1, Memorandum on the Stamp Duty of 2 per cent on Bearer Bonds, 2, 6.

[2] T160/470/F10549/1–2, Hopkins to Grigg, 23 April 1928; Churchill to Hopkins and Gowers, 4 July 1928; Hopkins to Financial Secretary, 27 November 1928; Phillips to Hopkins, 9 January 1929; Phillips to Hopkins, 9 July 1929; Hopkins to Grigg, 10 July 1929; Phillips to Hopkins, 6 February 1930; Leith-Ross to Hopkins, 24 March 1930.

[3] T175/4, Leith-Ross to Churchill, 6 October 1923; Hopkins to Norman, 10 October 1928.

[4] Clay, *Lord Norman*, 238. However, in 1930 Clay refers to a tightening of controls (368). The relevant passage of Snowden's speech ran as follows: 'I would like to make an appeal to City financial houses to exercise caution in regard to foreign lending where the exchanges are in favour of this country. I do hope that we shall be able to tide over the present situation without a further increase in the Bank rate ...' *Bankers' Magazine*, cxxviii (1026), September 1929, 416.

[5] T160/533/F13296/2, Warren Fisher to Chancellor, 30 November 1933.

It is substantially true that there has been some restriction on foreign issues in this country for a number of years. For a considerable time prior to the crisis in September 1931 the Governor, with the knowledge and concurrence of two successive Chancellors, was in the habit of discouraging foreign issues because of the strain imposed upon the exchange. No public Government announcement was made except for a reference to this subject by Lord Snowden in the course of a speech which he made in the City in 1929, but it was well understood in the City that this informal embargo had Government approval.

Norman noted in a discussion on foreign issues in February 1933 that 'we had had an embargo on this class of transaction [loans to foreigners for the purpose of placing orders here] imposed in one form or another for some five years'.[1]

Certainly in 1930 and 1931 there were few foreign loans, particularly when one excludes the Young and the Austrian Government International Loans of 1930 none of the proceeds of which were transferred abroad.[2] The two remaining loans were for coffee valorisation in Brazil (March 1930)[3] and for Greece (March 1931). Empire lending remained buoyant and unrestricted, except insofar as the growing economic crisis made investors unwilling to subscribe new money. Both the Bank and the Treasury continued to exercise a general scrutiny over such issues, but there is no recorded attempt to block such loans after 1925, although of course Colonial lending could be more easily controlled. Company borrowing fell off as well, but in this case economic conditions rather than controls appear to have been the prime reason.

Now how effective were these efforts to control overseas lending in its various forms? In answering this question, one must first emphasise that the controls were never extended to cover more than a few possible potential avenues for British overseas investment during the period. Thus insofar as other avenues remained open, British residents could increase their holdings of foreign assets by, for example, purchasing bonds in foreign markets and even holding them abroad to escape the 2 per cent duty. Moreover, if these other avenues offered securities with characteristics similar to those which might have been offered in London, the only impediments to investment might be higher transactions costs, reduced information and some element of exchange risk. Given that the use of moral suasion did not extend to the large institutional potential

[1]T160/533/F13296/1, Hopkins, Foreign Issues – Discussion with the Governor, 9 February 1933.

[2]Clay, Lord Norman, 368.

[3]For the background to this issue see J. W. F. Rowe, 'Studies in the Artificial Control of Raw Material Supplies, no. 3, Brazilian Coffee', London and Cambridge Economic Service, *Special Memorandum No. 35*, January 1932, 36, 37, 52, 56–7; H. Feis, *The Diplomacy of the Dollar 1919–1932* (New York, 1966), 31–2.

holders of foreign securities, such as insurance companies and investment trusts, the existence of these alternative avenues plus reasonably large supplies of securities that were reasonable substitutes for new London issues in their portfolios, the controls may not have stopped that much overseas investment. Instead, the controls may have merely changed the forms overseas investment took so as to reduce the incomes of City firms. Certainly City firms frequently opposed the controls for this very reason and their opposition made even the achievement of limited suasion more difficult.

To see whether these alternative avenues, particularly for fixed interest securities, existed, ideally one would like to have a fairly detailed knowledge of Britain's international capital transactions on a gross basis. However, Britain's international payments statistics are so inadequate for this period that one must rely on very rough, largely non-quantitative evidence. Certainly the possibilities for evading such controls as existed were so great that Governor Norman remarked that the embargo on loans to France resulting from her non-payment and non-funding of war debts meant 'that London had pro tanto found the capital and other countries have earned the commission and the profit', for French securities issued in Holland and Switzerland rapidly found their way to London.[1] In addition, in cases of joint London–New York issues, such as the Australian issue of July 1925, a large portion of the New York tranche normally found its way almost immediately to London. The reverse rarely, if ever, happened.[2] Moreover, the fact that almost £500 million of securities issued in London were held by foreigners meant that purchases of outstanding issues from foreigners might offset some of the balance of payments effects of an embargo on new issues of similar types.[3] The 'regular army of bond sellers' catering to the insurance and trust company markets' demand for foreign-issued securities also pointed to the existence of a large and profitable business in channels outside the controls,[4] as did the large volume of American

[1] T175/4, Norman to Warren Fisher, 2 October 1928. See also T175/4, Norman to Niemeyer, 21 February 1927; Middlemas and Barnes, *Baldwin*, 182.
[2] R. Kindersley, 'British Foreign Investments in 1928', *Economic Journal*, XL (158), June 1930, 176. As R. H. Brand, a director of Lazards, put it:
   When the Bank of England does agree and an international issue is made partly in London, partly in New York, and partly in Amsterdam, it is ten to one within six months London and Amsterdam have bought back nearly all the New York issue. The Americans do not hold it. They take the commission and make the issue, but they do not place it really like [*sic*] we do. They have a selling syndicate which holds it until they can sell it abroad very largely. (Keynes Papers, Macmillan Committee, Notes of Discussions, 28 November 1930, 21).
[3] R. Kindersley, 'British Foreign Investments in 1930', *Economic Journal*, XLII (166), June 1932, 193.
[4] Macmillan Committee, *Evidence*, Q. 1352, 1358, 6821-2.

transactions in securities with European markets including London[1]
Moreover, as British residents' portfolios of non-sterling, particularly
dollar, securities were relatively low in 1925, given wartime vesting and
official sales and the unattractiveness of American securities for other
than short-term speculation during the years 1919–25 when sterling
was expected to rise in value, a reduction in new supplies of foreign
issues in London might have induced a more rapid rebuilding of
American portfolios. If, in addition, there were changes in tastes as
between domestic and overseas issues or between types of overseas issues
during the period, the controls might have proved even less effective.[2]
The existence of a variety of channels for investment in overseas securities
and the internationalisation of the interwar security market thus probably
meant that controls on one segment of the market did not necessarily
lead to an equivalent improvement in the balance of payments, excluding
for the moment possibilities of any repercussions on such items as exports
or interest and dividends.

However, insofar as the controls did reduce overseas lending, they
probably reduced short-term pressure on the exchange rate and/or the
official gold and foreign exchange reserves. Any overseas loan initially
resulted in a deterioration in London's short-term international financial
position as domestic assets passed into the hands of foreigners. Thereafter,
the effect depended on the use of these assets by the foreigners concerned
(and on the sources of these assets in Britain). Assuming, for simplicity's
sake, that the assets were not transferred from London until the foreigners
involved actually spent them on goods and services and assuming that
the act of borrowing increased foreign demands for resources, let us concentrate on the effects of this increased foreign expenditure. If the loan
was spent entirely in Britain on British goods at the outset, the transfer
was easily effected. However, if the proceeds were spent in third countries
or initially were used to finance domestic expenditure in the borrowing
country, the process would be more roundabout and the initial weakening
of the exchange rate and/or the loss of reserves caused by the financial
transfer would not be offset by the repercussions of the increased ex-

---

[1]H. B. Lary and Associates, *The United States in the World Economy* (Washington,
   1943), 107, Table 10; Kahn, *Britain in the World Economy*, 163 (esp. footnote 15).
[2]During the 1920s, for example, life insurance companies, with the National Mutual
   in the vanguard, became more adventurous in their portfolio management and
   in some respects 'discovered' the New York Market. The aggregate statistics for
   all companies give little indication of this change, for it occurred outside the area
   of government issues, the only one even broadly classified as to origin, and largely
   in the area of debentures, preference shares, and, occasionally, ordinary shares.
   For the American and other overseas interests of the National Mutual whose
   overseas securities rose from 10.07 to 34.59 per cent of its security portfolio (rather
   than from 8.4 to 11.0 per cent as one might gather from the published balance
   sheet) between 1926 and 1929 see Keynes Papers, Files NM/1_4, 1_5, 3_1, 3_2, PC/1_1.
P

penditures abroad except after a considerable time lag. If the balance-of-payments position of the lending country was weak, the resulting loss of reserves might have necessitated official short-run deflationary measures.[1] Moreover, in an uncompetitive economy such as Britain's in the 1920s, it was highly unlikely that the secondary expansive effects on Britain resulting from the expenditure of the loan abroad would be anything but slight, particularly in the short period.

In addition, it was highly unlikely that British foreign lending in the 1920s actually increased British exports above the levels that they would have reached *if* some other financial centre had done the lending.[2] As recent research has suggested, direct overseas investment by U.K. (and U.S.) companies (which occurred to a limited extent in the 1920s) would probably not have led in the short term to a substantial offsetting of the initial effects of the financial transfer through increased exports and remitted profits.[3] Portfolio investment, despite its contribution to invisible earnings through commissions and issuing expenses would have been even less likely to do so, for a buy British bias would have been unlikely to be operative simply because the loan came from London.[4] However, insofar as potential borrowers might have been unable to substitute foreign for British loans, which might certainly have been the case after 1928 and which was the case for such schemes as Brazilian coffee valorisation,[5] British foreign lending might have been necessary to increase the volume of British exports. But in these cases, the export stimulation could have been increased by tying the loans which would have reduced, or eliminated, the initial financial deterioration and ensured that the increased demand for goods came to Britain. However, the Bank of England rejected tying as an alternative, as did City firms,

---

[1] Of course these deflationary measures might have only a small effect on domestic incomes and employment as the rise in interest rates needed to attract increased foreign balances might be very small.

[2] Assuming of course that the centre which made the loan actually held the securities after issuing them. See above, p. 214.

[3] W. B. Reddaway, et al., *The Effects of U.K. Direct Investment Overseas, Interim and Final Reports* (Cambridge, 1967 and 1968); G. C. Hufbauer and F. M. Adler, 'Overseas Manufacturing Investment and the Balance of Payments', *Tax Policy Research Study Number One* (Washington, n.d.).

[4] Thus the fact that 95 per cent of Indian Loans raised in the U.K. in the year ending 1 March 1923 were spent in the U.K. is not relevant in this context, for insofar as India would have spent the proceeds of, say, American loans in the U.K. the additional British exports to India would have occurred in any case. As it was the Colonial authorities who were borrowing, it would seem likely that the proportion spent in the U.K. would have been almost as large as if the funds had come from the U.S. R. B. Stewart, 'Great Britain's Foreign Loan Policy', *Economica*, N.S. v (17), February 1938, 53.

[5] As the American Government disapproved of such restriction schemes, the New York market was closed to such issues. See above, p. 213, n. 3.

who, lacking the intimate connections with industry characteristic of other financial centres, saw reduced earnings as the outcome.[1]

To sort out the full effects of restrictions on foreign lending, not only must we know the disposition of the funds involved and the alternatives, as outlined above, but we must also know the sources of the funds borrowed by foreigners. If the funds involved came initially from domestic dissaving or credit creation, the act of lending itself had no effects on the level of domestic activity and the process of effecting the transfer would result – in conditions of unemployment such as those which characterised Britain in the 1920s – in an increase in exports and a rise in domestic income, the savings from which would equal the increase in exports. If, on the other hand, the funds involved were diverted from domestic investment as a result of the operation of the capital market, effecting the transfer would only tend to restore the *status quo ante* and insofar as the transfer was undereffected, would leave Britain with a lower level of income than before. Thus, in conditions of unemployment, if the latter mechanism was operative, restrictions on overseas lending which resulted in other countries providing the necessary funds would enable Britain both to have a higher level of income and to avoid any additional deflationary pressures which might result from the financial transfer. If the former mechanism was operative, restrictions on British overseas lending merely avoided only the short term deflationary effects of the financial transfer.

In the discussions of the 1920s, the Treasury knights concerned tended to make a different set of assumptions. They assumed that the mechanism involved was classical (i.e. that the loan increased foreign expenditure and reduced domestic expenditure while leaving the level of income unchanged), that if London did not make the loan no one else would, and that the transfer was perfectly effected in such a short period as to rule the financial deterioration out of court. Working from these assumptions, they could see no improvement in the balance of payments or domestic employment as resulting from restrictions and no *a priori* reason for interfering with overseas lending. Thus R. G. Hawtrey could suggest: 'I think I *would* go so far as to say that in practice "no measures to restrict overseas issues would have any effect" [in improving the balance of payments]' and 'It is hardly going too far to say that (except when it is desired to facilitate Government borrowing in time of war) measures should *never* be taken to check external capital issues.' (italics in the original).[2] Similarly, the Treasury's 1929 White Paper

---

[1] T160/394/F11324, Harvey to Leith-Ross, 16 April 1931; D. C. M. Platt, *Finance, Trade and Politics in British Foreign Policy 1815–1914* (Oxford, 1968), 27. However, there may have been some implicit tying in the case of Colonial issues. See H. Feis, *Europe; The World's Banker 1870–1914* (New York, 1965), 94–5.

[2] T160/470/F10549/1, Hawtrey to Leith-Ross 1 December and 26 November 1927.

on the Liberal Party's election proposals could conclude that 'one would naturally expect that a great decline in the export of British capital must ultimately result in a decrease in our exports and an increase of imports,'[1] and believed that this argument, among others, made the Liberal proposals unworkable.

However, it is unlikely that this was an accurate description of the forces at work during the 1920s, for several reasons. First, it seems highly unlikely that the transfer mechanism worked as efficiently as the Treasury suggested. Second, it seems unlikely that foreign investment took place at the expense of home investment in the short to medium term. The capital market in which the process of bidding funds away from domestic uses would have to occur was not that important as a means of financing home investment and moreover, much overseas lending was, through the Trustee Acts, hardly competitive with domestic lending.[2] Third, as the economy was well below full capacity and full employment, it is highly unlikely that foreign lending, if it did not bid resources away from domestic uses in the capital market, would bid resources away through other means. Finally, it is not entirely clear that if controls had been effective and London had been unable to lend, even indirectly, that other centres would not have provided most of the funds. Where they did not, tying the loans might have raised British incomes and employment.

However, much of the above discussion is somewhat beside the point, as the Authorities' control over overseas lending in the 1920s probably only reduced the level of lending slightly, if at all. But, in certain periods, such slight overall reductions may have represented a significant proportion of the overseas lending for that short period and thus the

---

[1]*Memoranda on Certain Proposals Relating to Unemployment.* Cmd. 3331 (London, 1929), 51. See also pp. 48–9. Here it must be noted that the Liberal proposals were not at all clear on the mechanism involved, J. M. Keynes and H. D. Henderson, *Can Lloyd George Do It ? The Pledge Examined* (London, 1929), 37–8.

[2]The favouritism granted certain classes of overseas lending by these Acts, along with a belief that there was a divergence between private and social returns in overseas investment, lay at the root of Keynes' early suggestions for restriction. Later the grounds upon which he based his case for restrictions changed considerably, and became one of the safeguards to a programme of domestic expansion. J. M. Keynes, 'Foreign Investment and the National Advantage', *Nation and Athenaeum*, 9 August 1924, 586; 'Home versus Foreign Investment. Further suggestions for Revision of the Trustee List', *Manchester Guardian Commercial*, 21 August 1924; Committee on National Debt and Taxation, *Minutes of Evidence*, esp. Q. 4013–14; Keynes Papers, Macmillan Committee, Notes of Discussions, 6 March 1930, 8ff., 28 November 1930, 20ff.; Keynes, *Treatise on Money*, II, 311–15, 374–7. On the role of the capital market in industrial finance see Grant, *A Study of the Capital Market in Britain*, esp. Part III; Balogh, *Studies*, 274ff.; H. Clay, 'The Financing of Industrial Enterprise', *Transactions of the Manchester Statistical Society*, 1932.

restrictions may have helped get the Authorities over particular 'humps'. Thus, for example, in 1924–5 the controls on lending may have assisted the appreciation of sterling, for, so long as sterling was expected to rise against the dollar and such continental currencies as were stable, many of the routes for avoidance were closed both for new issues and outstanding securities. Similarly, after 1929 with alternative sources of funds closed, with many outstanding securities of uncertain prospect and with American financial problems so obvious and so pressing, the controls on new issues may have had more impact. However, in this case, tying new issues would have increased the effectiveness of the controls, for it would have allowed new issues which would have increased British incomes and employment. But in the remaining periods of their operation, the existence and size of the available loopholes probably made the controls ineffective and only served to reduce the City's invisible earnings. Moreover, the Authorities were loath to undertake further intervention to close the available loopholes – they only began to restrict the freedom of financial intermediaries to invest abroad and to reduce transactions in outstanding securities in the 1930s, and even the first year of the Second World War saw them trying to slowly complete their controls over the latter type of transactions.[1] Nevertheless, the experience of the 1920s did prepare the way for later extensions, represented a marked change in British international financial policy, and suggested the direction of future evolution in Bank of England–Treasury–City relations.

The Short-Term Capital Market

Moral suasion as an instrument of policy to influence the balance of payments did not stop at long-term issues, for given the relatively precarious nature of sterling's position after 1925, it was in the Authorities' interest to maximise their control of short-term market rates of interest as these were so influential in inducing movements of short-term funds. Although the rise of the Treasury bill gave the Bank an ideal instrument for open-market operations, one far superior to pre-war dealings in Consols and placements of India Council and other funds, the possibilities for open-market operations were limited. The Bank's supply of securities available for such operations was limited, particularly before 1928.[2] However, even if the Bank had held an 'unlimited' supply

---

[1] For developments, in the 1930s see Stewart, 'Great Britain's Foreign Loan Policy'; Balogh, *Studies*, 268–72. For war-time problems, plus a review of the 1930s, see Sayers, *Financial Policy*, Ch. VIII.

[2] The Banking Department's assets, as noted below (p. 257), were immobilised to a considerable extent by the need to provide sufficient income to pay a satisfactory dividend and to cover those running expenses not covered by Treasury grants for interest on the Government's debt to the Bank and for the management of the

of suitable open-market assets, the already-noted inhibitions as to the active use of Bank Rate often limited the level of possible short-term market rates to those resulting from the existing set of market conventions. Moreover, the Bank's control of market rates was somewhat uncertain, and small fluctuations in the volume of funds, or bills, in the market could, and did, threaten policies at crucial moments, even though the average level of rates remained high. To remove these limitations, the Bank throughout the period after 1924 attempted to increase its control of the short-term market so as to be able to influence rates without necessarily resorting to heavy open-market operations or changes in Bank Rate, both of which had domestic repercussions as well as international effects. These efforts towards increased control also represented attempts to change the conventions of the market so as to raise the effective international interest rates without raising the cost of funds to domestic industry. As such, they represented further efforts to insulate the domestic economy from the full impact of the Norman conquest of $4.86.

Technically the interwar Bank was in a favourable position to use moral suasion to influence short-term rates and market conventions. The Bank's acceptance of endorsements and its willingness to act as lender of last resort to certain firms served as the basis for these firms' existence, and moreover provided the Bank with extensive knowledge of their activities, knowledge which Norman made even more comprehensive.[1] The Bank, through operations to make Bank Rate effective, could provide additional sanctions,[2] for the process involved the firms concerned in additional costs for call money to avoid being driven into the Bank, in addition to the costs of Bank Rate plus $\frac{1}{2}$ per cent with a 5 per cent margin on the securities offered for a minimum of seven days upon being driven in, all these costs decreasing the profits on a portfolio of bills discounted at a lower rate. Moreover, the post-war market was superior to its predecessors as an object of control as its sources of funds were more concentrated. The amalgamation movement had reduced the number of British banks that could be sources of market funds; the railways which had provided large blocks of pre-war funds had

national debt. Before November 1928, moreover, the Issue Departments' holdings of Treasury Bills were very limited, as the bulk of the securities backing the note issue were in the Currency Note Account which does not appear to have been a vehicle for day-to-day money market operations. See T176/13, Note by Niemeyer, undated, but position in file suggests November 1925.

[1]Clay, *Lord Norman*, 276–7.

[2]In the case of the discount houses, this sanction could have short sharp effects which would not greatly offset the domestic economy, as would a rise in Bank Rate for the issuing houses. Moreover, the impact of such a device could be somewhat differentiated between firms insofar as the Bank was able to alter the definition of eligible securities or the duration of loans. See Artis, *Foundations*, 55–6.

entered less liquid and more difficult times; the German banks had disappeared from London and the funds available from the India Council had dwindled.[1] The decline in the number of sources of funds allowed oligopolistic forces to have increased impact in the setting of rates for loans to the market, while at the same time enhancing the possibilities of the Bank's suasion being effective. Again, wartime and post-war traditions of consultation and contact between the Authorities, the market and the main suppliers of funds, especially the banks, laid such instruments closer to hand than before 1914 when the 'hint from headquarters' occasionally had been successful.[2] After 1924, the Bank utilised these developments to make moral suasion almost a staple of the market.

The Bank's policy appears to have concentrated first on the rate at which the clearing banks lent money to the market in the form of fixtures.[3] As such sums represented at a minimum 50–60 per cent of the total funds available to the market and as the market had to make at least $\frac{1}{2}$ per cent over the cost of funds on its entire portfolio to break even, agreements in this area by determining a large part of the discount houses' costs could do much to influence bill rates, particularly as the fixtures rate was the pivot for expectations of rates paid on other discount houses' funds – even if these were determined by supply and demand.[4] After the war, the conventional margin between Bank Rate and the fixture rate was $1\frac{1}{2}$–$1\frac{3}{4}$ per cent.[5] With fixtures at this rate, the discount houses could quote rates for bills up to or over 1 per cent below Bank Rate and still successfully carry their bill portfolios, particularly as the existence of such rates would suggest that non-clearing bank market funds were plentiful and probably lower in price than fixtures. Under these circumstances, to make Bank Rate steadily effective might require continuous and extensive intervention through sales of securities. In these circumstances, the Bank's early concentration on fixtures' rates is understandable.

The first step to narrow the gap between the rate for fixtures and Bank Rate occurred in July 1924 in the course of the tightening of

[1]R. S. Sayers, *Gilletts in the London Money Market 1867–1967* (Oxford, 1968), 80–1; Balogh, *Studies*, 182ff.

[2]Sayers, *Bank of England Operations*, 43–4.

[3]Fixtures are the funds which are normally placed in the market for long periods by lenders. From the lender's point of view they represent a basic short-term reserve which they would not normally use and thus funds on which the market can generally rely.

[4]Macmillan Committee, *Evidence*, Q. 371; Sayers, *Gilletts*, 83; Balogh, *Studies*, 130; F.R.B.N.Y., Crane, Notes on Governor Norman's talk to Committee on Foreign Affairs, 7 January 1926, 2–3. On page 2 of this last document, Norman suggested a figure of 90 per cent for the proportion of fixtures to total funds, but this is the only source which puts it that high.

[5]Macmillan Committee, *Evidence*, Q. 1773.

market rates which followed Leaf's and Cassel's speeches favouring an early return to gold. At that time the margin was narrowed to 1¼ per cent.[1] The financial press differed in its exact interpretation of the change, but agreed that the move either had been 'inspired by the Bank of England' or had resulted from 'close co-operation between the Bank of England and the banks'.[2] Norman's correspondence with Strong at the time suggests that the Bank took the initiative.[3] This new relationship persisted through the March 1925 rise in Bank Rate, but in August 1925 the reduction of ½ per cent in Bank Rate was accompanied by a fall in the rate for clearing bank fixtures of only ¼ per cent. This change, *The Economist* noted would keep 'the market rate within reasonable distance of the official minimum' and give industry 'a certain relief' through a reduction in bank charges at a time when the Bank saw political advantages in a reduced Bank Rate but wished to maintain control of the exchanges.[4] This revised margin of 1 per cent below Bank Rate for fixtures remained unchanged until May 1931. Then, the decline in Bank Rate of ½ per cent was unaccompanied by any change in the rate for fixtures, thus increasing the incentive for the market to keep its rates up against Bank Rate at a time when bills were in short supply and outside money was somewhat more plentiful.[5] However, this arrangement was only temporary and the first crisis increase in Bank Rate in July saw the rate for fixtures rise by only ½ per cent thus restoring the old relationship at a time when non-bank funds were leaving London and the market's costs, being more closely determined by the fixtures rate, were moving the bill rate too close to Bank Rate to make the placing of Treasury bills an easy process.[6] There the position remained until the post-1931 policy of cheap money transformed relationships in the money market.

However, as these arrangements only covered a limited proportion of the market's funds, they limited its range of manoeuvre rather than eliminating it. Temporary money in the form of call loans, either from the clearing banks or outside sources could fetch less than the fixtures rate, and although the discount houses were under some pressure to take fixtures as a result of the need to maintain good relations with their major sources of funds,[7] they could alter their sources of supply somewhat to allow some reduction in rates and in the Bank's control of market

[1] *The Nation and Athenaeum*, 8 November 1924, 230.
[2] *The Economist*, 'Commercial History and Review of 1924', 3 January 1925, 7; *The Bankers' Magazine*, CXVIII (966), September 1924, 315.
[3] Above, p. 54.
[4] *The Economist*, 8 August 1925, 217–8; above, p. 164.
[5] *The Economist*, 16 May 1931, 34.
[6] *The Economist*, 25 July 1931, 158.
[7] Macmillan Committee, *Evidence*, Q. 1771–5.

rates in periods of plentiful outside funds. During the years after 1925, the Bank attempted to close off or minimise the effects of such loopholes through further moral suasion. By 1929, the clearing banks had extended their fixtures rate to call and overnight loans.[1] This combined fixtures rate and short money floor was considered quarterly or on changes in Bank Rate, and, although it meant that the banks had to be prepared to lose small amounts of interest income on occasions when non-clearing bank funds were plentiful, it did add a further barrier to the downward flexibility of rates.[2] Reginald McKenna's account of its introduction gives some indication of one possible means of consultation with the Bank in such matters and suggests that oligopolistic influences had some effect on the banks' discount market policies:[3]

As a matter of fact, when the rate was limited, in the first instance, we did speak to the Governor and told him what we proposed to do and asked him whether he would have any objection and he had none.

The motive was deliberate control of the bill rate as 'the unlent money draws the interest down $\frac{1}{2}$ per cent and the bill rate would not be maintained'.[4] This device set an additional floor on rates covering another 10–15 per cent of the market's resources and thus further reduced the possibility of the market's rates fluctuating widely.[5] However, as the discount market had additional sources of funds on occasion, the Bank still had incentives to make the process of pegging even more complete.

These additional attempts, rather than working on the sources of supply on the market's funds, took the form of working directly on the market itself. The Governor held regular meetings with members of the market throughout the period which, according to Clay, 'provided an opportunity for suggesting any modifications of practice which the credit position called for'.[6] From 1927 onwards, Norman's correspondence with the Federal Reserve Bank of New York, Clay's biography and the financial press indicate that it increasingly became the Governor's habit to instruct the market as to the appropriate level of rates. Thus Norman's Diary for September 1927 notes one such meeting:[7]

I urge them to maintain at all times a private rate of discount (as has been and is done in Paris, Berlin, etc.) irrespective of minor changes in gold holdings and of temporary easy money—say $4\frac{3}{16}$ with Bank Rate $4\frac{1}{2}$ as a minimum less broker's commission.

[1] Ibid., Q. 1773; Keynes Papers, Macmillan Committee, Notes of Discussions, 28 November 1930, 13.
[2] Ibid., 14.   [3] Ibid., 13.
[4] Ibid., 14.   [5] Sayers, *Gilletts*, 83.
[6] Clay, *Lord Norman*, 277.   [7] Ibid., 277.

At the same time, in his correspondence with Governor Strong, Norman mentions such arrangements for the first time:[1]

In so far as I can form plans for the future, they are to run along indefinitely with a $4\frac{1}{2}\%$ Bank Rate : a full $4\frac{1}{4}\%$ private rate of discount (I am trying to impress upon our dealers the need for a continuous and more or less rigid rate of private discount rather than a rate which fluctuates according to the passing value of short money): and short money averaging $3\frac{1}{2}-\frac{3}{4}$.

At the same time *The Banker*, among other financial journals, noted this 'departure from usual practice in the relations between the Bank of England and the money market' and attributed the desire for stability on the part of the Bank as occurring 'with a view to avoiding the necessity of a possible rise in the Bank Rate before the end of the year'.[2] Thereafter, reports of changes in the officially suggested rates appeared in the financial press, frequently at times of international stress or of a distinct change in trend.[3] On occasion, these rate suggestions appear to have been accompanied by understandings as to future Bank Rate policy, for reduced uncertainty would serve as an offset to the reduction in profit implied by the Bank's attempts at market control. Such arrangements and undertakings were also to the Authorities' advantage in times of stress, for they allowed the Treasury to place its bills in the market with greater ease if the understandings reduced the market's fears of loss from taking the bills up immediately prior to a change in Bank Rate. Thus in February 1931 *The Banker*, while recording the agreed rate, noted that the Bank would both sell bills to hold the level of rates and buy bills to keep the market out of the Bank and in August 1929 the Bank gave the market assurances as to the future level of rates to allow itself greater freedom of action in a difficult situation.[4]

However, the policy of moral suasion was of limited use on occasions. To make it successful the Bank had to preserve a rough equilibrium between the supply of funds and the supply of bills. In the latter case, the supply of Treasury bills was the crucial factor, particularly as commercial bills were always in heavy demand by foreign central banks which were required by their statutes to hold commercial bills when holding foreign balances and as the supply of such bills was exogenously determined.[5] Thus in 1930, when the fall in prices and in the volume of

---

[1] F.R.B.N.Y., Strong Papers, Norman to Strong, 10 October 1927.
[2] *The Banker,* IV (22), November, 1927, 389–90; *The Economist,* 7 January 1928, 5.
[3] *The Economist,* 11 August 1928, 270; 9 February 1929, 274, 275; 2 March 1929, 430; 31 January 1931, 213; 16 May 1931, 1034; *The Banker,* VII (32), September 1928, 204; XII (47) December 1929, 275; XVII (62), March 1931, 270; XVIII (63), April 1931, 2; XVIII (64), May 1931, 104; XVIII (65), June 1931, 210.
[4] *The Banker,* XVIII (63), April 1931, 2; XI (44), September 1929, 278; *The Economist,* 17 August 1929, 297–8; 24 August 1929, 342; Clay, *Lord Norman,* 253.
[5] Macmillan Committee, *Evidence,* Q. 1796.

international trade sharply reduced the value of commercial bills in the market, the Treasury's funding policy drove much short-term asset demand into the same market at a time when banks and many overseas governments were accumulating additional short-term resources. The resulting fall in interest rates is clear in Figure 4. The only possible solution for the Authorities, given their desire to fund, would have been to reduce the volume of funds in the market by shifting Government debt from the public to the private sector. This occurred, to some extent, from late 1930 onwards and the Bank thus regained control of the market to an extent sufficient to reintroduce suasion successfully. But the domestic costs of the lapse were high, as the decline in the money supply after 1930 indicates. Rates may have been recontrolled, but only at the cost of failing to insulate the domestic economy from international pressures.

The experience of short-term market control through moral suasion and pegging had one particularly unfortunate effect in the years after 1925, and particularly in 1929–30. The changes in the underlying operating conditions of the market and the narrowing of margins for profit implicit in the raising of borrowing rates meant that, despite attempts to peg market rates near Bank Rate, these years were very lean for the discount houses. As Mr R. H. Foa told the Macmillan Committee in 1930, 'The only thing left to us is hope.'[1] In these conditions, firms were forced to consider other investment possibilities. Professor Sayers records the faltering movement of Gilletts away from first class paper and into shipbuilding bills, trade bills, British, Colonial and Dominion bonds.[2] The Bank of England implicitly accepted some changes in the market's asset preferences when in 1930 it began to accept finance bills and occasional shipbuilding bills, two types of paper it had actively discouraged in the 1920s, but these were just the tip of the iceberg.[3] Many firms were less discriminating in their choice of assets in their attempts to maintain incomes, and this pressure, plus that on acceptance houses to expand their business meant that London's short-term position in terms of the assets it held probably deteriorated qualitatively, especially after 1929.[4] Firms, and the City, were less liquid in their overall positions, a factor which would be of some importance in crisis situations. This illiquidity was not completely the

---

[1] Ibid., Q. 1783.
[2] Sayers, *Gilletts*, 90–105.
[3] Clay, *Lord Norman*, 278; Macmillan Committee, *Evidence*, Q. 1722.
[4] P. Einzig, 'Finance Bills in the London Market', *The Banker*, xv (56), September 1930; Macmillan Committee, *Evidence*, Q. 1165–83; Balogh, *Studies*, 244–8. Commissions for acceptances fell substantially after the war as did the volume of business in traditional lines. As a result, the acceptance houses were under considerable financial pressure to expand the volume of their business. Ibid., 165–74, 244–6.

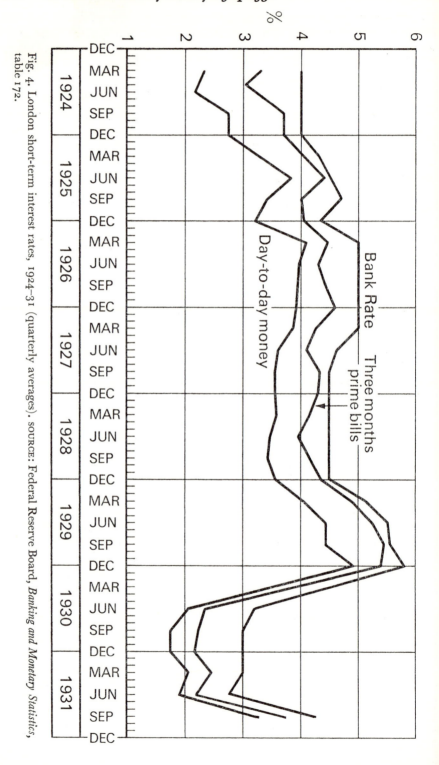

Fig. 4. London short-term interest rates, 1924–31 (quarterly averages). SOURCE: Federal Reserve Board, *Banking and Monetary Statistics*, table 172.

result of the Bank's discount market policy, but to some extent that policy encouraged the development of this situation.

Intervention in Capital Markets, the Overall Results

This concludes the examination of the Bank's (and to a much smaller extent the Treasury's) use of moral suasion in London's capital markets. Generally speaking, the experience was more 'successful' in the short-term market, largely because the Bank chose an area where suasion could be relatively effective. The stimulus to raising the cost of clearing bank finance worked in the interest of the increasingly oligopolistic banks and provided one element in the successful use of suasion on discount market firms, for lowered profit margins made the latter more willing to accept the Bank's guidance and a reduction in uncertainty in the area of lending rates. The experience in the long-term market was less 'successful' because the connections between self-interest and the objects of suasion were far from clear to those involved. Issues lost by London houses implied a fall in income and profits; foreign issues, to contemporary observers,[1] were associated with increased exports which loomed large during a period of difficulties; Imperial interests, on occasion, became closely involved; the controls fell very unevenly, given the possibilities for evasion. When to this basically hostile environment the Bank added an impression that it did not believe in what it was doing, the prospects for a successful policy of suasion were sharply reduced, for it was unable to play any educative function. Nevertheless, both sets of controls, to some extent and on certain occasions, served a useful function, the insulation of the domestic economy from international events and the consequences of 1925.

[1]See, for example, Committee on Industry and Trade, *Report*, 45–6.

10. CONCLUSION

The 'Norman Conquest of $4.86'[1] was ultimately an act of faith in an incompletely understood adjustment mechanism undertaken for largely moral reasons. It carried with it a belief that any overvaluation of sterling that did result would be removed by reductions in British, or rises in American prices and costs, that the results would be 'good for trade', if only by inducing stabilisations elsewhere by force of example, and that the resulting stable international environment would provide a basis for expanding trade which would benefit an internationally oriented economy such as Britain's.[2]

Once the decision was made and announced, there was no going back on it. The exchange rate chosen for sterling in 1925 probably overvalued sterling by at least 10 per cent, given the policy goals of the Authorities,[3] but once fixed, most observers generally accepted it. Most contemporaries, other than Ernest Bevin, viewed the prospect of a change in the exchange rate with horror.[4] The Conclusions of one of the last Cabinet meetings of the second Labour Government give some indication of the extremes this horror took.[5]

The Chancellor of the Exchequer informed the Cabinet of the nature of the

[1]This phrase first appeared in *The Nation and Athenaeum*, 8 November 1924, 230.
[2]In this connection, see the comments by Bradbury and Lubbock in Keynes Papers, Macmillan Committee, Notes of Discussions, 7 November 1930, 24–5.
[3]Above, p. 150; below, pp. 245–50.
[4]Above, p. 1. However, in the course of 1930–1, more people than Bevin began to see the advantages of exchange depreciation, as compared with the other available alternatives. Thus, although Keynes preferred to try other means of removing Britain's competitive disadvantage and solving her balance of payments problem in the first instance, he ultimately advised devaluation. Similarly, R. G. Hawtrey, by the early spring of 1931, was so convinced that devaluation or depreciation was the only available alternative that he refused to present memoranda justifying the maintenance of $4.86. See Keynes Papers, Macmillan Committee, Notes of Discussions, 7 November 1930, 15, 19; Letter to J. R. MacDonald, 4 August 1931; J. M. Keynes, 'Proposals for a Revenue Tariff', *New Statesman and Nation*, 7 March 1931 and ensuing letters; Conversation with Sir Ralph Hawtrey.
[5]Cab. 23/67, Meeting of 22 August 1931, Conclusion 3, 6.

consequences that would follow a departure from the gold standard. So far as he was concerned, he had no doubt whatever if he was compelled to choose between retaining the Labour movement in its present form and reducing the standard of living of the workmen by 50%, which would be the effect of departing from the gold standard, where his duty would lie.

This reaction was understandable, to some extent, for in the 1920s devaluation was 'a thing that no nation has ever in cold blood felt itself able to do, unless circumstances have forced it'.[1] Within the memories of those able to influence policy between 1925 and 1931, devaluations had occurred in advanced countries *only* after 1918 *and* only at times when any other course of action was impossible.[2] Even in these cases, the timespan for the adjustment of attitudes had been years, during which gold convertibility had been suspended: 'overnight' changes in official parities comparable to those since 1945 were unknown. With the examples of Germany and France fresh in men's minds and with the connotations of 'default' or 'bilking the foreigner' that were involved, consideration of devaluation (or depreciation) as a weapon of economic policy was impossible.[3] As Cecil Lubbock put it, 'a contract is, and always has been, sacred.'[4] Thus, until the events of August and September 1931 forced Britain from gold and any commitment to the maintenance of a fixed exchange rate, the 1925 decision had to be lived with by all concerned. Once sterling had fallen from gold, Treasury and Bank thinking became much more inventive and began to consider exchange rate movements as important instruments of economic policy,[5] but for the interim $4.86 was a 'given' in any policy.

It is in this light that the 1925 decision takes on its importance and in which one should evaluate the advice the Chancellor received. As noted above, that decision and the surrounding advice rested much more on beliefs than analysis. The underlying reasons for the success of Britain's pre-1914 gold standard experience were completely ignored: the discussants tended to assume that the gold standard was *the* reason for Britain's pre-war success and to leave it at that.[6] As a result, those

---

[1]Keynes Papers, Macmillan Committee, Notes of Discussions, 7 November 1930, 24–5.

[2]Even when the franc stood at or below one-fifth of pre-war par, many Frenchmen believed that it should and could be worked back to par and refused to accept devaluation. Above, p. 134.

[3]Cab. 24/233, C.P. 233 (31), Memorandum by Warren Fisher, 11 September 1931; C.P. 219 (31) (i), 'Sterling and the Gold Standard', 3 September 1931.

[4]Keynes Papers, Macmillan Committee, 7 November 1930, 18.

[5]See T175/56, Memoranda by Niemeyer, Bradbury, Hawtrey and Siepmann, September 1931.

[6]The first extensive study of financial policy before 1914 was not published until 1936. It was undertaken in reaction to the 'golden age' view of the pre-war world and the prevailing lack of analysis. Sayers, *Bank of England Operations*, vi.

considering the return to gold in 1925 had no idea of the strains the standard might be able to accept and still be successful from a national point of view.

To this lack of analysis of past experience, those advising the Chancellor in 1925 added almost no analysis of current conditions and problems. Except for the famous McKenna, Keynes, Niemeyer, Bradbury dinner party of 17 March, 1925, there was never an occasion when the extent and problems of adjustment to $4.86 were squarely faced. Rather euphemisms such as 'sacrifice' or 'inconvenience' tended to dominate discussions. There appears to have been a general presumption that money wage costs would show their post-1920 flexibility if deflation proved necessary, but this was assumed not analysed. Except for some rudimentary calculations of purchasing-power parity using wholesale prices, which were perhaps only half believed but which formed the basis for all implicit thinking on the stabilisation problem, there was no consideration of the adjustments necessary to make gold at $4.86 a success. There was no consideration of the trade position, in other than the most general terms, or of the time path of adjustment. As for the capital account, Churchill's advisers assumed that the return to gold would present few problems and that here, as elsewhere, alterations in Bank Rate could cope with both adjustment and future management. Thus, in many respects, misleading is perhaps too strong a word to apply to the advice tendered to Churchill in 1925, if only because it implies active consideration of the problems involved: non-existent might actually be more appropriate.

In fact, much of the case for a return to gold, as presented by Churchill's advisers depended on two expectations, one concerning price movements and the other concerning Bank of England policy. The expectation of inflation abroad removing any gap between British and foreign prices and costs was certainly very general. It extended to Keynes who had used the high probability of American inflation as one of the arguments for a managed currency; had welcomed the Gold Standard Act on a misreading which led him to believe that the Act removed the Bank's obligation to buy gold at a fixed price and thus, in theory at least, allowed the Bank to insulate Britain from inflationary movements abroad through exchange appreciation; and had found in an expectation of American inflation his ray of hope for an easy adjustment after the event.[1] Such an expectation depended on 'a nice balance ... between skill and want of skill on the part of the Federal Reserve Board', for it required 'that the Federal Reserve Board should lose control of their own situation and should then begin to exercise

---

[1] Above, p. 43; *The Nation and Athenaeum*, 2 May 1925; letter to *The Times*, 6 May 1925; Keynes, *Economic Consequences of Mr. Churchill*, 27.

skill just at the time that our own policy requires that they should'.[1] If it did not assume this, it was a ploy to 'give businessmen the tonic of a little inflation under highly respectable auspices'.[2] This expectation certainly weakened Keynes' case against returning in many eyes and it also precluded much serious analysis of the adjustment problem, as did one additional assumption.

This second important assumption underlying the 1925 discussions was that the Bank would, as a minimum, attempt to maintain any improvements in the exchange. If, in addition to this, one assumed that there was a substantial volume of speculative balances in London working on the hypothesis of a return to gold at $4.86 which would be withdrawn if expectations were not fulfilled, then one could argue that the Authorities, even if they did not return to gold, would have to take the same, or even stronger, measures to hold the exchange at $4.80 as they would to return to gold. Such a choice of assumptions effectively ruled out any consideration of the bulk of the exchange appreciation involved in returning to gold. In effect, this line of argument also obviated the need for analysing any specific adjustment problems connected with a return to gold in April 1925 as compared with, say, April 1927.

A final factor in 1925, and often thereafter, which heavily influenced policy discussions was what has since become known as the international role of sterling. However, this did not normally come into the discussions in the context of what was best for the international monetary system. Rather, it took the form, as often now, of an argument that the City and its institutions deserved special consideration in the formulation of economic policy, because invisible earnings played a large role in the balance of payments and because this role at the same time prevented conflicts between the City's and the national interest. As noted previously,[3] hints of this view were a part of the argument, particularly in the eyes of Niemeyer and Norman, for a return to gold in 1925, and after 1925 it played a considerable part in Keynes' rejection of devaluation as an alternative prior to August 1931.[4] In other circumstances, the argument was often implicit when phrases such as 'the national credit' found use as justifications for policy.[5] Moreover, this argument

---

[1] J. M. Keynes, 'Discussion on Monetary Reform', *Economic Journal*, XXXIV (134) June 1924, 174.

[2] J. M. Keynes, letter to *The Times*, 20 March 1925.

[3] Above, p. 99.

[4] Keynes Papers, Macmillan Committee, Notes of Discussions, 7 November 1930, 15ff. The refusal of the Macmillan Committee to consider devaluation extensively in its *Report* also had elements of this approach, but it took a wider 'internationalist' view as well (para. 255–7).

[5] See for example, Cab. 58/9, Overseas Loan's Sub-Committee, *Report*, para. 28, 30. For a view which is even more critical of such phrases, see Pollard, *The Gold Standard and Employment Policies*, 17–18, 22–3.

Q

has also found use in some *ex post* justifications of the exchange policy adopted in 1925.[1] This approach to the position of the City and the relationship between its interests and the national interest, in my opinion, fundamentally confused two issues: the fact that sterling had an international role and the means through which such a role developed and was maintained. The development of an international role for sterling some have suggested might 'be better called an accident'.[2] But economic theory provides some justification: the key in this case lying in the theory of portfolio selection.[3]

Individuals whose income or expenditure streams include foreign currency elements will tend to hold some foreign balances, if only to save on conversion costs. The exact size of these balances will, in addition, depend on the amount of these costs, relative interest rates and the volume of transactions. These do not account for holdings of one particular foreign currency. However, the economies of pooling income and expenditure streams in several currencies into transactions in one-vehicle currency to further reduce transactions costs and decrease the size of working balances provides a partial explanation. In addition, elements of risk and return will induce holdings of foreign currencies over and above working balances for an economic unit's country of residence is not necessarily the country in which it wishes to dispose of its wealth. The accumulation of assets in foreign currencies saves future asset exchange costs and also provides a hedge against future changes in the real value of wealth. Now where a country looms large in world trade, its currency will tend to be demanded for both transactions and asset-accumulation purposes. Even if wealth owners are uncertain as to their future commodity consumption patterns, the country offering the widest range of goods and services provides a useful first approximation to their possible future needs, subject to the principle of diversification to minimise risk. If this large trading country's currency possesses certain other advantages, over and above reducions in transactions costs resulting from the large volume of its foreign trade, it will tend to be still more favoured. If its financial markets are extensive, risk-averting investors will prefer it, for the probabilities of loss resulting from assets sales of a given size are lower than in a smaller market. If, in addition, its currency is not expected to fluctuate wildly or to depreciate in the long run, it will be preferred to other markets where this expectation is somewhat stronger.

This approach goes far to suggest why sterling developed as a vehicle

---

[1]Youngson, *The British Economy,* 234; Clay, *Lord Norman,* 169–71.
[2]Williams, 'The Evolution of the Sterling System', 266.
[3]What follows depends heavily on ideas advanced by A. K. Swoboda, 'The Euro-Dollar Market: An Interpretation', *Essays in International Finance No. 64,* February 1968, 5–11, 39–41.

and a reserve currency prior to 1914. The roots of development lay in Britain's trading position, her Empire, her policy of free trade and her dominance in world shipping and commodity transactions. To that base, over time she had evolved a financial system providing asset holders with a wide variety of assets, all easily traded in extensive markets, banking links into the domestic currency arrangements of many countries and a currency which was never scarce. Lastly, London's role as the major international capital market and almost a century of currency stability aided this process.

Given this background to the sterling system, the question arises as to whether the choice of an exhange rate other than $4.86 would have greatly affected London's position. The war left the basic institutions of the sterling system largely unchanged. Six years of fluctuating exchanges and almost ten years of inconvertibility of various types had interposed themselves between the pre-war system and any successor. This instability and inconvertibility had removed one advantage of London as an international financial centre and had probably contributed to the rise of New York as a possible competitor. In this situation, any exchange rate, so long as it was destined to be stable, would probably have served London's purposes. The British financial system was stable and Government finance was conducted by exemplary standards from the contemporary point of view. Thus a lower parity for sterling would probably not have triggered off expectations that Britain would follow Germany or France into severe inflation, despite the frequency with which that bogey saw use in official presentations. From a longer term point of view, and even in the short-term, a lower parity for sterling would have eased the City's position. Such a rate would have strengthened the underlying position of British industry in the international economy and made many services, such as shipping, more competitive. A lower rate for sterling would not have weakened London's position in the area of invisibles other than on Government account.[1] It probably would have increased the surplus on income account and hence eased the balance of payments problems that led to restrictions on certain types of transactions which, in all probability, weakened London's international position. On a longer term basis, it would probably have strengthened the real forces underlying Britain's international banking role by strengthening the forces beneath Britain's long-term growth. For ultimately, the role of London as a financial centre depended on the underlying strength of the economy, not the reverse. Invisible earnings were large, but they were not a major source of growth without a strong home economy which would allow unimpeded investment and intermediation.

[1]Above, p. 107; Below, p. 247.

However, as the adjustment problems were minimised or ignored by Churchill's advisers, the question of a rate for sterling other than $4.86 was never a live issue. Churchill, to a considerable extent, questioned many of his advisers' assumptions as to goals, but he was in a difficult situation, for intellectually he could see no alternative to a policy of drift, and politically he had to rely on support in official circles, the City, business and the country which were almost unanimous in its desire for the policy actually chosen.[1] Even the F.B.I., which might be regarded as one of the strongest critics of the details of the policy, both before and after April 1925, could see no alternative to drift, for it was committed to a return to gold, even at some discomfort to itself in the short-run, and regarded 'managed money' as only a stopgap.[2] The F.B.I. may not have been as fervent an advocate of gold in 1925 as Professor Sayers suggests, but it desired an end to uncertainty and admitted that 'considerations of high finance might make it so important that we should have to take the risk'.[3] Thus Churchill really had little alternative but to accept the advice generally offered, shortsighted though it was, and to adopt the gold standard at $4.86.

In fact, the decision-making style of the Authorities at the time is one of the most interesting aspects of the return to gold. Despite the amount of ink spilled in the course of the year before the decision, it can hardly be said that the decision was 'an exceptionally well-considered step' when so little attention was actually given to the analysis of the existing situation.[4] For a decision as to a rate of exchange not to involve a consideration of the current account and relative price implications of the step under consideration in relation to official policy goals seems almost foolhardy, as does the completely innumerate nature of the decision-making process. Similarly, although the tendency to ignore the adjustment problem, given the lack of analysis of the underlying situation and the expectations of those involved, is understandable to a considerable extent, it is still rather amazing. Churchill's memoranda had phrased the problems involved in a manner that cried out for analysis, but neither he nor anyone else really demanded it. Perhaps the best ex-

---

[1]Above, p. 95.

[2]Above, p. 96; 'F.B.I. and Currency Policy: A Restatement', *Manchester Guardian Commercial*, 29 October 1925.

[3]Sayers, 'The Return to Gold', 316; above, p. 47; T172/1499B, Glenday to Churchill, 17 March 1925, 3.

[4]Sayers, 'The Return to Gold', 316. Churchill himself took this line in the House of Commons when he stated (183 H. C. Deb. 5s. column 605):
There has never been any step of this character taken by any Government which, so far from being marked by undue precipitancy, has been more characterised by design, forethought, careful and laborious preparation ... We have taken every precaution which forethought, and patience, and long preparation could suggest.

planation of the non-analytical nature of the decision-making process lies in the apparent long run nature of most thinking at the time. Time and again in Niemeyer's briefs, the emphasis is on the long term: time and again this emphasis is used to circumvent short-term problems raised by Churchill. This long-term emphasis, plus an implicit belief that exchange rates once fixed were immutable, probably contributed heavily to the outcome. Once this was accepted, the actual exchange rate chosen did not matter, for in the long run the system would adjust and adjust successfully. However, other than Keynes and McKenna, no one really attempted to point out just how long and difficult the short run might be. One expects qualitative judgements ultimately to rule the roost in the formulation of economic policy – but for such judgements to dominate a policy decision, particularly when combined with an absolute minimum of analysis of its implications is most alarming.[1]

Once back on gold at $4.86, the Authorities were forced by their policy preferences to make the best of an evolving situation. Several possible outcomes could have made gold at $4.86 possible and, perhaps, even have reduced the element of overvaluation.[2] Of these, the widely expected inflation abroad did not occur: in fact, international prices tended downwards from early 1925. The General Strike removed the possibility of widespread reductions in money wages and costs, if only because attempts at reductions were too expensive socially and economically.[3] Thus the Authorities had to make the best of a system with two parameters, the level of money wages and the exchange rate.

Up to 1929, the Authorities could perhaps have claimed to have operated such a system successfully. Expanding overseas export demand, plus buoyancy in certain internal sectors, allowing the economy to offset the impact effects of the initial overvaluation and reach higher levels of

---

[1]Granted, *if* the return had proved successful and *if* Britain had successfully adjusted to gold at $4.86, the decisions of March and April 1925 might be considered differently by posterity. In that case, they might be considered a daring gamble which came off. However, even in these hypothetical circumstances, the decision making process should come in for criticism. Gambles made on the basis of the available facts and a careful balancing of probabilities on the part of officials perhaps deserve some acclaim: those made in blissful and often aggressive ignorance, as in 1925, do not. In this connection comparisons of 1925 with the 1945 Anglo-American Financial Agreement and the choice of a post-1945 exchange rate for sterling are instructive. Sayers, *Financial Policy*, Chs IX, XIV (vi) and XV; R. N. Gardner, *Sterling-Dollar Diplomacy* (Oxford, 1956), Ch. X and XI; J. M. Keynes, 'The Balance of Payments of the United States', *Economic Journal*, LVI (222), June 1946; Keynes' House of Lords speech of 18 December 1945, 138 H. L. Deb. Columns 777–94.

[2]Below, pp. 247–8.

[3]The fall in G.D.P. at constant prices in 1926 was four-fifths that of 1931 and could be attributed almost entirely to the general strike, given current trends.

employment and output. This output expansion was relatively respectable by historical standards and certainly an improvement on that
of the pre-war decade. However, unemployment remained stubbornly
high, at levels well above the pre-war average; sterling suffered from
fairly continuous exchange pressure; London's short-term financial
position deteriorated still further; and Britain's international competitive position weakened as unit costs fell as fast or even faster
abroad.[1]

After 1929, of course, all the pigeons released in previous years came
home to roost. World import demand fell dramatically, and Britain, a
marginal supplier at the best of times, found her export markets shrinking
more rapidly than those of her competitors. At the same time, rising
imports added a further deflationary twist to the domestic situation and
declining invisible earnings removed an important prop from beneath
the never healthy sterling exchange. Although high levels of consumer
and public expenditure helped to prevent the domestic situation from
deteriorating as badly as in, say, the United States, Germany or Canada,
the deterioration of Britain's external position and its repercussions
still left unemployment above 23 per cent at the end of the interwar
gold standard period. In these circumstances, Britain would have been
very hard-pressed to ride out the slump with the gold standard intact,
even had a liquidity crisis in the summer of 1931 not forced the suspension of gold convertibility, for even if she had managed to deflate
sufficiently to remove her 1931 payments deficit, the continuing
depression would have required further measures in 1932, if   the
depression continued, if Britain were to stay on gold.[2]

Official policy, faced with a 'chronic position of spurious equilibrium'[3]
which, at its most favourable, never saw unemployment fall below a
million and rarely saw London entirely free from exchange pressures,
was remarkably inactive. Throughout, it had a mildly deflationary bias
which intensified somewhat after 1928. However, it was never
sufficiently deflationary to improve the underlying competitive position

[1] In this respect, undervaluations abroad did not help Britain's competitive position,
but they were far from the only, or even the most important, element in the
situation after 1925.

[2] To achieve a reduction of, say, £60 million in imports by aggregate deflation,
national income would have to fall by approximately £200 million. This would
increase unemployment by 1 million or another 10 per cent. Such a measure of
deflation would remove the bulk of the pre-September 1931 current account
deficit. Of course, if Labour were not in power, tariffs might carry some of the
burden. Foreign repercussions on exports in both cases, would raise the basic
amount of improvement necessary to achieve a given end result. Cab. 58/18,
Provisional Board of Trade Estimates of Changes in the Balance of Trade, 3 September 1931; Balance of Trade, Memorandum by the Board of Trade, 21 September 1931.

[3] Keynes Papers, Macmillan Committee, Notes of Discussions, 21 February 1930, 6.

of the British economy and, as a result, tended 'to hamper without hitting, to injure without killing and so to get the worst of both possible worlds' – overvaluation and deflation.[1] At the same time, this policy in the Treasury and the Bank, and to a lesser extent in informed circles, tended to prevent a discussion of alternative aggregate policies. Instead, discussion tended to centre on particular problems in particular industries or areas, and especially before the slump tended to move away from public works or aggregate demand policies, which the balance of payments position probably made impossible.[2] Before 1930 however, there was little explicit realisation that any domestic expansion would be limited by external constraints unless attempts were made to insulate the domestic economy from external pressures.[3]

The appearance of deflation but refusal to deflate seriously, to some extent resulted from the political situation, in that the Treasury, afraid of the implications of increased unemployment which it believed to arise from a higher Bank Rate, tended to press for reductions and to oppose increases in the Rate. As a result, Bank Rate tended to be frozen and to be relatively useless as a short-term policy instrument. The situation also resulted from the policy attitude of the Bank which centred on certain short-term indices of financial conditions and tended to regard other areas of economic affairs as outside its competence or responsibility. Occasionally, the Bank realised the somewhat tenuous nature of the underlying situation and the weaknesses of an essentially short-term policy which depended, to a considerable extent, on foreigners' willingness to hold sterling balances and did not effectively adjust the economy to $4.86, but this recognition was fitful and did not lead to action.

Given this situation, with the adjustment mechanism jammed and with the most powerful instrument of financial policy, Bank Rate, partially immobilised as an instrument of long-term adjustment or short-term accommodation, the Bank, with Treasury approval in many cases, attempted to hold, and even to some extent relieve, the existing

---

[1]Ibid., 6.

[2]In the Treasury itself, public works were largely anathema. For presentations of the 'Treasury view' see *Memoranda on Certain Proposals Relating to Unemployment*; R. G. Hawtrey, 'Public Expenditure and the Demand for Labour', *Economica*, v (13), March, 1925. The 1929 Liberal election proposals were weak, however, on the balance of payments implications of the programme. J. M. Keynes and H. D. Henderson, *Can Lloyd George Do It?*, 36–8. For surveys of policy discussions during the period see Youngson, *The British Economy*, 239–51; Hancock, 'Unemployment and the Economists'; 'The Reduction of Unemployment as a Problem of Public Policy 1920–1929', *Economic History Review*, 2nd Ser., xv (2), December, 1962.

[3]Keynes Papers, Macmillan Committee, Notes of Discussions, 20, 21 and 28 February, 6 and 7 March 1930; 27 and 28 November and 5 December 1930; Keynes Papers, E. A. C. $_{14}$, Memorandum by Keynes, 21 September 1930; Skidelsky, *Politicians and the Slump*, Ch. 10.

position through the adoption of short-term palliatives. However, given the widespread adherence to *laissez faire,* such palliatives as found use depended for their success on being predominantly within the Bank's sphere of operations or on the successful use of moral suasion by the Bank. In the former area, the Bank resumed active gold market operations, undertook relatively extensive foreign exchange operations (both spot and forward) on its own account for the first time and co-operated extensively with foreign central banks to reduce the strains on London. In the latter area, the Bank attempted by suasion to control and to alter the relationship between domestic and international interest rates so as to increase the pull over the exchanges exerted by any given Bank Rate, to influence gold flows and to control some types of new overseas lending. Although this forging, or half forging, of new policy instruments was highly innovative in many respects, and incidentally foreshadowed (albeit without the same analysis) many of Keynes' 1930 proposals for improvements in the Bank's ability to insulate the domestic economy from international influences, it did not alter the underlying overvaluation of sterling : it merely masked it and made it somewhat more tolerable. Moreover, particularly in the area of controls on new overseas lending, it weakened the international position of that body which the return to gold had supposedly helped considerably, the City, and made something of a mockery of the liberal order which the return to gold was to symbolise.[1] As Keynes put it in a review of Bradbury's 'The Coal Crisis and the Gold Standard', expedients 'which in the old days would have shocked Lord Bradbury out of his skin' found use to defend the parity.[2] Bradbury, among others, was indeed shocked and most orthodox in his response.[3]

Official policy, after the gold standard's restoration, as in the course of the initial decision-making process displayed an important characteristic. Despite repeated protestations concerning the importance of the long-run, in the majority of cases, short-term, often instinctive, considerations normally held sway over an understanding of underlying forces and trends. The decision to return to gold was as much an outcome of these habits of thought as was London's management of the standard thereafter. The criteria for 'success' were invariably short-term, the level of the exchanges, the level of interest rates, the unemployment percentage. Difficulties tended to be met by assuming that foreign develop-

[1]In this connection, it was also rather ironic that the same Budget that brought the return to gold also saw the reintroduction of the McKenna duties and other measures of protection.

[2]J. M. Keynes, 'Our Monetary Policy', *Financial News,* 18 August 1925.

[3]Cab. 58/9, Overseas Loans Sub-Committee, *Report,* esp. para. 26–30; Macmillan Committee, *Report,* Memorandum of Dissent by Lord Bradbury, 263–81; T175/56, Siepmann, Note of a Conversation with Lord Bradbury, 24 September 1931.

ments would ensure their removal. Thus in 1925, the thrust of the case for action depended on short-term expectations of trends in American prices and (hopefully not) British money wages, on a short-term emphasis on the American exchange as the only one which mattered, on a short-term fear of the consequences of inaction and on a short-term view as to what policies would benefit the City. The crucial problem of adjustment was shifted abroad on the assumption that the exchange rate would be justified by American inflation and subsequent Continental rates for stabilisation. Similarly, at no point during the discussion was there any consideration of how the operating environment for the proposed policy might differ from that of the pre-war period – if only because nobody made any attempt to understand the pre-war system – or whether official policy might have to differ from pre-war, or of the possibilities of changing fundamental relationships. Similarly after 1925, short-time indices tended to be the criteria of success or failure. Specific difficulties met with short-term causal explanations and short-term palliatives or attempts to push the adjustment abroad.

The problem of French balances in London which threatened gold losses from London in almost every year after 1926 offers an outstanding example of these tendencies at work. At the time of the return to gold, the official expectations was that any future Continental stabilisations would occur in a manner which would not affect the viability of $4.86, or, to put it another way, that the French and others would make the same or compensating mistakes as the British in dealing with the stabilisation problem.[1] Of course, matters did not turn out that way and the exchange rate chosen for the franc from its *de facto* stabilisation onwards, undervalued it on a unit cost basis, in terms of sterling, by approximately 20 per cent.[2] It was this undervaluation, plus the large speculative balances that had moved out of France before stabilisation in 1926, that made life so difficult for London.

In the period after the *de facto* stabilisation, the movement of funds from London to Paris, and their counterpart of growing official French sterling balances, appeared to the Authorities as the result of overseas speculation on the rise of the franc stemming from the refusal of the French to move from a *de facto* to a *de jure* stabilisation.[3] Thus the effects of the previous flight from the franc and the possible implications of the rate of stabilisation were ignored. Given the initial official reasoning, the thrust of the Authorities' case suggested that the fault lay in Paris and the Bank of France demands for gold in London, which attempted to stem speculation as to the franc's ultimate exchange rate

---

[1]Above, p. 106.
[2]Brown and Browne, *A Century of Pay*, Figure 28.
[3]Moreau, *Souvenirs*, 27 May 1927, esp. 328–9, T176/29, Conversation with M. Quesnay, June 1927, 3ff.

by tightening credit conditions abroad, should not affect conditions in London. This was particularly important as the gold withdrawn by France would 'return in a few months' when the speculation ended and those involved took their profits or losses. The need for stability in London was particularly important 'now that our [wholesale] price level is right as compared with America'.[1] Thus the analysis and emphasis was wholly short-term and the dollar exchange dominant in the analysis of the problem. The solution adopted was also, characteristically, short-term.[2]

There matters appear to have stood for almost three years. In the interim, with one exception, the Bank of France's London balances remained roughly constant, the French Government's balances remained roughly unchanged and private French balances remained fairly stable, fluctuating slightly with interest differentials between London and Paris and banks' liquidity needs.[3] During this period, the Bank and the Treasury, seemingly unaware of the Bank of France's large holdings of forward sterling,[4] worried somewhat about the possibility of withdrawals of official French balances for political reasons, but did nothing.[5] However, heavy, almost continuous gold losses to Paris began towards the end of 1929 and became particularly regular in the spring of 1930 as London's interest advantage disappeared. The issue of the Paris tranche of B.I.S. shares, which was heavily oversubscribed, was the proximate cause of increased concern, because the stringency of the Paris market resulting from the event had resulted in a heavy withdrawal of balances and gold from London. The forthcoming issue of the Paris tranche of the Young Loan, which would probably produce similar pressures, heightened London's concern. The official British view of the situation, strongly influenced by Hawtrey, suggested that the pressure resulted from the heavy demand for transactions balances in France resulting from their diminution during the inflation, from the necessity to offset official surpluses deposited at the Bank of France and from limitations on the Bank of France's ability to conduct open-market operations.[6] Thus the thrust of the official British approach placed the sources of strain and the primary responsibility for appropriate policy

---

[1]Ibid., 8–9.
[2]Above, p. 135.
[3]Above, p. 138; T160/430/F12317/1, Memorandum by M. Escalier, 13 January 1931, 4–8.
[4]F.R.B.N.Y., Strong Papers, Memorandum on Bank of England–Bank of France Relations, 24 May 1928.
[5]Above, p. 164; F.R.B.N.Y., Strong Papers, Norman to Strong, 11 October 1927; T176/13, Hopkins to Grigg, 19 August 1929.
[6]Hawtrey set his views out in public in 'French Monetary Policy', *The Art of Central Banking* (London, 1932), 13ff. See also, T160/430/F12317/1, Leith-Ross to Waley, 30 May 1930.

responses squarely on foreign institutions. At that time, however, the Bank of England took the line that it was 'contrary to the prestige of London to make any representations to the French about these gold movements' and that any such approach by London would tend to create the impression that London wished 'the privileges of the World's Bankers without assuming the liabilities.'[1] This attitude effectively prevented any formal discussions with the French during the summer of 1930. In the interim, however, the Bank agreed to consider increasing the fiduciary issue to minimise the domestic effects of any continued drain, if that became necessary.[2]

Eventually, however, the Treasury did open discussions with its French counterpart.[3] Initially, it maintained its previous emphasis on French institutional factors as being the prime cause of the drain.[4] However, as the discussions proceeded the Treasury became more and more open, largely as a result of French prodding, to the idea that the underlying problem was one of the division of responsibilities for the adjustment of 'disequilibrium' in the balance of payments. It is unnecessary to say where the British believed that the burden should fall.[5] The change in viewpoint as to the causes of the gold loss, however, represented a significant concession on the part of the Treasury. It provided one more impulse in the movement towards a 'self-help' policy which developed in late 1930 and early 1931 :[6]

Professor Sprague emphasised the desirability of not appearing to ask favours[7] from the French and doubted the wisdom of palliatives which might conceal the true position and delay radical measures.

As regards the diagnosis of the present difficulties the Governor thought

---

[1]T160/430/F12317/1, Hopkins to Snowden, 5 June 1930; T176/33, Waley to Leith-Ross, 4 June 1930. The Bank's continued advocacy of the gold exchange standard also created this impression. O. E. Niemeyer, 'How to Economise Gold', Royal Institute of International Affairs, *The International Gold Problem* (London, 1931), 90–1.

[2]T176/33, Note by Hopkins, 21 June 1930.

[3]These discussions, however, resulted from a French initiative. Clay, *Lord Norman*, 370; T160/430/F12317/1, Leith-Ross to Hopkins, 2 December 1930; Leith-Ross, Note of an interview with M. Pouyanne and M. Rueff, 5 December 1930; Note of an interview with M. Pouyanne, 16 December 1930.

[4]T160/430/F12317/1, Memorandum on France and Gold, November 1930; Memorandum by Leith-Ross, 3 December 1930; Leith-Ross to Hopkins, 4 December 1930.

[5]T160/430/F12317/1, Leith-Ross to Hopkins, 19 January 1931.

[6]T160/430/F12317/2, Waley, Notes of a Conversation between Leith-Ross, Siepmann and Sprague, 30 January 1931; Leith-Ross, Talk with Hopkins and the Governor on Gold Movements, 16 February 1931. See also Macmillan Committee, *Evidence*, Q. 9231; above, p. 195.

[7]In addition to the technical changes in French money and capital markets under discussion, there was also some talk of a French loan to Britain to fund sterling balances and to provide some new money.

that while the technical market organisation in France could be improved[1] the main troubles of this country were due to the defects of our financial policy during the past few years and the consequent lack of confidence in British Government securities and in sterling.

However, between this realisation and sterling's fall from gold in September 1931, although this mood of pessimism remained most pervasive and influenced such documents as the May *Report*, the Authorities did remarkably little other than block, largely without analysis, all alternatives other than deflation and create a plethora of official committees to examine the problem in the hope that the problem would either go away or that, without public education, the Authorities would find it easier to do later what they didn't have the courage to do now.[2] Moreover, at no time in the succeeding months did 'our financial policy during the past few years' come to include the exchange rate decision of 1925. In fact, it is rather amazing that recognition of the weakness of Britain's international financial position at $4.86 in any vaguely comprehensive form took over five years. It is this recognition lag, rather than the ultimate perception of the underlying situation, which is of greatest interest, for it is most characteristic of the period.

To a considerable extent, the root of the policy problem in 1924–5 and thereafter lay in a lack of knowledge.[3] Policy-making depended almost exclusively on the use of rules of thumb, often disguised as general principles, derived from an earlier, less complicated and more benign age.

[1]At the time, Norman was promoting, with the Treasury's approval, a plan for an International Credit Corporation, to be organised through the B.I.S. This Corporation was designed to increase the volume of international lending, especially from Paris and New York. The plan floundered on American and French opposition and the events of the summer of 1931 buried it. See T160/398/F12377; Clarke, *Central Bank Cooperation*, 179–80.

[2]On the mood and the chops and changes of this period see, for example, Keynes Papers, Brand to Keynes, 30 January 1931; Henderson to Keynes, 14 February 1931; Macmillan Committee, *Evidence* (Professor Sprague, 18–19 February 1931), Q. 9246ff.; Cab. 58/14, The Economic Situation, 9 February 1931, 1–3; Royal Commission on Unemployment Insurance, *Minutes of Evidence*, 381–91; Moggridge, 'The 1931 Financial Crisis', 835–7.

[3]This lack of knowledge lay less in the absence of an appropriate theoretical framework for dealing with international payments adjustment, although this would have helped, than in the absence of information suitable for filling out existing notions. Thus, for example, the discussions of 1924–5 would have gained much from additional study of the problems faced on the pre-1914 gold standard, of the size of the existing cost differentials between Britain and her overseas competitors and of the behaviour of money wages in previous deflations–to name only some items. The same could be said for the period after 1925 as regards the volume of foreign funds in London, the balance of payments and the behaviour of relative costs. Whether this additional information would have made that much difference in the event is, of course, the relevant – and an open – question, which I believe would be answered in the affirmative.

It rested on instinct rather than analysis. Thus, for example, the target of £150 million for Britain's post-war gold reserves grew out of a rough guess by Lord Cunliffe which was later justified as being about right because it roughly corresponded to the gold holdings of the Bank of England, the clearing banks and individuals (in the form of sovereigns in their pockets) in 1913.[1] At no point was any attempt made to see whether this pre-1914 level would be suitable for the post-war world: it was merely assumed it would be. When policies devised in such an *ad hoc* manner produced problems, the Authorities tended to take further *ad hoc* and often innovative steps, again without analysis, to shore up the position – no more than that. These steps displayed characteristics similar to the overall policy pursued during the period: they were essentially short-term in their ability to 'solve' the problem at hand; they struck at a source of strain amenable to control by traditional institutions or instruments with minimal, if any, extensions; and they attempted to minimise the actual formal changes in institutions or habits of thought. The almost neurotic concern in 1925 with avoiding legislation at the time of the return to gold serves as a good example, as do the Bank of England's attempts to retain pre-war forms of administration, despite the obvious changes in the nature of the Governorship.[2] The atmosphere of policy-making is perhaps best illustrated by the Bank's approach to statistics and information, two essential bases for economic policy. Throughout the period, the Bank depended much much more on qualitative judgements by men passing through Norman's room than on any analysis of underlying trends. It was well into the 1920s before any individual was assigned 'to prepare charts illustrating current economic and financial conditions' and 1928 before the Bank hired a specialist in such matters as economic research and statistics. The first special Adviser was not appointed until 1926.[3] As late as 1928, Norman privately admitted that it would be ten or fifteen years before the Bank had a professional staff 'with a knowledge of the problems with which we are now dealing.'[4] Nevertheless, the impression created before the Macmillan Committee was one of complete adequacy.[5]

Chairman : . . . I would like to put a further question to you, Mr. Governor, if I may. You have at your disposal under your roof . . . a certain number of experts who were not formerly housed there. Having returned to a more or less normal period, I suppose it would always be the function of a Central Bank like the Bank of England to take very important financial decisions from time to time, and these decisions must have certain effects on industry

---

[1] Above, p. 18; Cunliffe Committee, *First Interim Report*, para. 41.
[2] Above, pp. 80, 83; Clay, *Lord Norman*, 299–317.
[3] Ibid., 300–1.
[4] Ibid., 311.
[5] Macmillan Committee, *Evidence*, Q. 9173–4.

and the general welfare of the country. Would it not be of use to you to have these experts at your hand in ordinary times, so that you may lay their special information under contribution when you are coming to these decisions on matters of policy ... ?

Mr. Norman : I do not think so. They are specialists you see ... I do not attach great importance to great elaboration of statistical information. In my opinion the requisite information is available.

This from the Governor of a central bank which did not have to hand information on the capital account of the balance of payments, except in the most rudimentary form, which did not know the active circulation of notes in the country but laid great stress on it, which did not know the magnitude of the external short-term liabilities against which it held reserves and which in periods of balance of payments strain could only make a rough guess at their sources or implications.[1] In an unchanged world, such attitudes might have been excusable, if only because the appropriate rules of thumb had probably evolved from extensive experience in the same environment. However, in a world in which the operating environment had undergone and was undergoing extensive and far-reaching changes, such attitudes and the lack of understanding that went with them left the basis of international financial policy at sea. As Sir Arthur Salter put it :[2]

Instinct works with a subtlety, a precision, an exactness, an ease, a regularity, that reason cannot rival—and with practical success, so long as the environment in which it works is unchanged. But our environment ... has changed.

Learning-by-doing in matters of high policy can be very expensive, particularly if, at times, one cannot find out exactly what it is that one has done and, in many instances, one is not terribly interested in trying.

---

[1] Macmillan Committee, *Report*, Part II, Ch. 5; Keynes Papers, Macmillan Committee, Notes of Discussions, 5 December 1930, 28.

[2] A. Salter, *Recovery* (London, 1932), 13.

APPENDIX 1

A NOTE ON POLICY GOALS AND THE IMPLICATIONS OF EXCHANGE RATE CHOICES

The goals of the Authorities with respect to foreign investment, trade and employment were discussed briefly in Chapter 4. At that time, no attempt was made to attach very precise estimates as to the effects of appreciating the exchange to $4.86 on these goals. Given below are some 'back of an envelope' estimates which provide a very rough indication of the orders of magnitude of the changes in the components of the current account balance involved in the appreciation of sterling from around $4.40 to $4.86 in 1924–5 and the implications of these for the policy goals of the Authorities. Throughout the discussion, the alternative exchange rate assumed is approximately 10 per cent below $4.86. Such a rate is plausible both from the 1924 exchange position and from the implications arising from the discussion of purchasing-power parity estimates and of changes in Britain's international economic position from that of a typical pre-war year in Chapter 2.

The discussion will proceed in two stages with: an indication of the impact effects, *ceteris paribus*, of the appreciation of the exchange rate by 11 per cent between 1924 and 1925 and (2) an indication of the implications of an exchange rate 10 per cent below $4.86 in a typical post-1925 year. In both cases, the impact effects of the changes on the balance of payments will be compared to those resulting from other developments or policy changes.

Both calculations, for their estimates of the effects of changes in exchange rates on the trade account, take advantage of the numerous estimates of the price elasticities of demand for exports and imports made since the 1930s, with full knowledge of all the difficulties involved.[1] For the present calculations, imports of goods are assumed to have a sterling price elasticity of demand of −0.5 (i.e. a 1 per cent fall in the sterling price of imports relative to other goods will raise the volume of imports demanded by 0.5 per cent) and exports of goods are assumed to have a foreign currency price elasticity of demand of −1.5.[2] Throughout the calculations which follow, unless otherwise stated, all reckoning is done in sterling.

[1]Harberger, 'Some Evidence on the International Price Mechanism'; Zelder, 'Estimates of Elasticities of Demand'; Maizels, *Growth and Trade*, 211–16; Scott, *A Study of United Kingdom Imports*; G. D. A. MacDougall, 'British and American Exports: A Study Suggested by the Theory of Comparative Costs', *Economic Journal*, LXI (244) December 1951; and LXII (247), A. J. Brown, 'The Fundamental Elasticities in International Trade', Wilson and Andrews, *Oxford Studies*; Z. Kubinski, The Elasticity of Substitution between Sources of British Imports 1921–1938; *Yorkshire Bulletin of Economic and Social Research*, II (1), January 1950.

[2]Both of these elasticities are, if anything, conservative, for they lie towards the lower end of the range suggested in the literature which will actually improve the balance of payments after a devaluation.

The estimates which follow are also conservative in another important respect

Effects of the Appreciation of Sterling in 1924–5

Assuming that all other things remain equal (employment, world demand, foreigners' prices in third markets, etc.) an estimate of the impact effects of an 11 per cent appreciation in the exchange value of sterling between 1924 and 1925 is possible. The 1924 current account figures (exports of U.K. produce, £801 million; retained imports, £1137 million; and invisible surplus, £409 million) provide a rough base on which to build the estimates.[1] Assuming that the appreciation resulted in some reduction in import prices which benefitted exporters and that exporters narrowed their profit margins in the face of increased foreign competition, export prices in foreign currency would rise by, say, 7 per cent as a result of appreciation. On the import side, assuming that foreigners took the opportunity to raise profit margins, prices in sterling would fall by 8 per cent. Given these changes in relative prices and using the elasticities given above, the implications for exports and imports are as follows :

	Exports	*Imports*
Percentage change in volume	− 10.5	+ 4.0
Percentage change in sterling value	− 14.1	− 4.3
Change from 1924 level in £ million	−112.9	−48.9

Thus on trade account, on the above assumptions, the appreciation of sterling by 11 per cent would imply a worsening of the trade deficit by £64 million.

On invisible account, as noted in Chapter 4, appreciation would result in divergent movements. Reckoning again in sterling, net shipping earnings could be expected to fall as foreign operators' costs fell relative to U.K. operators'; net income from short interest and commissions would fall as foreigners needed a smaller sterling amount to cover a foreign currency

which is masked by the *cateris paribus* assumption. They assume that any changes in Britain's exchange rate do not cause other countries to follow her. In reality, one would expect that most of the Empire and several 'outside' countries would follow sterling, as they did in both 1925 and 1931. If this occurred, the effects of the change in the sterling exchange rate on British exports would be reduced somewhat in as much as their competitive position *vis-à-vis* home produced goods in these countries would be unchanged, although their position *vis-à-vis* the exports of third countries in these markets would be affected in the manner suggested by the estimates. On the import side, in so far as substitution did not occur between imports moving to Britain from countries following sterling and imports from the rest of the world, the import effects of a change in the sterling exchange rate would also be reduced. As a result, the balance of payments impact of the appreciation of sterling would be smaller than that estimated below and, on the other hand, the size of the devaluation necessary to achieve a given improvement in the post-1925 British balance of payments would be increased.

As the discussion of the appropriate exchange rate for sterling in Chapter 4 above was set in terms of the flows of foreign exchange necessary to allow the Authorities to meet their goals as to imports, overseas investment, trade policy and foreign commitments, these considerations would serve to increase the estimates of sterling's overvaluation in 1925.

[1] Rough, if only because the range of exchange movements in 1924 certainly affected

transaction of a given size, and as the U.K. was a net exporter of such services; net income on overseas debt investment would remain unchanged as both debits and credits were predominantly denominated in sterling; net income on overseas equity investment would fall as credits were determined in foreign currencies by foreign conditions and debits were determined in sterling by U.K. conditions; net tourism earnings would remain roughly unchanged, as would other private invisibles; and net Government expenditure on war debts and other items would fall. As the major expenditure item to fall would be on Government account and would only be of the order of, say, £5 million; whereas, the income falls, particularly given that almost 30 per cent of U.K. overseas investment was in equity form which provided yields about $1\frac{1}{2}$ times those of debt investment,[1] would extend over a much larger area, in all probability the adverse change in the invisible account would be substantial, of the order of at least £15 million if one makes another conservative estimate.

Thus, on the 1924 current account figures, one would expect, *ceteris paribus*, that the balance of payments on current account would deteriorate by roughly £80 million (1924 surplus = £73 million) as a result of the impact effects of an 11 per cent appreciation in the sterling exchange. This would have meant a deficit on current account of roughly £7 million, to be considered in conjuction with new overseas issues of long-term capital of approximately £100 million.

To relieve the resulting strain on the balance of payments, the Authorities would have several possibilities open :[2]

(a) They could reduce employment and national income by an amount necessary to provide sufficient relief to allow the attainment of other goals. Each reduction in employment of 1,000 men, given net national income per person employed of £185.6, and a marginal propensity to import of 0.3, could be expected to reduce imports by £55,680.[3] To offset the whole effect of appreciation on the current account in this way would have meant adding 1.4 million to the existing number unemployed. Each reduction in employment would, moreover, imply moving further from the pseudo-full employment goal at a time when unemployment was over 10 per cent.

(b) They could hope that rises in overseas costs relative to U.K. costs would, through their effects on relative prices, increase U.K. exports and reduce imports. This could occur through exchange appreciations or inflationary developments abroad, the latter of course being commonly expected at the time of the return to gold. Each 1 per cent rise in foreign costs relative to U.K. costs, if fully passed on in foreign prices, would imply a 0.5 per cent rise in the sterling value of imports of goods (i.e. about £5.4 million, if one works from the 1924 trade figures adjusted for the effects of appreciation) and a 1.5 per cent rise in the sterling value of

the 1924 figures, making them only partially indicative of the implications of a stable exchange rate of approximately $4.38.

[1] R.I.I.A., *Problem of International Investment*, 148, 150, 152.
[2] Each of these is considered *ceteris paribus*.
[3] Brown and Browne, *A Century of Pay*, Appendix 3; Chang, *Cyclical Movements in the Balance of Payments*, Ch. VI.

exports of goods (i.e. about £10.3 million).[1] This implies that a relative rise of overseas costs of about 15 per cent would have been necessary to offset the full current account effects of appreciation. Of course, any declines in relative costs abroad, resulting from exchange depreciations, deflationary developments or unfavourable changes in wages and productivity, would have adverse effects.

(c) They could hope that the terms of trade would turn in the U.K.'s favour through a decline in the prices of non-competing imports, which would reduce the import bill. A fall of about 10 per cent in these prices, with export prices unchanged, would be needed to restore the *ex ante* current account surplus—provided one can ignore the effects of such a fall on U.K. exports and on domestic consumption patterns.

(d) They could hope that any increase in unemployment generated in (a) would reduce U.K. money wages (or hold them stable while foreign money wages rose) and that this, plus divergent rates of productivity growth would reduce sterling wage costs per unit of output, thus making U.K. exports and import competing goods cheaper relative to foreign goods so that (b) could operate.

(e) They could reduce overseas lending by intensifying controls on lending abroad by U.K. residents. Although this would mean some slight decline in U.K. exports, it would improve the overall balance of payments position. However, a reduction of over £80 million in overseas lending would virtually mean ending all foreign issues in London and giving up one of the Authorities' policy goals.[2]

(f) They could through increased protection reduce imports, although this would also imply giving up the free trade goal.

(g) They could hope that a rise in world import demand for goods and services would raise U.K. exports despite the latter's high relative costs. A 10 per cent increase in world demand for imported goods would raise the demand for U.K. exports by £69 million, all other things remaining equal.

This list by no means exhausts all the possibilities, which could be combined in various ways, for improving the balance-of-payments position and offsetting the deterioration implicit in the appreciation of the exchange between 1924 and 1925. Each of the calculations above, although made under restrictive assumptions which largely ignore repercussion effects, merely presents, in a simple form, an order of magnitude for each possibility. In 1924–5, the Authorities hoped that (b) and (g) would bear the primary burden in the ensuing adjustment process, and that (a), (e) and (d) would play a subsidiary role. However, given the general tendency throughout the discussions to avoid specifics and quantification, there was never any attempt to foresee exactly what burden the return to gold at $4.86 imposed on the adjustment mechanism. As a result, the Authorities ultimately gave up, in varying degrees, all of their goals in the hope, which analysis indicates was somewhat specious, that $4.86 rather than an equally stable lower rate would increase London's invisible earnings and

[1]Using the elasticity estimates given above and assuming no changes in foreigners' profit margins or U.K. export prices in sterling.
[2]New foreign issues in 1924–5 averaged £111 million, despite the existence of controls.

that the adjustment mechanism would so operate as to allow the achievement of other goals.

The Alternative Position in a Typical Post-1925 Year

Taking 1928 as a typical post-1925 year, one can also examine, in a similar manner, the balance of payments implications of an exchange rate 10 per cent below $4.86. 1928 provides a useful post-1925 year, because by that time most other currencies had been stabilised for a sufficiently long period to allow their effects to be felt, and on the realised British data it is a year relatively free from the disruptions of the General Strike and its aftermath and from the effects of the later depression. Under these conditions, it is worthwhile to take a rather timeless[1] look at the effects of an exchange rate 10 per cent below $4.86 using the British 1928 current account figures.[2]

Assume that if sterling had been at $4.38 in 1928, export prices for U.K. goods in foreign currencies would have been 6 per cent below their 1928 levels, the remaining effects of the lower exchange rate showing themselves in higher costs resulting from increased import prices and higher profit margins which would raise sterling prices. Similarly assume that sterling import prices would have been 9 per cent above their 1928 levels, allowing for some narrowing of profit margins. Using the same elasticities as above, on the goods side the import and export position would have appeared, *ceteris paribus*, as follows:

	Exports	Imports
Percentage change in volume	+ 9.0	− 4.5
Percentage change in sterling value	+ 13.3	+ 4.1
Change from 1928 level in £ million	+ 96.2	+ 44.1

This results in an improvement in the balance of trade of £52.1 million. If arguing on the same lines as previously, one allows for an improvement in the invisible account of, say, £15 million, the overall improvement approaches £70 million.

This relief on the balance on current account could have been used in various ways. For example :

(a) The Authorities could have achieved a higher level of employment without sacrificing other goals. In 1928, unemployment averaged 10.8 per cent, or 1,290,000. If it had stood at the pseudo-full employment level of 4.7 per cent, or 561,000 and if the remaining 729,000 men had found jobs and produced the national average net domestic income per person employed of £191.3,[3] assuming again a marginal propensity to import of

---

[1]Timeless because the analysis ignores the effects of the U.K. of an extended period at a lower exchange rate in terms of growth and of the possibility of avoiding the disruptions of 1925–6. In fact, this part of the exercise might better be considered as an exercise in estimating the effects of devaluation in 1928.

[2]Retained imports, £1,076 million; exports of U.K. produce, £724 million; surplus on invisibles, £475 million.

[3]Brown and Browne, *A Century of Pay*, Appendix 3.

0.3, the additional imports of £41.8 million could easily have been contained by the improvement in the trade balance resulting from this 'timeless' calculation of the implications of an exchange rate of $4.38. At the same time, a margin of over £25 million would be left for other objectives. Thus, if money wages had not risen, or if productivity had risen by an additional amount over the trend rate sufficient to enable some money wage increases without raising unit costs, a lower exchange rate would have allowed[1] the Authorities something approaching their goal and even have left some room for increase net foreign lending.

(b) Alternatively, the Authorities could have relaxed controls on foreign lending. The appropriate no-control level of overseas lending is probably impossible to estimate, given the rise of the United States as a lender and its increasing dominance in areas such as Latin America and Canada and other changes in the international economy. However, given the improvement in the current account postulated above and adding this to the 1928 surplus of £123 million, the possibilities for net foreign lending open to the U.K. exceed £190 million. Even allowing for the effects of a higher level of employment postulated in (a) above, the additional lending possible would have implied a higher level of net foreign lending than occurred at any time during the 1920s.

This list of possibilities could be extended in several directions — reserve accumulation, freer trade, etc. — but the basic outlines are clear. The return to gold in 1925 at $4.86, as compared with a return to gold at $4.38 with conservative assumptions as to price elasticities of demand for imports and exports of goods and the impact of exchange rate changes on invisibles, to name only two, removed from the Authorities' grasp the possibility of achieving certain goals. The two sets of calculations do not 'prove' anything as to the full extent of the possibilities foregone,[2] but they do provide useful additional criteria for an informed judgement as to the implications of a return to gold at $4.86 and provide a rough check on the hypothesis that 10 per cent would provide a reasonable first approximation to the extent of sterling's overvaluation in 1925 in relation to the policy goals of the Authorities.

---

[1] I use the term allow deliberately, for a changed exchange value for sterling would not necessarily ensure that pseudo-full employment came to pass, although it would have created pressures operating in the right direction.

[2] To work out the full impact of alternative exchange rate strategies for the British economy of the 1920s, one would need to know much more than the impact elasticities used in this Appendix. One would also need to estimate the effects of increased exports on British incomes and the effects of increased incomes on domestic 'absorption'. However, the analysis presented above does provide a starting point.

APPENDIX 2

THE BRITISH BALANCE OF PAYMENTS, 1924–1931

'Britain between the Wars was not only a country of excessive unemployment but of inadequate statistics.'[1] This was particularly true in the realm of the balance of payments. Official estimates went as far as to cover the current account, but the capital account and monetary movements other than gold were very much in the realm of speculation and guesses. At the official level, the element of guessing became painfully clear when towards the end of the 1931 crisis the Cabinet Committee concerned with the problem spent a large part of one meeting allowing the participants, including the Deputy Governor of the Bank, to make what can only be called guesses as to the volume of short-term claims on London.[2]

In the construction of the estimates presented in Table 7 I have also had to rely on guesses in many places. Earlier work, particularly that of A. E. Kahn[3] and the Royal Institute of International Affairs,[4] has aided the process, but as some specific estimates are at variance with previous work the following will attempt to explain their origins.

Current Account—These figures are taken from the Board of Trade's estimates without alteration, despite the obviously conventional nature of the estimates for 'short interest and commissions' and 'other receipts'.

Long Term Capital Account—The figures for 'New Issues' for 1924–8 come from the estimates published by the Midland Bank,[5] which exclude refunding issues and take no account of the portions of new issues taken up by foreigners. The 'new issues' estimates for 1929–31 and the 'repayments' estimates are those of Sir Robert Kindersley who adjusted the Midland Bank estimates to include foreign subscriptions and refunding issues.[6]

The estimates for transactions in outstanding securities for 1930 and 1931 are those of A. E. Kahn[7] who derived them from Kindersley's estimates of total British foreign investments. However, an examination of the American estimates for such transactions for the period suggests that these estimates are probably too favourable to the United Kingdom, as during the entire period the United States was a net exporter of securities, and as Britain was one of the major countries involved in such transactions.[8] Such a suggestion would be strengthened by the knowledge that British

[1]Grant, *A Study of the Capital Market in Britain*, vi.
[2]Cab. 27/462, Minutes of Meeting of 14 September 1931, 3ff.
[3]Kahn, *Britain in the World Economy*, Appendix I.
[4]R.I.I.A., *Problem of International Investment*, Appendix I.
[5]Midland Bank, *Monthly Review*.
[6]R. Kindersley, 'A New Study of British Foreign Investments', *Economic Journal*, xxxix (153), March 1929 and subsequent annual studies through 1933.
[7]Kahn, *Britain in the World Economy*, 297–8.
[8]This was true even in the years 1924–9 where the estimates are by implication o. Lary and Associates, *The United States in the World Economy*, 107, Table 10.

financial institutions would have been rebuilding foreign security portfolios which had been run down during the war after 1925 to meet liabilities in foreign currencies, particularly dollars.

The estimates are seriously deficient in that they take no account of direct investments abroad by British firms or foreign direct investments in the U.K.

Monetary Movements—The estimate for changes in short-term liabilities represents an adjustment of the figures presented in the Macmillan *Report*[1] for the periol June 1927 to March 1931. The Macmillan estimates covered the deposit liabilities to foreigners of the Bank of England, the Clearing and the Scottish Banks, the accepting houses and the discount market, as well as the sterling bills held on foreign account by these institutions. However, the Committee's estimates took no account of the deposit liabilities to foreigners and the bill holdings on foreign account of foreign and overseas banks operating in London or of the foreign deposits of British banks. Contemporary reactions to these estimates suggested that these omissions meant that London's foreign short-term liabilities were understated by £200–400 million, depending on where one drew the line in defining such liabilities.[2] The Cabinet Committee discussions prior to 21 September provide an additional estimate, on the Macmillan Committee's definitions, of £350 million for early September.[3] Thereafter, Macmillan Committee-type estimates are not readily available.

In 1951, the Treasury published a more comprehensive estimate of British external liabilities beginning with one of £411 million for December 1931.[4] Working backwards from this figure, Mr David Williams has estimated that London's total foreign liabilities in December 1930 stood at £705 million as compared with Macmillan Committee's estimate of £434.6 million.[5] In estimating London's short-term liabilities before 1931, I have converted the Macmillan Committee's estimate by multiplying them by 1.625, the factor necessary to make the December 1930 estimate comparable to Williams'. As a check, I have carried the same conversion factor forward to December 1931 to estimate a figure on the Macmillan Committee's definition. The resulting estimate, £253 million, is roughly £100 million below the early September estimate quoted by the Cabinet Committee and would seem plausible, given that the September figure excludes the final rush out of sterling before 21 September and the withdrawals of central bank and private funds to cut losses thereafter.[6]

---

[1]Macmillan, *Report*, Appendix I, Tables 9–11.
[2]J. M. Keynes, 'Reflections on the Sterling Exchange', Lloyds Bank Ltd, *Monthly Review*, April 1932, 148–9.
[3]Cab. 27/462, Minutes of Meeting of 17 September 1931, 3.
[4]*Reserves and Liabilities 1931 to 1945*, Cmd. 8354 (London, 1951).
[5]Williams, 'London and the 1931 Financial Crisis', 528.
[6]Bank of France balances in London at the time of the suspension were £62 million; Netherlands Bank balances £10.8 million and Bank for International Settlements balances £1.5 million. The greater part of these, plus considerable private balances were liquidated after September. T160/425/F11282/018, note by Siepmann, 13 November 1931; T160/403/F12666, Tyrell to Simon, 17 December 1931;

The estimates for acceptance on foreign account are those of the Macmillan Committee and the Royal Institute of International Affairs.[1]

The gold reserve figures are those of the Bank of England[2] which did not secretly hold gold earmarked abroad at any time during the period 1925–31.[3] The gold reserve figures for December 1923, 1924 and 1931 have been adjusted so as to reflect the depreciation of sterling at the time.[4]

The estimate for foreign exchange reserves covers the Bank of England's holdings of dollars and French francs but not minor holdings of other currencies. The estimate is that of the Bank of England and is carried at current exchange rates.

The estimate for central bank and other foreign assistance for 1930 represents the assistance from the Federal Reserve System outstanding at the end of 1930.[5] The estimate for 1931 represents the unpaid balance of the credits granted to the Bank and the British Government during the summer of 1931 outstanding at the end of 1931. The borrowing is valued at its original sterling value—i.e. before the depreciation of sterling—while the October repayment of two-fifths of the central bank credit is valued at the sterling cost of the resources involved, following the Treasury's conventions in this matter.[6] Any accumulations of exchange for repayments in 1932 are included under the change in the exchange reserves or in Government transactions depending on the accumulating body involved.

Balancing Item—The size of this item in almost every year during the period provides a warning of the tenuous nature of many of the above estimates. It reflects both incomplete coverage and inaccuracies in many individual items and contains many of the long and short-term capital items which are missing in the estimates, insofar as these did not cancel out.

T160/439/F12712, Aide Memoire left by the Netherlands Minister at the Foreign Office, 21 January 1932; Annual Report of the Bank of France, *Federal Reserve Bulletin*, XVIII (3), March 1932; Annual Report of the Netherlands Bank, *Federal Reserve Bulletin*, XVIII (9), September 1932. Other central banks also held reserves in London, but their later disposition is unknown. Against these and any private withdrawals must beset any increases in sterling balances resulting from sterling area surpluses or other foreign holdings of sterling.
[1]Macmillan Committee, *Report*, Appendix I, Tables 9–11; R.I.I.A., *Problem of International Investment*, 341.
[2]Except for 1924 where the gold holding of the Currency Note Redemption Account which was transferred to the Bank at the time of the return to gold is included in the Bank's 1924 reserve, raising it by £27 million.
[3]Letter to the author from M. J. Thornton, Bank of England, 11 August 1967.
[4]The revaluation adjustments for December 1923, 1924 and 1931 affect the reserve movements by +£16, +£4 and −£63 million respectively, thus making the changes at par equal −£1, +£6 and +£33 million respectively.
[5]Above, p. 192.
[6]T160/444/F12901, Lefeaux to Hopkins, 4 March 1932.

APPENDIX 3

NATIONAL DEBT ESTIMATES, 1925–1931

Foreign Holdings of U.K. Internal Debt

These tended to be concentrated in issues where tax was not deducted at source in the United Kingdom, particularly the 5 per cent War Loan 1929/47. However, there were significant holdings in other issues that tended to accept conversion into War Loan or the 4 per cent Funding Loan as they fell due.[1] Beyond this, it is very difficult to pinpoint these holdings. However, such indications as exist suggest that they tended towards the later maturities available. Given these tendencies and the stability of the total volume of funds involved, except at the very short end of the market where foreign holdings of Treasury bills are not covered by the Treasury estimates, it is reasonably safe to assume that changes in foreigners' asset holdings did not significantly affect the overall pattern of debt holdings of U.K. residents. As for foreigners' holdings of Treasury bills, although contemporary opinion suggested that they were significant,[2] estimates of changes in these holdings or their overall size are unavailable.

Official Holdings of the National Debt

Estimates of the maturity structure of official debt holdings must be confined to those of the Currency Note Redemption Account, the Issue Department of the Bank of England and the National Debt Commissioners whose holdings for 1925, 1929 and 1931 appear in Table 18. The Bank of England normally held predominantly Treasury Bills in the Issue Department, although it also held some foreign exchange assets and longer-term securities which it took in on conversion or an issue to ease market adjustments.[3] In the Banking Department the position is much less clear,[4] for the Bank would also probably hold sufficient long-term securities to provide the

[1]T160/398/F12394, Leith-Ross to Hopkins and Phillips, 9 February 1931.
[2]Committee on National Debt and Taxation, *Evidence*, Q. 8690.
[3]Macmillan Committee, *Evidence*, Q. 137. This was true in late November 1929 when Sir Ernest Harvey gave his evidence, for except during a new issue in January 1929, the Treasury Bill holdings of the Issue Department (plus occasional Ways and Means advances) had always stood above 73 per cent of total assets. However, in 1930–1 the proportion fell almost continuously to a low of 34.7 per cent in September 1931 in the face of conversion issues, the proceeds of crisis foreign borrowing (or sterling counterpart funds which had to be in commercial bills to meet central bank regulations in the United States and France) and possibly the attempts to offset the bill famine which made short term market control by the Bank so difficult in 1930–1. H.M. Treasury Issue Department: Bank of England, Treasury Bills and Securities to 28 February 1935; above pp. 143-4.
[4]Macmillan Committee, *Evidence*, Q. 297ff.

TABLE 17.   *Public sector, non-resident and private resident holdings of U.K. internal Government debt, selected years 1925–31 (£ million)*

31 March	Currency[a] Note Account (1)	Bank of[a] England Issue Dept. (2)	Bank of England Banking Dept. (3)	National[a] Debt Commissioners (4)	Total public holdings (1)–(4) (5)	Non-resident holdings (6)	Total (1)–(6) (7)	Total Internal Debt outstanding (8)	Total private resident holdings (8)–(7) (9)
1925	231	11	41	380	663	250	913	6,544	5,631
1929	0	243	51	426	720	280	1000	6,536	5,536
1931	0	236	30	477	743	250	993	6,516	5,523

[a] Government guaranteed securities excluded.

(1) Currency Note Redemption Account, securities and advances to H.M. Exchequer.

(2) 1925, Bank of England, Weekly Return. 1929 and 1931, H.M. Treasury, Issue Department: Bank of England; Treasury bills and securities to 28 February 1935, figure for 31 March.

(3) Bank of England, Weekly Return, Wednesday nearest 31 March.

(4) and (8) Pember and Boyle, *British Government Securities in the Twentieth Century*, 2nd ed. (London, 1950), 411, 415, 419, 489, 493, 495.

(6) T160/398/F12394, C. J. Gregg to Leith-Ross, 10 May 1927 and 4 February 1931. The figures of £250 and £280 million are given by Gregg to refer to January 1926 and January 1930. I have assumed some foreign sales of U.K. Government Securities in late 1930 and early 1931 to restore the total to the 1926 level.

TABLE 18. *Estimated security holdings of the Currency Note Redemption Account, the Issue Department of the Bank of England and the National Debt Commissioners by maturity, selected years 1925–31 (£ million)*

Type of debt	31 March 1925	% of issue	31 March 1929	% of issue	31 March 1931	% of issue
Floating debt	198.4	26.7	193.6	38.1	124.9	21.6
Under 5 years	71.8	7.0	109.8	18.8	136.0	27.1
5–15 years	41.8	12.5	16.6	8.5	38.3	8.8
15–25 years	63.0	2.8	1.8	0.1	17.0	0.8
Over 25 years	87.7	11.8	110.3	15.3	136.1	13.2
Optional redemption	76.1	7.5	104.8	7.2	87.9	6.2
Other debt	83.8	18.1	133.4	26.2	171.6	30.1
Government guaranteed debt	155.6	32.0	253.6	38.2	239.1	33.3
Total	778.2	9.5	923.4	11.0	950.9	11.3

Source: Pember and Boyle, *British Government Securities in the Twentieth Century*, 489, 493, 495.
Currency Note Redemption Account, securities and advances to H.M. Exchequer.
H.M. Treasury, Issue Department: Bank of England, Treasury bills and securities to 28 February 1935.

TABLE 19.   *United Kingdom internal national debt, selected years 1925–31 (£ million)*

Type of debt	31 March 1925	31 March 1929	31 March 1931
Floating debt	742	737	594
Under 5 years	1023	582	502
5–15 years	335	194	435
15–25 years	2276	2420	2087
Over 25 years	745	723	1033
Optional redemption	1009	1465	1411
Other debt	463	510	570
Total[a]	6593	6631	6632

[a] Include stock and bonds held against death duties; excludes Government guaranteed loans.
Source: Pember and Boyle, *British Government Securities in the Twentieth Century*, 407, 415, 419.

basic income for its shareholders' half-yearly dividend of 6 per cent and running expenses not covered by Exchequer payments[1] and it would also hold Government securities in other places (discounts and advances or any hidden reserve). The Currency Note Account appears to have followed a convention similar to that described by Harvey for the Issue Department except that, instead of Treasury bills, Ways and Means advances formed a large part of its assets before October 1928.[2] These funds, plus the holdings of the Commissioners for the Reduction of the National Debt,[3] were the major Departmental funds available to the Authorities for the management of the outstanding public debt, although some funds were also in the hands of the Paymaster General and other departments.[4] These smaller funds generally formed the basis for Ways and Means advances to the Treasury and one estimate suggests that they may have been as high as £70 millions, but as Professor Morgan suggests this 'seems to be only a shrewd guess'.[5] From the estimates of the holdings of the major Departmental Funds in Table 18, plus the overall maturity structure of the national debt presented in Table 19, rough estimates of resident private sector holdings are possible.

[1] To provide a 12 per cent per annum on its capital, the Bank would have to hold £35 million of War Loan 1929–47 or a similar security yielding 5 per cent. This dividend-producing holding would probably be fairly firmly held in most circumstances.

[2] T160/631/F14575, Leith-Ross to Churchill, 12 August 1927, 6–7; Niemeyer to Churchill, 8 July 1927; Currency Note Redemption Account, Securities and Advances to H.M. Exchequer, returns provided by H.M. Treasury.

[3] The Commissioners managed the funds of the Post Office Savings Bank, the Trustee Savings Banks, the Unemployment Insurance Fund Investment Account, the National Health Insurance Funds and other smaller funds or accounts. For a good description of their operation see E. Nevin, *The Mechanism of Cheap Money* (Cardiff, 1955), 176ff. As these funds do not publish holdings simultaneously, estimates for a single date are only approximations.

[4] Morgan, *Studies*, 125–6.

[5] Committee on National Debt and Taxation, *Evidence*, Memorandum by W. T. Layton, para. 10; Morgan, *Studies*, 126.

Perhaps more shrewd than Professor Morgan suspects. Taking the 1929 and 1930 Floating Debt Figures and Hopkins' internal figures for Treasury bills in the Departments (T175/46, Treasury Bill figures, undated) with the basic figures used to Table 18, one finds that, outside the areas covered, public sector holdings of Treasury bills totalled £22.2 and £21.1 million on 31 March 1929 and 1930 respectively, while unexplained Ways and Means advances for the same two years stood at £37 and £48.5 million. The totals for Treasury Bills and Ways and Means advances are thus £59.2 and £69.6 million for these Departments in the two years, remarkably close to that 'shrewd guess'.

APPENDIX 4

THE BANK OF FRANCE AND FOREIGN EXCHANGE
OPERATIONS

Many studies of interwar international finance have held that the Bank
of France after the *de jure* stabilisation of 25 June 1928 was no longer
able to buy or operate in the foreign exchange market.[1] However, not
all authorities follow this approach and conclude that the stability of
French foreign exchange holdings after 1928 was a matter of law rather
than of policy.[2] In fact, the Law of 25 June 1928 did abrogate the Law of
7 August 1926 which allowed the Bank to buy foreign exchange, gold and
silver coin at a premium over pre-war par and it did not allow the Bank to
use resources gained through exchange operations to count as backing for
the note issue. But the Law of 25 June 1928 did not remove the powers of
the Bank to hold foreign exchange in certain forms or to operate in
exchange markets as it had before 1914, both for its own customers and in
assisting the Bank of England on occasion.[3] This point was well brought
out on two occasions in 1930 :[4]

> In a general way . . . the bank has the power under its statutes to discount
> bills payable abroad, drawn in foreign currencies; it likewise has the
> power to buy and sell gold, and, by implication, to buy and sell foreign
> exchange representing gold.
>
> The abrogation of the law of August 7, 1926, did not restrict the
> bank's freedom of action; it merely put an end to a temporary system
> which had grown out of the inconvertibility of the currency, and which
> relieved the bank of any direct responsibility when it carried out opera-
> tions of this character.
>
> The law of June 25, 1928, by the mere fact that it had approved the
> convention which transferred to the bank, in full ownership, the stock
> of foreign exchange previously acquired for the account of the Govern-
> ment, authorised the bank to hold foreign balances and likewise to
> administer them in such ways as the General Council should consider
> best suited to the monetary policy which it proposed to follow . . .

[1]See, for example, League of Nation's, *International Currency Experience*, 36–8, M. Wolfe,
The French Franc between the Wars, (New York, 1951) 98; R. G. Hawtrey, 'French
Monetary Policy', 20, 30–1; R. G. Hawtrey, *The Gold Standard in Theory and Practice*,
5th ed. (London, 1947), 117–18; T. Balogh, 'The Import of Gold into France:
An Analysis of the Technical Position', *Economic Journal*, XL (159), September
1930, 456.
[2]Brown, *International Gold Standard*, I, 459–64.
[3]Bloomfield, 'Short-Term Capital Movements', 25.
[4]F.R.B.N.Y., Lacour-Gayet to Goldenweiser, 3 December 1930; Crane, Report of
Trip of September–November 1929. Conversations with Cariguel, Ricard and
others, quoted in Galantière to Crane, 29 December 1930. See also, F.R.B.N.Y.,
Goldenweiser to Lacour-Gayet, 25 October 1930 and Galantière to Crane,
29 December 1930.

Since June 25, 1928, the bank has felt that it would not be in accord with the intentions of the laws prepared by the Government and passed by the Chambers at the time of the stabilisation of the franc, for the bank to build up its reserves of foreign exchange by direct and systematic purchases in the open market.

Since the legal stabilisation of the franc it has not been the policy of the Bank of France to buy foreign exchange, although the Bank, of course, has the power to do so.

These statements are certainly in keeping with Moreau's decision recorded in his Diary entry of 22 June 1928,[1] and they were certainly implicit in the memorandum presented during the 1931 discussions between the British and French Treasuries by the French authorities.[2] They also allow for the Bank of France's purchases of sterling in 1930 and 1931, and its purchases of dollars in September 1931.[3]

[1]Moreau, *Souvenirs*, 22 June 1928.
[2]T160/430/F12317/1, Memorandum by M. Escalier, 13 January 1931, 3, 7, 13–14.
[3]F.R.B.N.Y., Harrison to Moret, 26 September 1931. On the whole issue, also see Clarke, *Central Bank Cooperation*, 137–8.

SELECTED DOCUMENTS

MOST SECRET

1. If we are to take the very important step of removing the embargo on Gold export, it is essential that we should be prepared to answer any criticisms which may be subsequently made upon our policy. I should like to have set out in writing the counter-case to the following argument:-

2. Gold is no longer a currency token, but simply a reserve guarantee or test of good faith between man and man and one country and another. If good faith were universal, Gold could be left to the fine arts. The higher the financial reputation of a community, the smaller the reserve of Gold required. Great Britain has a financial reputation which, if maintained by a strict financial policy and by healthy economic conditions, would uphold her credit independently of any large hoard of Gold in the vaults of the Bank of England. In fact at the present time the Pound Sterling is steadily advancing, and our paper notes are accepted without question although we are not on the Gold Standard and do not, and cannot, pay Gold for these notes on presentation. I see it stated that under the 'managed' currency of Great Britain we have enjoyed during the last three years a more steady level of prices than has been achieved in the United States on a Gold Standard. It is certain that the £150 million Gold Reserve bears no appreciable relation to our vast credit operations nor to the scale of our business. That business is mainly conducted by cheques, and our Gold and notes together play only a minor part. So long as we maintain a strict financial policy and a healthy trade, we could get on quite well with a much smaller Gold Reserve. A Gold Reserve and the Gold Standard are in fact survivals of rudimentary and transitional stages in the evolution of finance and credit.

3. We are now invited to restore the Gold Standard. The United States seems singularly anxious to help us to do this. But this generosity is not perhaps remarkable when we consider her own position. She has by her hard treatment of her Allies accumlated over £850 millions of Gold, probably nearly three-quarters of the public Gold of the world. She is now suffering from a glut of Gold. A large portion of this hoard is lying idle in American vaults, playing no part whatever in the economic life of the United States. The United States are therefore forced to export this Gold in the shape of loans to Europe and investments in European and other external securities; and this is the main cause of the decline of the Dollar in relation to the Pound Sterling. Naturally they wish, having got so much Gold, to make it play as powerful and dominant a part as possible. The question is whether our interest is the same.

4. Suppose we adopted an alternative course. Supose we declared that we would take no steps to establish a Gold Standard. Suppose we reduced our Gold Reserve from £150 millions to £50 millions. Suppose the British Government purchased the other £100 millions and shipped it to the United States in regular instalments over the next two years in payment of our American debt. In the first place we should reduce our payments to the United States by £3½ millions a year and substitute £4½ millions of internal debt charge for this far more onerous oversea burden. We should further increase the congestion of the United States with Gold. They would be forced to repel it in the form of further investments in European and British securities and in loans to Europe. They would thus emphasise the advance of the Pound and the decline of the Dollar. Why should the Pound stop short at parity? By this process it might be raised to a substantial premium, thus still further facilitating the payment of our American debt, reducing the burden of our necessary purchases from America, and compelling the United States to pay more for our rubber, etc. As the British Empire produces £60 millions of Gold a year, we ought to be able to continue over-feeding the United States with Gold; and the favourable reaction just mentioned would be stimulated.

5. The whole question of a return to the Gold Standard must not be dealt with only upon its financial and currency aspects. The merchant, the manufacturer, the workman and the consumer have interests which, though largely common, do not by any means exactly coincide either with each other or with the financial and currency interests. The maintenance of cheap money is a matter of high consequence. If a return to the Gold Standard, when restored, could be defended only by an increase of the Bank Rate to 5% or even 6%, a very serious check would be administered to trade, industry and employment. If the Government took positive action to restore the Gold Standard and this were followed by a rise in the Bank Rate, we should certainly be accused of having favoured the special interests of finance at the expense of the special interests of production. We should be told—whether it was true or not—that any rise in the Bank Rate subsequent to a decision to restore the Gold Standard, was a consequence of that decision. It would be difficult to rebut such a charge, the burden of which would fall upon the Chancellor of the Exchequer. Only very plain and solid advantages would justify the running of such a risk.

6. Moreover, it is not clear to me at present that there is any urgency for action It is true that the legislation prohibiting the export of Gold lapses in December. But such legislation could easily be renewed for one, two or three years. If it be true that we have succeeded in maintaining during the last three years a steadier price level on a 'managed' finance basis than the United States for all her Gold, why should we not continue this successful practice at any rate for another year? The three years during which the Treasury and the Bank of England have 'managed' the currency so skilfully have been years in which unprecedented political disturbance has taken place. There have been three General Elections, four changes of Government, five Chancellors of the Exchequer and the advent

of a Socialist Administration to power for the first time. Nevertheless in spite of these violent political convulsions, the economic and financial policy of the State has been steadfastly and rigidly maintained. We have now returned to an era of stable politics. We are reasonably entitled to look for three or four years of continuity. Why then should we not continue on the basis of a 'managed' finance? What risks shall we run? What evils shall we encounter? Apart altogether from any question of reducing our Gold Reserve or of compromising in any way our power of reverting to the Gold Standard should we later on become convinced that it is to our advantage to do so, why should we not leave well alone and let events take their course on the present basis? Very good reasons could be given to Parliament for prolonging the legislation against Gold export for at least another year. Meanwhile we should see what happened to the Pound and the Dollar and how the price levels on each side of the Atlantic were maintained. If the Bank Rate had in the ordinary course of events to be raised, no one could attribute it to the action of the British Government. It could with justice be said, had we restored the Gold Standard it would have had to be raised still higher.

7. If, further, I am right in thinking that it is greatly to the interest of the United States to bring as many nations as possible, and especially Great Britain, on to the Gold Standard, they will only become more anxious to persuade us to that course; and their persuasion may take the form of even greater facilities than are now offered. I notice in 'The Times' of Tuesday [27 January 1925] that 'typical New York banking comment on the problems of restoring the Gold Standard embodies the assertion that to maintain Sterling at par, England must be willing definitely to forego her former preeminent position as the market for long term foreign loans, and willing also so to conduct the Bank of England discount policy as to keep the London short term money market on a higher basis than New York.' If these effects resulted from overt action on our part, it would be extremely difficult to represent the re-establishment of the Gold Standard as a British achievement.

8. In setting down these ideas and questionings I do not wish it to be inferred that I have arrived at any conclusions adverse to the re-establishment of the Gold Standard. On the contrary I am ready and anxious to be convinced as far as my limited comprehension of these extremely technical matters will permit. But I expect to receive good and effective answers to the kind of case which I have, largely as an exercise, indicated in this note.

THE GOLD EXPORT PROHIBITION

SIR OTTO NIEMEYER   2 February, 1925

I

1. The decision which has to be taken on the question of gold is probably the most important financial decision of the present decade. It is not a decision which we can avoid by 'leaving things as they are'. The

criticism which His Majesty's Government would thereby incur would be almost as great as that which action will produce, and the consequences of inaction are quite as serious as those of action.

2. His Majesty's Government have ever since the Cunliffe Report in 1918 proclaimed that they proposed to return to the gold standard at the earliest possible moment. On every occasion, at international Conferences (Brussels, Genoa), at the Imperial Conference (Economic Conference 1923), and time and again in Parliament, this statement has been repeated by Governments of all political shades. At the present moment there is a general expectation both in Europe and America, that the return will be made very shortly. It is known that a decision must be taken with regard to the export prohibition of gold (which expires on *31 December 1925*): and it is realised that some considerable notice must be given in advance of that date in order that (1) manufacturers and exporters (2) those responsible for credit policy may fix their course with certainty against the appointed day.

3. So great is the expectation of a return that a decision to continue the export prohibition would not be a continuation of the present state, but would start us immediately in the opposite direction to that in which we are now travelling. It would reverberate throughout a world which has not forgotten the uneasy moments of the winter of 1923; and would be none the more convinced that we never meant business about the gold standard because our nerve had failed when the stage was set. The immediate consequence would be a considerable withdrawal of balances and investment (both foreign *and British*) from London; a heavy drop in Exchange; and, to counteract that tendency, a substantial increase in Bank rate. We might very easily thus reap all the disadvantages which some fear from a return to gold without any of the advantages.

With the engine thus reversed, no one can foretell when conditions, political, psychological, economic, would be such that the opportunity would occur again. It would certainly be a long time.

4. Apart from one or two theoretical advocates of 'a managed currency' —a strict application of which would incidentally have involved an increase over the present Bank rate several months back—there is nobody of opinion, either financial or industrial, in this country which does not wish for the restoration of the gold standard. Even those whose orthodoxy is most suspect, e.g. the F.B.I., would certainly maintain that they desired the gold standard, largely for the reasons eloquently adduced by Mr. McKenna in a recent speech. There is a difference of opinion as to *when* it should be restored, or, more strictly, whether sacrifices should be made for its restoration and what the extent of those sacrifices would be.

II

5. The late Chancellor of the Exchequer appointed in June last a Committee (Lord Bradbury, myself, Mr. Gaspard Farrer (of Barings), Professor Pigou of Cambridge, with (until he became a Minister) Mr. Austin Chamberlain as Chairman to consider the possible amalgamation

of the Bank of England and Currency Note issues. That Committee found at once that it could not deal with its reference without considering the question of gold standard. Our report, not yet signed, but practically agreed, is attached: and our definite recommendation is that His Majesty's Government should announce at a comparatively early date that the gold export prohibition will not be renewed and that in fact free licences to export gold sold by Bank of England should be given forthwith. Our witnesses included the Association of Chambers of Commerce and the F.B.I.

6. Our reasons for this recommendation may be put shortly as follows:-

(1) United Kingdom exports, visible and invisible, together with our income from foreign investments are clearly sufficient to cover imports and foreign debts, with something over for investment abroad. The primary conditions are therefore present.

(2) British and United States prices cannot be directly compared (owing to the differences in the bases of the published price indexes) but are probably within $4\frac{1}{2}\%$ of each other, if not nearer. Moreover at present United States prices are rising and the United Kingdom prices falling. So little more ($1\frac{1}{2}\%$) would be needed to maintain par, that the extra sacrifice (above that to maintain our present position) is negligible.

(3) South Africa has already announced that she will revert to gold standard in July. Australia will probably follow suit. United States is already on the gold standard: so are Austria and Sweden, and for practical purpose Germany. Holland will certainly revert in a few months and perhaps India. With this large body of traders on a stable currency, the United Kingdom cannot afford to remain fluctuating. A gold Bill for instance would replace the sterling Bill.

(4) We believe that an announcement that export prohibition would cease would put exchange to par at once. All experience, e.g. after Napoleonic wars—suggests that the way to resume is to resume and that in the event previous fears have generally proved to be exaggerated. But we do not disguise that there may be sterling held as a speculation for a rise, which will tend to take its profit when sterling has reached par *unless we can convince holders* that they will not lose by staying. It may therefore be difficult to maintain parity when reached, and this *may* involve a temporary increase in Bank rate (besides other measures mentioned below).

7. The Report does not mention, but we have necessarily had in mind certain other considerations.

(1) We have now a prospect of a period of stable Government *both in England and in United States*—a rare coincidence.

(2) We have every prospect of pretty *stable prices and money rates in United States*—a vital consideration as a considerable increase in United States money rates would inevitably drive up rates in London.

(3) We have a great desire (and considerable motives) in *United States banking and official circles to cooperate with us* in their domestic

money policy, and even assist us, with credits if necessary. (None of these things may reoccur; if we now hold off.)

(4) Obviously *the spring* when exchange demands are light rather than the months before December when exchange is heavy is the moment to move.

(5) We can secure considerable *cooperation not only from the Dominions but from Holland, Sweden and probably Switzerland*. This would not only lessen the speculative risk (for the movement would look more impressive) but will greatly facilitate the cooperation between the central Banks in accordance with the Genoa resolutions which is so necessary for keeping gold stable.

III

8. There are three main criticisms which will be brought against the Committee's proposal.

(a) that the United States holds most of the world's gold: that it is her interest not ours to reinstate gold (particularly as we are entitled to pay our war debt in gold bullion) and that by returning to gold we are enslaving ourselves to the New York money market.

(b) that the desire for the gold standard is a device of the Banks to enrich themselves by dear money at the expense of trade and employment.

(c) that in present conditions trade and employment cannot face a strait-laced money policy involving perhaps increased Bank rate. On the contrary it needs to be watered with cheap money (which would incidentally reduce Treasury Bill rates).

9. It is obviously true that the United States holds most of the world's gold (say £850 millions or about half the total world supply) and is anxious to see gold maintain its value.

But there are others who are interested in gold also. We ourselves hold some £150 millions: the British Empire produces £60 millions a year (70% of the world's output) : and we have very large foreign investments due to us in *sterling* (say £3,000 millions) the real value of which increases if sterling appreciates to gold. (This is apart from Allied War Debts due to His Majesty's Government).

Further we as a great exporting nation are vitally interested in stable exchanges. With United States, Germany and the main Dominions on gold, we cannot afford to fluctuate in relation to their prices.

Nor can we afford to let the sterling Bill, being of fluctuating value, be replaced by a Bill ($ or Mark) with a stable value.

Finally it is most probable that the effect of our stabilising on gold (on which alone *we* could stabilise) will be to force the Latin countries to devalue and stabilise also—a great step in the restoration of Europe for trade and commerce.

Much nonsense is talked in America about dethroning London finance. As we are a considerable debtor to America not only for war debts but for raw materials and food (cotton, tobacco, meat, wheat) and as we have during the war lost some £800 million of our American securities, we are in any circumstances largely dependent on America. A Return to gold, by strengthening our export trade and our London Bill seems more likely to diminish our dependence than otherwise.

10. It is quite a mistake to imagine that the Banks want dear money which makes but little difference to their profits. Cheap money (and rapid circulation) suits them much better. While dear money gives them a bit more on their Treasury Bills and on such advances as they make, it reduces the volume of their advances and tends to turn some outstanding advances into bad debts. Moreover they have to pay more for their deposits and their fixed securities depreciate in value (an important consideration when the Big Five hold some £300 millions of their resources in this form). No banker would ever for his own purposes advocate dear money.

The real antithesis is rather between the long view and the short view. Bankers on the whole take longer views than manufacturers. But the view is of what is good for trade and industry as a whole, on which after all the banks entirely depend, not of what may enable the Bank to bleed its trader.

11. The most serious argument against the return to the gold standard is the feared effect on trade and employment. No one would advocate such a return if he believed that in the long run the effect on trade would be adverse.

In fact everyone upholds the gold standard, because they believe it to be proved by experience to be best for trade. If it is agreed that we must have the gold standard, is it not better to get over any discomforts at once and then proceed on an even keel rather than have the dislocation (if dislocation there be) still before us?

No one believes that unemployment can be cured by the dole, and paliatives like road digging. Every party—not least Labour—has preached that unemployment can only be dealt with by radical measures directed to the economic restoration of trade, whether with Europe or with the Dominions. What could be worse for trade than for us to have a different standard of value to South Africa and Australia (i.e. pay more £ sterling for their wool etc.) or to Germany and the United States— fluctuating while they are stable inter se? On a long view—and it is only such views that can produce fundamental cures—the gold standard is in direct succession to the main steps towards economic reconstruction (Brussels Resolutions: Austrian and Hungarian Loans: Dawes Scheme) and is likely to do more for British trade than all the efforts of the Unemployment Committee.

12. I am myself much inclined to view that no very heroic steps will in fact be needed to maintain gold parity with the dollar, if we once take the bull by the horns. The great danger is that speculators may think that we cannot hold the position. What are our weapons against this form of attack?

(1) We have gold reserves of £150 millions and we should make it plain to the world that we mean to use them, if necessary to maintain the exchange, even though that may entail a temporary

increase in bank rate. The clearer we make this the less likely extreme measures.

(2) We already hold against our United States debt payments in June and December next of $160 millions some $110 millions—a fact not hitherto published but kept in reserve for the moment when we wish to use it.

(3) We shall march in company with Dominions and several European neutrals.

(4) We have assurances of American financial support if needed, beyond our own direct resources.

COMMENTARY

SIR OTTO NIEMEYER   2 February, 1925

(1) *Financial reputation, which, if maintained by a strict financial policy and by healthy economic conditions would uphold credit independently of any large hoard of gold.*

I firmly believe that a balanced Budget is the beginning of sound credit and currency; but it is equally true to say that unless you have a sound credit policy you can't maintain a balanced Budget. Unsound credit policy (i.e. inflation) inflates money (but not real) prices: makes taxes give a high return *in money* and directly encourages Budgetary extravagance. Then there arrives the moment when the bubble bursts and the Budget is left in ruins face to face not with paper money but with real costs (see debris scattered all over Europe in last 5 years).

No one values gold as a hoard : its only purpose is for use, not for internal circulation but as a basis of the credit structure and in particular a reserve for a balance of foreign payments. But the gold standard has nothing to do with hoarding gold. It[s] use is as a regulator of the degree in which remittances can be made to abroad.

(2) *The pound is steadily advancing.*

Why? Primarily because everyone believes we are going to revert to gold. It would soon cease to do so if this belief were damped down.

(3) *'Under the "managed" currency of Great Britain we have enjoyed during the last 3 years a more steady level of prices than has been achieved in the United States of America on a gold standard.'*

Mr. McKenna's actual figures of mean deviation from the average were:-

	England	United States of America
1922	2.87%	6.34%
1923	2.37%	2.99%
1924	2.58%	2.91%

Except in 1922 therefore the difference was very small : in 1922 the Federal Reserve Bank's were deliberately encouraging a credit expansion in order to increase prices after the slump in 1921.

Mr. McKenna's inference is ill-founded. The Federal Reserve Banks had in all this period *far* more than their legal gold requirements (100% to 150% more). Gold as a regulator of credit in the United States of America was every bit as inoperative as in the United Kingdom and the United States currency was as much and probably more a 'managed' currency as ours was. What slight difference there has been has been due to different objects of 'management': in no way to 'management v. gold.'

(4) *United States are forced to export this gold in the shape of loans … and this is the main cause of the decline of the $ in relation to the £.*

This is a very large overstatement.

United States has mainly used the gold not for loans (either foreign or domestic) but to substitute a 100% gold backing to her notes for a 40% backing. She has done this expressly to prevent her money prices rising as they would if credit (based on excess gold) increased with production of commodities not so rapidly increasing. This process costs the United States of America something (loss of interest on £850 million at 5% say £42 million per annum): but not more than she can afford to pay as an insurance against the dangers of a boom, almost for ever.

Foreign loans play an infinitesimal part in the big United States enclave. United States can absorb in internal development nearly unlimited amounts which in pre-war days she got from abroad and her investors are shy of foreign bonds. While she would like to send some gold out again in loans, it is going to be a long process and the amount will be comparatively small compared to the whole corpus. Even the United States share of Dawes loan was only £20 million.

The approximation of the £ and the $ is (1) partly natural, for the level of United States prices is close to that of the United Kingdom prices (United States Index 162, United Kingdom Index 170 or allowing for the exchange only about 4% difference): (2) partly due to return of sterling investments frightened into dollars by Montagu Barlow and fears of Labour in winter of 1923: (3) partly due to liquid United States money being attracted here by higher investment rates (Bank rate 4% against 3% in the United States): and only partly (4) to United States loans to Germany, France, Belgium and Europe generally, (5) because of the firm expectation that we are going back to par. It is a question how far (4) is offset by foreign balances (e.g. Holland) which are normally kept in sterling but of late have been kept in $.

(5) In the event of further gold shipments the United States 'would be forced to repel it in further investments in Europe.'

For the reasons under (4) this is a considerable overstatement.

(6) *As the British Empire produces £60 millions of gold a year, we ought to be able to continue over-feeding the United States.*

United States can stand a great deal of this diet without swelling much. The £60 million is produced by Australia, and more important, South Africa. Now South Africa is going on to the gold standard in July: probably Australia also. This means that, if the United Kingdom pound is below gold par it will cost us just as much to buy this gold as it would to buy $.

(7) *The merchant, the manufacturer etc. have interests . . . which do not exactly coincide with the financial interests.*

This is commonly said : I believe erroneously. The Banker has little desire for dear money. While it means he may get a little more on his short Bills (especially Treasury Bills), he will have to pay more on his deposits; he will have less demand for advances and some risk of losses on the advances he has made, and all his permanent investments (which are considerable) depreciate in value as ordinary interest rates go up.

The merchant etc. on the other hand are by no means unconcerned in stable exchange. The fluctuations of exchange—which mean that the exporter does not know what he is going to pay for them have been one of the prime causes of industrial depression.

(8) *Such legislation could easily be renewed for one, two or three years.*

This could be done—though there would be great disappointment and considerable opposition.

Such a course would, in my opinion, mean (1) a set back to financial reconstruction, followed inevitably by a great depression in exchange, (2) a world wide opinion that Great Britain did not really mean to return to gold, (3) not improbably a position in which Great Britain would not for a generation be *able* to return to gold the effects on British trade would be extremely bad.

(9) *What risks do we run?* (i.e. if we go on as here).

All the risks following reversing the engine.

(10) *'Typical New York banking comment . . . embodies the assertion that to maintain sterling at par England must be willing definitely to forgo her former prominent position on the market for long term foreign loans and to conduct discount policy so as to keep London short term market on a higher basis than New York.*

There is some truth: but it is nothing new and it would be equally true if we merely 'stayed where we were' and did not go to par. *Short term* money rates have been for many months more than in New York and it is essential that they should so remain. That is how we attract foreign money (and retain British money) at profit to ourselves. Long term money rates are *cheaper* here than in New York (and probably always will be because of our greater skill in foreign loan business). But it is almost certain that we are in fact over-lending to foreigners and this will in any event have to be corrected. The gold standard makes correction far more easy, because the ill effects of excessive lending become immediately apparent in reduced gold reserves instead of being obscurely reflected in exchange rates. We need have no fear that we should not always get quite as many foreign (& Dominion) loans as we wish, and nothing could be more desirable than that the United States should take some.

Para. 2. National Credit needs not only a strict financial policy and healthy economic conditions but also good faith and a liquid Reserve.

Gold is the guarantee of good faith.

A liquid Reserve must be internationally valid: there is no internationally valid Reserve except Gold (or its equivalent).

A Gold Reserve and the Gold Standard are steps in the evolution of Finance and Credit: as such they are necessary: so is a Police Force or Tax Collector : it is as dangerous to abandon the former as the latter.

The only possible alternative to Gold *was* a price-level scheme (Irving-Fisher and others). Now there *is* no alternative to Gold in the opinion of educated and reasonable men.

The only practical question is the Date.

The pound sterling on which paper Notes are based has advanced greatly because the date of free Gold is believed to be at hand. 'The financial reputation of Great Britain' is such that the world believes 1925 means 1925 and Gold in 1925 by Act of Parliament means Gold in 1925 in fact. Any other course means a declining pound.

Para. 3. In the past few years we here have taken steps to stabilise Austria, Hungary and Germany—in each case we have insisted (directly or indirectly) on Gold. Can we complain if the U.S. approves in our case the very same course which we have required in other cases?

One result of External Loans by the U.S. has been to cause the 'decline of the Dollar': another has been to provide cash against her Exports and greatly to liquidate her agricultural lock-ups.

The U.S. is suffering from a glut of Gold, which has been made harmless by her astute policy: the alternative policy in the U.S. would have been rising prices : a boom. No sane man anywhere (who lived through 1920 &c.) could recommend or even tolerate another boom.

In fact the policy of the Federal Reserve Bank of recent years has permitted general stability and given time for general reconstruction to begin. Any other policy would have reduced most of Europe to mediævalism.

On international questions of Finance the interests of Great Britain, of the U.S. and of most other countries are the same. You cannot permanently have 'patchy prosperity'.

Para. 4. It is quite possible and easy to reduce our Gold Reserves to £50 million and to ship the rest to America in payment of our approaching instalments.

In the first case, the result of so reducing our Gold Reserves would be psychological as well as financial : our Note-circulation would probably be discredited at home (as happened e.g. in Germany): specie payment would have to be formally suspended: Exchange would fall ... and fall: and the world-centre would shift permanently and completely from London to New York.

In the second case, the occasion has passed when it might have been possible to embarrass the U.S. by a congestion of Gold. The Federal Reserve Bank have learned how to sterilise any amount of Gold we could send and for the last few months have been exporting more Gold than, e.g., the relative service of our Debt.

There is no reason why the Pound should stop short at parity, if it be made *more* valuable (though this cannot last long). Its value depends on its continuous parity with Gold. But the suggestions in para. 4 are to make it less valuable—i.e., to prolong its divorce from Gold.

Broadly, the price we receive for rubber &c. balances (for us) the price we have to pay for wheat &c.: all such tend to move together.

Para. 5. In connection with a golden 1925, the merchant, manufacturer, workman, &c., should be considered (but not consulted any more than about the design of battleships).

Cheap money is important because 9 people out of 10 think so: more for psychological, than for fundamental reasons. Perhaps trade and industry are making greater strides in Germany than in Great Britain: *there* interest is 10% or 20%—*here* it is 4% or 6%.

The cry of 'cheap money' is the Industrialists' big stick and should be treated accordingly. Banking and Finance, as well as Industry, prosper from cheap money.

The restoration of Free Gold *will* require a high Bank Rate: the Government cannot avoid a decision for or against Restoration: the Chancellor will surely be charged with a sin of omission or of commission. In the former case (Gold) he will be abused by the ignorant, the gamblers and the antiquated Industrialists: in the latter case (not Gold) he will be abused by the instructed and by posterity.

Plain and solid advantages can be shown to exist which justify—and seem to require—this sacrifice by the Chancellor. He could hardly assume office with Free Gold in one country and watch half-a-dozen others attain Free Gold ... without his own.

Para. 6. There would be no urgency for action but for the expiry of the Act. If the Act did not happen to expire this year the urgency would hardly arise. The National Credit of this country presupposes that measure of good faith which has gradually induced the whole world to believe that when an Act expires, it expires.

While prolonging the Act would shatter our Exchange (worse than Barlow cum Labour in 1923) and our international Banking and Finance, there is no reason to suppose it would permanently benefit Trade and Industry.

These three years of 'managed' finance have been possible only because they have been made up of steps and deliberate steps—towards a golden 1925. These steps have been assisted, and supported, by successive Chancellors. When the publics have feared the Government might lose sight of this process our international position has temporarily worsened.

Our position must always be especially international: we have to buy before we can sell: we require foreign trade and foreign balances. The

Exchequer is able to borrow (directly or indirectly) these temporary balances held in London by Foreigners: this is needful.

Even 'managed' finance must be definite in object and time: its objective is being reached in 1925. If its objective is avoided—if 1925 is not golden—the opportunity is likely to pass for years. The prospect of three or four years of political stability is admirable for the change, which could never be made with a General Election on the horizon.

Some of the evils we should encounter by attempting to postpone the return to Free Gold until 1928 are set out (in answer to para. 4) in connection with the Reduction of Gold Reserves.

The demand for Foreign Issues in London cannot long be prevented by the present method of so-called persuasion. Half-a-dozen countries— with depreciated Exchanges—wish to borrow here. Whether or not we now return to Gold, a higher Bank Rate will therefore be necessary. If the Act is prolonged, the Bank Rate should probably be higher than if it is not prolonged—and certainly less effective. The pressure for Foreign Issues of itself demands at once a higher Bank Rate, for which the ignorant would doubtless blame the Chancellor.

Para. 7. The interest of the U.S. in this respect is identical with that of Great Britain and the world. The Gold Standard is the best 'Governor' that can be devised for a world that is still human, rather than divine.

The gradual distribution of Gold (now sterilised in America) will present great difficulties in a few years: a Gold-inflation in many countries is to be feared, but, compared with the inflation which has happened elsewhere, it will be the lesser of two evils.

The quotation from the 'Times' contains much truth. But London will forego her position as the market for long term Foreign Loans, not because of a golden 1925 but because the War has left her relatively poor. The same relative poverty will require (as already exists) a higher rate for money in London than in New York. Given similarity without delay in respect of Free Gold, it is likely that tradition and experience will gradually set London as high as New York as an international centre.

Para. 8. The above is an attempt to give brief but effective answers to the points raised: much of it is of course controversial: it should be elaborated verbally by question and answer in the case of any reader who is not familiar with the technique of the game.

THE GOLD STANDARD

LORD BRADBURY   5 February, 1925

'Gold is no longer a currency token, but simply a reserve guarantee or test of good faith between man and man and one country and another. If good faith were universal gold could be left to the fine Arts.'

This statement shows an entire misconception of the function which gold plays in international economics.

However little we may like it, gold is still the international standard of value and the medium in which, in the long run, any ultimate debt against one country in favour of another must, if it is to be liquidated at all, be liquidated.

It is quite easy to conceive a state of affairs in which each country would have a currency of its own, having the real value, in terms of commodities, of the commodities which it is capable of purchasing, which would be accepted by other countries in discharge of debts owing to them. It is conceivable, but not in fact feasible, since certain countries which are debtors on international account would never be able to resist the temptation to reduce the value of their currencies in order to diminish the real burden of their debts. For that reason a prudent creditor would never permit a debt due to him to be expressed in the currency of these countries.

It is also conceivable, and perhaps more nearly feasible in practice, that particular countries should enter into an agreement to maintain their respective currencies at a constant value, in terms of commodities and agree to accept payment of debts in each other's currency. Such an agreement would be perfectly possible in theory as between, say, Great Britain and the United States of America. If an agreement of this kind were arrived at between the two greatest commercial countries of the world, other countries would probably tend to adopt the currencies of these countries instead of gold as their own international standard. The result of this (if it worked) would be to abolish gold, both as a standard of value and as a medium for the settlement of international accounts, and leave the very large stocks of gold at present in existence to the Fine Arts. As the demand from the Fine Arts would undoubtedly be far less than the supply, the value of these stocks of gold, in terms of commodities, would fall to a very low figure. America, therefore, as the principal holder of the stocks of gold, could hardly be expected willingly to take a hand in the game.

Furthermore, existing international debts, according to the terms of the contracts which govern them, are, in the main, obligations to pay gold. To attempt to convert them into obligations to pay 'monopoly dollars' or 'monopoly pounds' would be regarded by the debtors, if gold depreciated in terms of those currencies, as a breach of faith. Even in regard to debts expressed to be payable in sterling money of the United Kingdom, it would be undoubtedly argued that the foreign debtor contracted his liability on the assumption that the law of the United Kingdom, under which an ounce of gold could be presented to the Royal Mint and converted into £3. 17. 10½d of sterling money without charge, would be maintained and that if it were altered he was entitled to discharge his debt by payment of the equivalent amount of gold at the Mint price.

It may be freely admitted that the unloading of gold by the United States of America, which is a possible consequence of the restoration of general international credit, is not unlikely to lead to a general rise in the prices of commodities, or, in other words, to a depreciation in the purchasing power of gold, and it is conceivable, though not, I think, probable, that this depreciation would be so serious that it would make it necessary for the world in general to protect itself against the superabundance of the gold supply.

It is not, I think, probable, because the interests of the United States are obviously against permitting such depreciation, and they have sufficient means at their disposal for preventing it.

So far as we are concerned, the only precaution we need take against it at the present moment, is to safeguard ourselves against becoming the dumping ground for surplus supplies of what may prove to be a depreciating article.

The restoration of the gold standard at the pre-war parity does not, of course, mean that we should be importers of gold on balance. Indeed, the recommendation of the Cunliffe Committee that our central gold reserve should be fixed at £150 million sterling was based on the assumption that a stock of gold to that amount as held in the United Kingdom before the war (in reserves and circulation taken together) and that in future the gold which had previously been in circulation would be replaced by notes of small denominations, the gold cover of which would be held in the central reserve.

The policy, therefore, stated shortly is to restore our national gold holding to the pre-war level, but not go beyond it.

It may, I think, be assumed that the United States are very unlikely to embark on a policy of demonetising gold, but that it is highly probable that they will continue to pursue the policy of aiming at stabilising gold, in terms of commodities, even at the expense of carrying the bulk of the existing gold stocks of the world and acquiring the new accretions.

It is also perfectly clear that they will do their best to make other nations share the expense of nursing this very inconvenient baby. Quite a large part of the American contribution to the Dawes Plan really consisted in an attempt to divert the contribution which Germany might otherwise have made to paying reparation, to this more or less laudable object, and it is not at all unlikely that America will devote a good part of anything she may get from her interallied debtors to the same purpose.

But this need not worry us, and the only reply we need return to any amiable invitations which may be given to us to assist in nursing the baby is that we think that the interest of our American friends in the health of the infant is really very much greater than ours.

In any case, however, the question whether, in certain contingencies, it might not be desirable to give sterling a higher value than gold is quite independent of the question whether it ought to be allowed to have a lower value.

When we have got back to the gold standard it may be useful and profitable to consider whether we should adopt a super-gold standard, but until we have got back to the gold standard the question is premature.

The idea that the 'pound' has some kind of intrinsic value dependent on the excellence of British credit is a pure hallucination. You can have a 'pound', the value of which, in terms of purchasing power, is equivalent to the quantity of commodities in exchange for which a mine in South

Africa can afford to produce a certain fraction of an ounce of gold, or some existing holder of that fraction of an ounce of gold will be prepared to part with it. That is the gold standard. You can have a 'pound' which has no intrinsic value whatsoever, but of which the supply is so carefully adjusted to the demand for it that, allowing for the play of the forces which determine the volume of domestic credit to be created from time to time, it will always purchase approximately the same quantity of a given commodity or group of commodities. That is the 'managed' pound. The 'managed' pound presupposes a deliberate restriction in the number of currency units created by the Government or by a central bank. The 'gold' pound pre-supposes an automatic increase in the number of pounds in circulation whenever gold is worth less than £3. 17. 10½ an ounce and an automatic diminution whenever it rises above that figure.

The supply of 'managed' pounds, if the purchasing power of the pound is to be kept stable, must be regulated according to the variation in the commodity price index. When the index tends to rise the supply must be stopped; when it tends to fall the supply can be increased. When the supply is stopped the same consequences will follow to trade and industry through restriction of credit as occur when you get an export of gold under the gold standard. When the supply is increased the credit cycle will follow the same course as when, under the gold standard, there is an influx of gold.

You do not, therefore, in any way eliminate the inconvenience of the 'credit cycle'. At best you can get rid of the disturbance which at present arises through fluctuations in the value of gold in relation to the general price level, and you only get rid of that if the index on which you work contains a smaller margin of error than the amount by which the real value of gold fluctuates: and to be quite sure of securing this advantage a good deal more labour would have to be expended on the preparation of the statistics than has up to the present been given.

The chief opponents, however, of the return to the gold standard are not the advocates of the 'managed' pound, but the inflationists pure and simple. The scientific advocates of the 'managed' pound will tell you quite dogmatically that the moment that your domestic prices give indications of rising more quickly than the domestic prices of other sound currency countries, you must turn off the currency tap and practice a policy of credit restriction. Indeed, the more thorough going apostles of the doctrine, who aim at price stability irrespective of whatever may happen elsewhere, would say that the moment your index figures show any sign at all of rising, this policy must be followed.

The other school of opponents of the return to the gold standard, on the other hand, say that when trade is improving more money is required, and credit should be extended rather than restricted, whether prices show a tendency to rise or not. Indeed, a rise in prices is the invariable concomitant of an improvement in trade.

They do not say, however, when, or how, the process is to end. So long as commercial sentiment is optimistic, banks and, other lenders are sufficiently human to continue to expand credit to the extreme limit which their cash reserves may appear to justify. If the currency issuing authority gives them all the cash they need, or think they need, they will go on expanding credit indefinitely and prices will continue to rise. As soon as the price level in the country is relatively higher than the price level outside, the country will cease to export and import intensively, unless and until equilibrium is restored by depreciation in the exchange value of its currency unit.

This is a simple *a priori* deduction from universally admitted economic premises, the truth of which has been demonstrated over and over again by practical experience.

It may be true that in the future gold is going to be too cheap to be a satisfactory international standard of value. But that is certainly no ground for rejecting it, because it is too dear.

It may equally be true that there is a reasonable probability that in the near future gold will depreciate to the present value of sterling and it would, therefore, be foolish to put up sterling to the value of gold merely for both to depreciate together afterwards.

There would be great force in this argument if there were, in point of fact, any appreciable difference between the value of sterling and gold at the present moment. The best conclusion, however, which it is possible to draw from a comparison of British and American index figures is that the current difference is not more than 2% or 3%—the fact that it is not possible to draw any precise conclusion is perhaps the most eloquent condemnation of the index figure as a working standard of value. It therefore appears to me that there is no advantage, and probably serious inconvenience, in waiting.

It is not unlikely that in the absence of any immediate announcement of the intention to restore the free gold market at any early date, there would be an appreciable set-back in the exchange value of the pound. Such a set-back would certainly tend to cause a rise in sterling prices, which, if we are to follow the policy advocated by the adherents of the 'managed' pound, would have to be met by credit restriction. It is not unlikely that such restriction would be far more severe than that which would be occasioned by a restoration of the free gold market, more particularly if the latter operation should take place at a time when dollar prices are rising in America. Indeed I should not be at all surprised if very shortly after the restoration of the free gold market a period of cheap money and easy credit becomes necessary to repel an influx of unwanted gold.

APPENDIX 6

DRAMATIS PERSONAE

Amery, L. S.—Secretary of State for the Colonies, 1924–9.

Anderson, Sir Alan—Director, Bank of England, 1918–46; Deputy Governor, 1925–6.

Baldwin, Stanley (later Lord)—Financial Secretary to Treasury, 1917–21; President of the Board of Trade, 1921–2; Chancellor of the Exchequer, 1922–3; Prime Minister, 1923–4, 1924–9.

Bevin, Ernest—General Secretary of Transport and General Workers Union, 1921–40; member Committee on Finance and Industry; member Economic Advisory Council.

Bewley, T. K.—Principal, H.M. Treasury.

Blacket, Sir Basil—Controller of Finance, H.M. Treasury, 1919–22; Finance Member of the Executive Council of the Governor-General of India, 1922–8; Director of the Bank of England, 1929–35.

Boothby, Robert (later Lord)—M.P. 1924–58; Parliamentary Private Secretary to Winston Churchill, 1925–9.

Bradbury, Sir John (Cr. Lord 1925)—Joint Permanent Secretary to H.M. Treasury, 1913–19; Principal British Delegate to Reparations Commission, Paris, 1919–25; member Committee on Currency and Foreign Exchanges after the war; member Committee on Currency and Bank of England Note Issues; member Committee of Finance and Industry.

Brand, Robert Henry—Director of Lazard Brothers & Co., merchant bankers; member of Committee on Finance and Industry.

Burgess, W. R.—employee Federal Reserve Bank of New York, 1920–33; Deputy Governor, 1930–6.

Cannan, Edwin—Professor of Political Economy, University of London, 1907–26.

Catterns, B. G.—Chief Cashier, Bank of England.

Chalmers, Lord Robert—Permanent Secretary, H.M. Treasury, 1911–13; Joint-Secretary to the Treasury, 1916–19.

Chamberlain, Sir Austin—Chancellor of the Exchequer, 1919–21; Secretary of State for Foreign Affairs, 1924–9; Chairman Committee on Currency and Bank of England Note Issues.

Chapman, Sir Sydney John—Permanent Secretary, Board of Trade, 1920–7; Chief Economic Adviser to Government, 1930–2.

Churchill, Winston—Chancellor of the Exchequer, 1924–9.

Cockayne, Sir Brien (Lord Cullen 1920)—Director, Bank of England, 1902–32; Deputy Governor, 1915–18; Governor, 1918–20.

Crane, Jay E.—Manager, Foreign Department, Federal Reserve Bank of New York, 1919–27; Assistant Deputy Governor, 1928–9; Deputy Governor, 1929–35.

Crissinger, D. R.—Chairman, Federal Reserve Board, 1923–7.

Cunliffe, Lord Walter—Director, Bank of England, 1895–1918; Governor,

1913–18; Chairman, Committee on Currency and Foreign Exchanges after the War.

Currie, L.—Managing Partner, Glyn Mills, Currie & Co.

Farrer, Gaspard—Director of Barings, merchant bankers; member of Committee on Currency and Foreign Exchanges after the War; member Committee on the Currency and Bank of England Note Issues.

Fergusson, J. D. (later Sir Donald)—Private Secretary to successive Chancellors of the Exchequer, 1920–36.

Fisher, Sir Warren—Permanent Secretary of H.M. Treasury and official Head of H.M. Civil Service, 1919–39.

Foxwell, H. S.—Professor, Political Economy at University College, London, 1881–1928.

Glenday, R. G.—Economic Adviser, Federation of British Industries.

Gilbert, S. Parker—Agent General for Reparation Payments, 1924–30.

Goldenweiser, E. A.—Assistant Statistician, Division of Research and Statistics, Federal Reserve Board, 1919–24; Assistant Director, 1925; Director, 1926–45.

Goodenough, F. C.—Chairman, Barclays Bank Ltd.

Goschen, Sir W. H. N.—Partner of Goschens & Cunliffe; Chairman National Provincial Bank Ltd; Director Chartered Bank of India, Australia and China.

Gowers, Sir Ernest—Permanent Under-secretary for Mines, 1920–7; Chairman of Board of Inland Revenue, 1927–30.

Gregg, C. J.—Director of Statistics and Intelligence Branch, Board of Inland Revenue.

Gregory, Theodore—Cassel Reader in International Trade, London School of Economics, 1920; Sir E. Cassel Professor of Economics, London School of Economics, 1927–37; member Committee on Finance and Industry.

Grigg, Percey James (later Sir)—Principal Private Secretary to successive Chancellors of the Exchequer, 1921–30; Chairman, Board of Inland Revenue, 1930–4.

Hamlin, C. S.—Member, Federal Reserve Board, 1914–36.

Harrison, George L.—Deputy Governor, Federal Reserve Bank of New York, 1920–8; Governor, 1928–36; President, 1936–40.

Hawtrey, R. G. (later Sir Ralph)—Director of Financial Enquiries, H.M. Treasury, 1919–45.

Henderson, H. D. (later Sir)—Editor of the Nation and Athenaeum, 1923–30; Joint Secretary to the Economic Advisory Council, 1930–4.

Holland-Martin, R.—Secretary, Bankers' Clearing House.

Hopkins, Sir Richard Valentine Nind—Chairman, Board of Inland Revenue, 1922–7; Controller of Finance and Supply Services, H.M. Treasury, 1927–32.

Horne, Sir Robert—Chancellor of the Exchequer, 1921–2.

Jay, Pierre—Chairman and Federal Reserve Agent, Federal Reserve Bank of New York, 1914–26.

Keynes, John Maynard (later Lord)—Fellow King's College, Cambridge,

1909–46; member Committee on Finance and Industry; member Economic Advisory Council.

Kindersley, Sir Robert Molesworth (later Lord)—Director, Bank of England, 1914–46; Governor Hudson's Bay Company, 1916–25; President National Savings Committee, 1920–46; Senior British member of Dawes Committee, 1924.

Kisch, C. H. (later Sir Cecil)—Secretary, Financial Department, India Office, 1921–33.

Lacour-Gayet, Robert—Director of Economic Research, Bank of France, 1930–36.

Lambert, Sir Henry—Senior Crown Agent for the Colonies, 1921–32; Acting Under-secretary for State for the Colonies, 1924–5.

Layton, Walter (later Sir)—Editor of *The Economist*, 1922–38.

Leaf, Walter—Chairman, Westminster Bank.

Lefeaux, Leslie—Bank of England, 1904–34; Assistant to the Governors, 1932–4.

Leith-Ross, Frederick William (later Sir)—Deputy Controller of Finance, H.M. Treasury, 1925–32; Economic Adviser to H.M. Government, 1932–46.

Lubbock, Cecil—Director, Bank of England, 1909–42; Deputy Governor, 1923–5, 1927–9; member Committee on Finance and Industry.

MacDonald, J. Ramsey—Prime Minister, 1924, 1929–35.

Macmillan, Lord (Hugo Pattison Macmillan)—Lord Advocate of Scotland, 1924; Lord of Appeal in Ordinary, 1930–9; Chairman, Committee on Finance and Industry.

McGarrah, G. W.—President, Bank of International Settlements, 1930–3.

McKenna, Reginald—Chancellor of the Exchequer, 1915–16; Chairman, Midland Bank, 1919–43; member Committee on Finance and Industry.

Mellon, Andrew—Secretary of the U.S. Treasury, 1921–32.

Mond, Sir Alfred (Cr. Lord Melchet 1928)—M.P. 1906–28; Joint Chairman Conference on Industrial Reorganisation and Industrial Relations.

Moreau, Emile—Governor, Bank of France, 1926–30.

Moret, Clement—Deputy Governor, Bank of France, 1928–30; Governor, 1930–5.

Morgan, J. P.—Partner J. P. Morgan & Co., 1891–1940; Senior Partner, 1913–40; American member, Committee of Experts on Reparations, 1929.

Nicholson, John Shield—Professor of Political Economy, University of Edinburgh, 1880–1925.

Niemeyer, Sir Otto—Controller of Finance, H.M. Treasury, 1922–7; joined Bank of England as Comptroller, 1927; Director, 1938–52.

Norman, Montagu (later Lord)—Director, Bank of England, 1907–44; Deputy Governor, 1918–20; Governor, 1920–44.

Osborne, J. A. C.—Secretary, Bank of England.

Parish, Sir George—Editor of *Statist*, 1900–16; Adviser to Chancellor of Exchequer, 1914–16.

Phillips, Frederick (later Sir Frederick)—Assistant Secretary, H.M. Treasury, 1919–27; Principal Assistant Secretary, 1927–32.

Pigou, A. C.—Professor Political Economy, Cambridge, 1908–43; member Committee on Currency and Foreign Exchanges after the War; member Committee on the Currency and Bank of England Note Issues.

Pinsent, G. H. S.—Principal, H.M. Treasury.

Poincaré, Raymond—French Premier, 1912, 1922–4, 1926–9.

Quesnay, Pierre—General Manager, Bank of France, 1926–30, General Manager, Bank of International Settlements, 1930–7.

Rist, Charles—Deputy Governor, Bank of France, 1926–9.

Rowe-Dutton, Ernest—Principal, H.M. Treasury to 1928; Financial Adviser, H.M. Embassy, Berlin, 1928–32.

Rueff, Jacques—French Financial Attaché, London, 1930–4.

Schacht, Hjalmar—President, Reichsbank, 1923–30, 1933–9.

Schuster, Sir Felix—Governor of the Union of London and Smiths Bank, 1859–1918; Director of National Provincial Bank, 1918–36.

Siepmann, H. A.—Head, Central Banking Section, Bank of England, 1926–36.

Snowden, Philip (later Lord)—Chancellor of the Exchequer, 1924, 1929–31.

Sprague, O. M. W.—Professor of Economics, Harvard University, 1913–41; Economic Adviser, Bank of England, 1930–3.

Sproul, Allan—Assistant Deputy Governor and Secretary, Federal Reserve Bank of New York, 1930–4.

Stamp, Sir Josiah (later Lord)—Chairman, London, Midland and Scottish Railway; Director, Bank of England, 1928–41; member Committee on National Debt and Taxation; British representative Dawes and Young Committees; member Economic Advisory Council.

Stewart, Walter W.—Director, Division of Research and Statistics, Federal Reserve Board, 1922–5; Economic Adviser, Bank of England, 1928–30.

Strong, Benjamin—Governor, Federal Reserve Bank of New York, 1914–28.

Sydney-Turner, S. A.—Principal, H.M. Treasury.

Vansittart, Robert Gilbert (later Lord)—Assistant Under-secretary of State for Foreign Affairs and Principal Private Secretary to the Prime Minister, 1928–30; Permanent Under-secretary of State for Foreign Affairs, 1930–8.

Waley, Sigismund David—Assistant Secretary, H.M. Treasury, 1924–31; Principal Assistant Secretary, 1931–9.

Young, R. A.—Chairman, Federal Reserve Board, 1927–30.

Young, N. E.—Assistant Principal, H.M. Treasury to 1928; Principal from 1928; Secretary, Committee on the Currency and Bank of England Note Issues.

Unpublished Papers
Chartwell Papers
Federal Reserve Bank of New York Archives (F.R.B.N.Y.) – including the Strong Papers and the Harrison Collection.
Keynes Papers.
Pigou Papers.
Public Record Office Papers – The full titles and call numbers of the items which have found use in the text are :
    Cab. 23. Cabinet Office. Cabinet Conclusions.
    Cab. 24. Cabinet Office. Cabinet Memoranda.
    Cab. 27. Cabinet Office, Cabinet. *Ad Hoc* Committees.
        Cab. 27/462, Committee on the Financial Situation, 1931.
    Cab. 58. Cabinet Office. Economic Advisory Council (Committee of Civil Research.)
        Cab. 58/1, Economic Advisory Council (Committee of Civil Research) Minutes, 18 June 1925–26 April 1928.
        Cab. 58/2, Economic Advisory Council, Minutes, 17 February 1930–15 January 1932.
        Cab. 58/9, Committee of Civil Research, Memoranda, (H) Series, nos 1–50, 29 June 1925–18 March 1926.
        Cab. 58/14, Economic Advisory Council, Staff Memoranda, The Economic Position.
        Cab. 58/18, Economic Advisory Council, Committee on Economic Information, Memoranda, nos 1–45, 14 September 1931–13 May 1933.
    T160. Treasury. Finance Files.
        T160/111/F4319/1, Issue in London of Foreign Loans.
        T160/149/F5742, French Gold Deposited in Great Britain as Security for War Advances.
        T160/153/F5904, Bank of France, Loan to, by Bank of England, Repayment of.
        T160/194/F7380/02, Colwyn Committee on National Debt and Taxation, Sir O. E. Niemeyer's Evidence.
        T160/197/F7528, Committee on the Currency and Bank of England Note Issues.
        T160/197/F7528/01/1–3, Chamberlain–Bradbury Committee on Gold Standard and Amalgamation of Treasury Note Issues with Bank of England Note Issue: Proceedings.
        T160/197/F7528/03, Return to the Gold Standard in U.K. Press Cuttings.
        T160/227/F8508, Revolving Credit for United Kingdom ($300,000,000) for a period of two years.
        T160/281/F11789, Sovereigns Held by Issue Department of Bank of England, Melting of.

T160/393/F11300/032/1–4, Germany and the Young Plan. Possibility of Moratorium and Demand for Revision.

T160/394/F11324, British Industry and the Fiscal and Banking Policy of Great Britain, Foreign Office Memo on.

T160/398/F12377, International Credit Corporation (Kindersley Plan).

T160/398/F12394, British Government Securities and British Companies' Stock, etc., Foreign and Colonial Holdings.

T160/403/F12666, Bank of France: Sterling Reserves.

T160/418/F6779/1–2, Treasury Exchange Transactions in U.S.A., General Memoranda.

T160/425/F11282/018, Bank for International Settlements, Sterling Balances.

T160/430/F12317/1–2, Conversations with France on Financial Relations, 1931.

T160/435/F12568/1–2, $200,000,000 Credit in U.S.A., 1931.

T160/439/F12712, Dutch Sterling Balances at Bank of England.

T160/444/F12899, Currency Crisis 1931, Repayment of Foreign Credits (America and France).

T160/444/F12901, Currency Crisis 1931, Bank of England Foreign Credits.

T160/463/F8362/1, Return to the Gold Standard.

T160/470/F10549/1–2, Foreign Loans Raised in London Market, Adverse effect of 2% Stamp Duty on.

T160/511/F8579/01, Currency and Bank Notes Act, 1928–Correspondence with Bank of England regarding (i) Cover for the Note Issue,(ii) Profits and Expenses of Issue Department.

T160/533/F13296/1–3, Restrictions on New Capital Issues, Memoranda 1932–3.

T160/551/F12570/1–3, French Credits to U.K. 1931.

T160/631/F14575, Treasury: (1) Submission of important matters dealt with by Finance Branch to Chancellor of Exchequer, (2) Summary of work done by 1D and 2D.

T163. Treasury. General Files.

T163/68/G3788, Gold Standard (Amendment) Bill 1931.

T163/130/G1942, Gold Standard Bill 1925.

T170. Treasury. Bradbury Papers.

T170/129, The Regulation of the Exchanges and of Gold Export, 1918.

T172. Chancellor of the Exchequer's Office: Miscellaneous Papers.

T172/1499B, Gold Standard 1925: Treasury Memoranda.

T172/1500A, Gold Standard 1925: American Credits.

T175. Treasury. Hopkins Papers.

T175/4, Embargo on French Loans, 1924–8.

T175/9, Proposed Return to the Gold Standard, 1925.

T175/11, Financial and Industrial Situations in Great Britain and Germany, 1927.

T175/46, B.I.S. Gold Guarantee, 1931.

T175/51, Crisis 1931, Drafts, Copies, etc.

T175/56, General Financial Policy, 1931–2.

T176. Treasury. Niemeyer Papers.

T176/5, Monetary Policy, 1920–9.

T176/13, Bank Rate, 1923–30.

T176/16, Gold Standard, 1925.

T176/17, Embargo on Overseas Loans, 1925.

T176/22, Internal Gold Circulation, 1925–7.

T176/29, Conversations with M. Quesnay (Bank of France) on French Monetary Policy and Inter-Allied Debts, 1927.

T176/33, French gold withdrawals from London, 1930.

T185/1–3. Treasury. Committee on Currency and Foreign Exchanges after the War, 1918–19, Proceedings.

Books, Articles, and Official Reports

Adler, J. H. (ed.) *Capital Movements and Economic Development*, London: Macmillan, 1967.

Aldcroft, D. H., 'Economic Progress in Britain in the 1920s', *Scottish Jouranl of Political Economy*, XIII (3), November 1966.

'Economic Growth in Britain in the Inter-War Years: A Reassessment', *Economic History Review*, 2nd Ser. xx (2), August 1967.

Aliber, R. Z., 'Speculation in the Foreign Exchanges: The European Experience 1919–1926', *Yale Economic Essays*, II (1), Spring 1962.

Amery, L. S., *My Political Life: War and Peace 1914–1929*, II, London: Hutchinson, 1953.

Artis, M. J., *Foundations of British Monetary Policy*, Oxford: Blackwell, 1965.

Aschheim, J., *Techniques of Monetary Control*, Baltimore: Johns Hopkins, 1965.

Ashworth, W., *An Economic History of England 1870–1939*, London: Methuen, 1960.

Atkin, J. M., 'British Overseas Investment 1918–1931', University of London, unpublished Ph.D. dissertation, 1968.

'Official Regulation of British Overseas Investment, 1914–1931', *Economic History Review*, 2nd Ser. XXIII (2), August 1970.

Balassa, B., 'The Purchasing Power Parity Doctrine: A Reappraisal', *Journal of Political Economy*, LXXII (6), December 1964.

Balassa, B., and Schydlowsky, D. M., 'Effective Tariffs, Domestic Cost of Foreign Exchange, and the Equilibrium Exchange Rate', *Journal of Political Economy*, LXXVI (3); May/June 1968.

Balogh, T., 'The Import of Gold into France: An Analysis of the Technical Position', *Economic Journal* XL (159), September 1930.

Studies in Financial Organisation, Cambridge: Cambridge University Press, 1947.

Barrett-Whale, P., 'A Retrospective View of the Bank Charter Act of 1844', *Economica*, N. S., XI (44), August 1944.

Bassett, R., *1931: Political Crisis*, London: Macmillan, 1958.

Baumol, W., 'The Transactions Demand for Cash: An Inventory Theoretic Approach', *Quarterly Journal of Economics*, LXVI (4), November 1952.

Bloomfield, A. I., *Monetary Policy under the International Gold Standard 1880–1914*, New York: Federal Reserve Bank of New York, 1959.

'Short-term Capital Movements under the Pre-1914 Gold Standard', *Princeton Studies in International Finance No. 11*.

'Patterns of Fluctuation in International Investment before 1914', *Princeton Studies in International Finance No. 21.*

Board of Governors of the Federal Reserve System, *Banking and Monetary Statistics,* Washington: Federal Reserve System, 1943.

Board of Trade, *Statistical Tables Relating to British and Foreign Trade and Industry (1924–30),* Part I, Cmd. 3737, Part II, Cmd. 3849, London: H.M.S.O., 1930 and 1931, (B.P.P., 1930–1 (3737 and 3849), xxxi, 21 and 399).

Statistical Abstract for the United Kingdom 1919–33, Cmd. 4801, London: H.M.S.O., 1935. (B.P.P., 1934–5 (4801), xxii, 1).

Boyle, A., *Montagu Norman,* London: Cassell, 1967.

Brand, R. H., 'A Banker's Reflections on Economic Trends', *Economic Journal,* LXIII (252), December 1953.

Brown, A. J., 'Britain in the World Economy 1870–1914', *Yorkshire Bulletin of Economic and Social Research,* XVII (1), May 1965.

Phelps Brown, E. H., and Shackle, G. L. S., 'British Economic Fluctuations 1924–38', *Oxford Economic Papers,* (2) May 1939.

Phelps Brown, E. H., and Browne, M. H., *A Century of Pay,* London: Macmillan, 1968.

Brown, W. A. Jr., *England and the New Gold Standard 1919–1926,* New Haven: Yale University Press, 1929.

The International Gold Standard Reinterpreted 1914–1934, 2 vols, New York: National Bureau of Economic Research, 1940.

Burns, A. F., and Mitchell, W. C., *Measuring Business Cycles,* New York: National Bureau of Economic Research, 1946.

Cairncross, A. K., *Home and Foreign Investment 1870–1913,* Cambridge: Cambridge University Press, 1953.

Canada, Royal Commission on Banking and Finance, *Report,* Ottawa: Queen's Printer, 1964.

Appendix Volume, Ottawa: Queen's Printer, 1964.

Cannan, E., 'Review of T. E. Gregory, *The Return to Gold*', *Economic Journal,* xxxv (140), December, 1925.

An Economist's Protest, London: P. S. King, and Son 1927.

Cassel, G., *The Downfall of the Gold Standard,* Oxford: Clarendon Press, 1936.

Caves, R. E., Johnson, H. G., and Kenen, P. B., *Trade, Growth and the Balance of Payments,* Amsterdam: North Holland, 1965.

Chandler, L. V., *Benjamin Strong, Central Banker,* Washington: Brookings Institution, 1958.

Chang, T. C., *Cyclical Movements in the Balance of Payments,* Cambridge: Cambridge University Press, 1951.

Chapman, R. A., *Decision Making,* London: Routledge & Kegan Paul, 1969.

Checkland, S. G., 'The Mind of the City 1870–1914', *Oxford Economic Papers,* N.S. IX (3), October 1957.

Clapham, Sir John., *The Bank of England: A History,* 2 vols, New York: Macmillan, 1945.

Clare, G., *A Money Market Primer,* 3rd ed., London: Effingham Wilson, 1931.

Clark, C. G., 'Statistical Studies of the Present Economic Position of Great Britain', *Economic Journal,* xli (163), September 1931.

Clarke, S. V. O., *Central Bank Cooperation 1924–31*, New York: Federal Reserve Bank of New York, 1967.

Clay, (Sir) H., *The Post-War Unemployment Problem*, London: Macmillan, 1929.

Lord Norman, London: Macmillan, 1957.

Committee on Currency and Foreign Exchanges after the War, *First Interim Report*, Cd. 9182, London: H.M.S.O., 1918. (B.P.P. 1918 (9182), VII, 853).

Final Report, Cmd. 464, London: H.M.S.O., 1919. (B.P.P., 1919 (464), XIII, 593).

Committee on Financial Facilities, *Report*, Cd. 9227, London: H.M.S.O., 1918, (B.P.P., 1918 (9227), X, 25).

Committee on the Currency and Bank of England Note Issues, *Report*, Cmd. 2392 London: H.M.S.O., 1925. (B.P.P., 1924–5 (2393), IX, 435).

Committee on National Debt and Taxation, *Report* Cmd. 2800, London: H.M.S.O. 1927, (B.P.P., 1927 (2800), XI, 371).

Minutes of Evidence, London: H.M.S.O., 1927.

Committee on Industry and Trade, *Survey of Overseas Markets*, London: H.M.S.O., 1925.

Committee on Industry and Trade, *Final Report*, Cmd. 3282, London: H.M.S.O., 1929. (B.P.P., 1928–9 (3282), VII, 413).

Committee on Finance and Industry, *Report*, Cmd. 3897, London: H.M.S.O., 1931. (B.P.P., 1930–1 (3897), XIII, 219).

Minutes of Evidence, London: H.M.S.O., 1931.

Committee on the Working of the Monetary System, *Report*, Cmnd. 827, London: H.M.S.O., 1969. (B.P.P., 1958–9 (827), XVII, 389).

Principal Memoranda and Minutes of Evidence, 4 vols, London: H.M.S.O., 1960.

Cooper, R. N., 'Macroeconomic Policy Adjustment in Interdependent Economies', *Quarterly Journal of Economics*, LXXXIII (330), February 1969.

Court of Inquiry concerning the Coal Mining Dispute, *Report*, Cmd. 2478, London: H.M.S.O., 1925. (B.P.P., 1924–5 (2478), XIII, 21).

Crowther, G., *An Outline of Money*, 2nd ed., London: Nelson, 1948.

Day, A. C. L., *The Future of Sterling*, Oxford: Clarendon Press, 1954.

Dunning, J. H., *American Investment in British Manufacturing Industry*, London: Allen and Unwin, 1958.

Einzig, P., *International Gold Movements*, 2nd ed., London: Macmillan, 1931.

The Tragedy of the Pound, London: Kegan Paul, 1931.

The Theory of Forward Exchange, London: Macmillan, 1937.

In the Centre of Things, London: Hutchinson, 1960.

Falk, O. T., 'Currency and Gold: Now and after the War', *Economic Journal*, XXVII (109), March 1918.

Feavearyear, Sir A., *The Pound Sterling: A History of English Money*, rev. ed., Oxford: Clarendon Press, 1963.

Feinstein, C. H., *Domestic Capital Formation in the United Kingdom 1920–1938*, Cambridge: Cambridge University Press, 1965.

Feis, H., *Europe the World's Banker 1870–1914*, New York: Norton, 1965.

The Diplomacy of the Dollar 1919–1932, New York: Norton, 1966.

Fellner, W., Machlup F., and Triffin R., et al., *Maintaining and Restoring*

Balance in International Payments, Princeton: Princeton University Press, 1966.

Fetter, F. W., *Development of British Monetary Orthodoxy 1797–1875,* Cambridge, Mass.: Harvard University Press, 1965.

Fleming, J. M., 'Guidelines for Balances of Payments Adjustment under the Par-Value System', *Princeton Essays in International Finance No. 67,* May 1968.

Ford, A. G., *The Gold Standard 1880–1914: Britain and Argentina,* Oxford: Clarendon Press, 1962.

   'British Economic Fluctuations 1870–1914', *The Manchester School,* xxxvii (2), June 1969.

Friedman, M., and Schwartz, A. J., *A Monetary History of the United States 1867–1960,* Princeton: Princeton University Press, 1963.

Gardner, R. N., *Sterling-Dollar Diplomacy: Anglo-American Collaboration in the Reconstruction of Multilateral Trade,* Oxford: Clarendon Press, 1956.

Gerakis, A. S., 'Effects of Exchange-Rate Devaluations and Revaluations on Receipts from Tourism', *I.M.F. Staff Papers,* xii (3), November 1965.

Goodhart, C. A. E., *The New York Money Market and the Finance of Trade, 1900–1913,* Cambridge, Mass.: Harvard University Press, 1969.

Gregory, (Sir) T. E., *The Return to Gold,* London: Ernest Benn, 1925.

   The First Year of the Gold Standard, London: P. S. King, 1926.

   Gold, Unemployment and Capitalism, London: P. S. King, 1933.

   'The "Norman Conquest" Reconsidered', *Lloyds Bank Review,* October 1957.

   'Lord Norman, A New Interpretation', *Lloyds Bank Review,* April 1968.

Grigg, Sir P. J., *Prejudice and Judgement,* London: Hutchinson, 1948.

Grubel, H. G., *Forward Exchange, Speculation and the International Flow of Capital,* Stanford: Stanford University Press, 1966.

Harberler, G., 'A Survey of International Trade Theory', *Princeton Special Papers in International Finance No. 1,* rev. ed.

Hancock, K., 'Unemployment and the Economists in the 1920s', *Economica,* N.S., xxvii (108), November 1960.

   'The Reduction of Unemployment as a Problem of Public Policy 1920–29', *Ecomonic History Review,* 2nd Ser., xv (2), December 1962.

Harberger, A. C., 'Some Evidence on the International Price Mechanism', *Journal of Political Economy,* lxv (6), December 1957.

Hawke, G. R., 'New Zealand and the Return to Gold in 1925', *Australian Economic History Review,* xi (1), March 1971.

Hawtrey, (Sir) R. G., *Monetary Reconstruction,* 2nd ed., London: Longmans, 1926.

   The Art of Central Banking, London: Longmans, 1932.

   A Century of Bank Rate, London: Longmans, 1938.

   The Gold Standard in Theory and Practice, 5th ed., London: Longmans, 1947.

   'The Return to Gold in 1925', *Bankers' Magazine,* xxix (1505), August 1969.

Henderson, Sir Hubert., *The Inter-War Years and Other Papers,* edited by Sir H. Clay, Oxford: Clarendon Press, 1955.

Hicks, J. R., 'Monetary Policy: A Symposium', *Bulletin of the Oxford University Institute of Statistics,* xiv (4–5), April/May 1952.

Hicks, U. K., *The Finance of British Government 1920–36*, London: Oxford University Press, 1938.

Hodson, H. V., *Slump and Recovery*, London: Oxford University Press, 1938.

Hufbauer, G. C. and Adler, F. M., 'Overseas Manufacturing Investment and the Balance of Payments'. U.S. Treasury, *Tax Policy Research Study No. 1*, Washington: Government Printing Office, n.d.

Iversen, C., *Aspects of the Theory of International Capital Movements*, London: Oxford University Press, 1935.

Johnson, H. G., *International Trade and Economic Growth*, London: Allen & Unwin, 1958.

Johnson, P. B., *Land Fit for Heroes: The Planning of British Reconstruction, 1916–1919*, Chicago: University of Chicago Press, 1968.

Jones, L. E., *Georgian Afternoon*, London: Rupert Hart-Davis, 1958.

Jucker-Fleetwood, E. E., 'Montagu Norman in the Per Jacobsson Diaries', *National Westminster Bank Quarterly Review*, November 1968.

Kahn, A. E., *Great Britain in the World Economy*, London: Pitman, 1946.

Katz, S. I., 'External Surpluses, Capital Flows, and Credit Policy in the European Economic Community, 1958 to 1967', *Princeton Studies in International Finance No. 22*.

Kenen, P. B., *British Monetary Policy and the Balance of Payments 1951–57*, Cambridge, Mass.: Harvard University Press, 1960.

Keynes, J. M., *The Economic Consequences of the Peace*, London: Macmillan, 1919.

A Tract on Monetary Reform, London: Macmillan, 1923.

'Discussion on Monetary Reform', *Economic Journal*, xxxiv (134), June 1924.

'Notes and Memoranda. The Committee on the Currency', *Economic Journal*, xxxv (138), June 1925.

The Economic Consequences of Mr. Churchill, London: Hogarth Press, 1925.

'The British Balance of Trade 1925–27', *Economic Journal*, xxxvii (148), December 1927.

A Treatise on Money, 2 vols, London: Macmillan, 1930.

Essays in Persuasion, London: Macmillan, 1931.

'Reflections on the Sterling Exchange', Lloyds Bank Ltd., *Monthly Review* April 1932.

Keynes, J. M., and Henderson, H. D., *Can Lloyd George Do It ? The Pledge Examined*, London: The Nation, 1929.

Kindersley, R., 'A New Study of British Foreign Investments', *Economic Journal*, xxxix (153), March 1929, and subsequent annual studies through 1932.

Kindleberger, C. P., *The Terms of Trade: A European Case Study*, New York: Wiley and Technology Press, 1956.

Economic Growth in France and Britain 1860–1960, Cambridge, Mass.: Harvard University Press, 1964.

Europe and the Dollar, Cambridge, Mass.: M.I.T. Press, 1966.

Kisch, C. H., and Elkin, W. A., *Central Banks*, London: Macmillan, 1928.

Krock, K., *A Study of Interest Rates*, London: P. S. King, 1929.

Kubinski, Z., 'The Elasticity of Substitution between Sources of British

T

Imports 1921–1938', *Yorkshire Bulletin of Economic and Social Research*, II (1), January 1950.

Lary, H. B., et al., *The United States in the World Economy*, Washington: Government Printing Office, 1943.

League of Nations, *The Course and Phases of the World Economic Depression*, Geneva: League of Nations, 1931.

International Currency Experience, Princeton: League of Nations, 1944.

Leith-Ross, Sir F. W., *Money Talks: Fifty Years of International Finance*, London: Hutchinson, 1968.

Lewis, W. A., *Economic Survey 1919–1939*, London: Allen & Unwin, 1949.

Lindert, P. H., 'Key Currencies and Gold 1900–1913', *Princeton Studies in International Finance No. 24*.

Lomax, K. S., 'Prioduction and Productivity Movements in the United Kingdom since 1900', *Journal of the Royal Statistical Society*, Series A, CXXII (2), 1959.

London and Cambridge Economic Service, *The British Economy: Key Statistics 1900–1966*, London: Times Newspapers, n.d.

Lund, P. J., and Holden, K., 'A Study of Private Sector Cross Fixed Capital Formation in the United Kingdom, 1923–1938', *Oxford Economic Papers*, N.S., XX (1), March 1968.

MacDougall, G. D. A., 'British and American Exports: A Study Suggested by the Theory of Comparative Costs', *Economic Journal*, LXI (244) and LXII (247), December 1951 and September 1952.

Machlup, F., 'Elasticity Pessimism in International Trade', *Economia Internazionale*, III (1), February 1950.

Macmillan, Sir Harold, *Winds of Change 1914–1939*, London: Macmillan, 1966.

Macrosty, H. W., 'Trade and the Gold Standard', *Journal of the Royal Statistical Society*, XCI (3), 1928.

'The Overseas Trade of the United Kingdom 1924–31', *Journal of the Royal Statistical Society*, XCV (4), 1932.

Maddison, A., 'Growth and Fluctuations in the World Economy 1870–1960', *Banca Nazionale del Lavoro Quarterly Review*, June 1962.

Maizels, A., *Industrial Growth and World Trade*, Cambridge: Cambridge University Press, 1963.

Mathias, P., *The First Industrial Nation: An Economic History of Britain 1700–1914*, London: Methuen, 1969.

Matthews, R. C. O., 'Some Aspects of Post-War Growth in the British Economy in Relation to Historical Experience', *Cambridge, Department of Applied Economics Reprint No. 240*.

'Why has Britain had Full Employment Since the War?', *Economic Journal*, LXXVII (311), September 1968.

McLeod, A. N., 'A Critique of the Fluctuating-Exchange-Rate Policy in Canada', *The Bulletin*, no. 34–35, April–June 1965.

Memoranda by Ministers on Certain Proposals Relating to Unemployment, Cmd. 3331, London: H.M.S.O., 1929. (B.P.P., 1928–9 (3331), XVI, 813).

Meyers, M. G., *Paris as a Financial Centre*, London: P. S. King, 1936.

Michaely, M., *Balance-of-Payments Adjustment Policies*, New York: National Bureau of Economic Research, 1968.

Middlemas, K., and Barnes, J., *Baldwin: A Biography*, London: Weidenfeld and Nicolson, 1969.

Ministry of Labour, *Eighteenth Abstract of Labour Statistics of the United Kingdom*, Cmd. 2740, London: H.M.S.O., 1926. (B.P.P., 1926 (2740), xxix, 1).

Mintz, I., *Deterioration in the Quality of Foreign Bonds Issued in the United States 1920–30*, New York: National Bureau of Economic Research, 1951.

Trade Balances during Business Cycles: U.S. and Britain since 1880, New York: National Bureau of Economic Research, 1959.

Mitchell, B. R., and Deane, P., *Abstract of British Historical Statistics*, Cambridge: Cambridge University Press, 1962.

Moggridge, D. E., 'The 1931 Financial Crisis: A New View', *The Banker*, cxx (534), August 1970.

The Return to Gold 1925: The Formulation of Economic Policy and its Critics, Cambridge: Cambridge University Press, 1969.

'Some Aspects of British International Monetary Policy 1924–31', Ph.D. dissertation, Cambridge University, 1969.

Morgan, E. V., *The Theory and Practice of Central Banking 1797–1913*, Cambridge: Cambridge University Press, 1943.

Studies in British Financial Policy 1914–1925, London: Macmillan, 1952.

Moreau, E., *Souvenirs d'un Gouverneur de la Banque de France*, Paris: Librairie de Medicis, 1954.

Morgenstern, O., *International Financial Transactions and Business Cycles*, Princeton: Princeton University Press, 1959.

National Bureau of Economic Research, Special Conference Series, *The Measurement and Behaviour of Unemployment*, Princeton: Princeton University Press, 1957.

National Monetary Commission, *Interviews on the Banking and Currency Systems of England, Scotland, France, Germany, Switzerland and Italy*, U.S. Senate, 61st Congress, 2nd Session, Document 405, Washington: Government Printing Office, 1910.

Nevin, E., 'Monetary Policy Again', *Bulletin of the Oxford University Institute of Statistics*, xiv (8), August 1952.

The Mechanism of Cheap Money: A Study of British Monetary Policy, 1931–39, Cardiff: University of Wales Press, 1955.

Nevin, E., and Davis, E. W., *The London Clearing Banks*, London: Elek, 1970.

O.E.C.D., *The Balance of Payments Adjustment Process*, Paris: O.E.C.D., 1966.

Orcutt, G. H., 'Measurements of Price Elasticities in International Trade', *Review of Economics and Statistics*, xxxiii (2), May 1950.

Peacock, A. T., and Wiseman, J., *The Growth of Public Expenditure in the United Kingdom*, London: Oxford University Press, 1961.

Pember and Boyle, *British Government Securities in the Twentieth Century*, 2nd ed., London: Privately printed, 1950.

Pigou, A. C., *Aspects of British Economic History 1918–25*, London: Macmillan, 1947.

Platt, D. C. M., *Finance, Trade and Politics in British Foreign Policy 1815–1914*, Oxford: Clarendon Press, 1968.

Pollard, S., *The Development of the British Economy 1914–1950*, London: Arnold, 1962.

(ed)., *The Gold Standard and Employment Policies between the Wars*, London: Methuen, 1970.

Pool, A. G., *Wage Policy in Relation to Industrial Fluctuations*, London: Macmillan, 1938.

Pressnell, L. S. (ed)., *Studies in the Industrial Revolution*, London: Athlone Press, 1960.

Rankin, M. T., *Monetary Opinion and Policy 1924–34*, London: P. S. King, 1935.

Reddaway, W. B., et al., *The Effects of U.K. Direct Investment Overseas, Interim and Final Reports*, Cambridge: Cambridge University Press, 1967/1968.

Richardson, J. H., *British Economic Foreign Policy*, London: Allen & Unwin, 1936.

Richardson, H. W., *Economic Recovery in Britain 1932–39*, London: Weidenfeld and Nicolson, 1967.

Richardson, H. W., and Aldcroft, D. H., *Building in the British Economy between the Wars*, London: Allen & Unwin, 1969.

Robertson, D. H., *Money*, 4th ed., London: Nisbet, 1948.

Britain in the World Economy, London: Allen & Unwin, 1954.

Robinson, J., *Essays in the Theory of Employment*, London: Macmillan, 1937.

'Monetary Policy Again: Comments', *Bulletin of the Oxford University Institute of Statistics*, XIV (8), August 1952.

Romans, J. T., 'Moral Suasion as an Instrument of Economic Policy', *American Economic Review*, LVI (5), December 1966.

Routh, G., *Occupation and Pay in Great Britain 1906–1960*, Cambridge: Cambridge University Press, 1965.

Royal Institute of International Affairs, *The International Gold Problem*, London: Oxford University Press, 1931.

The Problem of International Investment, London: Oxford University Press, 1937.

Salter, (Lord) A., *Recovery: The Second Effort*, London: G. Bell, 1932.

Slave of the Lamp: A Public Servant's Notebook, London: Weidenfeld and Nicolson, 1967.

Saul, S. B., *Studies in British Overseas Trade 1870–1914*, Liverpool: Liverpool University Press, 1960.

Sayers, R. S., *Bank of England Operations 1890–1914*, London: P. S. King, 1936.

Modern Banking, 2nd ed., Oxford: Clarendon Press, 1947.

Financial Policy 1939–45, London: H.M.S.O. and Longmans, 1956.

Central Banking after Bagehot, Oxford: Clarendon Press, 1957.

Gilletts in the London Money Market 1867–1967, Oxford: Clarendon Press, 1968.

Schacht, H., *The Stabilisation of the Mark*, London: Allen & Unwin, 1927.

The End of Reparations, London: Cape, 1931.

My First Seventy-Six Years, London: Allan Wingate, 1955.

Scott, M. FG., *A Study of United Kingdom Imports*, Cambridge: Cambridge University Press, 1963.

Select Committee on Nationalised Industries, Session, 1969–70, *First Report: The Bank of England*, London: H.M.S.O., 1970.

Skidelsky, R., *Politicians and the Slump: The Labour Government of 1929–31*, London: Macmillan, 1967.

'Gold Standard and Churchill: the Truth', *The Times Business News*, 17 March 1969.

Snow, E. C., 'The Relative Importance of Export Trade', *Journal of the Royal Statistical Society*, XCIV (3), 1931.

'Discussion on the Balance of Trade', *Journal of the Royal Statistical Society*, XCV (1), 1932.

Stolper, W. F., 'Purchasing Power Parity and the Pound Sterling from 1919–1925', *Kyklos*, II (3), 1948.

Svennilson, I., *Growth and Stagnation in the European Economy*, Geneva: United Nations, 1954.

Swoboda, A. K., 'The Euro-Dollar Market: An Interpretation', *Princeton Essays in International Finance No. 64*, February 1968.

Thomas, W. A., and Morgan, E. V. *The Stock Exchange: Its History and Functions*, London: Elek, 1962.

Tinbergen, J., *Business Cycles in the United Kingdom 1870–1914*, Amsterdam: North Holland, 1951.

Tobin, J., 'The Interest Elasticity of the Transactions Demand for Cash', *Review of Economics and Statistics*, XXXVIII (3), August 1956.

Triffin, R., 'The Evolution of the International Monetary System: Historical Reappraisal and Future Perspectives', *Princeton Studies in International Finance No. 12.*

'National Central Banking and the International Economy', *Review of Economic Studies*, XIV, 1945.

Truptil, R. J., *British Banks and the London Money Market*, London: Cape, 1936.

Tsiang, S. C., 'Fluctuating Exchange Rates in Countries with Relatively Stable Economies: Some European Experiences after World War I', *I.M.F. Staff Papers*, VII (2), October 1959.

U.S. Department of Commerce, *Historical Statistics of the United States from Colonial Times to 1957*, Washington: Government Printing Office, 1960.

Wheeler-Bennett, Sir J., *Action this Day: Working with Churchill*, London: Macmillan, 1968.

Whittlesey, C. R., and Wilson, J. S. G., *Essays in Money and Banking in Honour of R. S. Sayers*, Oxford: Clarendon Press, 1968.

Wicker, E. R., *Federal Reserve Monetary Policy 1917–1933*, New York: Random House, 1966.

Williams, D., 'Montagu Norman and Banking Policy in the Nineteen Twenties', *Yorkshire Bulletin of Economic and Social Research*, XI (1), July 1959.

'London and the 1931 Financial Crisis', *Economic History Review*, 2nd Ser., XV (3), April 1963.

'The 1931 Financial Crisis', *Yorkshire Bulletin of Economic and Social Research*, XV (2), November 1963.

Wilson, C., *The History of Unilever: A Study in Economic Growth and Social Change*, I, London: Cassell, 1954.

Wilson, T., and Andrews, P. W. S., *Oxford Studies in the Price Mechanism*, Oxford: Clarendon Press, 1952.

Withers, H., *Bankers and Credit*, London: Eveleigh Nash, 1924.

Wolfe, M., *The French Franc between the Wars*, New York: Colombia University Press, 1951.

Young, K., *Churchill and Beaverbrook: A Study in Friendship and Politics*, London: Eyre and Spottiswoode, 1966.

Youngson, A. J., *The British Economy 1920–1957*, London: Allen & Unwin, 1960.

Zelder, R. E., 'Estimates of Elasticities of Demand for Exports of the United Kingdom and the United States 1921–1938', *The Manchester School*, XXVI (1), January 1958.

Serial Publications

Bank of England, *Statistical Summary; Quarterly Bulletin*.

The Banker.

The Bankers' Magazine.

Board of Trade Journal.

The Economist.

Federal Reserve Bulletin.

League of Nations, *International Statistical Year-Book*.

London and Cambridge Economic Service, *Bulletin; Special Memoranda*.

Midland Bank, *Monthly Review*.

S. Montagu & Co., *Weekly Bullion Letter*.

The Nation and Athenaeum.

Various newspapers, particularly *The Times*.

INDEX

Note: Authors cited in footnotes appear only in the bibliography unless their views are discussed. The same is true for authors of cables or letters cited in the footnotes.